Transmitting the Spirit in Missions

Transmitting the Spirit in Missions

The History and Growth of the Church of Pentecost

AMOS JIMMY MARKIN

Foreword by J. Kwabena Asamoah-Gyadu

WIPF & STOCK · Eugene, Oregon

TRANSMITTING THE SPIRIT IN MISSIONS
The History and Growth of the Church of Pentecost

Copyright © 2019 Amos Jimmy Markin. All rights reserved. Except for brief quotations in critical publications or reviews, no part of this book may be reproduced in any manner without prior written permission from the publisher. Write: Permissions, Wipf and Stock Publishers, 199 W. 8th Ave., Suite 3, Eugene, OR 97401.

Wipf & Stock
An Imprint of Wipf and Stock Publishers
199 W. 8th Ave., Suite 3
Eugene, OR 97401

www.wipfandstock.com

PAPERBACK ISBN: 978-1-5326-6242-3
HARDCOVER ISBN: 978-1-5326-6243-0
EBOOK ISBN: 978-1-5326-6244-7

Manufactured in the U.S.A. JANUARY 29, 2019

Contents

Foreword by J. Kwabena Asamoah-Gyadu | vii
Preface | xi
Abbreviations | xiv

1. Introduction: Christianity, Mission, and Pentecostalism in Ghana | 1
2. Pentecostalism in Ghanaian Christianity | 27
3. A Post-Independence History of the Church of Pentecost | 50
4. Mission and Growth in the Church of Pentecost: A Case Study of African Pentecostalism | 130
5. The Church of Pentecost International Missions: Exemplary African Pentecostal Missionary Enterprise | 184
6. "Spirit and Mission"—Toward a Theology of Pentecostal Growth in Africa | 242
7. Summary and Conclusions | 273

Appendix A: Mission Report Form | 289
Appendix B: Photographs | 290
Bibliography | 301
Index of Names | 309
Index of Subjects | 317

Foreword

WE LEARN FROM THIS fine work by Apostle Dr. Amos Jimmy Markin that when the Spirit of the Lord moves, things happen. Thus, it is not for nothing that on the day of Pentecost the Spirit is said to have descended upon the disciples in the form of a "violent wind" and manifested as "tongues of fire." In both cases, the images deployed signify seismic change and transformation evident not just by the speaking in tongues but also in the boldness with which Peter articulated the message of the gospel focusing on Jesus Christ. We are accustomed to speaking of Pentecost in terms of the outpouring of the Holy Spirit, and that is not necessarily out of place. However, a careful reading of the full story indicates that the purpose of Pentecost was not simply to bring renewal and restoration, important as that was, but also to affirm Jesus Christ as Lord. In the message, Peter acclaims the resurrected Jesus as the one who poured out the Spirit of Pentecost. However, he then also proceeds to present him to the crowd as God's "Lord and Messiah." We read from Acts 2:32–33 and 36,

> This Jesus God raised up, and of that all of us are witnesses. Being therefore exalted at the right hand of God, and having received from the Father the promise of the Holy Spirit, he has poured out this that you both see and hear. . . . Therefore let the entire house of Israel know with certainty that God has made him both Lord and Messiah, this Jesus whom you crucified. (NRSV)

It was after this powerful theological statement on the meaning of the Pentecost-day proceedings that, following the message, thousands of souls came to faith and were baptized. The church of Jesus Christ was born on that day to do mission in the world.

In this work, the result of a doctoral thesis by Apostle Dr. Amos Jimmy Markin of the Church of Pentecost, we have a powerful case study of how this church, following the mandate of Jesus Christ and the force of the Spirit, has spread as a global denomination. The narrative is emic because it is coming from a critical insider. The Church of Pentecost, although pioneered in Ghana by the Irish Pentecostal missionary James McKeown, has developed as a world Pentecostal church that has branches and ministries not just in nearly every city, town, and village in Ghana but also across the world. It has become impossible to talk about African immigrant Christianity, especially in Europe and North America, without reference to the ministry of the Church of Pentecost. In Ghana their community-based church planting approach, prayer-driven services, liturgical vernacularization, simplicity of ministry, and the enforcement of biblical moral standards among members and clergy mean the Church of Pentecost has become one of the most important and highly regarded Christian denominations in the country. What we have in this study is a wide and comprehensive documentation and theological examination of the missionary strategies of a church whose commitment to the spread of the gospel and the church remains unparalleled in the history of Christianity in Ghana. The Church of Pentecost, in terms of church attendance, is arguably the largest single Christian denomination in Ghana today, and they have not stopped spreading.

It will be difficult, looking at the way Apostle Dr. Markin has explained this growth and ministry, to study mission from Pentecostal perspectives without reference to the models of the Church of Pentecost. In other words, Apostle Dr. Markin's work has successfully outlined for us what mission from an African classical Pentecostal viewpoint means, and at the heart of the success discussed here is the work of the Holy Spirit. Rather than rely on ecclesial structures, social intervention programs, and formal education as the sources of evangelization, the Church of Pentecost, we learn from this work, puts first things first. Formal education and medical care are important, but my reading of the work indicates that the preaching of the gospel, the making of disciples, and the planting of new Christian communities have been prioritized, with the others coming later.

Many churches today add the expressions "global," "international," and "worldwide" to their names, but they remain so only on paper. The Church of Pentecost is one of a few in Africa that can truly refer to itself as a global, international, or worldwide church. In evangelizing through soul-winning and by relying on prayer and the power of the Holy Spirit in mission, the Church of Pentecost, with all its weaknesses, would continue to serve as a model of what it means to build a twenty-first-century

Christian denomination. This work by Apostle Dr. Amos Jimmy Markin would serve as a useful text for seminaries and Bible schools seeking to understand what it means to be in mission for God through Jesus Christ and in the power of the Holy Spirit today.

Rev. Prof. J. Kwabena Asamoah-Gyadu, PhD, DD (HC), FGA
Baëta-Grau Professor of African Christianity and Pentecostal Theology
Trinity Theological Seminary, Legon, Ghana

Preface

AFTER I HAD BEEN a member for almost two decades of the International Missions Board of the Church of Pentecost (CoP), two considerations induced me to undertake this research and to publish this book. The first was that the worldwide growth and impact of the CoP—a Pentecostal denomination headquartered in the Sub-Saharan African nation of Ghana, with 2,516,147 adherents and congregations in 90 missions across the globe, including the Western world—deserves critical observation. I consider especially important the contributions that the denomination, as well as African Pentecostalism in general, is making towards the growth of global Christianity. One particular observation of mine was that various writings have skewed the origin and history of the Pentecostal movement towards the Western church and imply that Pentecostalism originated from the West without the contribution of African Christianity, particularly African Pentecostalism. However, many have observed African Pentecostalism's innovative and effective contributions in the current spread of global Christianity.

My second motivation was the need to update the history of the Church of Pentecost and to discover the ways and means by which the denomination thrives and grows. I do not seek to portray the CoP as in any way better than others or as having achieved what others have not. Neither do I attempt any comprehensive account of the mission of the Christian church in the broad sense. My concern is to discuss an institution whose leadership I am part of and to critically analyze the doctrines and practices related to its tremendous growth in Ghana and its worldwide spread and to suggest avenues for further growth. Doing so has led me to see that the Christian church as a whole must endeavor to pay particular attention to an important factor. My purpose, then, is to draw attention to the part the Holy Spirit plays in Christian church growth and missions globally and to warn of the implications of his neglect by the church, especially in this era. The attentive reader of this book will discover, among other factors (such as the religious and missiological), how the growth of the Pentecostal movement has come about through its theology of the Spirit, expressed in its spirituality based upon the experience of the Holy Spirit active in the adherents and in the corporate movement. The Pentecostal vitality that has brought revival, refreshing, and growth into the church since the beginning of the twentieth-century is purely the work of the Holy Spirit—the fulfillment of the promise of the Lord Jesus Christ in Acts:

> For John truly baptized with water, but you shall be baptized with the Holy Spirit not many days from now. . . . But you shall receive power when the Holy Spirit has come upon you; and you shall be witnesses to me in Jerusalem, and in all Judea and Samaria, and to the end of the earth. (Acts 1:5, 8)

This book comes to the conclusion that Pentecostal denominations such as the CoP are mushrooming across the global religious landscape due, above all, to their doctrine of and dependency on the Holy Spirit. I hope that the history, growth, and missions engagements of the Church of Pentecost (CoP), as a local version of African Pentecostalism that interprets the Pentecostal movement generally, will spur all of the present church to quickly come to terms with this reality and realign themselves with the Holy Spirit for further growth and development.

I take this opportunity to express my deep gratitude to the various contributors who in numerous ways enhanced this book. They include the Rev. Professor J. Kwabena Asamoah-Gyadu, who supervised this research and also graciously wrote the foreword. As a Methodist minister, his publications on Pentecostalism in general and issues on the Holy Spirit and his writings on the CoP have challenged and inspired me to this undertaking. Others who have been of great help include the Rev. Professor Elom-Dovlo, my former supervisor and lecturer at the University of Ghana, Department of Religion and Philosophy; Apostle Professor Opoku Onyinah, the immediate past chairman of the Church of Pentecost; Apostle Dr. Michael K. Ntumy, former chairman of the Church of Pentecost and the director of Literary Works of the church; Apostle Dr. Lord Elorm-Donkor, the principal of Birmingham Christian College, who read through my dissertation and offered very insightful suggestions and encouraged me to persevere; and Apostle Professor Emmanuel K.

Larbi, the founder and rector of Regent University College in Ghana, who supportively wrote blurbs for this book. My uttermost best regards to all who find this book helpful to their lives, ministry, and study.

The doctoral dissertation that was revised for this publication as a book included my expressions of gratitude to a number of people and groups whose names are not all given here. In addition to those named above, however, I do want to again express my gratitude to some persons for their important roles played in my life in this academic journey.

This work was inspired first and foremost by my inclusion on the International Missions Board of the Church of Pentecost. The privilege of being a member of this august board for over seventeen years and the insight of knowing and associating with the international missions directors, their secretaries, and missionaries and gaining knowledge of general trends and affairs in CoP missions spurred me on. In this regard I am most grateful to Apostle B. K. Arthur, who spotted me from afar and probably instigated my inclusion on the board.

My profound indebted gratitude goes to the staff at the CoP statistical department, Elder Daniel Tetteh and his team, the Secretariat of the International Missions Directorate, and the secretaries at the General Secretariat's office, especially Pastor Abraham B. Agyemang. My personal administrative secretary at the Evangelism Ministry Secretariat, Miss Theresa Louisa Obadzen, is to be commended for her tireless contributions and errands. The Publications Department team, headed by Pastor Isaac Annor and Brother Prince Asare, needs commendation. I am grateful to many precious colleagues and friends, to the field pastors at Bolgatanga, who offered a great deal of help in data collection and other discussions, and to my regular prayer intercessory team, my driver, Cosmos B. A. Kwaw, and my assistants at home.

Finally, I am eternally grateful to my dear wife, Mavis, and our children, Loretta, Jeshurun, Coretta, and John Kingsley, for their patience, sacrifice, and tenacity in the seasons of long hours of study. Their sacrifices enabled me to complete this study, by the grace and manifold gifts of God in his Son Jesus Christ through the Holy Spirit.

Abbreviations

ACF	African Christian Fellowship
ACG	Apostolic Church of Ghana
ADB	African Development Bank
AEAM	Association of Evangelicals in Africa and Madagascar
AIC	African independent church / African-instituted church / African-initiated church / African indigenous church
CAC	Christ Apostolic Church
CBCB	community-based church building
CM	Charismatic movement
CoP	Church of Pentecost
CP	classical Pentecostal/Pentecostalism
EFK	Evangelical Fellowship of Kenya
ELICOP	Elim Church of Pentecost
FAD	finance and administrative director
GEC	Ghana Evangelism Committee
GHAFES	Ghana Fellowship of Evangelical Students
GPC	Ghana Pentecostal Council
GPCC	Ghana Pentecostal and Charismatic Council
ICCC	International Christian Chamber of Commerce
IMD	international missions director
IFES	International Fellowship of Evangelical Students
ITI-PENSA	Inter-Tertiary Institution PENSA
KNUST	Kwame Nkrumah University of Science and Technology
LIC	Legon Interdenominational Church
LPU	Legon Pentecostals' Union
NRTVMC	National Radio and Television Ministry Committee
NGO	non-governmental organization

NOM	Northern Outreach Ministry
PAUKE	Pentecost Association of UK and Eire
PEMEF	Pentecost Men's Fellowship
PEMEM	Pentecost Men's Ministry
PENCO	Pentecost Cooperative Mutual Support and Social Services Society
PENSA	Pentecost Students and Associates
PENTSOS	Pentecost Social Services
PENTWAS	Pentecost Welfare Association
PENTYEM	Pentecost Youth and Evangelism Movement
PIWC	Pentecost International Worship Centre
RCC	Regional Consultative Council
SC	spiritual church
SU	Scripture Union
UNDP	United Nations Development Programme
UNIFIL	United Nations Interim Force in Lebanon

1

Introduction
Christianity, Mission, and Pentecostalism in Ghana

THIS STUDY FORMS PART of an effort to unravel the innovations, challenges, and achievements of Pentecostalism and its global Christian missions over the last century, particularly from the perspective of African Pentecostalism. It undertakes a historical-theological analysis of a particular African classical Pentecostal denomination: The Church of Pentecost (CoP), headquartered in Ghana. The CoP, though originally part of an African indigenous initiative, locates its historical roots in the British Apostolic Church, in Bradford, England. It was established through the collaborative endeavors between an Irish missionary, James McKeown, and his African counterpart, Peter Newman Anim. Since its inception, the CoP has grown into a vibrant, independent, indigenous classical Pentecostal denomination with a strong missionary orientation. It has emerged as the largest Protestant church in Ghana, and has many recognizable assemblies all over the world, including Britain, the location of its roots.

PENTECOSTALISM AND GLOBAL CHRISTIANITY

Pentecostalism has been acknowledged by current studies and research as the most influential and fastest-growing form of Christianity, spearheading global Christian mission outreach and the changing character of Christianity in the 21st century.[1] Allan Anderson identifies it as the fastest-growing religious movement in the world today, whose significance and effects on the global Christian mission enterprise, now and in the future, cannot be underestimated.[2] He asserts that even apart from its massive growth, a fact accepted by all informed observers, no observer of Christianity can deny the significance of Pentecostalism in today's religious landscape. He further states that the premise for understanding the primary motivation of Pentecostalism for global church expansion throughout the 20th century is that it is a missionary movement.[3] He writes, "The many varieties of Pentecostalism have contributed to the reshaping of the nature of global religion itself, with enormous implications."[4]

Harvey Cox has also written on the growth of Pentecostalism worldwide in his publication *Fire from Heaven: The Rise of Pentecostal Spirituality and the Reshaping of Religion in the Twenty-First Century*. In an earlier publication, *The Secular City*, Cox had tried to work out a theology for the "post-religious" age in which some theologians and sociologists had predicted the waning or extinction of religion and the "death of God" due to the rise of secularism.[5] In his later encounter with Pentecostalism, of which he wrote in 1995, the sheer enormity of its numbers made him concede that "it is by far the largest non-Catholic grouping, accounting for one in every four Christians. It is also the fastest-growing Christian movement on earth, increasing more rapidly than either militant Islam or the Christian fundamentalist sects with which it is sometimes confused."[6]

Since the beginning of this century, Pentecostalism has attracted massive academic and scholarly attention. Walter J. Hollenweger first drew the world's attention to the development and potential of modern Pentecostalism. He suggested that the astronomical growth of the Pentecostal movement from its inception to date is unique in church history, and that should warrant academic investigation. Hollenweger, in *Pentecostalism: Origins and Developments Worldwide*, stated, "The stupendous

1. Anderson, *To the Ends of the Earth*, 1; Robert, "Shifting Southward."
2. Anderson, *To the Ends of the Earth*, 1–2.
3. Anderson, *To the Ends of the Earth*, 2.
4. Anderson, *To the Ends of the Earth*, 3.
5. See Cox, foreword to *Pentecostals after a Century*, 8.
6. Cox, *Fire from Heaven*, 14–15.

growth of Pentecostalism/Charismatism/independentism from zero to almost 500,000,000 in less than a century is a growth which is unique in church history, not excluding the early centuries of the church."[7] One database indicates that the numerical figure of 614,000,000 adherents in 2010 makes this group a quarter of the world's Christian population.[8]

In addition to being a global movement, Pentecostalism has emerged as a Third World or non-Western phenomenon.[9] Significantly, it has risen concurrently with the massive growth of Christianity in Africa. Theologians and scholars of religion agree that this century has seen a tremendous shift of the center of gravity of Christianity from its previous home in the North to the South.[10] This shift had been rightly predicted by Andrew F. Walls, Kwame Bediako, and David Barrett.[11] We now see a vibrant Christian church in southern locations such as East Asia, Latin America, and Africa. For instance, since the 1970s, Barrett has predicted the permanent transformation of Christianity into a non-Western religion based on its tremendous numerical surge. The annual statistics in his *World Christian Encyclopedia* reads as follows:

> Since 1900 Christianity has become massively accepted as the religion of the developing countries in the so-called third world, particularly in Africa. In Africa, Christians have mushroomed from nine million nine hundred thousand (9.9 million) in 1900 (0.6% of the world's population then of 1,619,886,760) to two hundred and three million (203 million) in 1980 (4.7% of 4,373,917,535 world population) and three hundred and ninety-three million (393 million) by 2000 (19.5% of 6,259,642,000 world population). The net increase of Christians on the African continent as of 2000 is six million (6 million) new Christians a year (16,400 a day).[12]

Based on Barrett's analysis, Walls then drew attention to its implication by suggesting that what happens within the African churches in this generation will determine the whole shape of church history for centuries.[13]

7. Hollenweger, *Pentecostalism*, 1.
8. Barrett and Crossing, "Christianity 2010," 29–36.
9. Anderson, *To the Ends of the Earth*, 1.
10. Hanciles, *Beyond Christendom*, 3.
11. See Walls, *Missionary Movement*, 68–75; Walls, *Cross-Cultural Process in Christian History*, 31–34, 47; Bediako, *Christianity in Africa*, 158, Barrett, "AD 2000," 39–54.
12. Barrett, Kurian, and Johnson, *World Christian Encyclopedia*, 25.
13. Walls, *Missionary Movement*, xviii.

True to their observations and analyses (Walls and others), at the beginning of the 21st century, religious phenomenologists accept that Christianity has become a non-Western religion.

The growth and transformation of African Christianity in this century has almost entirely been ascribed to the impact and influence of Pentecostalism.[14] The historical growth of the Christian church in Ghana underscores this same point. Researchers clearly see Pentecostalism, including that practiced by the CoP, as the dominant Christian form influencing the growth of Ghanaian Christianity today.

FOCUS OF THE STUDY: THE CHURCH OF PENTECOST

This study focuses on the CoP as a local version of world Pentecostalism that provides a specific base from which to further discuss the influence and impact of African Pentecostalism in the growth of African and global Christianity. The denomination is recognized as having a massive presence in Ghana and conspicuous establishments in the diaspora and many other places in the world Christian landscape, which provide "ongoing missions" outside its original African context. Its mission in the United States, for instance, has been identified as one of the better-organized African immigrant churches.[15]

Statistically, as of December 2016, the CoP has branches in 91 nations around the globe, with 2,516,147 congregants from 18,426 local assemblies or congregations. These congregations are administered by 112,347 lay leaders, 35,711 of which are elders, 49,681 deaconesses, 26,955 deacons, and 1,995 ministers or clergymen. Out of the 1,995 total ministers, 1,934 are stationed in Ghana, and 61 are missionaries outside Ghana.[16] The total number of registered congregants in Ghana, which is 2,122,076, is estimated to be around 8.5 percent of the national population of the country of 27,000,000.

In spite of these CoP growth statistics, it has not been the subject of much scholarly research until recently. One reason may be that its brand of Christianity, unlike that of the independent Charismatic churches, raises few controversies that would excite Western authorities on African

---

14. Asamoah-Gyadu, *Contemporary Pentecostal Christianity*, 2; Asamoah-Gyadu, "Pentecostalism and the Missiological Significance," 30.

15. Asamoah-Gyadu, "'On Mission Abroad," 89–102.

16. CoP, Summary Statistics Worldwide, June 2017.

studies.[17] The other reason is that, until recently, the CoP had raised few or no research theologians from its own fold, who would be interested in doing theological and scientific research on its development. The only formal scholarly publication on the CoP was published in 2001 by E. Kingsley Larbi, a member of the church. He wrote comprehensively on the origins of Pentecostalism in Ghana and traced its development and diffusion before 2000.[18] He discussed the CoP from its historical inception and other formative structural developments (the church's ethos, doctrine, worship pattern) up to the early 1990s.[19] Since then, no further update has been done on its historical growth and developments. The factors contributing to the CoP's growth have not yet been fully and scientifically analyzed and discussed.

This present writer holds that one of the main causes of the growth of Pentecostalism is the "pneumatic factor," the part played by the Holy Spirit. This is the main focus of this study. For instance, as will be shown later in this chapter, the current outlook of Christianity in Ghana is predominately Pentecostal and Charismatic. This observation implies that a "pneumatic factor," the role of Holy Spirit—as has always been associated with the movement—plays a key role among the factors underpinning Christianity's growth in the nation. Asamoah-Gyadu has noted that "a critical point in terms of understanding the work of the Holy Spirit in the life of the church is to see Him, that is, God the Holy Spirit, as God's empowering presence among His people."[20] The CoP's growth and missions is no exception to this observation.

This book aims to demonstrate the hypothesis that, among a number of reasons, the major factor underpinning the growth and mission of the CoP is the experience of the power of the Holy Spirit—the "pneumatic factor" operating in the church. In fact, discussions on the growth of the Pentecostal movement, since its inception, have always engaged the "pneumatic factor." This study's hypothesis aligns with other observations, such as Asamoah-Gyadu's statement, "in the Twenty-First Century, the Christian theology that seems to have become characteristic of the African church including Ghana is that which takes seriously the pneumatic experiences of the Bible in general and the New Testament in

17. Asamoah-Gyadu, "Renewal within African Christianity," 34.
18. See Larbi, *Pentecostalism*.
19. Larbi, *Pentecostalism*, 99–294.
20. Asamoah-Gyadu, *Holy Spirit Our Comforter*, 229.

particular,"[21] referring to Pentecostalism, particularly in Ghanaian Christianity today. Thus, more detailed research on the theological factors that promote the phenomenal success of CoP as an African Pentecostal denomination is overdue.

Also in support of this thesis, current African theologians and historians such as Jehu J. Hanciles, Afe Adogame, and Asamoah-Gyadu point to the fact that the growth of Christianity in Africa is mainly among Pentecostals.[22] Moreover, African Pentecostalism is not only growing in Africa but is spreading into other continents as well.[23] These researchers examine various issues including globalization, transnationalism, migration, reverse flow, reverse missions, and many other religious transmission issues affecting African Christian presence in many parts of the globe, including the West. They particularly examine the implications of these trends on the future global Christian church, as well as their effect on Africa's contribution in global evangelization. For instance, in his *Beyond Christendom: Globalization, African Migration and the Transformation of the West,* Hanciles argues that contemporary globalization embodies the most transformative processes of all times. And, most significantly, when people move they carry their ideas, beliefs, and religious practices with them.[24] The fact that the southern shift in global Christianity's center of gravity coincides with the epochal reversal in the direction and flow of global migration (South to North) is of historic consequence.[25]

Scholars also assert that the presence of African migrant churches in the West, for example, is reengaging the church in missions in much the same fashion as the Western missionaries brought the gospel to Africa.[26] In this regard, Hanciles contends that the religiosity of the CoP plays an integral part in these new missionary engagements because of its global spread and immigrant congregations in the diaspora, which draw attention to this new mission movement. Asamoah-Gyadu affirms the uniqueness of CoP and other African migrant churches, especially in the diaspora, arguing that they have set a new agenda for studies in Christian

21. Asamoah-Gyadu, *African Charismatics*, 18.
22. Asamoah-Gyadu, *Contemporary Pentecostal Christianity*, 9.
23. See Adogame and Spickard, *Religion Crossing Boundaries*.
24. Hanciles, *Beyond Christendom*, 2, 4.
25. Hanciles, *Beyond Christendom*, 6.
26. Adogame and Spickard, *Religion Crossing Boundaries*, 14–15; Hanciles, *Beyond Christendom*, 5.

mission that should engage scholarly attention.[27] Thus, this study also investigates the CoP's global missionary enterprises. Specifically, it updates, discusses, and analyzes the history, growth, and mission of the CoP and, in doing so, identifies the salient and essential factors that promote its growth both locally and in its missions abroad. The history of Christianity in Ghana, however, predates the Pentecostal churches and the CoP.

Brief Historical Trajectory of the Growth of Christianity in Ghana

The history of Christian mission and church planting in Ghana can be organized chronologically into four major church forms: Roman Catholic mission, Protestant mission enterprise, African independent churches, and Pentecostal and Charismatic church forms.

Beginning from the early 20th century, Pentecostal expressions of Christianity were introduced and have developed in Ghana, overlapping with the four church forms. These have emerged in five noticeable streams: (1) as a revivalist movement preceding the emergence of African Christian initiatives, (2) as independent indigenous spiritual movements or churches, (3) as different Pentecostal denominational church forms, (4) as renewal movements injecting vibrancy into the older historic or mainline denominations, and (5) as recently proliferating Charismatic church forms and other parachurch movements across the country.[28] The extent of Pentecostal growth and influence since its emergence compared to the other three church forms is phenomenal. An examination of the historical trajectory of Christianity in Ghana demonstrates this tremendous contrast.

Roman Catholic Mission

Christian missionary activity in the Gold Coast (Ghana)[29] dates back to the 15th century through Roman Catholic mission. Their first attempt at church planting did not come to fruition.[30] The second and more fruitful

27. Asamoah-Gyadu, "On Mission Abroad," 102.

28. See Omenyo, *Pentecost Outside Pentecostalism*; Asamoah-Gyadu, *African Charismatics*.

29. Until it became independent of British rule in 1957, Ghana was known as the Gold Coast.

30. Sanneh, *West African Christianity*, 19, 21.

attempt at evangelization and church planting in Ghana in terms of "disciple-converts" came in the 19th century. After 40 years of restarting the missions work in Ghana, the church recorded 35,000 baptisms, 25,000 catechumens, 10 parishes, 364 out-stations, 301 chapels, 22 priests, 13 sisters, and 85 schools with 4,734 boys and girls on the rolls.[31] The population of Ghana was 2,300,000 at that time.

Protestant Missionary Enterprise

The modern phase of Christian missionary enterprise into sub-Saharan African commenced in earnest from the second half of the 18th century and continued through much of the 19th and 20th centuries.[32] In Ghana, this era marked the emergence of European Protestant missionary societies whose efforts culminated in the forming of the present mainline Protestant churches.[33] Between 1787 and 1893, various European nations such as England, Holland, France, Denmark, Sweden, and Germany erected considerable settlements in forts and castles along the coast of Ghana. These explorers used the services of Protestant chaplains. Beginning from this era, various Western missionary societies, predominantly evangelical, sent their missionaries and chaplains to work in Ghana.[34] They included the Moravian United Brethren Mission, Netherlands Reformed Missions (1742–1747), the Church of England's Society for the Propagation of the Gospel (1751–1816), the Basel Evangelical Missions Society (1828–1918), Wesleyan Methodist Missionary Society (1831–1961), North German Missionary Society (1847–1916), and the United Free Church of Scotland (1914–1918).[35] Out of these societies emerged the various mainline Protestant churches, such as the African Methodist Episcopal (AME), Zion Church, Ewe Presbyterian Church (now the Evangelical Presbyterian Church), Presbyterian Church of Gold Coast (now Presbyterian Church of Ghana), Wesleyan Methodist Church (now Methodist Church of Ghana), English Church Mission (Anglican Church), and others. These named formed the Christian Council of Gold

---

31. Omenyo, *Pentecost Outside Pentecostalism*, 47.
32. Sanneh, *West African Christianity*, 21.
33. Omenyo, *Pentecost Outside Pentecostalism*, 48.
34. Adogame and Spickard, *Religion Crossing Boundaries*, 4.
35. The dates refer to the periods spent on the Gold Coast. For a more detailed work on the Western missions, see Omenyo, *Pentecost Outside Pentecostalism*.

Coast (now the Christian Council of Ghana) on October 30, 1929, as the largest Protestant ecumenical body in the country.[36]

Few religious historians will disagree that decades of missionary endeavor in this era produced only a small number of African converts.[37] Writers of Christian history and missions agree on the reason: the missionary activities of these societies did not genuinely encounter the African and, for that matter, the Ghanaian context.[38] However, Omenyo confirms that some of the rich heritage of the missionary societies later became a strong drive in the proliferation of African independent churches and Pentecostalism in Ghana.[39]

African Independent or Indigenous Churches in Ghana

One African response to the Western missionary encounter in the late 19th century and the 20th century resulted in the emergence of African-initiated or -instituted or independent churches (AICs) from 1914 to 1937 and on.[40] The subsequent expansion of Christianity in Ghana from the 20th century on has largely been driven by AICs. These began through the preaching of some dynamic charismatic African figures such as William Wadé Harris and Kwame Sampson Oppong, who emerged between 1914 and 1920.

Subsequently, the 1920s and 1930s witnessed a second wave of new Ghanaian Christian independent churches—referred to in Ghana as spiritual churches (SCs)—as a spontaneous development after the effective preaching of these charismatic figures. The spiritual churches were basically prophetic and healing movements that demonstrated pneumatic experiences. They include the Musama Disco Christo Church (MDCC, 1922), Cherubim and Seraphim (1925), the Twelve Apostles Church, the Apostles Revelation Society, the Saviour Church, and the African Faith Tabernacle congregations.[41] The number of these indigenous churches

36. "C.C.G History," Christian Council of Ghana website, christiancouncilgh.org/history.htm.

37. See Adogame and Spickard, *Religion Crossing Boundaries*, 4; and Kalu, *African Christianity*.

38. Bediako, *Christianity in Africa*, 69; and Omenyo, *Pentecost Outside Pentecostalism*, 63.

39. Sanneh, *West African Christianity*, 114.

40. Omenyo, *Pentecost Outside Pentecostalism*, 67.

41. Adogame and Spickard, *Religion Crossing Boundaries*, 5. See also Bäeta,

seems to have declined since the 1970s, a trend attributed, among other reasons, to the emergence of other, more pragmatic church forms with the same emphasis on pneumatic experience,[42] specifically, the Pentecostal and Charismatic Christian groups, which present a similar brand of indigenous Christian church forms on the Ghanaian religious landscape.

Classical Pentecostals and Charismatic Churches in Ghana

The classical Pentecostal and Charismatic movements have been prominent church forms on the Ghanaian landscape since the 1930s. They include some Pentecostal denominations of entirely foreign origin, such as the Assemblies of God, Foursquare Gospel churches, the classical Pentecostal denominations that emerged from the 1930s onward and their progeny, and the Charismatic movements (CMs), which emerged in the early 1970s. They have infiltrated the mainline churches in their various Charismatic wings and the larger Ghanaian Christian landscape as independent CMs. The independent Charismatic churches appear to be the most widespread and are enjoying enormous growth and influence in Ghana today. The CM churches in Ghana include Christian Action Faith Ministries International, International Central Gospel Church, Global Revival Ministries, Resurrection Power Ministries, Word Miracle Church International, Living Praise Chapel International, and Lighthouse Chapel International, to name a few of the earlier ones that emerged.[43]

Defining African Pentecostalism

Pentecostalism's variations and diverse forms make it difficult to define.[44] Generally, it refers to the stream of Christian forms that emphasize pneumatic phenomena. Douglas Jacobson suggests that, in a general sense, being Pentecostal means that one is committed to a Spirit-centered, miracle-affirming, praise-oriented version of the Christian faith, but he is quick to add that there is no meta-model of Pentecostalism.[45]

Prophetism in Ghana.
    42. See Asamoah-Gyadu, *African Charismatics*, 29–30.
    43. See Asamoah-Gyadu, *African Charismatics*, 35.
    44. Anderson, "Varieties, Definitions and Taxonomies," 13–29.
    45. Jacobson, *Thinking in the Spirit*, 11–12.

Historically, Pentecostalism worldwide has been interpreted as standing in direct continuity with the experience of Charles Fox Parham's and William J. Seymour's Azusa Street movements of 1901 and 1906, respectively.[46] This presumed historical link has two problems, though. First, other incidents of the Spirit's experience occurred before Azusa Street, such as documented in India's experience, which predates the North American initiative by at least 40 years.[47] The second is the fact that making it a Western experience minimizes the origins of the movement from other contexts across the globe, making it look like an innovation not suitable for other cultural contexts such as African ones. Asamoah-Gyadu has rightly argued that religious movements are shaped by the cultural and political milieu in which they arise. He and others, such as Hollenweger, advocate an intercultural interpretation that considers the Spirit's experience as universally normative for Christian history.[48] He posits that the movement has generated a global culture with shared effects despite the cultural, ethnic, linguistic, and theological diversities. Asamoah-Gyadu then proposes an intercultural working definition for Pentecostalism, based on its origins in the early church as found in the Acts of the Apostles, thereby making it more universal. This study considers his definition apt as coming from an African cultural context and taking a universal outlook. Adopting Asamoah-Gyadu's definition as a working definition throughout these discussions, Pentecostalism, including African Pentecostalism, encompasses

> Christian groups which emphasize salvation in Christ as a transformative experience wrought by the Holy Spirit and in which pneumatic phenomena, including "speaking in tongues," prophesies, visions, healing and miracles in general, perceived as standing in historic continuity with the experiences of the early church as found especially in the Acts of the Apostles, are sought, accepted, valued, and consciously encouraged among members as signifying the presence of God and experiences of his Spirit.[49]

This definition embraces large movements that require further distinctions and classifications. Anderson delineates three general distinctive

---

46. Asamoah-Gyadu, *African Charismatics*, 10.
47. McGee, "Pentecostal Phenomena and Revivals in India," 112–17.
48. Asamoah-Gyadu, *African Charismatics*, 10–12.
49. Asamoah-Gyadu, *African Charismatics*, 12.

classifications: classical Pentecostals; older church Charismatics including Catholics, Anglicans, orthodox; and neo-Pentecostals or neo-Charismatic churches.[50] The CoP is classified as a classical Pentecostal (CP) denomination. The roots of classical Pentecostalism trace from early 20th-century evangelical revivals and missionary movements, particularly from the Western world.[51]

However, among classical Pentecostals, further distinctions can be made according to theological differences: (a) Holiness Pentecostals, whose roots are in the 19th-century holiness movement with belief in a second work of grace called "sanctification" and a third stage called "baptism in the Spirit"; (b) "Finished Work" Pentecostals, who differ in their approach to sanctification, seeing it as a consequence of conversion to be followed by Spirit baptism as a second work of grace; (c) Oneness Pentecostals, who reject the doctrine of the Trinity and posit a unitarianism that includes the deity of Christ; and (d) Apostolic Pentecostals, both Oneness and Trinitarian, who emphasize the authority of present-day "apostles" and "prophets" and are especially strong in West Africa. The Church of Pentecost, with its roots from the Apostolic Church in Britain, belongs to the last group, the Apostolic Pentecostals.[52] All of these groups have a theology of a subsequent experience of Spirit baptism usually accompanied by speaking in tongues.[53] However, throughout this study the terms "Pentecostal" and "Charismatic" refer to all types of such pneumatic movements mentioned above.

PURPOSE, SCOPE, AND METHOD OF THIS STUDY

In view of the tremendous growth and influence of Pentecostalism in Africa, including Ghana, the factors accounting for it warrant further examination. The part played by "pneumatic phenomena" elicits particular interest: "people in the CoP will tell you the church has grown because of the Holy Spirit."[54]

Two recent works related to the study of CoP growth factors are Daniel Okyere Walker's PhD thesis, presenting models of mission

---

50. Anderson, *To the Ends of the Earth*, 4–10.
51. See Synan, *Holiness-Pentecostal Tradition*.
52. Anderson, *To the Ends of the Earth*, 7.
53. Anderson, *Introduction to Pentecostalism*, 45–57.
54. Leonard, *Giant in Ghana*, 6.

activities of the CoP, and Lord Abraham Elorm-Donkor's theological analysis on an aspect of CoP spirituality: Christian morality. Alongside religious and theological factors that account for the expansion of the CoP—the focus of this study—writers Christine Leonard and E. K. Larbi single out administrative and ministerial structures in the CoP.[55] This current research further demonstrates how and the magnitude to which such administrative and ministerial structures of this African institution have contributed to its global expansion.

Afe Adogame and others suggest that world Christianity must be examined in local contexts since the local context is now seen as a manifestation of the global context, both in Africa and in diasporic movements.[56] Thus, it is also important to answer the question of whether these factors only apply locally for CoP as a Sub-Saharan Pentecostal movement or also contain viable applications for general Pentecostal growth.

In addition to the need for research on the factors accounting for CoP growth, we also lack documentation of major historic developments in the ministry of the CoP since 1962, when the denomination became autonomous from its parent body, the Apostolic Church UK. Its more recent post-independence history in the period after 1982 is especially important because the the Rev. James McKeown, the CoP missionary founder, handed over CoP leadership to indigenous Ghanaians in 1982.[57]

Under the broad purpose of understanding how the CoP has moved from the periphery to the center of church life in Africa and has also moved beyond its local context into other parts of the globe, including the West, this study has the following specific objectives:

a. To update the history of the CoP and her international missions from 1962 to 2012 and beyond

b. To identify and analyze the theological and missiological factors influencing the global expansion of the CoP

c. To discuss the administrative and ministerial structures through which the CoP is governed and managed as a missional church

---

55. Leonard, *Giant in Ghana*, 122–27; Larbi, *Pentecostalism*, 180.

56. Adogame, Gerloff, and Hock, *Christianity in Africa and the African Diaspora*, 3.

57. See Larbi, *Pentecostalism*. Larbi's work does not discuss the CoP beyond 1982.

d. To analyze the growth and influence of African Pentecostalism within the present discussion of world Christianity, using the CoP as a case study

This study affirms Pentecostalism not only as being the main thrust behind the shifting of Christianity's center to the southern continents but also as influencing its spread and expansion towards the North by bringing new innovations, including missions and missionaries, from the South to the North. This book points toward and helps to interpret the role of African Pentecostalism in global church evangelization in the 21st century.

Scope

This study focuses on approximately the last 50 years of the CoP's existence, beginning from 1962. The period since 1982—where Larbi's history ended—through 2012 and into the present receives particular attention.

Regarding the scope of the research, the study centers on two locations: first, its development in and from Ghana, the main African country where the institution started and has its headquarters. Second, its mission in the United Kingdom (UK) and a few other nations is examined as representative of her foreign missions. Throughout the study, however, reference is made to other international contexts, including other African countries and parts of the globe where the institution is present. The purpose of mentioning the UK first is that, apart from the fact that it serves to reflect the pattern of CoP's foreign missions, it also demonstrates how a non-Western church, brought forth through missionary effort from a Western country (the UK in this instance), could now return to that same Western country as a missionary church.[58] This also makes it possible to evaluate the CoP's contemporary developments side by side with the UK Apostolic Church that pioneered its establishment in the late 1930s and also with the Elim Pentecostal Church of UK, which has been affiliated with the CoP since 1971.[59]

---

58. The indigenous nature of the CoP is primarily inferred from its early historical link to Anim's group before the arrival of McKeown and also its early severance of ties with the British Apostolic Church.

59. See Larbi, *Pentecostalism*, 196.

Method

This historical-theological research employs a case study approach using a qualitative research method. The advantage of the case study approach is that it allows the researcher to retain the holistic and meaningful features of the real-life events of the context being studied, and it is more appropriate for answering the "why" research questions.[60] The history has been obtained through structured and semi-structured interviews and reliable literary works. The literary works include publications relevant to the study and, in the fourth and fifth chapters, which discuss church growth methods and patterns, church records. The church records include the minutes of management meetings, annual council meeting records, historic data from church archives, the history of the CoP in the various nations collated by the mission's directorate, pastoral letters, circular letters, addresses by important church leaders, documentary sources, conference materials, church statistics, brochures for programs, and program outlines.[61]

Oral information came from individuals who witnessed some of the historical events as well as those who played key roles in the church's growth. Interviewees include the leadership of the church, comprising the principal officers at the CoP headquarters (the chairman, general secretary, and international missions director), significant personalities who served in the missions directorate, some directors of ministries, some heads of CoP churches both local and international, and significant individuals involved with the church in particular geographical locations, including the national head of CoP–UK. The interviewees provided relevant information on the religious, theological, and missiological factors responsible for the growth, as well as salient input on the history that augmented other sources needing further clarification and confirmation.

Buttressing all this, the writer presents this research as an insider who brings to bear 25 years of experience in the organization as an ordained minister of the CoP, an apostle and an area head of a designated area of the church, as well as a member of the CoP's International Missions Board for over 16 years. This position accorded the researcher more opportunities for a constructive position on the facts than would otherwise be possible. It could be contended that an insider's reflections

---

60. Yin, *Case Study Research*, 2, 6–7.

61. These are located at the church's headquarters and are available to researchers and others from the various countries in which the church operates.

might be biased. To the best of this writer's knowledge, he has been very critical in presenting the facts. Again, the writer's position afforded him relatively unfettered access to church data and all interviewees, who are close associates, as well as the opportunity to visit some of the churches of the CoP across the globe. Eight weeks in June and July 2014 were spent visiting some of the CoP branches in the UK. The advantage of using participant observation as a qualitative research method is that the researcher is able to observe and at the same time participate in the process of the research.[62]

LITERATURE REVIEW

Christine Leonard's book *A Giant in Ghana: 3,000 Churches in 50 Years*, published in 1989, widely acknowledged as the foundational history of the CoP, focuses on the life and missionary efforts of the Rev. James McKeown, considered the missionary founder of the CoP in Ghana.[63] Leonard acknowledges McKeown's work as a collaboration with indigenous efforts, and she affirms that the CoP was entirely formed, governed, run, and financed by Africans. She documents that at its fiftieth anniversary in 1987, the CoP had grown from a small number to a membership of 270,000 and a network of 3,000 local churches covering almost every town and village in Ghana. In addition, at that time it was growing at an average of five new assemblies a week.[64] Based on these statistics, the CoP experienced comparatively greater growth and expansion within this period than the earlier established missionary societies over the same number of years; the CoP has also received wider acceptance and participation from the Ghanaian populace.[65]

Leonard asserts that the church thrives on seven factors: the influence of the Holy Spirit; the James McKeown leadership factor; priority given to evangelism and missions; consistent prayer; effective sacrificial giving, a key to their financial self-sufficiency; a non-compromising stance against any attitude considered sinful (reversion to cultic practices,

---

62. Zelditch, "Some Methodological Problems," 169.
63. Leonard, *Giant in Ghana*, 3.
64. Leonard, *Giant in Ghana*, 6.
65. See the brief history of Christianity in Ghana in this introduction; Leonard, *Giant in Ghana*, 11.

sexual sins, drunkenness, etc.); and their total love for Jesus.⁶⁶ Her book suggests other factors as well that promote the church's growth, such as healings, signs and wonders, and miracles observed in the church through prayer and from its established healing camps.⁶⁷ Others contributors include the role of women in spreading the gospel,⁶⁸ the church's resonance with African culture and cosmology, the involvement of Africans in its leadership,⁶⁹ structures of administration that promote supervision and accountability,⁷⁰ and the character of the adherents, exhibited, for example, by holiness, love towards one another, and care for the needy.⁷¹ Leonard asserts that McKeown's understanding of missions, especially the manner in which he engaged with local and indigenous people as a missionary, "stands out" in relation to his success compared to previous missionaries.⁷²

The earliest scholarly work available on the CoP is Larbi's PhD thesis published under the title *Pentecostalism: The Eddies of Ghanaian Christianity*, which provides a thorough and extensive scientifically researched history of Pentecostalism in Ghana from 1914 to 1992.⁷³ The book examines how salvation is perceived and appropriated by the Pentecostal movement through holding out the gospel as a response to a traditional Ghanaian worldview: "one of the major factors leading to the remarkable success of Ghanaian Pentecostalism is that its cosmology and soteriology are in consonance with the primal concepts of reality."⁷⁴ Larbi examines Pentecostalism's continuity with the Ghanaian primal religious imagination, showing where they interconnect and where they differ.⁷⁵ With this in focus, Larbi traces the religious reasons for the emergence of Ghanaian Pentecostalism. He affirms, though, that the socioeconomic and political factors at the time provided a fertile environment for the growth of the movement.⁷⁶ The book discusses the history, development

66. Leonard, *Giant in Ghana*, 6–9.
67. Leonard, *Giant in Ghana*, 36–37.
68. Leonard, *Giant in Ghana*, 55–56, 145.
69. Leonard, *Giant in Ghana*, 69, 116.
70. Leonard, *Giant in Ghana*, 122–26.
71. Leonard, *Giant in Ghana*, 109–11.
72. Leonard, *Giant in Ghana*, 7.
73. Larbi, *Pentecostalism*, 58.
74. Larbi, *Pentecostalism*, xii, 3–13, 425; quotation from p. 3.
75. Larbi, *Pentecostalism*, 7–13.
76. Larbi, *Pentecostalism*, 49–50.

of the administrative structures, and the doctrinal understanding of Pentecostals in Ghana, which promote its growth.[77]

Particularly pertinent to this study is the fact that Larbi makes a very helpful comparative historical study of the major classical Pentecostal churches (the Christ Apostolic Church, the Apostolic Church, and the CoP) and their growth in Ghana.[78] He writes specifically on the CoP's history beginning from its roots in the meeting between Peter Anim and James McKeown in 1937 all the way to 1982, when African leadership took over.[79] He points out that the growth of the CoP as a non-Western, indigenous, independent Pentecostal church with such a dynamic evangelization strategy warrants further investigation.[80] The entire CoP denomination, he affirms, sees itself as a missionary force and, because of this, every member regards him or herself as a missionary, and they establish churches wherever they find themselves.[81] He considers the emergence, development, and growth of the CoP to be phenomenal in the history of Christianity in Africa, and it must be understood within the broader context of the modern missionary efforts and the process of Pentecostal renewal in Africa since the middle of the 20th century.

Nevertheless, Larbi's work on the CoP ends at 1982, and he treats it in the larger context of Ghanaian Pentecostalism. He bases the CoP's numerical growth primarily on her uncompromising stand in prayer, discipline (in terms of ethical rigor), and evangelism.[82] Larbi also includes the effectiveness of the organizational structure; the disciplinary measures in the CoP's structures; the zeal of the early evangelists, Bombing group, Witness Movement; and signs and wonders.[83] He observes the early transfer of members from Anim's group into the CoP due to doctrinal difference on the use of medication and from the historic churches due to their observation of the demonstration of the Holy Spirit.[84] Other factors suggested by Larbi include McKeown's missiological approach and teachings centered on Christ, leadership involvement with the indigenous

77. See, for instance, Larbi, *Pentecostalism*, 108–71, which discusses the CAC; 175–294, on the CoP; and 295ff., on neo-Pentecostalism in Ghana.

78. Larbi, *Pentecostalism*, 108–71.

79. Larbi, *Pentecostalism*, 106–294.

80. Larbi, *Pentecostalism*, 204.

81. Larbi, *Pentecostalism*, 250.

82. Larbi, *Pentecostalism*, 180.

83. Larbi, *Pentecostalism*, 181–88.

84. Larbi, *Pentecostalism*, 181–82.

Ghanaians, use of print and electronic media, Pentecost Students and Associates (PENSA), Pentecost International Worship Centres (PIWCs), and the emergence of the prayer camps.[85] The current study builds on Larbi's work on the CoP, taking off from where he stopped.

Asamoah-Gyadu, an African scholar keen on African Pentecostalism, is another scholar who has written on issues related to the CoP. His article "Pentecostalism and the Missiological Significance of Religious Experience in Africa Today: The Case of Ghana 'Church of Pentecost'" discusses the importance of religious experience as a nonnegotiable element of Christian mission using the CoP as a paradigm.[86] He argues that all the reasons for the phenomenal impact of the CoP's missionary endeavors are motivated by the unique personal experiences of the Holy Spirit. Pentecostal Christianity has performed well in most parts of Africa, "partly because Pentecostalism provides ritual contexts within which people may experience God's presence and power in forceful and demonstrable way."[87] Asamoah-Gyadu's article further discusses the current state and structure of the CoP as a Sub-Saharan African Pentecostal denomination at the forefront of global evangelization in the 21st century. He does not discuss, however, how the Spirit is involved in the CoP through the individual's spiritual experiences to forge its missions, and how this spiritual experience works through the church's various administrative, missional, and ministerial structures. Although his article centers on only one aspect of the factors that promote the CoP's growth, his work does enhance the main idea behind this study, laid out particularly in its sixth chapter: how the pneumatological experiences found in the life of the CoP (both individually and corporately) promote her growth and missions.

In his earlier publication *African Charismatics: Current Developments within Independent Indigenous Pentecostalism in Ghana*, Asamoah-Gyadu continues Larbi's work on Ghanaian Pentecostal history and theoretical analysis. He outlines Pentecostal emergence in Ghana as occurring in three phases, the first being the AICs, the second the Western mission-related Pentecostal denominations, and finally the neo-Pentecostal movements.[88]

---

85. Larbi, *Pentecostalism*, 185, 199, 201–3, 407–11.
86. Asamoah-Gyadu, "Pentecostalism and the Missiological Significance," 30.
87. Asamoah-Gyadu, "Pentecostalism and the Missiological Significance," 31.
88. Asamoah-Gyadu, *African Charismatics*, 16–35.

Another article by Asamoah-Gyadu, "On Mission Abroad: Ghana's Church of Pentecost and Its USA Missions," discusses the CoP's international missions using Ghanaian immigrant congregations in North America as a case study.[89] He identifies the CoP as an African Pentecostal organization with some of the best-organized churches in the West.[90] In addition, he claims, the CoP has a "Pentecostal Pattern of Spiritual Life" that is recovering the existential experience of the Holy Spirit for the contemporary church.[91] The current research further investigates this assertion.

The 2010 thesis of Daniel Okyere Walker, a CoP pastor and a lecturer at the Pentecost University College in Ghana, entitled "The Pentecost Fire Is Burning: Models of Mission Activities in the Church of Pentecost," examines the development of missionary activities of the CoP from 1917 (era of Peter Anim) to 2008 (era of Ntumy), using five mission models: local, regional, migrational, reverse, and reflux.[92] He asserts that CoP missions—in contrast to the general pattern of missionary organizations that normally direct mission activities from a higher board—are shaped and formulated from the grassroots.[93] Walker suggests what he calls the "economission" model, which draws on economic principles enabling the mission practitioner to assess, evaluate, identify, and apply the appropriate model to a particular mission context.[94] Walker's thesis was helpful in the fifth chapter of this work, which focuses on the CoP diaspora missions, drawing on his historical analysis from the CoP–UK missions.[95]

Over a decade after Larbi's *Pentecostalism*, Opoku Onyinah published *Pentecostal Exorcism: Witchcraft and Demonology in Ghana*, which aims at contextualizing an aspect of African Christian theology—deliverance and exorcism and African witchcraft exorcistic practices—observed from the African Pentecostal perspective, using the CoP as a case study.[96] Exorcism has become a major topic of Ghanaian Pentecostal spirituality,

---

89. Ludwig and Asamoah-Gyadu, introduction to *African Christian Presence in the West*, 10–18.

90. Asamoah-Gyadu, "On Mission Abroad," 91.

91. Asamoah-Gyadu, "On Mission Abroad," 93.

92. Walker, "Pentecost Fire," 79–271.

93. Walker, "Pentecost Fire," 7.

94. Walker, "Pentecost Fire," 274–75, 299.

95. Walker, "Pentecost Fire," 188–244.

96. Onyinah, *Pentecostal Exorcism*, 5.

especially as practiced among the Akan traditional people.[97] Onyinah addresses the current Pentecostal deliverance ministry as a contextualization of the gospel to the African audience. He concludes that the CoP has not yet intellectually systemized its faith and practice into theological categories, but its normal church activities nevertheless express them.[98] His work is particularly relevant to this study in its attempt to formulate an African Pentecostal theology for the 21st century.

In response to some of Onyinah's queries on Christian character and deliverance, we have Lord Abraham Elorm-Donkor's 2011 PhD thesis, "Christian Morality in Ghanaian Pentecostalism: A Theological Analysis of Virtue Theory as a Framework for Integrating Christian and Akan Moral Schemes."[99] His research explores whether and how Ghanaian Pentecostals' appropriation of the African worldview into Christian praxis might account for the observed paradox of enthusiastic Christian spirituality that appears to be separated from social morality, and he proposes a deeper integration of the Christian and Akan traditional moral schemes. He asserts that there has been no serious reflection on the relationship between the African traditional worldview and African Christian moral practice in the Ghanaian context.[100]

Elorm-Donkor recognizes Ghanaian Pentecostals' "deliverance theology" as the source of Pentecostalism's tremendous growth.[101] He argues, however, that the "deliverance theology" of Ghanaian Pentecostals involves significant misrepresentations of the Akan traditional scheme, which causes many Christians to focus on religion as a means to meet one's needs rather than to transform one's inner disposition for moral character formation.[102] He advocates integrating the Wesleyan account of the Christian truth and reinterpreting the Akan view of humanity, thereby transforming the deliverance theology to portray the Christian life as a pneumatological characterology. The Wesleyan account of Christian anthropology holds that, by the grace of God, humanity can unite with God through the acts of the Holy Spirit in effecting repentance,

---

97. Onyinah, *Pentecostal Exorcism*, 4.
98. Onyinah, *Pentecostal Exorcism*, 138.
99. Elorm-Donkor, "Christian Morality in Ghanaian Pentecostalism," 11.
100. Elorm-Donkor, "Christian Morality in Ghanaian Pentecostalism," 13, 15.
101. Elorm-Donkor, "Christian Morality in Ghanaian Pentecostalism," 18, 46–48.
102. Elorm-Donkor, "Christian Morality in Ghanaian Pentecostalism," 27–29.

justification, and sanctification that ultimately enable humans to embody the character of God as revealed in the character of Jesus Christ.[103]

In his *Looking Back, Moving Forward: Transformation and Ethical Practice in the Church of Pentecost*, Girish Daswani analyzes the growth and mission of global Pentecostal Christianity, but from the viewpoint of an anthropological study of ethics. He uses the CoP's mission both locally in Ghana and in its diaspora mission in the UK to focus on Pentecostal transformation and ethical practice. He writes,

> Pentecostal transformation is productively understood as a reflective process that involves dual movements of looking back reflectively and moving forward in time through an ethical practice that is located in the conjunction or movement between explicit commitments to shared Pentecostal values and implicit practices and changing circumstances.[104]

Daswani holds that Pentecostal transformation should be seen as an ethical practice that emerges through a moral framework in which Pentecostals are mediating and evaluating everyday situations, different cultural and socioeconomic environments, their ambitions to travel abroad, and their relationship with multiple others, including the Holy Spirit.[105] By including the Holy Spirit among the "multiple others," Daswani raises a challenge and critique to the proposal of other theological writers such as Asamoah-Gyadu, who argues that religious experience such as the personal transformative experience of the Holy Spirit in the Pentecostal movement is the major factor for its growth. As this literature review suggests, all these writers on the CoP, such as Leonard, Larbi, Asamoah-Gyadu, and others, propound the role of the Holy Spirit as the pivot for Pentecostal transformation and missional growth. Daswani's perceptions discount this view thus:

> Ghanaian Pentecostals have to wrestle with their own personal destiny and the present expectations of a future in this world. They have to act now, in the time before the end of the world, for themselves and for others. The near future, and the role of the Holy Spirit in this future, is an unknown presence

---

103. Elorm-Donkor, "Christian Morality in Ghanaian Pentecostalism," 305.
104. Daswani, *Looking Back, Moving Forward*, 201.
105. Daswani, *Looking Back, Moving Forward*, 203.

that interrupts a Christian life and sometimes surprises church members in unexpected ways.[106]

By this, Daswani runs counter to the aims of this study, particularly chapter 6 on the role of the Holy Spirit in the growth of the CoP. This book, however, argues to the contrary in chapter 6 in order to demonstrate the transformative effect of the Holy Spirit in the Pentecostal movement.

Nevertheless, some of Daswani's observations regarding the future growth of the CoP need to be noted. He acknowledges the CoP's development from among mainly poor and uneducated members into a congregation of rising middle-class Ghanaians. He observes that, unlike many Charismatic churches located in urban areas, the CoP has an effective rural base that serves as the first point of contact for Ghanaians, and he sees the effectiveness of its strong organizational structure.[107] He also notes current CoP leaders' concern and critique about matters involving the changing public sphere, globalization, and cultural change.[108] On the whole, Daswani's book brings together the anthropology of Christianity and the ethical dimensions of a Christian life focusing on Pentecostal transformation as ethical practice in the face of the multiplicity and the heterodoxies of religious experience and practice.[109]

In late 2015, Benjamin Ali, a minister and lecturer at Pentecost University College, published *Prophetism in the Church of Pentecost in Ghana*, which discusses the use of prophecy as a source in and part of the governance practice in the CoP. He suggests that the CoP forms a distinct denomination within Ghanaian Pentecostalism on account of its practice of "divine government,"[110] to appoint people to higher offices, transfer church workers, and give directions generally. While the practice has sometimes caused negative responses due to its unchallengeable nature, it has also averted states of confusion in the church that otherwise would have ensued.[111]

Ali traces the roots and origins of prophetism as found in the CoP to the British Apostolic Faith Church dating from 1916. He notes the CoP's distinction between prophecy as a gift available to all believers and

---

106. Daswani, *Looking Back, Moving Forward*, 205.
107. Daswani, *Looking Back, Moving Forward*, 15–16.
108. Daswani, *Looking Back, Moving Forward*, 17.
109. Daswani, *Looking Back, Moving Forward*, 205.
110. Ali, *Prophetism in the Church of Pentecost*, 14.
111. Ali, *Prophetism in the Church of Pentecost*, viii.

prophecy as a ministry limited only to ordained prophets in the church. His information on how the CoP nurtures ministerial gifts such as prophecy is very helpful to this present work.[112] He identifies such ministerial gift formation as part of the unique ways the CoP grows and sustains its missionary churches. Ali's work also draws attention to the church's reliance on prophecy as one of the reasons that drives its adherents and the corporate church into global evangelization, a fact also alluded to by other writers on the CoP, such as Leonard and Larbi.[113]

STRUCTURE OF THE BOOK

Following this introductory chapter, chapter 2 centers on the historical developments of Pentecostalism in Ghana. It focuses on Ghanaian Pentecostalism as part of African Pentecostalism, which is seen as a unique stream within global Pentecostalism.[114] Its discussion of the emergence, growth, and influence of Ghanaian Pentecostalism includes the different forms of emergent Pentecostal denominations in Ghana and concludes by tracing the contemporary face of Pentecostalism in Ghana and its significance, especially of and for the CoP today.

Chapter 3 examines the history of the Church of Pentecost, especially developments after its break from the British Apostolic Church fraternity and its evolution into a classical Pentecostal denomination in Africa. It highlights the post-independence history of the CoP by building on the initial history captured by Larbi's work, discussing and updating the historical developments of the CoP from 1962 to 2012 onwards, the period of the CoP's mission expansion. This chapter demonstrates how the denominational structures that have developed through its historical trajectories account for her growth.

The fourth chapter, "Mission and Growth in the Church of Pentecost: A Case Study of African Pentecostalism," builds on the third chapter by using the CoP as a case study to demonstrate the growth and missional strategies of African Pentecostalism. This chapter examines the methods, patterns, and principles used to promote the CoP's growth and expansion into missions—in Ghana and onto the international scene. It

---

112. Ali, *Prophetism in the Church of Pentecost*, 111.
113. Larbi, *Pentecostalism*, 250.
114. See Asamoah-Gyadu, *Contemporary Pentecostal Christianity*.

also evaluates some patterns and methods of church growth that previous writers on church growth set out since the 1970s.

Chapter 5 examines African Pentecostal missionary enterprise through the Church of Pentecost international missions, tracing the genesis of CoP international missions both within and outside of Africa, in Western and non-Western nations. The chapter analyzes the emerging patterns and missiological factors promoting the CoP's growth, showing how the external missions of the CoP have emerged as an example of African Pentecostal mission engaged in "reverse missions" and global evangelism. Other missionary patterns unique to the CoP are also discussed.

Chapter 6 highlights the main hypothesis of this book under the title "'Spirit and Mission': Toward a Theology of Pentecostal Growth in Africa." The chapter addresses the theological factors, ethos, and characteristics underpinning the spirituality of the CoP that promotes her growth. It likewise discusses the role of the Holy Spirit and argues that it is the major influencing factor behind the growth of African Pentecostalism. The chapter further discusses how the experience of the Holy Spirit in the life of the individual adherents and the corporate body drives the mission focus of the CoP through its historic growth patterns in spite of the numerous challenges it faces as a denomination coming from sub-Saharan Africa. Finally, it uses this analysis and understanding to formulate the theological factors promoting the growth of the CoP and, for that matter, African Pentecostalism.

The conclusion, chapter 7, summarizes the analysis from the previous chapters and makes recommendations based on them. It provides a summary of the findings regarding the religious, missiological, and theological factors that are promoting the CoP's growth. It draws conclusions about limitations and implications for the growth of African Pentecostalism and global Christianity.

This introductory chapter begins from the fact that Pentecostalism is the fastest growing Christian form influencing the global Christian outreach in this century and is a missionary movement. It is receiving massive academic attention due to its current influence. A Third World phenomenon, Pentecostalism's tremendous growth has coincided with the shifting of the global church's center of gravity from the North to the South. In Africa particularly, this growth and shift has been attributed to the influence of Pentecostalism. The African Pentecostal denomination that this study focuses on, the Church of Pentecost, is widespread, with branches in the African diaspora. Yet systematic research on the factors accounting for its growth has not been adequately done. This chapter has described the background, the research purpose and method, and the existing literature on the CoP as an indigenous African Pentecostal denomination that exemplifies African Pentecostalism's growth and mission. The next chapter presents an updated overview of Pentecostalism's emergence on the Ghanaian Christian religious landscape and its contemporary developments.

2

Pentecostalism in Ghanaian Christianity

THE INITIATIVES, CONTRIBUTIONS, AND impact of Pentecostal Christianity on the growth of Christianity in Ghana in the 21st century cannot be overemphasized.¹ This chapter further authenticates this observation by tracing the movement's history, diffusion, and different forms on the Ghanaian Christian landscape. With its overview of the Pentecostal movement in Ghana, the chapter also shows the place of and part played by the CoP.

Following the brief history of Pentecostal Christianity in Ghana, the chapter explores the emergence of Pentecostalism's different streams and forms and then reviews its contemporary impact on the Ghanaian Christian landscape and on international Christian missions in this era of globalization and transnationalism.

BRIEF HISTORY OF PENTECOSTALISM IN GHANAIAN CHRISTIANITY

An understanding of the historical antecedents of Ghanaian Pentecostalism and its various forms will prepare for an informed analysis of the reasons for past growth and directions for future development.

The most concrete and the initial evangelical effort to develop the Christian church in Ghana was in the 19th-century Western missionary

---

1. Asamoah-Gyadu, "Born of Water and the Spirit," 388–409.

expeditions. Many writers on Christian history and missions agree that these missionary activities did not genuinely encounter the African context. Bediako and Hollenweger have both evaluated the encounter as being neither dialogical nor situational. Though the missionaries sincerely presented what they had, they could not grapple with the issues of African culture, traditional worldview, and spirituality.[2] Hollenweger castigates their activity as being "a truncated and distorted form of evangelism because the colonial evangelist takes his or her culturally-conditioned interpretation of the gospel to be the gospel for everybody."[3] Moreover, between 1880 and 1920 when European imperialism was at its height, the mission task became synonymous with the transplantation of Western civilization. As a result, African converts were taught to repudiate African culture in its entirety and assume the new status of a "Europeanized African."[4] Nevertheless, the efforts of African initiatives and input sustained Christian missions in this era. Omenyo implies that the effects of the evangelization and church-planting efforts during this era would have been unremarkable if not for the timely intervention of some African initiatives.[5]

Despite the failures, the missionary societies in this era did in fact leave an enormous legacy for later developments in evangelization and church planting. As part of this legacy, Christian missions took a broader view of their work—to think of the whole of Africa—and various agendas were drawn up towards future reaching of the whole continent.[6] They made education and training their priority, which opened the way for educated Africans to take their place alongside Western missionaries.[7] Africans, therefore, became translators, evangelists, and later, ministers and leaders of the churches.[8] African languages were learned and put in writing in order to translate the Scriptures and to provide effective instruction in the schools that the missions established.[9] Omenyo confirms that the rich heritage of translation into the vernacular—for example, in

---

2. Bediako, *Christianity in African*, 69; Omenyo, *Pentecost Outside Pentecostalism*, 63.

3. Hollenweger, "Evangelism," 110.

4. Sanneh, *West African Christianity*, 106.

5. Omenyo, *Pentecost Outside Pentecostalism*, 63.

6. Sanneh, *West African Christianity*, 111–14.

7. Omenyo, *Pentecost Outside Pentecostalism*, 60–61.

8. Omenyo, *Pentecost Outside Pentecostalism*, 55.

9. Sanneh, *West African Christianity*, 111.

Ghana the Fanti, Ga, and Ashanti Bibles—later became a strong factor in the proliferation of African independent churches and Pentecostalism in Ghana.[10] Trade and legitimate commerce were encouraged in the struggle to suppress the slave trade and make slavery unattractive. Westerners imposed administrative order on African societies in the hope of facilitating peaceful progress towards the ideal of an abundant life.[11]

The input of African partnership allowed endeavors of the Western mission societies to survive. Sanneh wrote, "the missionaries from the West, aware of the significance of the local springs of religious vitality, could no longer dispense with African agents and would themselves have to clothe their thinking in the indigenous cultures of their endeavors, if they were to bear any lasting fruit."[12] It has been suggested that the African factor, more than any other consideration, sustained the Christian and humanitarian initiative in the development of the continent, including Ghana.[13] From the 20th century on, an evangelistic and church-planting effort by some African evangelists emerged on the Ghanaian Christian scene and later produced African churches independent of the Western-founded churches.[14] These African independent churches eventually led to the rise of Pentecostal movements and the Pentecostalization of Christianity on the continent.

African Independent or Indigenous Churches

Thus, an African attempt to reconcile the contradictions thrown up by Western missions in the African context produced a new phase of indigenous and independent Christianity in Africa known as African independent or indigenous churches—AICs.[15] Historians see the AICs as an African response to the effects of the Western European missionary encounter in the late 19th and early 20th centuries, a response that sprang up from 1914 to 1937 onwards.[16] AICs were established solely by

---

10. Omenyo, *Pentecost Outside Pentecostalism*, 55.
11. Sanneh, *West African Christianity*, 114.
12. Sanneh, *West African Christianity*, 106.
13. Omenyo, *Pentecost Outside Pentecostalism*, 42.
14. Sanneh, *West African Christianity*, 168.
15. See Omenyo, *Pentecost Outside Pentecostalism*, 65–75, esp. 75.
16. Omenyo, *Pentecost Outside Pentecostalism*, 67.

local players or through a partnership of foreign and local initiatives.[17] The earliest references to AICs in the literature speak of churches that separated from the existing mission churches because of a number of irreconcilable issues, such as discrimination against local actors, disputes over resources, and a general feeling of marginalization among educated Africans and others. Such churches were referred to in West Africa as "African churches" beginning in the 1890s.[18]

African Charismatic Revivalists

The stream of AICs that affected Ghana, however, commenced through the evangelistic initiative of some African Charismatic evangelists between 1914 and 1920. The dynamic, charismatic African figures who engineered these revivalist movements in Ghana during this era were completely autonomous and had no link with the Western mission enterprise. Andrew Walls observes that their presence and work on the Ghanaian scene provided the key to the success of the African church, that is, the participation of local players. Since the turn of the 20th century, Walls notes, "Modern African Christianity is not only the result of movements among Africans but it has been principally sustained by Africans and is to a surprising extent, the result of African initiatives."[19] Even the "missionary factor" in African Christian growth, he argues, must be viewed from that perspective. Further comparing these charismatic persons to older AICs, such as the earlier "African churches," Walls maintains that these charismatic African figures owed little in any direct way to Western church mission and nothing to any commission from them.[20]

The most prominent among these preachers was the Liberian prophet William Wadé Harris (1860–1929),[21] whose preaching especially affected the western region of Ghana beginning from 1914. His preaching caused many, including a former fetish priest, to abandon their old ways and traditional worship for Christianity.[22] Shank asserts that an

---

17. Kalu, "Ethiopianism in African Christianity," 258.
18. Adogame and Spickard, *Religion Crossing Boundaries*, 5.
19. Walls, *Missionary Movement*, 86.
20. Walls, *Missionary Movement*, 86.
21. Shank, "William Wade Harris"; Shank, "Legacy of William Wade Harris," 170–76.
22. See Haliburton, *Prophet Harris*, 3.

estimate of over 100,000 people from more than a dozen ethnic groups in the Ivory Coast and thousands more in the Gold Coast (Ghana) were baptized during his mission.[23]

The activities of another Charismatic preacher in this period, Kwame Sampson Oppong (1884–1965), aided greatly in the raising of the Methodist Church in the Ashanti region of Ghana. An illiterate and a self-acclaimed ex-convict, Oppong was asserted to have been called into the preaching vocation through an encounter in a vision, when he did not have any knowledge of the Christian faith. His dramatic preaching within a span of five to six years brought an estimated 20,000 people under the care of Methodist missions.[24] Other evangelists of this category include John Swatson (a convert of Harris), Prophetess Grace Tani, and Prophet John Nackabah (a former traditional priest converted through the preaching campaign of Harris). Grace Tani and John Nackabah were the people behind the formation of the Twelve Apostles Church after Harris's campaign.[25]

Spiritual Churches in Ghana

Subsequently, the 1920s and 1930s witnessed a second stream of new beginnings within Ghanaian Christian independent churches. These were referred to in Ghana as spiritual churches (SCs), and were a spontaneous development after the effective preaching of these charismatic figures.[26] Asamoah-Gyadu argues that these spiritual movements were the genesis of pneumatic Christianity on the Ghanaian scene, and he holds that they share the ethos of Pentecostal movements worldwide:[27]

> In the experiences of the indigenous prophets and their followers, renewal took place in the form of personal, often dramatic, conversions, miraculous acts demonstrating the power of the Holy Spirit and the manifestation of Pentecostal

---

23. Shank, *Prophet Harris*, 4.
24. Omenyo, *Pentecost Outside Pentecostalism*, 71–72.
25. See Omenyo, *Pentecost Outside Pentecostalism*, 69–74; and Baëta, *Prophetism in Ghana*.
26. Adogame and Spickard, *Religion Crossing Boundaries*, 5.
27. Asamoah-Gyadu, *African Charismatics*, 19–21.

phenomena, embodying charismatic and spiritual gifts into Christian practice.[28]

He therefore, presents the SCs as the premier form of Pentecostal phenomena in Ghana after the early African preachers, whose revivals included Pentecostal phenomena. The SCs are basically prophetic and healing movements, which became popular in Ghana, according to Asamoah-Gyadu, because they affirmed the reality of God and other supernatural entities. Their growth is acknowledged as the most dramatic aspect of 20th-century Christianity in Sub-Saharan Africa.[29]

The SCs' doctrines emphasize the centrality of the Bible, ecstatic prayers, healing, prophecy, visions and dreams, elaborate rituals, flexible modes of worship and liturgies, and Charismatic leadership shaped by a particular African brand of Christianity.[30] They typically embrace a functional theology and a pragmatic approach to life, which endear them to many Africans. Though they utterly condemn and reject traditional religion as fetish and demonic, their belief systems and ritual structures share some affinities with African cosmologies. As a result, members come not only from the mainline churches but also from other Christian and non-Christian groups, including Islam and the various traditional religions.[31]

Despite these similarities, the various SCs differ in their social and historical origins. Each has its own religious dynamics, specific doctrines, and ritual acts and performances. They typically emerge from the mainline churches as a prayer band or group or are founded through the visionary experience of a charismatic figure. The SCs include the Musama Disco Christo Church (MDCC, 1922), Cherubim and Seraphim (1925), the Twelve Apostles Church, the Apostles Revelation Society, the Saviour Church, and the African Faith Tabernacle.[32]

The SCs seem to have decreased since the 1970s,[33] possibly for the same reasons as the West African AICs. Asamoah-Gyadu proposes other reasons for their decline as well, such as the emergence of other,

---

28. Asamoah-Gyadu, *African Charismatics*, 37.
29. Baëta, *Prophetism in Ghana*, esp. foreword by Asamoah-Gyadu, xiv.
30. Omenyo, *Pentecost Outside Pentecostalism*, 51–52.
31. Adogame and Spickard, *Religion Crossing Boundaries*, 5.
32. Adogame and Spickard, *Religion Crossing Boundaries*, 5. See also Baëta, *Prophetism in Ghana*.
33. See Asamoah-Gyadu, *African Charismatics*, 29–30.

more pragmatic church forms that have the same pattern of pneumatic expressions.[34] The mode of operation or church praxis of these new Pentecostal movements either forced the SCs out of existence, or as he suggests, caused them to modify their outlook in keeping with the new or modern trend.[35] Thus, in the trail of the SCs' decline we see a sporadic mushrooming of a similar brand of indigenous Christian church forms on the Ghanaian religious landscape, designated as Pentecostal and Charismatic Christianity. The Pentecostal and Charismatic churches, like their counterparts, the SCs, take pneumatic experiences seriously.

Pentecostal and Charismatic Movements in Ghana

The Pentecostal denominations and their progeny, the Charismatic movements, comprise the major church form shaping the Christian religious landscape of Ghana today. They include, first, classical Pentecostals, considered by some an alternative to the SCs; next, renewal or revivalist movements within the mainline Western mission congregations, and finally, neo-Pentecostal movements. The neo-Pentecostal movements include the Charismatic churches and other parachurch movements.

The Pentecostal and Charismatic movements share religious and theological tendencies with the SCs, as stated above. However, some aspects of the SCs' ethos they consider cultic. But though considered cultic by these emerging Pentecostal and Charismatic movements, Asamoah-Gyadu argues that the SCs were equally Pentecostal: "Not only do AICs share religious and theological tendencies and emphasis with indigenous classical and contemporary Pentecostal movements but also, many of their practices previously condemned as belonging to the occult have been reinvented in contemporary Pentecostal spirituality."[36]

In addition to keeping Pentecostal practices such as devotion to Bible reading, prayer, evangelism, and manifestations of the Spirit (the very phenomena for which people seek the intervention of the SCs), the Pentecostal and Charismatic movements became more appealing than the SCs because they added more innovations. These include strict moral ethics, a very high standard of pastoral care, and a liturgical simplicity that commands a very high level of integrity and administrative orderliness.

---

34. Asamoah-Gyadu, "Renewal within African Christianity," 35.
35. Asamoah-Gyadu, *African Charismatics*, 30.
36. Asamoah-Gyadu, *Contemporary Pentecostal Christianity*, vii.

These are observed especially in classical Pentecostal denominations such as the CoP.³⁷

Classical Pentecostalism in Ghana

Historically, the classical Pentecostal denominations (CPs) emerged after the SCs in Ghana in the 1930s as the third stream of Pentecostalism—characterized as Western-related Pentecostal denominations. They include some Pentecostal denominations that have entirely foreign origins (such as the Assemblies of God and the Foursquare churches) and some that initially had indigenous roots but were later affiliated with Western-related Pentecostal denominations. To distinguish between the two, those with indigenous roots will be designated in this section as "indigenous classical Pentecostals."

Those denominations with indigenous roots began as independent indigenous initiatives but linked up quite early with foreign Pentecostal missions. They comprise the Christ Apostolic Church (CAC), the Apostolic Church of Ghana (ACG), and the Church of Pentecost (CoP). They emerged from an initiative of a Ghanaian Pentecostal and his subsequent collaboration with the British Apostolic Church. Larbi's *Pentecostalism* chronicles beautifully the beliefs, ethos, and theology of each group under what he calls "Life and Faith."³⁸ Their classification, ethos, and theology are almost identical and are also akin to that of the Apostolic Pentecostals classified in chapter 1.³⁹ They are, however, very quickly developing into large denominations of their own, with branches all over the country, in both the rural and urban areas, and have established other mission posts outside the country.

The "indigenous classical Pentecostal denominations" in Ghana first originated from a church-planting initiative of a Ghanaian Pentecostal, Peter N. Anim, in the early 20th century.⁴⁰ In 1935, the group became affiliated with the Apostolic Church of the UK, headquartered in Bradford, UK. Through this collaboration, the British Apostolic Church sent missionaries, James McKeown and his wife, Sophia, to Ghana in 1937 to

---

37. Asamoah-Gyadu, *African Charismatics*, 88–89.
38. Larbi, *Pentecostalism*, 142, 243.
39. See Larbi, *Pentecostalism*; Anderson, *To the Ends of the Earth*, 37–62.
40. Wyllie, "Pioneers of Ghanaian Pentecostalism," 110.

supervise the group as their branch in the Gold Coast.[41] Relations between James McKeown and Peter Anim and his group broke down due to doctrinal differences. Later, an intractable relationship developed with the parent church, the Apostolic Church in the UK. These fissures eventually led to the formation of three distinct classical Pentecostal churches in Ghana.[42]

The Anim group first disengaged from the collaboration with the British Apostolic Church headed by McKeown, and they took the name Christ Apostolic Church. The remnant from the split became the local branch of the British Apostolic Church under the leadership of McKeown. This became the Apostolic Church of Gold Coast, a local branch of the British Apostolic Church. Subsequently, due to a rift between the British Apostolic Church and McKeown, the church had to divide again. Thus, in 1953, out of the Apostolic Church of Gold Coast emerged the Gold Coast Apostolic Church, led by James McKeown and independent from the UK Apostolic branch. This group was later referred to as Ghana Apostolic Church.[43] The name change came after the nation of Ghana gained political independence from its former colonial master, Britain, and changed its name from Gold Coast to Ghana in 1957. The Ghana Apostolic Church was later renamed the Church of Pentecost in 1962.

Thus, by August 1962, the classical Pentecostal denominations in Ghana with indigenous roots had become three distinct groups: Christ Apostolic Church, the Apostolic Church of Ghana and the Church of Pentecost. Since then, the classical Pentecostals, through their beliefs, ethos, doctrines, and other pragmatic church practices, have outpaced the growth of the SCs. It has also sparked Pentecostalization in the historic mainline churches and in other parachurch organizations, including those in the schools and universities, and has led to the emergence of the neo-Pentecostal movements.

Neo-Pentecostal Movements

The exuberance of the CPs from the 1930s sparked the Pentecostalization of Ghanaian Christianity. However, from the 1950s to 1970s, another stream of movements, characterized as neo-Pentecostals, further

---

41. See Leonard, *Giant in Ghana*, 3–4.
42. Asamoah-Gyadu, "Pentecostalism and the Missiological Significance," 35.
43. Asamoah-Gyadu, "Pentecostalism and the Missiological Significance," 35.

influenced the cause of the nation's Pentecostalization and Charismatization. They included parachurch Christian associations in Ghana and all the current Charismatic movements (CMs).

The parachurch Christian associations, such as the Student Christian Movement in the universities, Inter-College Camps, and Scripture Union (SU), initially carried out school-based outreach as interdenominational Christian camps and fellowships.[44] Their influence and impact in the schools and colleges and, subsequently, in the mainline churches, led, on one hand. to revivals or renewals within the churches. On the other hand, their misunderstood stance, especially in regard to teachings, doctrines, and some experiences of the Holy Spirit, in some cases led to the breaking-away of members of these groups to form new groups, most of which became the Charismatic churches.[45] These, coupled with later developments, led to the establishment of other independent Charismatic churches. This later Pentecostal movement emphasized the "gifts of the Holy Spirit" (Greek: *charismata pneumatika*) spelled out by Paul in 1 Corinthians 12 and 14 as applicable to every believer. Hence, they are referred to as "Charismatics."

Parachurch Associations in Ghana. The parachurch associations in Ghana were nondenominational Christian fellowships, prayer groups, gospel music teams, and individuals whose evangelistic activities aimed at augmenting the efforts of the mission of existing churches in gospel witness and Christian nurture. According to Barker and Boadi-Siaw, the years prior to the independence of the nation from British colonial rule and immediately after—1945 to 1965—witnessed two scenes: the expansion of education at all levels and a slackening of Christian spirituality, especially among the mainline churches. They state,

> In 1945 the Gold Coast was on the brink of a twelve-year movement towards independence from British rule. Between 1945 and 1965 there would be a tremendous expansion of education at every level. The number of secondary schools and training colleges would grow from less than a dozen in 1945 to some 200 in 1980, and to over 470 by the end of the century. Three university colleges would be founded, and each would ultimately become a full university in its own right. By 2000 there were five public universities and two private ones. But the spiritual foundations had grown weak over the years—the churches needed

---

44. Barker and Boadi-Siaw, *Changed by the Word*, 16–28.
45. Barker and Boadi-Siaw, *Changed by the Word*, 87–88.

reminding of the clear gospel message brought by the early missionary pioneers.[46]

These parachurch groups sprang up as an intervention in the churches' spiritual slackness at that time, particularly mainline churches. Most of these groups and fellowships were affiliated with the Scripture Union (SU) or were independent groups. The SU was founded in December 1951 through a fellowship of some British Christians in Ghana led by Tony Wilmot.[47] A nondenominational fellowship set up in Ghana under the auspices of the UK-based parent organization, the SU has the aim of equipping Christians with Bible knowledge and encouraging responsible membership in the churches. By the 1960s the SU had established nondenominational groups with a wide membership in all the post-primary educational institutions, secondary schools, and other community fellowships. In the tertiary educational institutions, the prevailing parachurch organization was the Ghana Fellowship of Evangelical Students (GHAFES), the largest conservative evangelical movement in Ghana.[48] Other nondenominational associations were not necessarily made up of students, such as the Full Gospel Men's Fellowship, Ghana Congress on Evangelism (GHACOE), GHACOE Women's Fellowship, and Women's Aglow.

By the early 1970s, it became evident that members of the SU and its affiliate organizations were becoming increasingly Pentecostal in character and orientation. Its teaching at the time emphasized the baptism of the Holy Spirit, with speaking in tongues, prophecies, healings, and miracles.[49] The speakers invited for campus programs held more Pentecostal orientations, and their teachings greatly affected the movement. In addition, some of the front leaders were very influential classical Pentecostals. The Pentecostal posture of the SU became a matter of concern for school authorities, who were mostly Western-mission-related Christians, and for authorities of the SU body.[50] As a movement with a Western European heritage, the SU had reservations about Charismatic phenomena such as speaking in tongues and other experiences. The persistent hostility of

---

46. Barker and Boadi-Siaw, *Changed by the Word*, 12–13.
47. Barker and Boadi-Siaw, *Changed by the Word*, 16.
48. Asamoah-Gyadu, *African Charismatics*, 103.
49. Asamoah-Gyadu, *African Charismatics*, 103, 105.
50. Asamoah-Gyadu, *African Charismatics*, 105.

SU authority to pneumatic phenomena alienated the movement from its local patronage and reduced its influence in Ghanaian Christianity.[51]

By the 1970s, the mounting gap between the officials of the SU and their grassroots members became evident. Parallel to this, the evangelical leaders from the pre-1970s generation warned people to be wary of these experiential phenomena, and the Ghanaian evangelical movement then disregarded the Pentecostal spirituality emerging at that time in both the fellowships and the established churches.[52] By this time, the SU group was gradually developing certain practices that represented a shift from conservative evangelicalism. Examples include the formation of prayer warriors from 1974, the rise of youth gospel drama and music groups (such as Joyful Way Incorporated, Calvary Road Incorporated, Abundant Life Ministries, New Creation Singers, and Jesus Generation), who started using modern Western instruments to recover the taste for percussion instruments in Ghanaian indigenous Christian worship, and the formation of other fellowships not under the umbrella of the SU.[53] The SU and her affiliated institutions failed to provide a satisfactory response to the Pentecostal phenomena—emotion in public worship, prayer, and speaking in tongues. This led to the development of a host of parachurch evangelical groups outside the SU network, which includes the Ghana Evangelistic Society (GES), the Hour of Visitation Choir and Evangelistic Association, Tears of Jesus, and Upper Room Fellowship.[54]

Charismatic Movements in Ghana. While these circumstances led to the decline of the SU and her affiliated institutions, the CMs appeared on the Ghanaian religious landscape in the late 1970s.[55] All the groups mentioned above apparently became part of the current CMs. Thus, the historic roots of many Charismatic churches in Ghana can be traced back to the parachurch evangelical associations of the 1950s–1970s.[56]

The mass movement of adherents of the older mainline Protestant churches into the CMs paralleled this development. Those of the SU and its associates who opted to heed the advice of the SU to remain in their churches sparked within them a resurgence of renewals, characterized by

---

51. Asamoah-Gyadu, *African Charismatics*, 106.
52. Asamoah-Gyadu, *African Charismatics*, 105–6.
53. Asamoah-Gyadu, *African Charismatics*, 105–6.
54. Asamoah-Gyadu, *African Charismatics*, 108–11.
55. Asamoah-Gyadu, *African Charismatics*, 107.
56. See Adubofour, "Evangelical Para-Church Movements."

Pentecostal phenomena. They became the Bible study and prayer groups in the Protestant churches and the Catholic Charismatic movement in Roman Catholic settings. Asamoah-Gyadu contends—and this writer agrees—that the recent proliferation of independent CMs in Ghana is partly a culmination of years of imbibing an evangelistic and Pentecostal spirituality that was bound to look for expression outside existing churches and denominations.[57] Their emergence sparked a new move within Ghanaian Christianity that effected several restructuring projects in the existing mission-related churches. It also informed other developments in the older classical Pentecostal denominations, whose younger generation especially were thought to be shifting to CMs whose modernity and flamboyance appealed to those from otherwise traditional indigenous settings.[58]

The discussion above shows that the CMs in Ghana form part of the current indigenous innovations appropriating Pentecostalism in the Ghanaian context; this fact makes them African in nature. Some scholars, such as Steve Brouwer and Paul Gifford, contest their true indigenous character, contending that the CMs were an American importation. They base this contention on the CMs' taking inspiration from American neo-Pentecostal culture, portrayed particularly in Ghana through their Bible school culture, media consciousness, and also their cherished value of their transnational and international networks.[59] This writer agrees with Asamoah-Gyadu that the core message of Ghanaian neo-Pentecostals does not reflect the American content. Rather, the way in which it is expressed appears to be an imitation of American media evangelistic style, and the international outlook may be an inevitable consequence of religious globalization.[60] The Ghanaian neo-Pentecostal churches include Christian Action Faith Ministries International, International Central Gospel Church, Global Revival Ministries, Resurrection Power and Living Bread Ministries International, Word Miracle Church International (now Perez Chapel), Living Praise Chapel International, and Lighthouse Chapel International, to name a few of the earlier ones that emerged.[61]

---

57. Asamoah-Gyadu, *African Charismatics*, 102.
58. Larbi, *Pentecostalism*, 201–4.
59. Brouwer, Gifford, and Rose, *Exporting the American Gospel*, 178.
60. Asamoah-Gyadu, *African Charismatics*, 99.
61. Asamoah-Gyadu, *African Charismatics*, 35.

CONTEMPORARY GHANAIAN PENTECOSTALISM: OUTLOOK AND IMPACT

The emergence and influence of Pentecostalism in Ghana since the turn of the 20th century has inspired a Pentecostalization of the Ghanaian Christian landscape that we have seen in three specific streams: first, in the fast growth and extensive development into denominationalism of the classical Pentecostals; second, in its serving as a catalyst for renewal in the historic mainline churches; and third, in the sporadic spread of neo-Pentecostal movements such as the indigenous Charismatic churches and parachurch movements all over the country. This Pentecostalization has had an impact not only on Ghanaian religious life but also on corporate civic life.

Impact on Ghanaian Religious Life

Evidence of the Pentecostalization and Charismatization of Ghanaian religious life can be measured by the massive and impressive Pentecostal congregations and church buildings sprouting up everywhere in the country, including the numerous congregations meeting in classrooms, cinema halls, and other rented premises. The CoP alone recorded 13,050 congregations in 2013. They had 1,652 permanent church buildings, 3,682 uncompleted permanent church buildings, 4,118 temporary structures, and 158 rented halls, as well as 342 congregations worshipping in free accommodations: 2,079 in classrooms, 899 under trees, and 120 in other nondefined places.[62] Whereas the classical Pentecostal congregations engage in services every day, including Sundays, the major CM churches in Ghana hold services at least twice on Sundays and have one or more weekday meetings.[63] The noticeable, colorful signposts, particularly of the CoP and Lighthouse Chapel congregations, springing up everywhere in Ghana, in the major urban cities and the rural villages, attest to this "Pentecostalization."

An example of Ghanaian acceptance of Pentecostalism—attested by both Larbi and Asamoah-Gyadu—is its special appeal to the up-and-coming youth, both the highly educated and less well educated, who are considered the future of the nation's development. Since the 1950s and

---

62. CoP, Growth Statistical Report, June 2013.
63. Asamoah-Gyadu, *African Charismatics*, 5.

1970s, the SU and other fellowships in the schools have attracted young people; Pentecostal movements still do today.[64] Evidence of Pentecostals' and Charismatics' impact can also be seen in their media ministries that reach and are accessible to the Ghanaian populace. Pentecostalism's dominance not only includes religious messages and sermons, but also its profound cultural significance of its the musical creativity and video productions. Their music has become almost more widely accepted at all functions—domestic, traditional, or national, irrespective of purpose—than Highlife music, which is considered Ghana's own particular form of music.[65] Their well-advertised programs constantly proclaiming success, healing and deliverance, and empowerment have become more or less a religious buffet frequented by many.[66]

Currently, another significant development noted for its contemporary popularity is the establishment of university colleges initiated by Pentecostal/Charismatic organizations, such as the Central University College of Mensah Otabil's International Central Gospel Church, Pentecost University College of the CoP, Dominion University College of Duncan Williams's Christian Action Faith Ministries, and Perez University College of Agyin-Asare's Perez Chapel. All of these were formerly Bible centers and seminaries, and they have now metamorphosed into university colleges patronized by young people.[67] These university colleges become avenues for continuing education in their tertiary institutions as direct alternatives to government institutions, which have a limited intake. A principal aim of these university colleges is to advance the cause of Christianity through Pentecostal orientation in higher education.[68]

Ghanaian Pentecostalism, it is argued, has been innovative in developing its experiential and versatile spirituality to serve the contextual needs of Ghanaians. This is evident from its emphasis on prayer, music, and the appropriation of new forms of worship that are Pentecostal-oriented, and also from the reintroduction into Ghanaian church life of the presence and ministry of the Holy Spirit.[69] In contemporary Ghanaian Pentecostal culture, prayer as a means of religious interaction be-

64. Asamoah-Gyadu, *African Charismatics*, 101–4; Larbi, *Pentecostalism*, 295.
65. Gifford, *Ghana's New Christianity*, 35.
66. Asamoah-Gyadu, *Contemporary Pentecostal Christianity*, 15.
67. Asamoah-Gyadu, *Contemporary Pentecostal Christianity*, 15.
68. See the College Manual of Pentecost University College indicating vision, as well as its mission statements.
69. Asamoah-Gyadu, *Contemporary Pentecostal Christianity*, 18, 60.

tween the natural and supernatural realms has served as a theological interventionist strategy in all Christian streams. These types of prayer interventions range from weekday prayer services and all-night vigils to revival services, healing camps, and prayer centers. They seem to have created a ritual space for supernatural attention for all classes of people, including the sick, deprived, politicians, and traditionalists. The Ghanaian Christian scene has adopted many venues established for Pentecostal and Charismatic appropriation of new prayer services currently patronized by all and sundry: members of historic churches, traditionalists, and others of Islamic orientation. They include "Jericho Hour" at Action Chapel International, "Hour of Miracles" at Perez Chapel, and many others advertised daily in the media.[70]

The acceptance of Pentecostal-type inclusive congregational worship can be seen alongside other Ghanaian indigenous religious practices and traditions.[71] Social functions such as festivals, child namings, funerals, family gatherings, and others, which were previously organized with traditional rituals and ceremonies, are today laced with or completely taken over by Pentecostal prayers, worship, and liturgy.

Likewise, we see the influence of Pentecostal and Charismatic trends in worship on the historic mission churches' mode of worship, which have adapted it for their services. The historic churches had to restructure to avoid decline in the face of such Pentecostal resurgence, as well as allow pneumatic phenomena in their churches in response to Pentecostalism.[72] The historic churches demonstrate a pattern of Pentecostalization of their worship. For instance, in some of the historic churches, offertory time is accompanied by enthusiastic choruses, generally identified as originally Pentecostal, along with clapping and dancing. Some mainline churches have replaced the opening services with Pentecostal-type "intercession" and "praise and worship" sessions. Apart from the singing of hymns and reading of Scriptures, it is argued, the entire liturgy in some of the historic mainline churches has given way to Pentecostal expressions in the church's mode of worship.

Further, the Pentecostal emphasis on the manifestation and use of the gifts of the Holy Spirit as a grassroots experience now appears across the religious landscape. This emphasis finds support from the teaching of

---

70. See Asamoah-Gyadu, *Contemporary Pentecostal Christianity*, 35–41.

71. Asamoah-Gyadu, *Contemporary Pentecostal Christianity*, 19.

72. Asamoah-Gyadu, *Contemporary Pentecostal Christianity*, 31–32.

the "priesthood of all believers," which is particularly evident in contemporary Pentecostalism.[73] This has encouraged the churches' recognition of and the participation of lay leaders—church members who minister particular graces to communities of believers, thus promoting growth.[74]

Another avenue of noticeable influence by Pentecostalism is its ecumenical organ, the Ghana Pentecostal Council (GPC). The GPC, which originally consisted of the earlier classical Pentecostal denominations, has been extended to include other emerging independent Charismatic churches, so that it is now known as the Ghana Pentecostal and Charismatic Council (GPCC). The total number of individual churches registered in the GPCC was 214 as of December 2015.[75] This is apart from the major Charismatic churches not aligned with them or that have their own associations, such as International Central Gospel Church, Action Faith Church, Lighthouse Chapel International, and several others. Thus, with regard to national religious issues, political advocacy, and national welfare issues, the GPCC has emerged as another formidable Christian ecumenical force apart from the Ghana Catholic Secretariat and the Christian Council of Ghana. The GPCC's 2015 report states:

> The GPCC continues to play a part on the Advisory Board of the Civic Forum Initiative and the Coalition of Domestic Election Observers (CODEO). While our President continues to serve on the Board of the National Peace Council (NPC), the General Secretary also continues to serve on various committees of the Ghana AIDS Commission (GAC) during the period under review.[76]

Impact on Ghanaian Corporate Civil Life

The impact of the contemporary Pentecostal and Charismatic movements in Ghana extends to all levels of Ghanaian civil and public life. Almost every mundane space of Ghanaian communal life feels it, such as in education, politics, and the socioeconomic sphere.[77] Birgit Meyer has commented on Pentecostal/Charismatic churches generally as be-

73. See Dayton, *Theological Roots of Pentecostalism*.
74. Asamoah-Gyadu, *Contemporary Pentecostal Christianity*, 60.
75. GPCC, National Secretariat Annual Report, January–December 2015.
76. GPCC, National Secretariat Annual Report, January–December 2015, 3.
77. Gifford, *Ghana's New Christianity*, 13–43.

ing central to the globalization of Christianity in our time. She writes, "The contemporary archetype of Christianity is 'a community without an institution,' but a community of a new type, proper to the forms of diffuse, individualized, and nonisomorphic forms of connectedness in our globalized world."[78]

Paul Gifford has shown how the Ghanaian Pentecostal movement, especially the current Charismatic brand that he refers to as "Ghana's New Churches," has thrived by taking advantage of the historical economic and socio-political situation of the nation since colonial rule.[79] He draws attention to the fact that, in the two decades since 1979, the nation of Ghana has in many ways been eclipsed by religious developments quite novel to the mainline historic churches: These Pentecostal and Charismatic developments became evident due to their claim of economic intervention. He writes, "Everyone is aware of Charismatic prayer centers, their all-night services, crusades, conventions and Bible Schools, new buildings, bumper stickers, banners and particularly the posters that everywhere advertise an enormous range of forthcoming activities."[80] Moreover, "they grow because they claim to have answers to Ghanaians' existential problems and especially to their most pressing existential problem: economic survival."[81] Notwithstanding the intent of his comments, he rightly affirms the contemporary impact of Pentecostal and Charismatic Christianity on the Ghanaian civic and public environment. The movement has pervaded the Ghanaian terrain through providing or aiding in social functions that were previously the preserve of traditional structures, such as arranging marriages, child-naming, funerals, and others.[82] It also provides social interventions with material assistance, employment, and healthcare services.

In the political arena, Pentecostal and Charismatic churches in Ghana play both functional and dysfunctional roles. Their leadership is involved in various nongovernmental and political assignments in the country such as the National Peace Council, the Council of State, and the AIDS Commission.[83] Some of these bodies have statutory positions

---

78. Meyer, "Aesthetics of Persuasion."
79. See Gifford, *Ghana's New Christianity*.
80. Gifford, *Ghana's New Christianity*, 23.
81. Gifford, *Ghana's New Christianity*, viii–ix, ix.
82. Markin, "Ghanaian Christian Missions," 96.
83. GPCC, National Secretariat Annual Report, January–December 2015.

earmarked for the Christian community that persons from the GPCC such as its president or general secretary can occupy. The leaders from the GPCC play valuable roles in Ghanaian politics: for instance, as neutral forces not from the political parties, they act as advocates or an independent voice in the nation's political issues. In the past, clergy from the mainline denominations officiated at functions of governmental importance, even when appointed from the army. However, in 2008, the induction service for the Ghanaian president elect, John Evans Atta-Mills (2008–2011), was officiated by a known Pentecostal/Charismatic preacher, the Rev. Eastwood Anaba of Fountain Gate Chapel.

Pentecostal- and Charismatic-oriented clergy also serve as chaplains in the Ghana Army. The chairman of the CoP, in the 2007 State of the Church Address, recorded that four of its ordained pastors were seconded as service personnel to the Ghana Armed Forces and prisons as chaplains.[84] Others report the GPCC Executive Council's taking the initiative to organize periodic church services in the presidential residence or seat of government during President John Evans Atta-Mills's term of office.[85] Given all its religious, political, and civic roles, the movement's recognition within the Ghanaian environment, as well as some of its practices and excesses, has engendered wide discussions, criticisms, and speculations in the Ghanaian media. Of particular note is the behavior of some of its practitioners, such as pastors and prophets, and the general affluent lifestyle of its Charismatic brand.[86]

Impact on International Missions

On the international front, the Pentecostal and Charismatic movements in Ghana, through their immigrant congregations abroad, have joined their African Pentecostal counterparts in making known their presence through transnational networks in the diaspora. They are said to be bringing vitality to the otherwise declining state of Christianity in the

---

84. CoP, Chairman Apostle Dr. M. K. Ntumy, State of the Church Address, presented at the opening ceremony of the 11th session of the Extraordinary Council meetings held at Pentecost University College, Accra, April 26, 2007.

85. Presented by GPCC General Secretary S. Y. Antwi, February 22, 2013, at Bolgatanga.

86. Ghana daily news has many such reports, including the 2016 ongoing impasse between Bishop Obinim and Bishop Owusu Bempah, both Charismatic church leaders, which became a regular discussion topic in both print and electronic media.

northern hemisphere. Asamoah-Gyadu, writing on the CoP's missions abroad, states that their Pentecostal spirituality, with its emphasis on personal transformation, prayer, evangelism, holiness, healing, deliverance, and community, suits the religious needs and aspirations of African immigrant communities.[87] He further asserts that African immigrant congregations, of which there are many such as the CoP, have strong missionary intentions.[88] Through their presence in the West, they appear to be changing religious transmission in those areas by promoting "reverse missions" to the West.[89]

THE CURRENT PLACE OF CLASSICAL PENTECOSTALISM AND THE COP

Generally, the AICs and the neo-Pentecostals have received enormous scholarly attention in the last century. More work has been done on them, particularly in Ghana, than on the CPs. Asamoah-Gyadu and Omenyo, who have researched and written on Ghanaian CMs and renewal movements, have bypassed the classical Pentecostals—who can be considered the forerunners—and instead focused on the CMs and others. Although both scholars did mention the classical Pentecostals as precursors to the CMs, they did not discuss much of their current challenges or successes in light of the contemporary Pentecostal resurgence in Ghana.[90] However, in Ghana, the classical Pentecostals seem to be commanding a greater influence than the CMs, given their internal growth and expansion, structural development, financial self-sufficiency, and international mission outreach, evidenced by the greater presence of their Ghanaian immigrant congregations abroad.[91]

Since 1962, the indigenous classical Pentecostal denominations in Ghana have become three distinct denominations: Christ Apostolic Church (CAC), the Apostolic Church of Ghana (ACG), and the CoP, not including those with foreign links such as the Assemblies of God. Also since 1962, the CoP has grown to become the largest Protestant

---

87. Asamoah-Gyadu, "On Mission Abroad," 91.
88. Asamoah-Gyadu, "On Mission Abroad," 97.
89. See Ter Haar, *Halfway to Paradise*.
90. Asamoah-Gyadu, *African Charismatics*, 88–92.
91. See GEC, *Survey of Churches in Ghana*, 2010; and Markin, "Ghanaian Mission in the Diaspora."

denomination in Ghana and is also acclaimed as the fastest growing. From the end of 1962, the CoP membership of 26,000 (by a conservative estimate) increased tremendously to almost a tenth of the national population by 2013.[92] It has developed a better structure, both administratively and ministerially, than its contemporaries. As an indigenous institution that is financially self-sufficient, it is capable of maintaining its local churches and also providing for its missions abroad. Its influence and impact in the country, particularly on other church forms, Western-related mainline churches or orthodox churches (as they are referred to in Ghana), and other Pentecostal/Charismatic churches and organizations, cannot be underestimated. Its standard of spirituality, particularly in its ethics and morality, is said to be the standard for other religious institutions. Noted earlier, Asamoah-Gyadu argues that the CoP's standard of spirituality and religiosity contributed to the decline of some of the earlier institutions, such as the SCs in Ghana; the CoP had a more pragmatic orientation in terms of church praxis than the SCs, although they have the same orientation regarding pneumatic phenomena. Asamoah-Gyadu discusses the reasons for the decline of the SCs in Ghana:

> The other religious development accounting for the decline of the "Sunsum Sore" [spiritual churches] is the presence of the CoP. The CoP has emerged as a Pentecostal denomination with rigorous evangelistic programmes, an extensive geographical spread, a community church planting method, a diversified ministry including provision for children and youth, with a strong women's movement and an emphasis on Pentecostal phenomena. The CoP therefore stands for what may be perceived to be a more accessible and "more respectable option" in indigenous Pentecostalism. It is more accessible than other classical Pentecostal churches like the Assemblies of God.[93]

Recently, however, scholars such as Asamoah-Gyadu are arguing that though the SCs appear to be declining, the very outlook of the contemporary CMs suggests a reinvention of the same rituals and characteristics of the SCs. This observation poses questions regarding the very existence and future growth of the CPs. One such question is what effect the development and current appeal of the CMs will have on the CPs' growth, specifically their Pentecostal tradition and spirituality and continuous numerical growth, particularly in Ghana. Daswani, an anthropologist,

92. CoP, Statistical Department Data, 2013.
93. Asamoah-Gyadu, *African Charismatics*, 88.

aware of the effects of the CoP's Pentecostal spirituality on Pentecostal growth in Ghana, and having observed the rising influence of CMs currently in Ghana, has drawn attention to that effect. He writes, "The recent capitalism of the Protestant-Pentecostal spirit in Ghana is seen to be promoting a set of neo-liberal values that pose a threat to the CoP's Pentecostal tradition."[94] This questions the very survival and growth of the CPs (including CoP) in relation to the current emergence of the CMs on the Ghanaian scene. By "Pentecostal tradition," Daswani refers to the Pentecostal spirituality associated with the CPs, which was previously identified as the cause for the decline of the SCs and, to some extent, for the sparking of renewal in the mainline churches.

Other observations that require examination are the doctrinal emphases and some characteristic features of the CMs. Apart from those alluded to by the working definition in the introduction, the doctrinal emphases of the CMs are their prosperity gospel, emphasis on the promise of health and wealth, and focus on the relevance of ancestral curses, coupled with the exhibition of an affluent lifestyle.[95] This doctrinal emphasis has been described by Asamoah-Gyadu as a "theology which lacks the theology of Christian suffering," which makes CMs look "this-worldly." He wrote, "In many ways, contemporary Pentecostal theology we have noted, promotes a theology of glory with sometimes very little to say to those who are weak or suffering."[96] Daswani has further inquired whether the present CMs' affluent lifestyle in Ghana poses a threat to CoP's Pentecostal tradition and growth.[97]

In light of these observations, this study focuses on showing how CP institutions, such as the CoP, have developed the resources for sustaining their growth. In other words, it asks, How are the CPs developing or have developed measures or growth initiatives to sustain and continue the church's present growth? This study will, in the next chapters, demonstrate how a CP institution, specifically the CoP, has developed enough interventions (religious factors for its growth) to maintain its relevance and continuous growth on the Ghanaian scene, as well as on international terrain. It will also consider whether classical Pentecostalism, through the CoP, is raising alternatives in terms of theology, ethos, and

---

94. Daswani, *Looking Back, Moving Forward*, 17.

95. Asamoah-Gyadu, *Contemporary Pentecostal Christianity*, 17; Gifford, *Ghana's New Christianity*, viii–ix.

96. Asamoah-Gyadu, *Contemporary Pentecostal Christianity*, 112.

97. Daswani, *Looking Back, Moving Forward*, 17.

other structures that could serve as a check on some of the characteristics of CMs considered excessive. Daswani has pointed out that, in engaging with personal and social changes, "the CoP leaders today are concerned with, and critical of, matters that involve the changing public sphere, globalisation and cultural change."[98] Thus, it could well be that the CoP institution has, at this point in its history, developed, or is developing, interventions aimed at remedying such anomalies.

The next chapter builds on this chapter's history of the emergence and current streams of Pentecostalism and its impact on the Ghanaian Christian religious landscape and on the Ghanaian civic and public sphere, including its political, educational, and socioeconomic life, through its various engagements such as its media culture. Yet currently, the innovations and appropriations of the CMs are noticed to be influencing the religious paradigm of the nation. This is regarded as a threat to the growth of the earlier CPs such as the CoP, previously considered the standard for the other churches, especially in terms of ethical morality and other praxis. Further analysis of the history of the CoP is used to identify and evaluate the religious and theological factors engendering and sustaining her growth. The next chapter also gives updated information and analysis of the historic growth of the institution from 1962 onwards. These religious and theological factors can be used to evaluate the CoP as a distinct institution, Ghanaian classical Pentecostalism in general, and the entire contemporary Pentecostal movement.

---

98. Daswani, *Looking Back, Moving Forward*, 17.

3

A Post-Independence History of the Church of Pentecost

WE HAVE TRACED AND analyzed the trajectory of the various streams of Pentecostalism on the Ghanaian Christian landscape, as well as their contemporary outlook and the impact of the current Pentecostalization of Ghanaian Christianity—argued to also be the case for the rest of the church in Africa.[1] The CoP, as part of these Ghanaian Pentecostal church forms, has emerged as a distinct, independent, indigenous classical Pentecostal denomination since the latter part of the 1930s. This chapter now engages the CoP's history, especially its post-independence history, as a prime example of a growing African Pentecostal denomination, in order to analyze the religious and theological factors that account for its growth, and for that matter, the general emergence of African Pentecostalism in the 20th century and the present.

The phrase "post-independence history of the CoP" refers to the period in the denomination's history since it disengaged affiliation with its parent body, the British Apostolic Church, in 1962. This independence of the CoP from its parent body must not be misconstrued to mean the political independence of the nation Ghana from British rule in 1957. Since becoming officially independent from the British Apostolic fraternity in 1962, the CoP has continued to expand in growth and mission both locally and internationally and has taken on a distinct character and form. Various conflicts and acrimonies in its early history initially

1. Asamoah-Gyadu, *Contemporary Pentecostal Christianity*, 9.

threatened to truncate its progress, but they rather led to the forming of other indigenous classical Pentecostal denominations and also aided in the firm grounding, stability, and growth of the Church of Pentecost. Though it is still the fastest growing Protestant Pentecostal denomination, the current Charismatization, the recent mushrooming of Charismatic-type churches (which are still "Pentecostal"), may pose a threat to its classical Pentecostal tradition. This chapter therefore discusses the post-independence developments, engagements, and growth of the church as a continuation of its early history—in order to address its future growth and the church's global Christian evangelization and mission in this era. The content has been divided into two main headings: Pre-Independence Historic Analysis of the CoP (1937–1962), and Contemporary History of the CoP (1962 to the present).

PRE-INDEPENDENCE HISTORIC ANALYSIS OF THE COP (1937–1962)

The Genesis

The origin of the CoP as an indigenous Ghanaian Christian initiative came out of the work of a Ghanaian Pentecostal, Peter Newman Anim, from a remote part of the Eastern Region of Ghana, Asamankese, around 1917. Peter Anim, originally a Presbyterian, was disenchanted with the spiritual staidness of the local Presbyterian church where he was a preacher. His zeal and yearning for a more satisfying spiritual experience led him to form a Christian prayer group. His readings led him to encounter and later become affiliated with two USA-based Christian institutions, which changed his life and that of his group for good. His first encounter was with the Philadelphia-based Faith Tabernacle movement through the reading of their periodical, *The Sword of the Spirit*,[2] from which he developed his doctrine on faith in biblical miracles and healing without medication. Second, reading another magazine brought him under the influence of the Apostolic Faith, another USA-based Pentecostal movement, that teaches, among other things, the relevance of the Pentecostal experience for every believer, accompanied by "speaking in

---

2. Wyllie, "Pioneers of Ghanaian Pentecostalism," 110.

tongues" as evidence and manifestation of the rest of the gifts of the Spirit as indicated in Acts 2 and 1 Corinthians 12.³

Around 1930 and 1932, the group experienced turnarounds that greatly affected its growth pattern. This growth was attributed to the personal experience of the empowerment of the Holy Spirit accompanied by speaking in unknown tongues and other manifestations of the apostolic promises such as prophecies. The group referred to this phenomenon as the outpouring of the Holy Spirit. According to Larbi, this period in the life of the Anim group has been characterized as the Holy Spirit's dispensation. The phenomena attracted all sorts of followers who became members, many from other denominations (historic mission denominations), including church leaders. This outbreak of experiences, seen as the Holy Spirit revival of 1932, spread to other parts of the country such as Ashanti, Togoland, Fanti, and other towns in the eastern region.⁴

Encounter with the British Apostolic Church

The earliest encounter of Anim's group with the British Apostolic Church was in June 1935. The group subsequently adopted the name the Apostolic Church of Gold Coast as a local branch of the Apostolic Church of the UK. Peter N. Anim was subsequently ordained a pastor into the Apostolic denomination by Pastor Perfect of the Apostolic Church–UK, in Asamankese.⁵

It must be noted that, before its affiliation with the British Apostolic Church, Anim's group was already functioning according to its own mode of operations. They had developed their own ethos and set of beliefs, beginning from their previous associations, mentioned earlier. These included a strong emphasis on prevailing prayer, a strong belief in divine healing without recourse to any form of medication (preventive or curative), the experience of glossolalia, and a very strong evangelistic ethos.⁶ This information is vital since it would inform the stability of the merger in later years. The two groups (British Apostolic and Anim's group) shared many similarities in their history and beliefs. The difference, however, is that, though the British Apostolics believed in the glos-

---

3. Asem, *History of the Church of Pentecost*, 18.
4. Larbi, *Pentecostalism*, 105.
5. Asem, *History of the Church of Pentecost*, 20.
6. Larbi, *Pentecostalism*, 108.

solalia phenomenon and divine healing, as did Anim's group, they did not believe in non-medication as a doctrine of biblical faith.

The James McKeown Factor

The Anim group subsequently requested, in October 1936, a permanent resident missionary from the Apostolic Church–UK.[7] The missionary and his wife, James and Sophia McKeown, were sent in response to this request. The CoP considers James McKeown its missionary founder. McKeown himself recorded his arrival in the Gold Coast, Accra, on March 7, 1937, as the premeditated resident missionary asked for by the Apostolic Church of Gold Coast and Pastor Peter N. Anim. His primary mission was to be a superintendent missionary for the Apostolic Church of Gold Coast, headquartered in Asamankese, establish it in the doctrine and practices of the Apostolic Church, and further evangelize the nation.

The summary of McKeown's total mission to the Gold Coast, in this writer's assessment, turned out to be akin to that of the biblical prophecy given by Simeon concerning Christ in Luke 2:34: "Behold, this Child is destined for the fall and rising of many in Israel, and for a sign which will be spoken against." The arrival of the McKeowns as the resident missionaries from the Apostolic Church–UK to their newfound daughter church in the Gold Coast was the commencement of a great sign. However, his presence initially generated acrimony and many conflicts as a sign being spoken against. Later, his efforts led to the establishment of a large tree rooted in African soil—truly, indigenously African, moving out into the rest of the world—and this tree is the CoP. McKeown's presence also led to the breaking up of the original Apostolic Church of Gold Coast, which according to the present writer, is in line with the Bible quotation above. The breakup of the Apostolic Church led to the rise of many other churches. It became the pioneering source or root for the indigenous classical Pentecostal denominations in Ghana today: CAC, ACG, and especially the CoP, now the largest Protestant denomination in Ghana, with branches around the globe.

---

7. Larbi, *Pentecostalism*, 107.

Doctrinal Conflicts, Other Internal Conflicts, and Secessions

Doctrinal Conflict

Shortly after his arrival, James McKeown had some disagreements with Peter N. Anim and his group due to doctrinal differences. The Anim group, as stated earlier, held tenaciously to a doctrine of faith healing without recourse to medication.[8] McKeown, in spite of his belief in divine healing through prevailing prayer, also believed in the potency of medication and did not think its use went against biblical instruction. In May 1937, barely two months after his arrival at Asamankese, McKeown took ill with malaria,[9] which became very severe. McKeown was reported to have been taken, semi-conscious, to the European Hospital (Ridge Hospital) in Accra in the company of Apostle Anim. However, upon his return, the congregation and leadership of the church that he led felt betrayed because their missionary—who should be trusting God for his healing—would use medication. The church and its leadership lost their trust in him.

McKeown realized that the church leadership no longer trusted him, and he was also dissuaded from preaching the gospel in outlying communities lest he pollute them with his use of medication.[10] Two years after McKeown's arrival, the faith-healing debate had generated a series of disagreements, mistrust, rancor, and confrontations between Anim and McKeown, which ended with the two leaders parting company and each forming his own group. The part of the group that followed Anim took the name Christ Apostolic Church.

In June 1938, McKeown moved the headquarters of his group from Asamankese to Winneba and continued his missionary work in the name of the Apostolic Church of Gold Coast. Some members from Asamankese, the church in Akroso and Winneba, and others from Anim's group in the Ashanti, Eastern, and Central regions adopted the name The Apostolic Church, and all these churches followed McKeown. They formed the starting point of McKeown's work after the exit of Anim and his group. The leaders from the Akroso branch, such as J. S. Gyimah, C. K. Frimpong, J. A. Bimpong, R. H. Dwuma, Philip Annor, Kwaku Asare, J. W. Amoako, and K. Nyarko, were all with the McKeown group.

8. Asem, *History of the Church of Pentecost*, 6.
9. Larbi, *Pentecostalism*, 108.
10. Asem, *History of the Church of Pentecost*, 31.

Evidence suggests that McKeown had a larger following than the Anim group, with two main reasons given. First, some members of the Anim group already had reservations about the anti-medication doctrine. The stance of McKeown only served as a way to release them. The other reason, especially from the Akroso group, was that no concrete references in the Bible support the faith-healing-without-medication doctrine, and they did not consider it a sin to take medication. The first convention of the Apostolic Church of Gold Coast after the secession from Anim was attended by about 200 members.[11] Thus, from this point, two distinct classical Pentecostal denominations were established in Ghana: the Christ Apostolic Church and the Apostolic Church of Gold Coast as the affiliate of the Apostolic Church–UK.

The Apostolic Church of Gold Coast and Other Conflicts

The beginning of the Apostolic Church of Gold Coast as a branch of the Apostolic Church–UK with James McKeown as its superintendent and without links to the Anim group is reputed to have been in June 1938.[12] By the year 1952, the church had spread throughout the country, with statistics estimating a membership of 10,512 and 53 ordained pastors.[13]

While the conflict with the Anim group was dying down, McKeown's own relationship with his parent church started going sour. The issues had to do mainly with church governance in the mission field and also McKeown's reservations concerning the Apostolic Church's belief in directive prophecy.[14] The relationship became intractable when the Apostolic Church of Gold Coast went ahead to invite a revival movement from the United States, the Latter Rain Evangelistic Team, led by Dr. Thomas Wyatt, for a revival program in 1952. This invitation went against the refusal of the Apostolic Church–UK. The final agitation that led to the severing of his ties with the parent body was his refusal to sign an amendment to the church's constitution that disallowed a black apostle to have oversight over a white apostle. Nevertheless, it was rather the objection of the Home Committee to the proposed visit of the Latter Rain team that caused resentment in McKeown. This resentment was

---

11. Larbi, *Pentecostalism*, 180.
12. Asem, *History of the Church of Pentecost*, 31.
13. CoP, Statistical Department Data, 1952.
14. Asamoah-Gyadu, "Pentecostalism and the Missiological Significance," 36.

shared by the brethren in the Gold Coast Church.¹⁵ All these together informed the dismissal of James McKeown from the fellowship of the Apostolic Church in May 1953. However, McKeown had played a very vital role sustaining the Apostolic Church of Gold Coast as a proactive missionary. His pro-African attitude and accurate timing for events can be considered good missionary strategy.

Secession from the Apostolic Church of Gold Coast

Upon McKeown's dismissal from the fellowship of the Apostolic Church–UK, the Apostolic Church of Gold Coast seceded from the mother Apostolic Church in the UK on May 21, 1953, and formed its separate independent body, the Gold Coast Apostolic Church.¹⁶

The group then, in a communiqué, invited McKeown to come and continue as their leader. However, other members or assemblies from the main body later rescinded the decision to secede from the Apostolic Church–UK and chose to remain with the parent body. These maintained the name Apostolic Church of Gold Coast. Through a series of painful, intractable conflicts lasting almost a decade, the two groups of the Gold Coast Apostolic Church finally separated into two different permanent bodies with the Apostolic Church of Gold Coast affiliated with the mother UK branch. Thus, from 1953 there have been three separate Apostolic churches in the Gold Coast: the Christ Apostolic Church with Anim as its head and headquartered in Asamankese, the Apostolic Church of Gold Coast as a local branch of the Apostolic Church–UK, also headquartered at Asamankese, and the Gold Coast Apostolic Church, with McKeown as its missionary founder, headquartered at Winneba. The term "missionary founder" differentiates McKeown from the indigenous founder, Peter Anim, and signals the church's difference from that of its initial history.

Internal Crisis and Change of Name

The conflict between the Apostolic Church of Ghana (renamed after the country's independence and change of name to Ghana in 1957) and McKeown's Ghana Apostolic Church (likewise renamed in 1957) persisted and escalated to national dimensions. In the meantime, while

15. Larbi, *Pentecostalism*, 222.
16. Asem, *History of the Church of Pentecost*, 99.

the issues with Bradford, UK, still continued, an internal crisis surfaced within the Ghana Apostolic Church between 1960 and 1962.

The cause of this crisis primarily concerned the leadership of McKeown and an agitation for African leadership. Later on some people attempted to reunite the Apostolic Church of Ghana and the Ghana Apostolic Church, which had parted company in 1953. In 1960, amid the controversy, McKeown went on furlough. During his absence, J. A. C. Anaman acted on his behalf as the chairman of the Ghana Apostolic Church, an assignment for which the church's General Council recommended Anaman.[17] While McKeown was still on furlough, an African chairman for the Ghana Apostolic Church was elected. It was proposed that McKeown act as the spiritual father of the organization by an emergency General Ministers' Council convened at Merry Villas, Accra, on October 18, 1960. J. A. C. Anaman was unanimously voted as McKeown's successor, and he duly accepted the nomination and started work, pending the arrival of McKeown, towards his inauguration. The new appointment was published in the national daily newspapers and all local assemblies of the church. The appointment sparked dissension and misunderstanding between some church members not in total agreement with this development.[18] The elders in the Ashanti Region passed a resolution expressing their dissatisfaction, resolving not to recognize or comply with the chairmanship of Anaman until McKeown returned.[19]

While the issues with the African chairmanship had not completely died down, another popped up on the need to reconcile the Apostolic churches. Some members from Ghana Apostolic Church, the McKeown group, initiated a process of reconciliation between the two groups—McKeown's Ghana Apostolic Church and the Apostolic Church of Ghana. A seven-man committee headed by E. D. Ocansey from Ghana Apostolic Church and J. R. Asiedu, then the speaker of the national assembly, was appointed. The meetings and deliberations yielded no positive results. The matter was then referred to the intervention of the government of Ghana.

The Ghanaian minister of education at the time appointed a commission on December 9, 1961, to resolve the impasse and see to the reconciliation of the two factions. The minister appointed the Honorable

---

17. Larbi, *Pentecostalism*, 217.
18. Larbi, *Pentecostalism*, 220.
19. Larbi, *Pentecostalism*, 220.

J. B. Blay as the deputy minister of education to chair the committee. The other members of the committee were James S. Kesseler, superintendent of the Assemblies of God Mission, and George Ankra Badu, acting synod clerk of the Presbyterian Church of Ghana.[20] Before the report of the Blay Commission could be made public, the McKeown faction of the church petitioned the then head of state, Osagyefo Dr. Kwame Nkrumah, regarding publication of the report.

On July 21, 1962, in the presence of four representatives, two from each group, the head of state ruled on the matter. The final ruling said that the two groups should remain as separate bodies. All properties acquired by the churches before May 21, 1953, the date of McKeown's secession, should go to the Bradford, UK, side. Every other property acquired by each group after that date should remain that group's property. The McKeown group was also advised to adopt a different name. The Ghana Apostolic Church, in obedience to the suggestion by the head of state, changed its name to the Church of Pentecost on August 1, 1962.

Effects of the Doctrinal and Other Conflicts and the CoP's Independence

The position of the present writer is that the conflicts and challenges in the CoP's early history, and the developments thus chronicled, shaped the organization into a formidable force. They established its doctrinal beliefs and forged its religious practices and characteristic ethos. For instance, the formation of some of its developmental structures, such as functional ministries and administrative and ministerial structures (yet to be discussed) are informed and influenced by the fallout and decisions arrived at from these early engagements. Thus, they acted as very important factors that contributed to her growth—initially and in the years since.

Larbi corroborates this view in his comment on the various secessions in the history of classical Pentecostalism in Ghana. He observed that, instead of undermining the growth and development of the movement, the secessions rather appear to have contributed to its growth and vitality.[21] Wyllie earlier asserted this same notion: "We cannot entirely accept the idea that the dissension and fission that seethed around the activities

---

20. Bredwa-Mensah, "Church of Pentecost in Retrospect," 37.
21. Larbi, *Pentecostalism*, 79.

of McKeown and Anim were necessarily drawbacks in the development of Pentecostalism in Ghana. Out of the various disputes and conflicts, new groups were created and, it may be suggested, contributed to the vitality of the Pentecostal movement as a whole."[22] In Bredwa-Mensah's view, the reason the CoP is a strong and major Pentecostal force may be in part its historical ability to overcome the many complex and difficult crises that confronted it from its inception.[23]

Overview of Developments from 1937 to 1962

The period in the CoP's history between 1937 and 1938, the first break with Anim's group, and subsequent developments between 1953 and 1962, characterized by various painful acrimonies and court cases, should not be deemed wasted years. These conflicts served as avenues for real, deeper commitment by some of the members. They developed empathy for and commitment to their church in a manner that enabled them to voluntarily help the organization with material and financial support. This challenge can be understood as the genesis of the sacrificial giving observed as part of the ethos of the denomination, which eventually made it self-supporting, without much recourse to or dependence on any aid from foreign donors.[24] The members, having gone through such difficulties, had learned to be dependent on God and committed to their church. What defined the conduct of the members and spurred them on for evangelism was their love for God and the factor of James McKeown.[25] In this vein, the CoP maintained a pattern of not only being self-supporting or self-financing but also self-governing, self-propagating, self-theologizing, and self-sustaining.[26]

That era in the organization did include financial difficulties. One Mrs. Christiana Obo Mends was moved to give her precious ornaments to be sold by McKeown to support the church's financial obligations. She was said to have put up a building to house him and the pastors when they were on trek. She was able to pay for the pastors' allowances when

22. Wyllie, "Pioneers of Ghanaian Pentecostalism," 110.
23. Bredwa-Mensah, "Church of Pentecost in Retrospect," 43.
24. Asem, *History of the Church of Pentecost*, 68.
25. Interview with Mrs. Grace Lucy Yeboah, National Women's Director, Asuamah, February 5, 2014.
26. Larbi, *Pentecostalism*, 136–37.

the church had no adequate funds to do so.[27] Mrs. Obo was supported by other women, including Prudence Anaman from Saltpond.[28] Some leaders in Accra donated as much as £500 to aid a new pastor's settlement in Accra. Some gave lands and properties, just to mention a few. The spirit of giving for the cause of God informed the character of the church.[29] The church that emerged from this time has been a self-supporting organization that sends missionaries sponsored from Ghana to every part of the globe.

The CoP, amid the various dissensions, secessions, and acrimonies in this era, developed formidable administrative and evangelistic structures as well as its own unique governing structures to protect its integrity. Asamoah-Gyadu identifies the administrative structures (polity of the church) of the CoP as the one vital, positive strength that informs growth, especially in congregations located in the United States.[30] Larbi, however, argues that it is rather the discipline (in terms of ethical rigor) of its leadership towards the individual members and the ministers (field pastors) that drives the CoP ahead. He argues that the same administrative structures are used by other classical Pentecostals such as the CAC, which has the same root as the CoP, yet the CoP outgrew them. He suggests that the CoP's growth is rather due to its adoption of strict discipline.[31] Both factors (administrative structure and strict discipline) suggested by these two writers, Asamoah-Gyadu and Larbi, contributed to CoP's development and growth. Both factors are fallout from the CoP's early historic challenges and are characteristics that have become part of its cherished values.

This work argues that the factors that led to the growth of the CoP do not seem to have emerged from intentional strategic planning. They were measures to address these challenges as the denomination proceeded through its history. These measures, aimed at correcting the problems, became part of the religious and theological factors that eventually promoted its growth.[32] For instance, the matter of "strict discipline" could be traced to the strict disciplinary measures the early leadership, including

---

27. Asem, *History of the Church of Pentecost*, 68.
28. Larbi, *Pentecostalism*, 187.
29. Larbi, *Pentecostalism*, 178.
30. Asamoah-Gyadu, "On Mission Abroad," 90–101.
31. Larbi, *Pentecostalism*, 180.
32. Bredwa-Mensah, "Church of Pentecost in Retrospect," 43.

James McKeown, adopted due to the mistrust of some previous alliances or members.[33] In the present writer's opinion, much of the initial administrative setup can be attributed to the work and ministry of James McKeown and his early leaders as they led the movement through its experiences during this era.

Following this period of doctrinal differences and divisions among various bodies, from 1962 on the real evangelistic initiatives and missionary endeavors of McKeown's mission to Ghana began to bear fruit through the now-established CoP. First of all, the separation between the Apostolic Church of Gold Coast and the Anim group brought others from the Faith Tabernacle churches and the Apostolic Church in Akroso, together with their leaders, into McKeown's group.[34] Second, the structures of the organization (secretarial, administrative, and ministerial) became more stable and formidable, leading to the opening of more congregations and expansions into other nations beginning from neighboring African countries.[35]

The CoP at this time of its history, having undergone diverse conflicts and disagreements, produced highly conscientious Christians among its membership. The ordinary members had learned both to be dependent on God and to be committed to the organization and evangelistic activities.[36] The members themselves, through their own initiatives and finances, established local churches and requested the main church's recognition. As a result of these historic trajectories, the CoP developed its own practices and liturgy, theological beliefs, ethos and characteristics, as a distinct indigenous classical Pentecostal church. The church developed structured governance and an administrative organization, boards and committees, and various functional ministries. The structures established during this period informed its next dimension of growth after 1962.

Another factor identified as originating during these years of challenges is that the movement relied on some messages received as prophetic utterances. These, it is assumed, inspired its leadership and members alike to further growth, especially in missions outside the country. As a Pentecostal institution, the CoP believes in the validity of prophetic

---

33. Bredwa-Mensah, "Church of Pentecost in Retrospect," 82.
34. Asamoah-Gyadu, "Pentecostalism and the Missiological Significance," 40.
35. Leonard, *Giant in Ghana*, 122–27.
36. Asamoah-Gyadu, "Pentecostalism and the Missiological Significance," 40.

utterances. Some of the prophetic utterances recorded from those periods might have come to relieve adherents' fear about future extinction during the intense acrimonies.[37] Larbi has recorded that some such prophetic utterances conveyed that the church would spread into Africa as a light from black Africa; subsequent prophecies seemed to include the rest of the world.[38] Apparently, some specific prophecies directed towards areas to be evangelized and others indicated the bright future of the movement. These prophetic messages have been perceived as validating and believed to affirm the church's unique or special covenant relationship with God that sets them apart as unique from all others. Larbi contends that this belief has become the main focus or drive behind the CoP's growth and current international missions.[39] It has become a point of reference, as an extension to the biblical mandate of evangelism in Mark 16:15–18, which reminds the members concerning their responsibility to evangelize the world. This has become a major part of the spirituality and beliefs of the organization, one that drives its followers to sacrificial giving and charity, personal and group evangelism, church planting, and other voluntary engagements for the church.

CONTEMPORARY HISTORY OF THE COP (1962 TO THE PRESENT)

The CoP's developmental history during the period between 1962 and 2014 compared to the period discussed above can be characterized as one of stable administration, aggressive evangelism, church planting, and external Christian mission outreach beyond the borders of Ghana into other African countries and other continents, including the West. The church experienced astronomical growth within this period. For instance, it claimed 26,000 adherents in 1962, after its break from the British Apostolic fraternity. Fifty years later, as of December 31, 2012, it reported a total membership of 1,938,411 locally and a total worldwide of 2,252,228, with mission posts in 86 other countries apart from Ghana.[40] This is an increase of over 800 percent in half a century. This growth in

---

37. Larbi, *Pentecostalism*, 218.
38. Larbi, *Pentecostalism*, 250–51.
39. Larbi, *Pentecostalism*, 252.
40. CoP, Statistics Department Data, 2012.

number of adherents is in addition to growth in non-personnel and movable and immovable structures and developments.

Furthermore, the church's growth can be seen in its established functional ministries, such as in its Witness/Evangelism, Women's, Youth, Children's, and Men's Ministries, the Pentecost International Worship Centres, and Northern Outreach Ministries. Other indicators include structures for church governance, administration, and finance, which have changed or are appraised periodically; the raising of indigenous leadership (especially when the indigenes took over from McKeown in 1982); the development of human resources, training and education; social services; and print and electronic media. Other growth indicators that cannot be overlooked include major theological factors such as its belief in pneumatic phenomena (such as Holy Spirit baptism, gifts, and fruits), signs and wonders, the effects of prayer camps and hosting structures (church buildings, mission houses), and church corporate assets. We can learn much about the CoP's growth trends in this period by analyzing how these ministries and structural developments emerged and grew.

Functional Ministries

Thus, this work proposes that the starting point for CoP growth and development, especially after her independence, can be located within the vibrancy and dynamism of its functional ministries. Some of the CoP's leadership has suggested that the vibrancy of the church depends on the dynamism and effectiveness of the local congregations. Opoku Onyinah, the current chairman of the denomination, in an address to the church's leaders across the world, commented on the need to strengthen the local congregations as part of their vision for growth up to 2018. He stressed that the local assembly in the CoP is the focal point of the church and must be seen as such.[41] However, the functional ministries had become the engines behind the growth of the local assemblies in the entire CoP.[42] Seven distinct functional ministries have evolved in the CoP over the past years: Evangelism, Women's, Youth, Children's, Men's, Northern Outreach, and the PIWCs. Larbi suggests that the Evangelism and Wom-

---

41. Opoku Onyinah, Chairman of CoP, explaining some excerpts from the *Vision 2018* manual at the Area Heads' meeting, November 2012; see CoP, *Vision 2018*.

42. Larbi, *Pentecostalism*, 187.

en's Ministries are the agencies that largely contributed to the growth of the emerging church from the 1940s.[43] Thereafter, other historic developments have led to the creation of other ministries to further promote the growth of the church.

Evangelism Ministry

The Evangelism Ministry is the body that promotes the evangelistic drive of the organization. The CoP's evangelistic nature characterized its existence as a revival movement from its inception, with its roots from Anim's group.[44] The church had on record ordinary members, both men and women, up front in vibrant evangelism as a sign of having experienced truly the phenomenon they call baptism in the Holy Spirit. Individuals and groups in the CoP are reported to engage in aggressive evangelism in villages, towns, and communities as part of normal church life. Records also tell of recognized, seasoned ordained evangelists and preachers such as R. O. Hayford and his team from Saltpond, the twin brothers Yaw Atta Panyin and Yaw Atta Kakra from Abura Dunkwa, S. W. Duffour of Banko, S. H. Ankama, and S. T. W. Frimpong, to name a few, who traveled extensively in the 1940s throughout the nation and outside establishing churches with great signs and wonders following them.[45] Evangelist R. O. Hayford was instrumental in opening assemblies in the Assin and Twifo Areas in 1946. The church also organized rallies and conventions, all with an evangelistic orientation. Asem wrote that "organised rallies and conventions were the means by which the church grew, beginning with the first General Convention at Winneba in 1939."[46]

Around this period in the 1940s, these evangelistic efforts brought many to the church, including young people. The entrance of young people between 16 and 25 years necessitated the establishment of the Young People's Movement in the early 1940s. These involved very energetic young men and women desiring to be active in evangelism. The prime aim of the movement was to mobilize and train the young people for evangelism and to prepare them for various positions of leadership in the church. Around 1950, interest in the movement had increased

---

43. Larbi, *Pentecostalism*, 183.
44. Larbi, *Pentecostalism*, 187, 183.
45. Asem, *History of the Church of Pentecost*, 76–77.
46. Asem, *History of the Church of Pentecost*, 90.

tremendously due to its evangelistic ethos. The name was changed from Young People's Movement (*Mbrantsekuw*, in the Akan language) to the Apostolic Witness Movement, and the membership age was waived to include any interested person.[47]

The Witness Movement became the drive behind evangelism in the entire denomination. Membership and participation were later used as a yardstick for measuring individual commitment when anyone was being considered for promotion into leadership or into full-time ministry. The structure of the movement became pronounced and much more recognized as a wing in the church. The first general leader of the movement was S. L. Adotey.[48] Then, sometime around 1950, Pastor Stanley M. Hammond, a missionary from the UK, was appointed the leader. Stanley M. Hammond was said to have introduced the name Witness Movement. Since then, the movement has undergone several name changes corresponding to the church leadership's perception of the direction of evangelism at the time and the nature of its participants. Various other offshoot evangelistic groups sprouted out of the Witness Movement in many of the regions. A very instrumental group in the evangelizing of the Accra community and its environs was the Bombing group.

The Bombing group was a group of Witness Movement young men who mobilized themselves for evangelism in the church around 1945. The name was derived from the Second World War air raids of the allied forces. It was expected that the group would be dealing with the devil through evangelistic activities the same way the allied forces dealt with their enemies. The group initially counted about 12 members. Their leaders included S. L. Adotey, Johnny Mallet, S. Y. Diaba, J. Egyir-Paintsil, J. W. Sackey, and C. C. A. Hushie. This group was credited with starting assemblies at Merry Villas, Mamprobi, Korle Gonno, Achimota, and Teshie, all in Accra. They also started assemblies in Ada Foa, Big Ada, Somanya, Akuse, Mamfe, Aburi, and Nsawam. Almost all these young men except Johnny Mallet later became field workers in the church.[49] This discussion shows that though the whole church considers itself an evangelistic movement and every member part of the Witness Movement, in practice the young people are the ones most involved in the movement and in frontline evangelism. This practical reality has had a

---

47. Larbi, *Pentecostalism*, 183.

48. Larbi, *Pentecostalism*, 183.

49. Larbi, *Pentecostalism*, 184.

very important effect on the progress, pattern, and developments in the church, especially with regard to the evolving of other ministries and to evangelism in general.

The activities of the Apostolic Witness Movement of Gold Coast centered on equipping the young people for witnessing to the gospel of Jesus Christ. It was also apparent from its various early handbooks that the movement was responsible for the Bible study outlines that guided, trained, and equipped church members, especially the young people.[50] In its *Witness Syllabus* for 1966, the Witness Movement held class meetings once weekly for prayers, witnessing, Bible study, Bible quizzes, and singing or learning of songs.[51] The movement also embarked on personal evangelism and gospel rallies. In 1979, for instance, the movement held 929 gospel rallies, which yielded over 10,000 souls.[52] These gospel rallies were arranged by the local assembly's witness leaders.[53]

The national leader of the wing was referred to as the General Witness Leader. He had the responsibility of coordinating all the affairs of the movement, including updating the *Witness Syllabus* with the church's literature committee and organizing "general witness rallies."[54] He was the chairman of its national meetings and conventions. Successive General Witness Leaders of the church and their dates of service are as follows: Elder S. L. Adotey (from the beginning to 1949), Pastor S. W. Hammond (1949-1955), Apostle F. D. Walker (1955-1967), Apostle A. T. Nartey (1967-1980), Apostle D. K. Arnan (1980-1982), Apostle Patrick Asiamah (1982-1988), and Pastor J. K. Appiah (1988-1991).[55] Others who were later all designated directors instead of general witness leaders are Apostle Peter Ayerakwa (1991-1996), Apostle J. S. Gyimah (1996-2000), Apostle Kingsford Kyei-Mensah (2000-2008), and Apostle Michael C. Aseidu (2008-2016).

By the 1970s, a younger generation had emerged in the church. Many of these younger generations and their parents aspired to an education, especially tertiary education. At this time in the nation's history, the government initiatives for the expansion of education at all levels were

50. Apostolic Church, *Apostolic Witness Movement Gold Coast.*
51. CoP, *Witness Syllabus.*
52. CoP, Report of the Witness Work, December 31, 1979.
53. CoP, *Witness Syllabus.*
54. CoP, Report of the Witness Work, December 31, 1983.
55. CoP, Reports of Witness Work, 1955-1991.

at their peak.⁵⁶ Many of these young people found themselves in colleges and other tertiary institutions, which led to the springing up in the late 1970s of a youth movement for the tertiary institutions: Pentecost Students and Associates (PENSA). When the programs and membership of the Witness Movement and PENSA began to conflict, it became evident that the commitment of the youth, especially those in higher education, leaned towards PENSA. This development eventually led to forming of a new, unified group to accommodate both groups. Thus, Pentecost Youth and Evangelism Movement (PENTYEM) was created in 1991. On the campuses, however, PENSA still operates as a campus wing under the PENTYEM.

The PENTYEM, according to its handbook, comprises all the youth of the church and all who have the strength and mind to carry on with the Great Commission of the Lord Jesus Christ, irrespective of age. The functions of PENTYEM include carrying out evangelism and training members for it, enabling the youth to participate fully in the programs and activities of the church, and further exposing them to the various ministries within the church. Further, it is to afford the youth opportunities to plan and organize programs and activities for evangelism in schools, colleges, universities, and in the cities and to bring out the gifts and leadership qualities in them.⁵⁷ To this end, the aim of merging these two to form the PENTYEM, according to its manual, was to build bridges with other movements in the church to complement each other's efforts towards growth and also to help the leadership identify the particular needs of the youth and create an atmosphere for their equipping.⁵⁸ In this regard, the original operations, activities, and aims of the Witness Movement and the PENTYEM have not changed much.

The restructuring had been for purposes of organization and effectiveness, but the operations of the movement as a wing for evangelism and training into leadership remain the same as from its beginning. To buttress this observation, PENTYEM was later separated again into two groups: Youth Ministry and the Witness Movement, bringing back the previous Witness Movement. More recently, the name Witness Movement has been changed to Evangelism Ministry. The Evangelism Ministry, from the 1980s on, went through various challenges regarding its

---

56. Barker and Boadi-Siaw, *Changed by the Word*, 12.
57. CoP, *Handbook for Pentecost Youth*, 2–3.
58. CoP, *Handbook for Pentecost Youth*, 2.

structures, constitution of its membership, and mode of operations, especially due to its separation from the Youth Ministry. This makes sense given the fact that its original composition had always been predominantly the youth. Thus, beginning around the 1970s, the structures of the Witness Movement and the Evangelism Ministry have overlapped and intertwined with the newly developing Youth Ministry.

Youth Ministry

Among the major developments in the CoP between 1962 and 2014 is the Youth Ministry, which includes PENSA and its progeny, the ITI-PENSA. The CoP was basically a grassroots movement until the 1970s.[59] The majority of participants had been people from the lower educational and social strata, with very little or no formal education. A few highly educated people had been attracted to join the church through interventions such as the need for healing from sicknesses or some other prayer need. Some of these few elites were Mrs. Christiana Obo Mends, the first Women's Leader, and Kafui Asem, one of the early contributors to *Pentecost Fire*—the church's periodical.[60] From 1970 on, many children of members had been born into the church, and they had received or were going through secondary- and tertiary-level education; many church members sought to give their children the highest levels of education. This and other factors led to the presence of a large number of young people in the church, both on school campuses and in church congregations.

The formation of global Christian student groups to bear witness to the Lord Jesus Christ in universities dates back to the 1930s. It produced the International Fellowship of Evangelical Students (IFES), formed in 1947 as an international campus ministry with the aim of reaching students worldwide.[61] The Ghana Fellowship of Evangelical Students (GHAFES), an arm of IFES in Ghana, was formed in 1966 in the University of Ghana. At that time, the Inter Hall Christian Fellowship, formed in 1956, was already 10 years old on Kwame Nkrumah University of Science and Technology (KNUST) campus. On the University of Ghana campus, a similar group, the Legon Interdenominational Church

---

59. Larbi, *Pentecostalism*, 197.

60. Larbi, *Pentecostalism*, 189.

61. See the website for the International Fellowship of Evangelical Students (IFES): www.ifesworld.org.

(LIC) was formed in 1978 to provide an opportunity during vacation for students to worship God. The first pastor was Professor Emeritus K. A. Dickson.[62] The Legon Pentecostals' Union (LPU) was also founded, in October 1976, to bring together all students of the Pentecostal fraternity into student Christian fellowship with Pentecostal worship. The founders of the group included the president, W. N. Kissiedu, Peter Ohene Kyei, J. A. Larkai, William Adjei, and Mrs. Kate Asiseh.[63]

However, many of the CoP youth on the campuses were not attending the nondenominational Christian fellowships on campus. Concern about this trend led to the birth of PENSA as a student wing for the CoP in 1979.[64] Those who introduced and started the PENSA on campuses included Peter Ohene Kyei, W. N. Kissiedu, Joshua Adjabeng, J. S. Gyimah, R. Ato Addison, Peter Ayerakwa, Offei Awuku, and Stephen Ampofo. A three-man delegation made up of Peter Ohene Kyei, J. A. Larkai, and J. S. Gyimah was sent to discuss the issues with the general secretary Apostle Egyir-Paintsil in 1979.[65] The general secretary appointed Elder Ntiri to be the first officer to oversee the students' affairs. The first Pentecost Students' Delegate Conference was held at Accra Academy in August 1979.[66] The church, through the general secretary, Apostle Egyir-Paintsil, donated a sum of GHC1,500 to the group. The name PENSA was adopted at this delegates' meeting. The church leadership, including Apostle Egyir-Paintsil, Frederick Diabene Walker, Fred Stephen Safo, and A. T. Nartey, all supported the PENSA. The first institution to set up PENSA on its campus was University of Science and Technology (now KNUST) in 1979, with 33 members.[67]

The movement spread very fast to other campuses as PENSA was established in many tertiary institutions and secondary schools. On August 23, 1980, a general conference was held at Prempeh College, Kumasi, and PENSA was formally inaugurated and its working constitution was published. By the close of the 1980s, PENSA had gone through some growth challenges, as most organizations do at various stages. Larbi asserts that

62. Legon Interdenominational Church, history file, Legon, January 2011.
63. Culled from Legon Pentecostals' Union website: thelegonpentecostalunion.blogspot.com.
64. CoP, "Short History of PENSA KNUST."
65. CoP, "Short History of PENSA KNUST."
66. Lawrence Otu-Nyarko, "PENSA in Retrospect," paper presented at ITI-PENSA retreat for tertiary schools, Kumasi, June 2007, 1.
67. CoP, "Short History of PENSA KNUST."

a cross-section of the elders, pastors, and the leadership of the Witness Movement became suspicious of the motives of the PENSA. A pioneer leader of PENSA thought the conflict was about the patronage of the young people drawn to PENSA, believed to be undermining the activities of the Witness Movement and, in some places, the local assemblies. Evaluating the PENSA after 10 years of existence, the national executives at the time stated that the movement had been struggling to survive. In this period, some of its achievements included internal discipleship of the students, evangelism at the three universities and other schools and colleges, and literacy training for some illiterate members of the church. Its members also contributed to the writing of devotional articles for the church's devotional guide.

Restructuring in the PENSA. By the end of the 1980s and into the 1990s, the activities of the Women's Ministry, PENSA, and Witness Movement started conflicting. The three ministries were asserted to be soliciting the patronage of the same group of people, especially the youth. Evidently, the interest of the young people was shifting towards the PENSA, thereby decreasing the patronage of the other ministries. Some form of restructuring in the organogram in the church was called for, which the PENSA leaders interpreted as a threat to abolish their movement.

The structural change proposed a merger between the then Witness Movement and PENSA, and the resulting body was named Pentecost Youth and Evangelism Movement (PENTYEM). The General Council appointed Apostle Peter Ayerakwa as the director of PENTYEM in 1991.[68] The Rev. L. A. Nyarko was made the patron; the deputy director was Elder E. A. Boate; Prophet Ebenezer Appiah-Agyekum, Pastor I. J. K. Adeti, Elder Peter Ohene Kyei, Elder Henry Koranteng, Elder W. N. Kissiedu, and Elder E. Y. Torso were all members of the PENTYEM committee.[69] This composition suggests a blend of leaders from both the Witness Movement and PENSA. By September 1991, PENSA had ceased to exist as a distinct, separate body.[70] The student leadership did not consider the move favorable on the campuses. After many deliberations, it was agreed that PENSA should operate only in tertiary institutions, while PENTYEM would function in the mainstream church. This development informed the formation of the Inter-Tertiary Institution PENSA (ITI-PENSA) in

---

68. CoP, General Council Decisions and Appointments (white paper), 1991.
69. CoP, PENTYEM Handbook, 1991.
70. Larbi, *Pentecostalism*, 200.

1991 as a means of continuing the PENSA vision in the higher education institutions. Its maiden program was held on March 22, 1992, at the University of Ghana. The first coordinating team was made up of five members from KNUST. Since then, the coordination of ITI-PENSA has been on rotation among KNUST, University of Ghana, University of Cape Coast, and recently University of Development Studies. The aims and objectives of the ITI-PENSA, among others, are to foster interaction among members within the various campuses for proper integration of students and alumni of tertiary institutions into the Church of Pentecost, to help establish PENSA in all secondary and tertiary institutions, to curb the drift of PENSA students and alumni into other churches, to gather resources for field and missionary work, and to ensure effective communication between ITI-PENSA and the Church of Pentecost.[71]

Another Restructuring. In 1996, other structural changes took place, motivated by the same two reasons already discussed: first, the many young people flocking to the church, and second, the need for effective evangelism. The very contemporary challenges and needs of the youth had to be addressed. PENTYEM, which is responsible both for the youth and evangelism, was remodeled into two separate groups, comprising the CoP Youth Ministry and the Witness Movement. The idea was to place the young people of the church and the evangelism efforts under separate umbrellas of leadership. This change aimed to primarily address the specific needs of youth pertaining to postmodernity's complexities, while also allowing the Witness Movement to continue with its basic assignment and vision for evangelism and training. In 1997, the General Council appointed Apostle D. K. Noble-Atsu as the first director for the Youth Ministry.[72] His assignments included training young people for evangelism, discipleship, counseling, and others. Then PENSA was officially placed under the Youth Ministry of the CoP and the ITI-PENSA automatically went under the leadership of the Youth Ministry. The activities of the ITI-PENSA were restructured to include PENSA from the secondary institutions, and thus, in 2011, ITI-PENSA had to change its name again, now to PENSA-Ghana. The president of ITI-PENSA who took over the coordination of PENSA-Ghana automatically became a member of the National Youth Executive and also a councilor to the General and Extraordinary Council meetings of the church.

71. CoP, *ITI-PENSA Constitution*, 2009, article 2.

72. CoP, General Council Meeting Minutes, 1997; his working executives included Elder Amos Kelvin-Annan as deputy director.

PENSA-Ghana Traveling Secretaries. At the church's 34th General Council meeting held in May 2003, the council appointed the first two traveling secretaries to oversee PENSA activities in the schools and campuses under the youth directorate of the church. They were Pastor Franklin Agbovi-Hushie and Pastor E. K. Acquah.[73] Pastor Franklin Agbovi-Hushie was responsible for five political regions in southern Ghana, while Pastor E. K. Acquah was responsible for five political regions in the northern territories. The rising student population, coupled with the importance of the proximity of the traveling secretaries to their sectors of operation compelled the leadership to create additional sectors. Three more secretaries were added in 2005: Pastor Samuel Otu Appiah for the Central and Western Regions, Pastor Seth Acquaye for the Eastern Region, and Pastor Philip Osei-Korsah for the Northern Sector.[74] In 2006, three more were added to make it eight. They were Pastor Patrick Kwabena Bremansu for Brong Ahafo Region, Pastor Maxwell Adubofour Asiedu for the Volta Region, and Pastor Daniel Sackey for the Western Region.[75] One more was created in 2011 for the Northern and Upper Regions combined under the care of Pastor David Amankwaah.[76] When the Northern and Upper Regions were divided in 2012, Pastor Gideon Yirenkyi-Boadu took over the Upper East and West Regions.[77] By this time all regions in the nation were covered by a traveling secretary.

The assigned duties for these traveling secretaries include the following: interacting with the students on campuses of the tertiary and secondary institutions with the view of giving them direction and support in their evangelistic activities; identifying leadership potential, gifting, or callings of the youth for recommendation into full-time ministry and making the necessary recommendations to the leadership of the church for appropriate actions; providing pastoral counseling and meeting the felt individual and corporate needs of the youth; conducting leadership training programs for the student leadership as well as potential leaders

---

73. CoP, General Council Decisions and Appointments, released at the close of the 34th session of the General Council meetings, May 2003, contained this information. This white paper is a document containing transfers, appointments, and callings of the church. It is released by the Executive Council at each General Council meeting of the church.

74. CoP, General Council Decisions and Appointments, 2005.

75. CoP, General Council Decisions and Appointments, 2006.

76. CoP, General Council Decisions and Appointments, 2011.

77. CoP, General Council Decisions and Appointments, 2012.

in the institutions; helping to promote the CoP Youth Ministry devotional guide and other church literature in collaboration with the PENSA-Ghana coordinators; providing pastoral care and services to the students such as baptism; identifying and encouraging final-year students of the tertiary institutions to voluntarily opt for national service in the CoP's designated needy areas; and facilitating the integration of final-year students of the tertiary institutions into the alumni body of PENSA and the mainstream church to curb the elite-exit syndrome from the CoP.[78]

In 2004, the General Council reviewed the mandate of Apostle D. K. Noble-Atsu and the National Executive Committee, replacing them by the following people, who assumed duty from October 2004: Apostle Dr. Opoku Onyinah as the patron; Pastor Emmanuel Kwesi Acquah as the youth director; Elder Amos Kevin-Annan as the deputy director; Pastor S. O. Asante, Mrs. Mary Kutin-Buah, Elders S. K. Amegah and E. Y. Torso as members; and Pastors Frank Agbovi-Hushie and Emmanuel Ofei Ankrah-Badu as co-opted members.[79] By this time, the activities of the Youth Ministry had assumed a dimension of their own, not dependent on the Evangelism Ministry. Two major challenges faced the Youth Ministry, as stated in their 2014 Annual Report: first, how to build youth-friendly churches without sacrificing the church's core values, which include evangelism, and second, how to promote the awareness that the youth are not only future leaders of the church but an active part of the church and its leadership. The ministry therefore rolled out activities and projections aimed at addressing these issues. They included youth creativity and inventions, leadership trainings, building of youth resource centers, peer counseling training, and Pentecost Youth Missionaries projects.[80] The Executive and General Councils of the church demonstrated very important attachments to the youth ministry and its various accessories. The chairman's opening address at the 2009 ITI-PENSA Conference captures this relationship:

> On this occasion, I wish to, on behalf of the Executive Council, express heartfelt appreciation to the past and present leaders for their dynamic and dedicated leadership. Their zeal coupled with the grace of God has made PENSA a beacon of light on the various campuses. I follow with keen interest the giant strides

78. CoP, ITI-Travelling Secretaries Guidelines and Responsibilities from General Secretaries as in Appointment Letters, 2013.

79. CoP, Youth Ministry Annual Report, 2004.

80. CoP, Youth Ministry Annual Report, 2004.

you are making in your evangelistic activities on the campuses and outside the schools. Your involvement in the local churches is also gratefully acknowledged. . . . I am happy to remind you that the intention of the Executive Council in appointing ITI-PENSA Travelling Secretaries is to bring Pastoral care closer to PENSA so as to make them perpetually accessible.[81]

To augment the evangelism efforts of the Youth Ministry, the youth leadership introduced additional functions to the work of PENSA. Though already massively involved in mainstream evangelism, leadership believed the added functions could be carried out easily through PENSA. These involved ministry among drug addicts, Rastafarians, prostitutes, street kids, and physically and mentally challenged people. The efforts of the Youth Ministry in terms of the CoP's growth, especially among young people, are described by its leaders as heart-warming. In April 2008, the chairman of the church, Apostle M. K. Ntumy, indicated that the youth ministry undertook 4,970 evangelistic outreaches, won 25,561 converts, evangelized 660 schools and colleges, and saw 19,959 people receive the baptism in the Holy Spirit. He commented thus: "It is heart-warming to note that the CoP has 18,084 members in secondary and tertiary institutions. Surely, by his grace, we can say the future is very bright."[82]

Ministry leadership changed in 2010: Pastor David N. Hayfron, a product of PENSA, was brought into the CoP pastorate and appointed as the director to replace Pastor E. K. Acquah, who was sent as a missionary to the Republic of South Africa. Apostle Eric Nyamekye was the patron for the ministry. Since then, other initiatives have been added as needed by the movement. They include teen services for youth under 13 years, Pentecost Youth Missionaries Outreach, Mega Youth All-night Services, School of Youth Ministry, School of Apologetics, PENSA Leaders Summit, Pentecost Writers Contest, Mega Crusades, Virtuous Ladies' Conference, and Youth Wave Radio and Television Recording. By the end of 2015, Youth Ministry recorded its membership as 750,320, comprised of 329,847 teens and 420,473 young adults; PENSA membership was 76,267.[83] As of the end of 2016, the Youth Ministry membership is recorded at 842,019: 372,038 teens, which is 44 percent, and 469,981

---

81. CoP, PENSA Conference brochure, 2009.

82. CoP, Chairman Apostle Dr. M. K. Ntumy, State of the Church Address, presented at the opening ceremony of the 37th session of the General Council meetings, Pentecost University College, Accra, April 24, 2008.

83. CoP, Youth Ministry Annual Executives Report, January–December 2015.

young adults, or 56 percent. The membership of PENSA was recorded as 83,036.[84] In his 2016 State of the Church Address, Apostle Opoku Onyinah, the chairman of the church, observed that the overall membership analysis implies that 71 percent of the CoP membership in Ghana is made up of children and youth, which indicates how the CoP is thriving:

> The overall analysis implies that 71% of the CoP membership in Ghana is made up of children and youth (up to thirty-five years). This is a healthy sign and an indication that the Church of Pentecost is a thriving church with a great future. It is therefore imperative for the church leadership, at all levels, to focus its programmes and activities towards effective mentoring and nurturing of young people to prepare them for leadership responsibility, both within the church and in the nation as a whole.[85]

In support of this assessment are observations that this age bracket especially (16 to 25 years) has been up front in evangelism in the church and in the Evangelism Ministry. Having switched allegiance from Evangelism Ministry to Youth Ministry, the church must endeavor to strategically include in their mentoring and nurturing orientation, awareness, and drive for evangelism. Such mentoring will maintain and sustain the evangelistic drive acknowledged as the core value of the church.

The youth ministry as of 2016 is led by a nine-member executive with Apostle David N. Hayfron as the director, Elder Amos Kevin-Annan as the deputy director, Pastor Daniel Sackey as member, Elders Omari Siaw and Makafui Nyamadi as members, Mrs. Gifty Otu-Appiah and Mrs. Georgina Asante as members, Emmanuel Ayisi Manu as the PENSA coordinator, and Pastor Ben Noye, co-opted youth ministry executive, as traveling secretary. The ministry has 15 traveling secretaries in 15 different sectors and recently started developing the youth pastor concept to care for the youth in the churches. The PENSA traveling secretaries are Pastors Ben Noye (Koforidua sector), Seth Asare Ofei Badu (Asokwa Sector), Gideon K. Boadu-Yirenkyi (Upper East Sector), Ebenezer Hagan (Greater Accra Sector), Philip Anane (Kwadaso Sector), Ebenezer Agyapong (Takoradi Sector), Abraham N. Boateng (Central Sector), Emmanuel Antwi Boasiako (Lower Volta Sector), Benedict Eghan (Suhum Sector), Samuel Yankey (Upper West Sector), Michael Peasah (Upper

---

84. CoP, Youth Ministry Annual Executives Report, January–December 2016.

85. CoP, Chairman Apostle Opoku Onyinah, State of the Church Address, Pentecost Convention Centre, May 5, 2017.

Volta Sector), Kwadwo Obeng (Northern Sector), Eric Abeiku Quainoo (Tarkwa Sector), Stephen Safo Nsiah (Mampong Sector), and Godwin Ako-Awuku (Sunyani Sector). The appointment of youth pastors, which is in its early stages, has commenced with four pastors stationed in four areas: Pastors Eric Asare (Madina), Isaac Osei (La), Kwabena Darko Mensah (Akim Oda), and Shadrack Addo (Asokwa).[86]

Current State of the Evangelism Ministry. The growth and effectiveness of the Youth Ministry and its accessories such as PENSA, ITI–PENSA, traveling secretaries, and the youth pastors concept have become more appealing to the upcoming educated youth. This, to some extent, has a negative effect on the dynamism of the church's other functional ministries, including the Evangelism Ministry. This is because the young and educated members, especially students, who have been the fulcrum of evangelism activities in the church from its inception, have since the late 1970s switched allegiance towards the youth ministry. In this vein, even though evangelism as an activity still continues in the church, the Evangelism Ministry as a functional ministry has been struggling, especially in regard to patronage and also duplication of activities with the other ministries such as the Youth Ministry.

From 1991 on, the Evangelism Ministry has undergone challenges that informed the restructuring of the movement with the growth of PENSA and the Youth Ministry, becoming PENTYEM. From 1997 on, the major activities of the Evangelism Ministry, since its name reverted to the Witness Movement, were organizing gospel crusades to the demarcated areas, specific evangelistic outreaches, and specialized target evangelism towards specific groups. These have included area crusades, event outreach at festivals such as the Kwahu Easter Festival, the Winneba Aboakyir Festival, and specialized outreach to politicians, chiefs, Rastafarians, and deaf ministry conventions.[87] There have also been rallies and conventions. Its other earlier functions such as Bible study, writing of study materials, witness classes, and special all-night or extended prayer meetings had been taken over by other ministries and committees such as Bible Study and Home-cell Committee and the Lay-leadership Training School. This development eventually led to a lower patronage of the Evangelism Ministry at the local assembly level.

---

86. CoP, Youth Ministry Annual Executives Report, January–December 2016.
87. CoP, Evangelism Ministry Report, December 2015.

In 2008, Apostle Michael Collins Aseidu replaced Apostle Kyei Mensah as the evangelism director. His National Executive Committee included Pastors F. Yaw Adu as the deputy director, Ben Ampea Badu as secretary, Chief Superintendent (CSP) James Tetteh, Elders S. Y. Peasah, P. Y. B. Frimpong, and Joseph Siaw-Adjapong. During this period, attempts were made to have the ministry revamped or restructured. For instance, on November 21, 2013, a joint meeting of all functional ministries in the church was held at the Tesano transit quarters. The minutes recorded the purpose of the meeting as follows:

> Giving the purpose of the meeting, Apostle Aseidu informed the house that at the recent Heads Meeting a draft copy of the Vision 2018 was discussed. In the process, the Ministries of the Church were given the opportunity to meet and come up with our inputs into the Vision Policy so that we can all be on the same page and share in the ownership of the document. He further mentioned that the vision document enjoins Ministries to review their functions. We had therefore met to discuss how the Ministries can restructure themselves so that evangelism could become a core focus of each ministry. In view of this, the leadership had asked the Ministries to look at the issues and present a document on the position of the Ministries. The idea was floated that the Evangelism could be restructured to become a department in the church and not a ministry. It means that it will not be doing evangelism directly but serve as a resource base to have inroads into all Ministries.[88]

This joint meeting of the leaders of all functional ministries concluded that the Evangelism Ministry should be left intact to stand as a functional ministry of the church and be restructured to fit into the Vision 2013–2018 policy under review at the time.[89] The meeting suggested that it was necessary for every member of the church to become a witness for the Lord and that the mandate of the Evangelism Ministry should be expanded to enable it to work and strengthen evangelism in the other ministries and in the local assemblies. It further suggested that the Evangelism Ministry should be charged with the responsibility of developing training manuals, training and providing resources for evangelism, and providing a guide to discipleship and follow-up for the converts through

---

88. CoP, Meeting of Executive Committees of All Ministries.
89. CoP, Meeting of Executive Committees of All Ministries.

the other ministries.[90] This writer agrees with these provisions intended to stop the church from viewing evangelism as a preserve of only a few (such as some designated evangelists or preachers) but instead to make it a conscientious mobilization of the entire church populace as in the New Testament. As Michael Green has noted, "Whenever Christianity has been at its most healthy, evangelism has stemmed from the local church and has had a noticeable impact on the surrounding area."[91] Strengthening the Evangelism Ministry in the local assemblies (and in the ministries, especially Youth Ministry) as they were previously, would render many of the evangelistic campaigns, missions, and crusades much more effective. The Evangelism Ministry in the CoP, though going through these challenges and restructuring, continues to thrive under its mandate to save souls for the kingdom of God. In December 2016, the Evangelism Ministry reported that 147,271 people made decisions for Christ; 73,755 received baptism in the Holy Spirit; 325 new local churches were planted or opened; and 2,547 new evangelism classes were conducted. This happened as a result of 31,795 rallies and conventions held nationwide, with other forms of evangelism such as dawn broadcasts; house-to-house evangelism; market, street and artisan's workshop evangelism; distribution of gospel tracts; and cinema van outreach.[92]

Women's Ministry

An important functional ministry counted as a factor in the phenomenal growth of the CoP is its Women's Ministry. It is argued, apart from the experiential evidence of the Holy Spirit in the personal life of the individuals in the CoP, the driving force behind the growth of the organization is the "women factor," which the Women's Ministry promotes.[93] Since its inception, the success of the CoP owes much to the active role and various contributions of its women. This affirms Mercy Oduyoye's correct observation that, in the African context, women are religion's chief clients.[94] The role of women in the CoP's growth cannot be underestimated.

---

90. CoP, Meeting of Executive Committees of All Ministries.
91. Green, *Evangelism through the Local Church*, preface.
92. CoP, Evangelism Ministry Report, December 2016.
93. Interview with Mrs. Lucy Yeboah-Asiamah, current Women's Ministry director, February 5, 2014.
94. Oduyoye, *Daughters of Anowa*, ch. 5.

The pattern of such participation by women, in the Ghanaian context, was laid by the older African-initiated churches (AICs), which broke the male hegemony in Christian ministry in Ghana.[95] Even though the CoP does not ordain women into full-time ministry, it does not deny women full participation in the life of the church. It has a very well organized Women's Ministry with a full-time female director at the church's headquarters.[96] The formal organized front of the women of the CoP began in 1945 with T. Adam McKeown, a brother of James McKeown.[97] The ministry was officially inaugurated as a movement of the church in 1952 during a General Council meeting held at Winneba.[98] The women wielded strong support behind McKeown throughout his entire ministry in Ghana. The CoP statistics always showed the women outnumbering the men.[99] Church membership statistics for 2013 indicate that approximately two thirds of the church are women.[100]

The activities of the Women's Movement initially centered on group prayer and Bible study, and later developed into evangelistic outreaches, which became a dominant feature. Later, various vocational trainings, such as sewing, cooking, and housekeeping, were incorporated. This training was reportedly started by Mrs. Sophia McKeown, who was a professional seamstress. In the formative years of the church, she occasionally gathered the women to give them lessons on how they could keep and maintain their homes.[101] Larbi asserts that this vocational training always turned into various spiritual exercises such as prayer meetings. He posits that the women performed better in the organization of prayer meetings and evangelistic activities and conventions than in these women-oriented issues.[102]

The Women's Movement is one movement in the church whose modus operandi has not changed much. It has, for instance, maintained its name (Women's Movement) and its organization of its Tuesday-evening classes. Traditionally, Tuesday evening is synonymous with Women's

95. Sanneh, "Horizontal and Vertical in Mission," 7.
96. See CoP, *Constitution*, 2010, 83.
97. Larbi, *Pentecostalism*, 184.
98. CoP, Women Directorate Write-Up, 2014.
99. CoP, Women's Ministry Report, 2013.
100. CoP, Statistics Department Data, 2013, put women at 63 percent of adult membership (854,716) and men at 37 percent of adult membership (504,639).
101. Asem, *History of the Church of Pentecost*, 67.
102. Larbi, *Pentecostalism*, 185.

Movement in the CoP. The name was changed recently, in 2012, from Women's Movement to Women's Ministry, in order to bring it into conformity with the contemporary usage of "ministries" in other similar church organizations and denominational groups. But for the earlier adherents of this ladies wing, the word "movement" connotes its vibrancy.[103]

Beginning from 1965, the ministry was headed by General Women's Leaders who spearheaded its affairs. These General Women's Leaders were males, and their deputies were females. It has been asked why men should be leaders in a women-oriented organization, and two answers were given. First, it follows the arrangement of the traditional pattern of leadership in most Ghanaian societies in which leadership is male dominated. The second is that leadership in the CoP is predominantly male. Nevertheless, there seems to be no particular reason for following these arrangements. This study argues later that these arrangements were temporary and used to prepare future leaders for the movement who would be competent to handle the affairs of the movement. An interview with the current elite female leadership of the movement suggests that the arrangement was not only unnecessary but also a byproduct of male chauvinism.[104]

The succeeding general women's leaders and their years of service are as follows: the Rev. G. A. Woode (1955–1957), the Rev. A. K. Yaw (1957–1962), the Rev. F. S. Safo (1962–1967), the Rev. D. Y. A. Owusu (1967–1976), the Rev. E. D. Aninkorah (1976–1983), the Rev. T. C. Amoah (1983–1988), and Prophet J. K. Ennumh (1988–1993). The pattern was changed in 1994 to allow women to be the substantive leaders while the men acted as their patrons. Perpetual Owusu was the first women's director, from 1995 to 2004. Since then are Mrs. Beatrice Kwaffo (2004–2012) and Mrs. Grace Lucy Yeboah-Asuama (2012–present). The substantive deputy general women's leaders were Mrs. Christiana Obo Mends (1941–1958), Mrs. Eunice Addison (1958–1983), and Mrs. Esme Siriboe (1983–1994). In this arrangement, the succeeding women's patrons were the Rev. R. Asomaning Sarpong (1994–1996), Apostle S. K. Ofosu (1996–2005), Apostle S. L. Agyin (2005–2007), Prophet James Osei Ampofo (2007–2012), and Apostle Jacob Narh Affum (2012–2015). The church's November 2015 Area Heads' meeting, with apostles, prophets,

103. Interview with Mama Susuana Ampomah (a former CoP Women's Ministry leader), Takoradi, February 5, 2014.

104. Telephone interview with Mrs. Lucy Yeboah-Asiamah (current Women's Ministry director), February 5, 2014.

and directors of ministries in attendance, scrapped the use of patrons for the Women's Ministry[105] because the ministry was thought to be mature enough at this level, with competent female leaders to handle its own affairs.

The growth of the church, coupled with changes in contemporary roles of women both in the society and the church necessitated a review in the operations of the movement to meet contemporary challenges. This may have been compelled by the demands of the young professional ladies on the church's current landscape to upgrade the Women's Ministry to meet their aspirations. Though the core values of the movement have not changed much from those of its early beginnings, modes of operations have been enhanced. In addition to their original focus on prayer, evangelism, Bible study, and vocational training, they have included literacy drives, skill training and entrepreneurship, and ministering to and winning other businesswomen, queen mothers, sex workers, lady politicians, and female professionals.[106] The ministry has established a few schools such as Kasoa Pentecost Preparatory School and Gbawe Pentecost Vocational Training Institute.[107]

The first professional ladies' club was officially inaugurated in August 2011 at KNUST, Kumasi.[108] The purpose, according to the director, is to keep these women in fellowship and also organize women of the same profession to come together to share ideas to boost their professions or businesses. The ministry's activities have been extended from Tuesday class meeting and conventions to include more regular retreats, seminars, workshops, and periodic conferences. This boost in its regular activities also addresses the challenge of making the ministry attractive for the younger ladies, especially the educated and professionals. As for the Evangelism Ministry, the challenge of the Women's Ministry had been the younger women's lack of interest. The director, Mrs. Grace Lucy Yeboah-Asuama, asserts that this later generation of women in the church wants to be addressed as ladies and not Women's Ministry.[109] They consider the Women's Ministry to be the preserve of the older women, the married, and the uneducated. They find the programs of the Women's

---

105. CoP, Proposal for amendment of the Constitution, March 31, 2015.
106. CoP, Women Directorate Write-Up on the Movement's Operations, 2013.
107. CoP, Women Directorate Write-Up on the Movement's Operations, 2013.
108. CoP, Women Directorate Write-Up on the Movement's Operations, 2013.
109. Interaction of the writer with the women's director, Mrs. Grace Lucy Yeboah-Asuama, in the office of the general secretary of the CoP, April 19, 2017.

Ministry, especially in the rural areas, uninformed, archaic, and shaped for the illiterate and nonprofessionals. They prefer to be with the ladies' wing in PENSA and Youth Ministry, whose programs are tailored to suit their needs and aspirations. A further setback came from enforcement of Vision 2013–2018, which requires each member to choose a functional ministry to which to belong.[110] The policy seems to skew the younger ladies' patronage of the functional ministries towards the Youth Ministry. The Youth Ministry also has provision for teenage girls, who later associate with the Youth Ministry. Nevertheless, these changes and variations in women's programs is enhancing interest in the Women's Ministry among younger women.

With regard to evangelism in this period, the chairman's State of the Church Address at the 2008 council meeting, for instance, noted that the Women's Ministry in the CoP cannot be overlooked. They were recorded to have held, in 2008, 1,716 evangelistic outreach programs, won 13,564 converts, and saw 2,820 receive the baptism in the Holy Spirit.[111] The statistical report form for the National Women's Ministry's annual report has six columns, which show the number of areas, districts, rallies held, souls won, Holy Ghost baptisms, and membership. These indicate that in the particular year under review the Women's Ministry ultimately looks out for souls evangelized. The annual reports indicate that these figures have increased consistently every year. For instance, in 2014, the recorded numbers of rallies held was 4,411, souls won 21,748, Holy Ghost baptisms 14,259, and members registered were 575,032. In 2015, rallies held numbered 7,023, souls won 27,855, Holy Ghost baptisms 21,339, and members registered were 762,211. At the end of 2016, rallies numbered 9,819, souls won 25,441, Holy Ghost baptisms 22,574, and membership registered increased to 858,102.

The Women's Ministry since 2012 has been led by a National Executive of 7: Mrs. Grace Lucy Yeboah-Asuama as the director; Deaconess Mrs. Margaret Osei as deputy director; and members Mrs. Georgina Osei Amaniampong, Mrs. Comfort Quampah, Deaconess Mrs. Victoria Aboah, Deaconess Juliana Asare Debrah, and Deaconess Gladys Atujona. In 2016, Mrs. Georgina Osei Amaniampong, after serving 12 years on the Executive Committee, was replaced by Mrs. Rebecca Assabil. The

---

110. CoP, *Vision 2018*, 35.

111. CoP, Chairman Apostle Dr. M. K. Ntumy, State of the Church Address, presented at the opening ceremony of the 37th session of the General Council meetings, Pentecost University College, Accra, April 24, 2008.

composition of the leadership in the National Executive does not have representation from the younger class of women. This would have been helpful for the involvement of younger ladies in the ministry, as discussed above. The Women's Ministry of the CoP is, however, a vibrant movement that has been replicated, as have the other functional ministries, in other nations where the church is located.

Children's Ministry

The initial coordination of the children in the CoP into fellowship is linked to Mrs. Margaret Mills, the wife of the Elim missionary David Mills. She was said to have traveled extensively across the nation in order to put the fellowship in place. In 1972, the General Council of the church formally regulated the organization as a movement at its meeting in Kumasi.[112] The decision that was taken, according to the meeting minutes, was that there should be proper organization of the children. Prior to that time, the children were randomly gathered and given instructions as the leadership of the local assembly deemed necessary.[113] Until 1972, there were virtually no formal statistical records for the children in the CoP. The church membership records include adults of 18 years and above. Part of the reason is that the CoP does not baptize children below 13 years of age. The other reason is that the traditional values in Ghana place more emphasis on adults than on children.

Until 2013, the CoP church buildings in both urban and rural areas did not have spaces for children's classes. The children attended classes on Sunday afternoons after the adults' services had ended because many of the churches did not own the buildings they occupied on Sundays. They worshipped in rented apartments, classrooms, under trees, and the like. Financial constraints made it impossible to build structures to accommodate both children and adults. Recently, the PIWC in Kumasi built a separate auditorium to make room for children and youth activities. According to the children's director, this discussion surfaces at every consultative meeting with the leadership of the church.[114] This challenge notwithstanding, the ministry has made great strides in its organization.

---

112. Leonard, *Giant in Ghana*, 156.

113. CoP, Children's Ministry History Document, 2014.

114. CoP, Children's Ministry directors' discussion at Area Heads' meeting, Pentecost Convention Centre, May 4, 2017.

After launching the Children's Ministry at a meeting in Kumasi in 1972 through the initiative of Margaret Mills, the council appointed Apostle C. E. Apau-Asante to be the general leader with Mrs. Margaret Mills as his deputy and Mrs. Esme Siriboe as secretary.[115] A general meeting of all national and regional officers of the movement drawn from all regions in the country was held at the Morning Star School in Accra on January 14, 1974. At this meeting, the name of the fellowship was proposed to match that of the Women's Movement, and they adopted Children's Movement. The mission of the movement is to bring up children to grow mentally, physically, socially, and spiritually to take up future leadership roles of the church. The following aims and objectives guide the movement: to lead children to a personal knowledge of Christ as their Lord and Savior (2 Tim 3:15), to teach children to read and understand the Bible, to prepare them to take their place in the body of Christ in a responsible way, to prepare children to integrate into the Youth, Evangelism, and Women's Ministries and into church membership after water baptism, to instill in the minds of the children the desire to live honestly and righteously, and to encourage the spirit of good citizenship in the children. The ministry advocates a thought-out strategic and developmental plan as necessary to build a strong church. This plan must be in line with God's own "master plan." His master plan tells us we should not leave the next generation behind with regard to salvation (Ps 78:1–8; Matt 18:14).

The name for the movement, its mission statement, and its aims and objectives were approved by the General Council in its sitting at Asamankese in 1974. Subsequently, other leaders, such as regional leaders and their assistants, were appointed from the regions, districts, and also the local assemblies. These leaders were to augment the work of the teachers in the children's classes.

The major activities of the movement since 1974 revolve around running training courses for the teachers and leaders. The movement does this in connection with Child Evangelism Fellowship, a worldwide nondenominational fellowship founded in 1937, headquartered in Warrenton, Missouri, USA. Child Evangelism Fellowship claims to be the world's largest evangelistic outreach to children. It has reached over 14,000,000 children in 183 countries. Its branch in Ghana has been a resource to many Ghanaian denominations with regard to training for children's work. The activities of the Children's Movement include

---

115. CoP, Children's Ministry History Document, 2014. All data in this and the next two paragraphs come from this document.

conventions, evangelistic rallies, and children's camp meetings. Every three years, scriptural quizzes are conducted nationally. As part of their activities, every September 12 is celebrated as Founder's Day in remembrance of James McKeown and to thank God for the children and the ministry. This is organized as a National Children's Day in the church. Between 1972 and 1986, Christine Leonard indicated that the movement had involved 71,000 children in Ghana.[116]

In the initial stages, the church appointed what they call general leaders to oversee the ministry. These were skilled area apostles who had previous experience with children's ministry work. They acted as general leaders for the children's ministry as a responsibility added to their assignments as area heads. The general leaders have been Apostle S. K. Ansong (1972–1983) and Apostle J. K. Essel (1988–1994).[117] The general leadership was changed to a permanent headquarters directorate in 1994.[118] The General Council, through the recommendation of the Executive Council, set up a directorate for the movement at the church's headquarters to oversee it. The members of the first successive Executive Committee were Pastor C. N. Kissiedu as the director, Pastor Adjei Badu and Pastor B. A. Adobah as members, Pastor Agyemang-Baduh as a coopted member (Literature Committee representative), and Apostle Robert Acquaah as the patron. The church assigns a patron who is an apostle to every national movement that does not have an apostle or prophet as its director. Overseer Daniel Walker, Andrews Oduro-Ampaw, Elder Fred Tiakor, Deaconess Grace Yamoah, and Deaconess Faustina Sarfo-Appiah were all executive members. These were all inducted into office on September 10, 1994.[119] In 1998, a deputy director, an elder, was also introduced.

From 1998 to 2004, the successive Executive Committee members for the ministry were Prophet J. E. Ameyaw as patron, Pastor C. N. Kissiedu as the director, Elder S. Ankamah-Lomotey as the deputy director, Pastors Andrews Oduro-Ampaw and Fred Tiakor and Mrs. Faustina Ofosu-Koramoah as members, and Mrs. Georgina L. Awuku as a coopted member. The Executive Committee members from 2004 to 2008 were J. E. Ameyaw as patron; Pastor B. A. Adobah as the director; Elder

---

116. Leonard, *Giant in Ghana*, 156.
117. CoP, Children's Ministry History Document, 2014.
118. CoP, General Council Meeting Minutes, 1974.
119. CoP, Children's Ministry History Document, 2014.

S. Ankamah-Lomotey as deputy director; Pastor J. G. Quardson, Elder S. E. A. Pobee, Mrs. Grace Aniakwaah, and Mrs. Rita Yedu as members, with Mrs. G. L. Awuku a co-opted member. From 2008 to 2012, they were Prophet B. A. Adobah as the director, Elder S. Ankamah-Lomotey as the deputy director, Pastor J. G. Quardson, Pastor R. S. Nii Anang, Elder K. Asare Twerefuor, Mrs. Grace Aniakwaah, and Mrs. Rita Yedu as members, with Mrs. Adelaide Owuo as a co-opted member (Literature Committee representative). Since 2012, Executive Committee members for the ministry have been Apostle J. W. D. Cudjoe as patron; Pastor Fred Tiakor as director; Elder Stephen Ankamah-Lomotey as the deputy director; Pastor Nii Anang as secretary; and Pastor Robert Sowah, Pastor P. G. Andoh, Elder Kwadjo Asare Twerefuor, Mrs. Victoria Abeo-Tetteh, and Mrs. Rita Yedu as members.[120]

In 2011, the Executive Council recommended to the General Council to change the word "movement" in its name to "ministry." They gave these reasons for the change:[121] "Ministry" is easily understood and really gives a broader picture of the activities of the wing than does "movement," which must always be defined in context. "Movement" in the name of the wing reflects a more secular theme than that of child work. The current activities or operations of child work in the church appeals more as a ministry than a movement.

Children's Ministry has a very important role with regard to the church's future growth and development. In his book *Why Evangelize Children?*, Doherty commented:

> That every worker among young people needs to have spiritual bi-focals. He evangelizes young people because he sees their present need for Jesus Christ and His Salvation. But he also evangelizes them because he sees their potential for the future and he is investing in that future.[122]

From 1972, the Children's Ministry grew steadily. By the end of 2012, the annual statistical report of the Children's Ministry in Ghana reported 621,768 children in regular fellowship.[123] By the end of 2013, the records show 778,689 children in regular fellowship, 61,294 dedicated, 34,926 evangelized for Christ, 27,143 transferred to the teenage group, and

---

120. CoP, Children's Ministry History Document, 2014.
121. CoP, Children's Ministry History Document, 2014.
122. Doherty, *Why Evangelize Children?*, 1.
123. CoP, Annual Statistical Data, 2012.

26,339 teachers had been trained.[124] A challenge during this period was how to maintain an intergenerational ministry where children occasionally join the adult services in order to learn from them.[125] This provision was part of the Vision 2013–2018 policy adopted by the church and aimed at impacting the generations to continue with the church's mandate.

The Children's Ministry also embarks on evangelism of children. In 2016 they visited some selected communities in the northern regions. The mission brought together 3,731 children, out of which 1,123 were discipled and retained in the church. At the end of 2016, their fellowship claimed a total of 774,641 children registered. They were supervised by 36,788 teachers nationwide, overseeing 14,551 classes.[126] The report showed that 1,744 assemblies do not hold classes for the Children's Ministry. This large number calls for urgent attention. The Children's Ministry in the CoP augments the growth of the church through sustaining the children born to members to remain in the church and discipling them to become committed Christians through their various training programs.

Men's Ministry

The CoP Men's Ministry is a late development in the church. Its antecedents in Ghana can be traced to other denominations such as the Methodist and Roman Catholic Men's fellowships. The CoP Men's fellowship started as a local fellowship of a group of men in the church. In the urban areas, the men apparently dropped off their wives and young ladies on Tuesdays at the Women's Ministry meetings and went back for them later. Some local assemblies used the opportunity to organize the men into fellowships alongside the women's meetings. It was not recognized as an organized wing, however.[127] The move to organize men into a Men's Fellowship was initiated by Pastor Samuel Badu Nyarko in 1985 at Sankore, in Brong Ahafo Region. He was then the Sankore District pastor.[128]

Badu Nyarko asserts that he observed the inactivity of the men in his district who were 40 years old and above. He noticed they did not attend the Witness Movement meetings and had no interest in receiving

---

124. CoP, Children's Ministry Annual Report, 2013.
125. CoP, Children's Ministry Annual Report, 2015.
126. CoP, Children's Ministry Annual Report, 2016.
127. Interview with National Men's Ministry Director, February 6, 2014.
128. Interview with Apostle Samuel Badu Nyarko, February 6, 2014.

the baptism of the Holy Spirit. In response to his observation, the older men attributed this to the fact that the Witness Movement had become a gathering for younger men, and therefore they could not mingle with them. Badu Nyarko therefore used the opportunity to organize the men who were 40 years old and above into a distinct group. He replicated the process in Mim District in 1987.[129] Subsequently, at a National Witness Movement Retreat at Mim, Brong Ahafo, in 1987, the group was called upon to sing. At this meeting the organization of the men came to the attention of the then acting chairman of the church, Apostle D. Y. A. Owusu.[130]

The following year, in 1988, at the General Council meeting, the current acting chairman, Apostle Owusu, put forward the issue of forming a men's fellowship, which the council accepted. The Men's Fellowship started official operation in 1991. At the beginning, it was created as a local fellowship to deal with contemporary issues concerning men in the church. These issues included relational problems in marriage, fostering business acumen, and inheritance. Later, the Men's Fellowship objectives as spelled out in their handbook were to organize seminars, workshops, and lectures in areas concerning marriage and family, domestic laws, business management, church history, current affairs, leadership and responsibility of men in the home, the church, and the state.[131]

To facilitate the growth of the fellowship and its organization, the first National Executives were inaugurated by the church's Executive Council in March 1997.[132] Their duty was to provide a forum for the men to gather to facilitate the aforementioned teaching. The first National executives were Apostle Moses Ladejo as the national leader; Elder Professor Addae as the assistant leader; and the Rev. Andrew Tetteh, the Rev. A. Y. Kumi, Elder P. Owusu-Antwi, Elder E. K. Asamoah, and Elder M. T. Ayitey as members. The Rev. J. B. A. Ghansah and Elder V. C. T. Antwi, who were residing in the Accra metropolis at that time, were co-opted to facilitate the work of the committee, which had no secretariat at the church's headquarters. This first committee provided the *Study Guide, Volume One* for the Men's Fellowship in January 1999.

---

129. Interview with Apostle Samuel Badu Nyarko, February 6, 2014.
130. Narration from Apostle Samuel Badu Nyarko, February 6, 2014.
131. CoP, Men's Ministry Handbook, 2009.
132. CoP, Men's Ministry History Write-Up, 2013. The information in this paragraph and the next comes from this document.

A second National Committee was appointed in October 1999 due to the retirement of the leaders Apostle Moses Ladejo and the Rev. Andrew Tetteh from active service of the church, both at the age of 65. The new committee included Prophet Appiah-Agyekum as its national leader; Elder Professor Addae as the assistant leader; and the Rev. A. Y. Kumi, Elders P. Owusu-Antwi, E. K. Asamoah, and M. T. Ayitey as members, who were inducted into office in March 2000. The group was granted permission by the Executive Council to organize the first National Pentecost Men's Fellowship (PEMEF) Leadership Training Conference in August 2000 at the Central Cafeteria of the University of Ghana. The theme for the conference was "The New Man and the Kingdom—Ephesians 2:15." Facilitating the exposition on the theme were Prophet M. K. Yeboah (chairman of the CoP, 1988–1998), Apostle M. K. Ntumy, the Rev. John Waller, Apostle Noble-Atsu, Apostle S. K. Ansong, Mr. Sam Boateng (president of International Christian Chamber of Commerce [ICCC] Ghana), and Lawyer Agyei-Agyiri of SSNIT Assembly, CoP, Accra. Part of the reason for this conference was also to launch the first PEMEF Study Guide. The participants at this conference included all representatives from every district of the church. A follow-up to this national conference was held in January 2005 at Pentecost University College, Sowutuom, Accra, under the theme "Men Excelling in the Demonstration of God's Power." The speakers included Apostle M. K. Ntumy (chairman), Apostle Alfred Koduah (general secretary), Mrs. Beatrice Kwaffo (Women's Movement director), Lawyer M. Z. Glover, Apostle F. E. Antwi, Apostle Opoku Onyinah, and Apostle D. K. Noble-Atsu.[133] These two conferences promoted the expansion and vitality of the movement.

The General Council of the church recognized it as a full-fledged ministry in 2008[134] and established a directorate for the movement and appointed a director in the person of Apostle N. A. O. Amegatcher.[135] This culminated in the third National Executive Committee of the movement: Apostle N. A. O. Amegatcher as director; Elder Prof. A. K. Addae as deputy director; Elder Dr. Yao Yeboah as secretary; and Pastors A. P. Mensah, I. K. Amoako, Onyinah Gyamfi, and Elder Raymond Opoku as members.[136] Their tenure of service was changed in 2012, and at the

---

133. CoP, Men's Ministry History Write-Up, 2013.
134. CoP, Men's Ministry History Write-Up, 2013.
135. CoP, General Council Decisions and Appointments, 2008.
136. CoP, Men's Ministry History Write-Up, 2013.

2012 General Council of the church, the National Executive Committee was reconstituted or reviewed as follows: Apostle J. F. Asante-Ayeh as director; Elder Professor Stephen Owusu Kwakye as deputy director; Elder Dr. Yao Yeboah as the secretary; Pastors Joseph Quaicoo, Joseph K. Agbemor, Anthony Peter Mensah, and Elder Raymond as members.[137] In 2015 Elder Professor Stephen Owusu Kwakye was replaced by Elder Ebenezer Asamoah Nyarko as the deputy director.

Currently, the wing has redefined its scope of ministry to include other men of various capacities. For instance, it has extended ministry towards male professionals, businessmen, politicians, traditional rulers, alcoholics, chief executives, and bachelors, with media evangelism and counseling; poverty alleviation programs; breakfast, lunch and dinner evangelism; and other related ministry avenues for men.[138] The challenges identified in Pentecost Men's Ministry (PEMEM) annual reports for the running of the ministry have always shown the same issues: lukewarm attitude towards PEMEM activities, poor attendance at meetings, some presiding elders replacing the ministry's meeting periods with other programs, and lack of devoted leaders. The major challenge reported in 2016 by the leaders was general apathy towards PEMEM activities at all levels in the church. However, the patronage of the ministry, shown in active members attending fellowship, has gradually increased over the years. For instance, it numbered the active members attending fellowship in 2014 at 142,005. This figure increased to 172,326 in 2015. As of December 2016, PEMEM's active membership had grown to 204,068. The efforts of the ministry have at least occupied the men in the church and engaged them in some form of evangelistic drive. In 2016, for instance, the number of those who made decisions for Christ through the PEMEM was put at 24,446, and 16,904 were baptized in the Holy Spirit.

Pentecost International Worship Centres

The most recent development in the setup of the CoP is the creation of branches referred to as Pentecost International Worship Centres (PIWCs). These seek to create Bible-based contemporary churches to meet a specific audience. These identified groups include highly qualified professionals and academicians, young people who are drifting to

---

137. CoP, Men's Ministry Annual Report, 2012.
138. CoP, Men's Ministry Annual Report, 2012.

other denominations due to unfamiliarity with the local or traditional languages and the form of liturgy, and others who cannot communicate or understand the native languages in their locality such as diplomats, missionaries, and expatriates.

The PIWCs are a follow-up or development of the work of the ITI-PENSA in the schools and campuses. The PIWC provides a conduit for continuing service for the younger generation who have become accustomed to worshiping in English and in a particular worship style after being on campus for a period of time, especially for those who would have lost their taste for the traditional liturgical forms of CoP worship for any reason. Larbi has suggested that the PIWCs are a response to adapt to modern demands, away from traditional forms regarding aspects of the ethos and liturgy of the traditional CoP worship by the younger generations:

> The situation with the predominantly younger, literate segment of the society, with the taste for the western value system, is different. Many people in this group do not find aspects of the ethos, liturgy and the medium of communication of CoP and similar churches attractive. They are more attracted to the neo-Pentecostal churches, mainly because of their characteristic life style.[139]

In response to these concerns, the CoP, in the mid 1980s, decided to build cross-cultural churches suitable for people with the orientation described above, especially those from non-Ghanaian backgrounds and those who prefer to worship in English or another foreign language.

The first effort created English-speaking assemblies in the major cities. Three were first created, two in Accra and one in Kumasi. After a period of time, they were observed to be operating just as the traditional local assemblies, except for the language change to English. Subsequently, the regional apostle of Greater Accra at the time, Patrick Asiamah, in consultation with the Greater Accra Executive Committee merged the two English assemblies to form the first Accra International Worship Centre on April 29, 1993.[140] Later, another was formed in Kumasi, thus creating two such churches in the two largest metropolises in the country. The originator of this concept was Apostle Opoku Onyinah, the first international missions director of the CoP.

139. Larbi, *Pentecostalism*, 201.
140. Larbi, *Pentecostalism*, 202.

The Accra International Worship Centre eventually became the Pentecost International Worship Centre. The first resident pastor was Apostle Opoku Onyinah, who was assisted by the Rev. John Waller, the principal of the CoP Bible Training Centre.[141] Subsequently, this move was duplicated in all regions and most important towns and communities in the country. For instance, there are PIWCs in Kumasi, Cape Coast, Takoradi, Tema, Sunyani, Bolgatanga, and Tamale. Some large metropolises now have more than one PIWC.

In the personal view of the present writer, the future outlook of a model CoP congregation will take the form of today's PIWCs because of the desire of its younger generation for such change. They see the PIWCs as offering an alternative form of service to the CMs in Ghana, which are considered appealing to the current educated youth in Ghanaian society. Recently a round-table conference of all leaders of the PIWCs across Ghana and from some of the church's international branches was held at the Pentecost Convention Centre, March 17–19, 2016. According to the chairman, the church's aim in organizing the conference was to explain the role and rationale behind the formation of the PIWC ministry in the CoP and to discuss its current challenges and the steps to forge ahead.[142] E. Kingsley Larbi, one of the speakers at the conference, sharing on the practices of excellence in the PIWCs, stated that in his view only one of the PIWCs could be said to be close to the set goal with regard to the excellent practices expected from them. His remark seems to make reference to the practices of other similar institutions such as some of the CMs.[143]

Northern Outreach Ministry (NOM)

A contemporary initiative in the internal missions outreach,[144] which has become another avenue for the growth of CoP in this era, is the Northern Outreach Ministry. In the early 1940s, the CoP extended evangelistic

---

141. Larbi, *Pentecostalism*, 202.

142. CoP, brochure of the Conference of Pentecost International Worship Centre Officers, Pentecost Convention Centre, March 17–19, 2016.

143. CoP, speech given by E. K. Larbi, Conference of Pentecost International Worship Centre Officers, Pentecost Convention Centre, March 17–19, 2016.

144. Internal Missions is the CoP's missions in the Northern and Upper Regions, as well as some parts of the Afram Plain.

activities towards the Northern and Upper Regions of Ghana, considering them part of its internal missions areas.

People in this part of the nation are of diverse ethnic backgrounds. More than 40 different dialects are spoken. The landscape is predominantly savannah/tropical grasslands. It was considered a missions' area due to its low socioeconomic development and the perception of strong Islamic and traditional religious domination. People of the northern regions, since the precolonial era, have migrated to southern Ghana in search of better living standards. They end up as low-income workers, such as porters, security men, farm laborers, and housekeepers.

In 1989, a national survey on Christian outreach was conducted by the Ghana Evangelism Committee (GEC) led by Ross Campbell. The report discovered that more people of northern descent live in southern Ghana than in the north, and the majority of them are unreached with the gospel. For instance, the report indicated that people of northern descent form 30 percent of the total population of Brong Ahafo Region, 35 percent in the Ashanti Region, and 21 percent in the Greater Accra Region.[145] In 1993 the report showed that, out of 3,600,000 northern people living in southern Ghana, 2,300,000 had not been reached with the gospel.[146] The report also showed that the population of people from the north living in the south is larger than the population of the three northern regions in Ghana (Northern, Upper East, and Upper West) put together. These had been perceived to be Muslim due to connection with the Zongo communities and because of their low socioeconomic conditions.[147] Yet many may have been Christian converts from the north or of other faiths. Based on this background, the CoP in January 1997 launched a mission toward people of northern descent living in the south. Among the prime objectives for this ministry was to reach out to them with the gospel through literacy classes and vocational training in their dialects and to establish congregations for them along cultural and linguistic lines.[148]

Pioneering work in the CoP's Northern Outreach was initiated by the Rev. Patrick Aseyero, with three local assemblies in Accra Old

145. GEC, *Survey of Churches in Ghana*, 1989.

146. GEC, *Survey of Churches in Ghana*, 1993.

147. Zongo communities are a kind of slum neighborhood in Ghana largely associated with northerners, Muslims, and the deprived or low-status in the Ghanaian community; they are also associated with many vices.

148. Anank, "Impact of the Northern Outreach Ministry."

Fadama (Konkomba Assembly), the Anumle and Point One assemblies. Together these had a total membership of 420, with 25 church leaders (leaders, deacons, and deaconesses).[149] By the year 2000, it had grown to places such as Nungua, Ashiaman, Timber Market, Nima, Madina, Ablekuma, and Dome—all in Accra. It spread to other parts of the country beginning in 2001, which required other ministers to come on board. Between 2001and 2005, Pastor Beddim was stationed in Kumasi, and under him five assemblies were opened: Bantama, Moshie Zongo, Adom, Kokode, and Aboabo. Other ministers were subsequently recruited to open and man new places: Pastors Robert Gyinase (2004) in Accra, Kojo Mahama (2004) in Techiman, Micheal Zinah (2005) in Sunyani, Elisha W. Nambu (2007) in La-Accra, S. Amos Adams (2007) in Nima-Accra, James Magyam (2007) in Madina-Accra, Amos Dindiago (2008) in Kwadaso-Kumasi, James K. Yinger (2008) in Asokwa-Kumasi, Emmanuel Akay (2005) in Techiman, and Francis Anank (2007) in Techiman.[150] By the end of 2010, the National Northern Outreach Report showed a total adult membership of 4,859, with 2,155 children and 277 leaders in 66 assemblies.[151] Its achievements at the end of 2013 included a total membership of 11,500 (an adult membership of 8,100, and 3,400 children), nine districts, and 105 local assemblies.[152]

After 20 years of establishment, in line with organizational review, the Executive Council of the church reviewed the NOM. Though the ministry had achieved remarkable successes, it was saddled with many challenges that required a second look at its activities. They included supervision challenges by pastors, perception by some from the larger church body that NOM was not part of the CoP, lack of support by some areas and districts, a feeling of segregation by some NOM members, lack of interest by people of northern descent in associating with the NOM, and the difficulty of some of the designated pastors in reaching their assemblies.[153] In this writer's assessment, such challenges of the NOM in the CoP are inevitable because the character of the church from its outset has always promoted integration of all tribes and people groups in every aspect of its activities and in its organogram. The church has northern-

149. Anank, "Impact of the Northern Outreach Ministry."
150. Anank, "Impact of the Northern Outreach Ministry."
151. CoP, Northern Outreach Ministry Report, 2010.
152. CoP, Northern Outreach Ministry Report, 2013.
153. CoP, Proposal to Integrate NOM into the Mainstream Church Structure, 2014.

ers as pastors and area heads over large congregations in the south and vice-versa. For instance, in 2014 Apostle Patrick Aseyero, an apostle from Navrongo in the Upper East Region, was posted from Walewale Area to be the area head at Bompata Area in the heart of the Ashanti Region.[154]

In this situation of the CoP, a farmhand or laborer who is a northerner can be a presiding elder over his landlord who is a southerner. Though structures like the NOM system appear to be thriving in other churches such as the Presbyterian Church of Ghana, the CoP struggles with it. In 2013 the coordinator of the NOM, Pastor Osei-Wusu Brempong, along with Elder Micheal Kodum were tasked with investigating and evaluating the operations of NOM and to provide a way forward. They presented a report on January 2, 2013,[155] which recommended a review of the operations of the NOM concept and the integration of their activities into the mainstream churches. Accordingly, the NOM assemblies were integrated into the closest districts within the communities to serve as one of the assemblies in the districts.[156] The Evangelism Ministry was mandated to support all NOM activities from local assemblies. Area heads and district ministers who have NOM assemblies were to report on them in their half-year and annual reports.

Analyzing the Emerging Structures for Growth from the Functional Ministries

The functional ministries in the CoP, as discussed, emerged as answers to specific needs of managing the growth of the church at particular periods in its history. They emerged particularly in situations in which they had to exert influence on the evangelistic drive and the numerical growth of the church in that period. Then, further structural organization within the functional ministries, such as choices of leaders, names for the ministries, functions and objectives, to mention but a few, became the structural mechanisms through which the church grew and managed her growth.

For instance, the Evangelism Ministry emerged due to the zeal of the early adherents to witness to others about their faith. Although avenues such as personal evangelism, street and community rallies or campaigns,

---

154. CoP, Chairman's Circular Letter to All Assemblies, June 13, 2014.
155. Kodum and Brempong, "Evaluation of NOM Operations."
156. CoP, Chairman's Circular Letter to All Assemblies, June 13, 2014.

and various conventions existed for the purpose, other groups and individuals also rose up, such as the "Bombing group." Responses to these splinter groups were based on the conviction that evangelism as an important focus in the church should be properly managed.

In the same way, the other functional ministries such as the Women's, Youth, Children's, and Men's Ministries emerged as a response to factors affecting these individual groups with regard to their sustenance and effectiveness. Whereas the Northern Outreach Ministry was a means for winning the misplaced people from the northern regions in Ghana, the PIWCs cater to the contemporary worshippers in the church who are not conversant with its traditional form of worship. The activities and management of these ministries and their functions invariably grow the church.

The idea of the functional ministries emerging out of very specific needs poses relevant questions: If they evolve out of particular needs, can they also be obsolete when the needs are met? Answering this question involves managing the functional ministry. For instance, the Northern Outreach Ministry was dissolved in 2014 and reabsorbed into the mainstream congregations. Thus, management of the ministries over time with regard to their sustainability provides the structures that invariably grow or manage the growth of the church.

The church exercises a great deal of discretion in managing these functional ministries. For example, the history of the Men's Ministry shows that choices when finding leaders for the ministry are made with regard to the maturity and ability of the candidates; even though Pastor Badu Nyarko seems to have initiated the whole concept of the Men's Ministry, the church took it over and appointed others to manage the fellowship without him. There may be many reasons for this decision, possibly his unavailability at the time. The trend observed for all the functional ministries, however, is that the church owns and manages them. For each functional ministry, if the leader is not an apostle—a mature senior minister—a patron of that caliber is put in place to guide the leaders. This system guides the functional ministry until such a time as matured leaders are found or nurtured.

Another observation concerns the changing of the names of functional ministries periodically, such as with evangelism and youth ministries; name changes such as Witness Movement, PENTYEM, Youth Ministry, ITI-PENSA, and PENSA-Ghana all serve as management mechanisms. Through these arrangements and mechanisms, the leadership manages the growth of the church and establishes effective structures.

The functional ministries, therefore, apart from aiding in extending the growth of the church, serve as a check to maintain its existing membership. In its more recent history, we observe the CoP raising specific functional ministries as measures to correct any perceived anomaly restricting any area of her growth, especially with regard to specific groups of people (such as women, youth, men, or children). Thus, the CoP's functional ministries, past or present, act as engines that promote its growth.

CoP's Growth Mechanisms

The above analysis and discussion of the history of these functional ministries in the CoP point towards one prominent factor: growing the church through active evangelistic efforts, which is also the church's purpose for establishing the functional ministries. Evangelism, the main thrust of the church's corporate intention, must be engaged in not only by a specific group, such as Evangelism Ministry, but by all. This, in the present writer's opinion, makes the setting up of a special ministry such as Evangelism Ministry a duplication. As the other ministries such as Youth and Women appear to have same focus, there is bound to be some conflict of interest and competition, as has been shown already between the Evangelism Ministry and the Youth Ministry, culminating in changes of names and functions over the years.

In order to avoid such clashes, this study proposes that the Evangelism Ministry in the CoP be structured as an outfit for mobilization, training, and instruction for evangelism for all the other functional ministries and in the local assemblies. Evangelism therefore becomes imperative for every member of the church. This will enhance the main focus of the functional ministries, which is evangelism, by avoiding duplication of duties and unnecessary competition for a certain group of members such as the young people. This proposal will be highlighted in chapter 7 as part of the recommendations for further growth of the church.

This book argues, as does Asamoah-Gyadu, that these functional ministries, as the engines driving the growth of CoP local assemblies, have thrived because of the personal working of the Holy Spirit in individual members and in the corporate church. Asamoah-Gyadu has written, "There is a definite relationship between personal experiences of the Spirit and commitments to the cause of Christ and his mission through the church. Such a commitment arises out of a sense of belongingness that develops within the individual as a result of that intense encounter with the Holy Spirit."[157]

It is this experience of encounter with the Holy Spirit since the early 1930s by the Anim group that has influenced and still influences the CoP's current growth. The influence of the Holy Spirit encountered by individual members produces the zeal and vibrancy for all the voluntarism associated with the functional ministries and thereby encourages subsequent growth. Thus, the historic narrative of the CoP as a classical Pentecostal institution indicates that the "Holy Spirit factor" drives, motivates, energizes, and empowers it for growth and mission.

The Pneumatic Phenomena in the CoP

The historic mainline churches had, over the years, also developed functional structures such as women's ministry, men's fellowship, young people's guilds, and the like. What makes the functional structures of the CoP different and effective can be located in its pneumatic emphasis. The major initial factor in the CoP's history that catalyzed its growth as a Pentecostal institution is the pneumatic phenomena, "the Holy Spirit factor." Through the Spirit, great signs and wonders sometimes accompany the CoP's evangelistic drive.

Larbi enumerated a number of such signs and wonders in his writing when analyzing the evangelistic strength of the church during the 1930s and 1940s.[158] According to him, in that era the blind saw, cripples walked, insane people received restoration of their minds, and dead were brought back to life. Leonard had already confirmed that the early history of the CoP was laced with remarkable miracles.[159] But her comment asserted that, unlike what happens in recent times in many parts of the world where church growth is intricately linked with signs, wonders, and miracles, the CoP does not emphasize these. The reason is that the early leaders, especially James McKeown, placed greater emphasis on personal salvation and a subsequent encounter with the Holy Spirit (in baptism in

---

157. Asamoah-Gyadu, "Pentecostalism and the Missiological Significance," 30.
158. Larbi, *Pentecostalism*, 186.
159. Leonard, *Giant in Ghana*, 27.

the Holy Spirit, as it is called) than on physical healing and miracles.[160] It is argued that in places with very prevalent disease and the dread of evil, such as Africa, inevitably some might place their faith entirely on the healings and signs and wonders.

Notwithstanding, many of the church's outreach programs have been characterized by astounding healings, signs and wonders, and miracles, attributed to the presence and work of the Holy Spirit. The church's annual statistical report forms, completed by the districts, includes a column specifically for reporting healings, signs and wonders, and miracles, under the heading "spectacular events." For example, both the National and Missions Reports are laced with spectacular events.[161] The recorded spectacular events are so many that annual appendices are created for them behind the main report. A scan through the spectacular events shows the blind having their sight restored, dead coming back to life, barren women giving birth, people saved from accidents, and other supernatural occurrences. In the 13th session of the Extraordinary Council meeting, the chairman's State of the Church Address reserved a heading for miracles. He wrote:

> The church continues to enjoy the supernatural workings of God in the form of miracles, signs and wonders during the period under review. The dead were raised to life, the dumb and mute were healed, women who had fibroids and other gynaecological dysfunctions were healed, the paralyzed received healing, the blind had their sight restored, the mentally challenged received sanity and others were miraculously delivered from the hands of kidnappers.[162]

These spectacular events prompt an integral discussion on the factors that promote the CoP's growth. Again, the statistical report form for the annual review of progress in the field requires a record of membership, souls won, converts baptized, children dedicated, some statistics on physical acquisitions, and Holy Spirit baptism. This column on Holy Spirit baptism evidenced by the Pentecostal phenomenon of speaking in tongues (glossolalia) is held in high esteem. Many consider its emphasis

---

160. Leonard, *Giant in Ghana*, 36.

161. See CoP, Missions Comprehensive Report, 2013, for records of several signs and wonders in the nations.

162. Chairman Opoku Onyinah, State of the Church Address, 13th session of the Extraordinary Council meeting, Pentecost University College, Sowutuom, Accra, May 14–18, 2012.

on this spiritual experience to be one of Pentecostalism's distinctive features, if not the major one.[163] An apostle of the church asserts that the entire success of the movement as a Pentecostal denomination is linked to the personal experiences of the individuals in light of this spiritual experience.[164] Green's assertion buttresses this observation; he notes that in the early church, it was the Holy Spirit who guided, empowered, and led the infant Christian community into growth. He writes:

> He [the Holy Spirit] it was who so worked within the lives of the Christians individually and the Church corporately that they began to be conformed more and more to the character of Jesus. And it was the Spirit who gave his followers remarkable spiritual gifts, prophesy, tongues (interpretation), healing and exorcism were the most prominent in apostolic and sub-apostolic days alike. People did not merely hear the gospel: they saw it in action, and were moved to respond.[165]

In much of its statistical reporting, the figures accounting for number of converts baptized by the Holy Spirit are above or close to the number of converts baptized in water. This indicates the emphasis the church places on this spiritual experience. Much of the reason many people left the mainline churches and some intellectuals joined the CoP stems from a quest for some form of supernatural encounter or receiving of divine healing.[166]

Thus, "signs and wonders" as part of the fundamental characteristics of the CoP's Pentecostal heritage are defined as giftings such as healing, miracles, casting out of demons, prophecy, and speaking in tongues. The development of this experience (Holy Spirit baptism) and the pursuit of the miraculous (including healings, signs, and wonders) explains the emergence of prayer camps on the religious landscape of the CoP. Larbi has stated categorically that the CoP established more prayer camps in Ghana than any other denomination.[167] They provide interventionist avenues for people believed to be under the taunt of evil, instead of resorting to consult a fetish. Several prominent people in the CoP today came through the prayer camps. Though James McKeown did not accede to

---

163. Asamoah-Gyadu, "Pentecostalism and the Missiological Significance."
164. Woode, Lectures at Pastors and Wives Conference.
165. Green, *Evangelism in the Early Church*, 25.
166. Larbi, "Church of Pentecost."
167. Larbi, "Church of Pentecost."

their expansion in the church, they nevertheless continue to grow.[168] His reservations on the ascendency of the prayer camps may be due to the history of problems associated with their management in the past. The church has, therefore, provided special guidelines for biblical and ethical operations of the prayer camps that are accepted as its procedures.[169] The system seems to have become part of the church's practices despite efforts to curb its existence.

This researcher's personal opinion on the evolving of the prayer camps in the CoP is twofold. First, the church should further aid these centers to be developed into well-resourced forms of rehabilitation centers, with pastoral, clinical, and psychological counseling units, places of rest, waiting on the Lord, and spiritual retreats. This will involve training the leaders of the camps in some of these aspects and helping to develop the physical infrastructure to suit this purpose and modern trends. This will make the camps suitable for both spiritual and physical purposes. Second, the place of the prayer camp leader in the structure of the church polity must be defined and structured for proper management. The CoP prayer camp leader is a lay evangelist, who, when in the local assembly, inspires faith, demonstrates healings, and works miracles. The Apostle Paul speaks of this role in Ephesians 4:11, "He Himself gave some to be apostles, some prophets, some evangelists, and some pastors and teachers." The other biblical text is 1 Corinthians 12:28, "And God has appointed these in the church: first apostles, second prophets, third teachers, after that miracles, then gifts of healings, helps, administrations, varieties of tongues." Comparing these two texts side by side, the place of the evangelist in the local assembly seems to be represented by "gifts of healings and workings of miracles." However, since the only pattern these prayer camp leaders have seen is that of the prayer camps system, they tend to operate in that pattern. Identifying their place and acknowledging it in the structure of the whole church will help its regulation and also curb unhealthy excesses associated with prayer camps' operations in the church.

---

168. Interview with Chairman Apostle Opoku Onyinah, February 10, 2014.
169. CoP, *Minister's Handbook*, 2014, 32.

Structural Developments

The experience and working of the Holy Spirit as a Pentecostal phenomenon within the CoP does not function in the abstract or only on the personal level. It also informs the church's structural developments as the movements grow. One of the CoP's leaders, an earlier apostle, commented in the Ghanaian language Twi, *Pentecosti som ye nyansa som*, meaning "the Holy Spirit movement is also a sensible movement." The Holy Spirit also aids and guides in "sound administration," as the Apostle Paul indicated it as one of the ministries in the church, the body of Christ (1 Cor 12:28).[170] The Holy Scriptures have pointed out that the Spirit is orderly and does not work in chaotic conditions or in any state of confusion (see 1 Cor 14:40).

The period of the CoP's history from 1962 on has seen the development of structural and administrative organization. The governance of the CoP since 1962 is reinforced with well-defined and integrated administrative and management structures. These ensure accountability and administrative and pastoral discipline. They evolved mostly as a response to the numerous crises (conflicts, secessions, and court cases) since its inception.[171] Clear management structures are important for the survival and credibility of any church organization, especially within a context where secession is a primary option in dealing with differences that arise within its local leadership.[172] By June 14, 1971, the CoP had been duly registered under its board of trustees as a religious nonprofit organization in Ghana.[173] The constitution, according to which the church is governed, the general policy framework, had been written and accepted.

Church Governance

The governing structures of the CoP as a church started taking shape after the 1960–1962 crises described above. The CoP, unlike some Pentecostal denominations with a congregational system of governance,

---

170. Comment made by Apostle Patrick Asiamah, one of the early fathers of the church, at an annual fasting and prayer event at PIWC in 1997.

171. See Larbi, *Pentecostalism*, 231, which describes how the formation of the Executive Council began. It was originally an ad hoc institution as a response to the conflict involving the placement of an African as chairman.

172. Asamoah-Gyadu, "On Mission Abroad," 91.

173. CoP, *Constitution*, 2010.

has a strong central governance system. This central governance system can be seen in two streams that work in tandem. The first is the general administrative governance and management, which sets policies for the church, and the second is the ministerial governance, which oversees the congregations through implementing the policies.

The church's administrative governance and management structure operates through a central hierarchy. The highest authority in the CoP central governance is the General Council, which works through a 14-(formerly seven-)member International Executive Council, chaired by an executive chairman. Christine Leonard observed that the chairman of the CoP operates like an executive president of a republic.[174] The International Executive Council meets more often, but its major decisions are to be ratified by the General Council. The decisions taken by the International Executive Council filter down to similar executive committees in the nations, regions or areas, districts, and the local congregations (assemblies) for implementation. The nations may be divided into regions or areas, which are further divided into districts. The districts are comprised of clusters of community-based local congregations known as assemblies. All these (nation, region, district) have their executive committees. The local assembly is run by the local presbytery.

This form of government was adopted through consensus by the local leadership and James McKeown. E. Kingsley Larbi wrote that this system is in consonance with some Ghanaian traditional patterns of leadership, such as the Akan.[175] Emmanuel Gyasi Addo, the international missions director of the church, has stated that the type of church governance observed in the CoP is patterned after a typical Ghanaian paramount chieftaincy. The paramount chieftaincy type of governance has chiefs and other subchiefs, each in his own rank, overseeing or ruling the towns and communities and reporting to the paramount chief.[176] The executive chairman's mode of operation could be likened to a typical Ghanaian traditional ruler or a king as a paramount chief. He has authority over all matters, subject to the approval of the elders or kingmakers. As Kwame Gyekye pointed out, in an African state such as Ghana, traditionally, the king is both the political and the religious head.[177] The

174. Leonard, *Giant in Ghana*, 123.

175. Larbi, *Pentecostalism*, 204.

176. Comments made by Emmanuel Gyasi Addo during a meeting with the church in Burkina Faso and its leaders, June 2, 2016.

177. Gyekye, *African Cultural Values*, 109.

CoP's governance system can be likened to it;[178] the chairman is both the political and religious head of the administration.

General Ministerial Governance

Ministerial governance in the CoP refers to the operation or use of the New Testament apostolic ministry giftings, which govern or oversee the running of the congregations. The CoP, with its roots in the British Apostolic Church, follows the leadership pattern prescribed by the apostolic ministry gifts in the New Testament (Eph 4:11, 2 Cor 12:27–28), that is, apostles, prophets, teachers, pastors, elders, deacons, and deaconesses.[179] In this regard, apostles, prophets, or evangelists are considered head over the rest of the callings. They exercise control and leadership over national, regional, or area jurisdictions of the church. They are not all of the same rank, but any could act in the same capacity. The apostle is ranked higher in terms of ministry and administration than the prophet and evangelist, but any of them could be national, regional, or area heads of the church. The pastors oversee the districts, while the elders and the rest of the leaders oversee the local congregations.

These two streams, the general administrative governance structure and the ministerial governance, intertwine to form the governance structure of the church. The general administrative setup could be seen as the policy-making body, while the other acts as the implementation body. In its day-to-day running in the field, the same system applies: the head (national, regional, area, or local) takes responsibility both for the managerial and ministerial administration. For instance, the head of a national political area of the CoP who is an apostle, prophet, evangelist, or a senior pastor doubles as the head of the ministerial administration. Whereas the apostles and prophets, and in some cases senior ministers (as evangelists or pastors), head the nations and regions, the districts are manned by the district ministers.[180] At the grassroots level, the local congregation is governed by a presbytery of elders, deacons, and deaconesses, who are headed by a presiding elder, who in turns reports to his district minister.

---

178. Nukunya, *Tradition and Change in Ghana*, 67–76.
179. See Worsfold, *Origins of the Apostolic Church in Great Britain*, 86.
180. See CoP, *Constitution*, 2010.

General Administrative Governance and Management

In practice, the CoP, as stated earlier, is governed through a General Council, which is the highest policy-making body. The General Council is composed of all CoP ministers, missionaries, directors of functional ministries, chairmen of boards and committees, regional and area deacons (laymen who manage the finances), and some elders representing various presbyteries (national or regional).[181] The General Council was set up in 1948, and it meets once a year.[182] Major decisions of the body such as the calling of ministers, transfers, creation of areas and districts, financial policies, and doctrinal issues affecting the church are deliberated and decided on by the General Council. The International Executive Committee implements the policies of the General Council through the local assemblies.[183]

The highest executive body, the Executive Council, deals with the daily and regular management of church affairs ahead of the General Council. It is made up of an executive chairman, who is the head of the management of the church, a general secretary, an international missions director (IMD), a representative from each African Francophone area, and representation from the Western world. The executive chairman, general secretary, and the IMD of the church act as headquarters' officers, while the rest of the executives serve as administrative heads in designated areas or nations.[184] The council's membership was expanded in 2015 to include some additional members, increasing the headcount to 14.[185] This came in response to the growth of the church, which has required the administration in Ghana to be further regionalized for easier administration.[186] The general secretary serves as the administrative head of the headquarters' management under the chairman, while the IMD serves as the executive secretary of the Missions Board, which is chaired by the executive chairman.

The Executive Council was established in 1964 in response to the crisis between 1960 and 1962.[187] The rationale for these structures was

---

181. CoP, *Constitution*, 2010, 7.
182. Leonard, *Giant in Ghana*, 123.
183. For details, see CoP, *Constitution*, 2010.
184. CoP, *Constitution*, 2010, 7–10.
185. CoP, General Council Meeting Annual Report, 2015.
186. CoP, Chairman's Circular Letter to All Area Heads, May 26, 2010.
187. See Larbi, *Pentecostalism*, 231–35. Initially the executives where to work for

to allow power sharing rather than control by a single individual.[188] It appears that the management of the CoP provides supervision for every stakeholder. The system allows for participation by both lay leaders and the clergy in its operation. The most sensitive places such as financial management at the headquarters are headed by responsible professionally trained staffs (who are either pastors, elders, or responsible church members).

This form of central administration trickles down to the grassroots. The nations are divided into manageable administrative blocks classified as regions or areas. These used to be referred to as regions, in line with the political divisions of Ghana, but were changed to areas with the growth of the church when a political region could not be managed by a single individual.[189] Recent growth has required creating more areas in the regions, informing the creation of a Regional Consultative Council (RCC) made up of a number of areas in a designated location such as in a common region.[190]

The nations, regions, or areas have a presbytery as the highest decision-making body. The area presbytery comprises 11 representatives, each from a domain classified as a district. The national, regional, or area executive committee is chaired by an area head who is an experienced minister of the church (a senior pastor, evangelist, prophet, or apostle). The area executive committee is made up of seven members. It has the area head as its chairman, a secretary, two pastor members, an area deacon (a responsible elder who supervises the financial administration of the area), and two elders.

The district is made up of a cluster of local congregations (referred to as assemblies). The district presbytery consists of all elders, deacons, and deaconess (church leaders). The district is represented by seven executives: the district pastor, district secretary, financial chairman, and four other elders. This arrangement in turn applies to the local congregation (designated as an assembly). The assemblies have a presbytery made up of the body of elders, deacons, and deaconesses, and headed by a presiding elder, a reviewable position run by the elders every two years. The presiding elder chairs the local congregation in the absence of the district

---

12 months after which the position was to be reviewed.

188. Interview with Chairman Apostle Opoku Onyinah, February 10, 2014.

189. Interview with Chairman Apostle Opoku Onyinah, February 10, 2014.

190. CoP, Chairman's Circular to All Area Heads, May 26, 2010; September 9, 2010.

minister. The strength of the whole organization lies in the vitality of the local assembly, which forms the nucleus of the church populace. The establishment of the home cells and Bible study groups extends around the nucleus so the church consists of the cell units of the local assembly.

The Headquarters' Management

The headquarters' management has the general secretary as its head. He is the head of the secretariat that manages the various segments of the administration. He answers to the executive chairman, who is the executive chairperson or an ex officio member of every board. The general secretary has responsibility for the welfare of the field ministers as well as for the running of the head office departments. The departments are run by professional department heads. The head office departments include the Secretariat, Finance and Administration, External and Internal Audit, General Services, Human Resources, Public Relations or Protocol, Statistics, Audio-visual, Radio, Publications, Archives, Ministry Directorates, Transport, and Security.[191]

Boards and Committees

In addition to the head office departments, other boards and committees also help in the running of the various sections of the church. They include the Missions, Finance, and Pensions Boards, and the Ministerial, Literature, History, and National Music Committees, and an electoral commission. Their various names indicate their mandates.[192] These committees make policies or directives regarding what they have been mandated to do or tasked with by the General Council, to be approved or ratified by the General Council. The committees are formed as either ad hoc or standing committees to deal with pressing issues as they arise, and they report to the General Council through the Executive Council. The church has used such committees since its inception. They are not to do any other business outside the church's setting. The boards, which are more permanent, according to Abua-Ayisi, a former finance and administration director (FAD) of the church, evolved out of the committees.[193]

191. CoP, *Administrative Manual*.
192. See CoP, *Constitution*, 2010.
193. Interview with Elder Abua-Ayisi, former Finance and Administration Head,

For instance, the finance board used to be a finance committee, which was later made a permanent board with a four-year mandate, renewable for other terms. The persons appointed on the board are provided by the International Executive Committee, which also reviews the board when its mandate expires.

Missions Directorate

A separate department within the head office administration exists solely for the church's missionary enterprise. It is managed by a missions board, through an elected international missions director, who is an apostle of the church. Historically, the missions directorate needed to be created because of the growth and outreach of the church after 1962. The Missions Board is a policy-making body and has the executive chairman of the church as its chairman. It meets officially twice in a year and has other meetings as necessary. The international missions director, as the secretary of the board, is also the headquarters' officer in charge of the daily running of the church's missions engagements. His scope of work comprises missions in Ghana and all other mission posts in the other parts of the world. He has a detailed directorate run by a very competent secretariat and financial administrators. Details of this important outfit will be discussed in chapter 4, which deals exclusively with the church's missions.

Raising and Equipping of Indigenous Leadership

Much of the distinctiveness of the contemporary CoP owes to the history since 1982, the period in the church's history when indigenous Ghanaians took over the leadership and administration after James McKeown's retirement in 1982. His immediate successor as the executive chairman of the church was Apostle F. S. Safo, who was considered his direct mentee.[194]

James McKeown had been in leadership as long as his missionary endeavor in Ghana. Beginning with his relationship with the Anim group in 1938 and throughout the history until 1982, he had been up front in leadership. A common question asks whether or not he was

---

CoP head office, February 27, 2014.

194. Leonard, *Giant in Ghana*, 104.

being paternalistic.[195] Opoku Onyinah, the current chairman of the CoP, answered this question in his lecture at the 50th Anniversary lectures of the CoP in 2004 that centered on the person and ministry of James McKeown. In his view, if Bosch's discussion on paternalism implies "conditions under which the younger churches could not reach maturity due to the overshadowing of the Missionary either by staying too long or otherwise," then McKeown might not be paternalistic. Onyinah buttressed his conviction with the definition of paternalism given by Pentecostal historian McGee, "denying the indigenous an access or exercising the gifts of administration and leadership," according to which McKeown is rather far from being paternalistic.[196] His long stay, Onyinah implies, "provided an access for the younger generation to rather exercise their gifts of administration and leadership."[197] He suggests that McKeown's long stay should be seen in the context of his dismissal from the Apostolic Church–UK. McKeown, having been dismissed from the apostolic fraternity in the UK, had nowhere else to go and therefore chose to stay in Ghana. However, historically, before his dismissal there was already an incitement within the group to have him replaced or reassigned. This indicates that part of the group might have felt he had overstretched his stay.

The personal conviction of the present writer is that McKeown's leadership style from its inception had been a unique incentive for raising up true indigenous leadership of integrity, sacrifice, and self-confidence. This pattern differs from that of the early missionary societies that seem to have managed the indigenes as mere objects of the missionary enterprise.[198] Larbi affirms Onyinah's comment that one of McKeown's major legacies was his ability to provide selfless leadership. He summarizes in these words:

> In spite of the fact that CoP was founded through the missionary activities of the Rev James McKeown, the church has fully developed as an indigenous, independent evangelical Pentecostal church. . . . The success story appears to have been possible because McKeown in his capacity as the founder of the movement trusted in the ability of the local people.[199]

195. See Bosch *Transforming Mission*, 295; also Luzbetak, *Church and Culture*.
196. McGee, "Pentecostal Missiology."
197. Onyinah, "Man James McKeown," 71.
198. Bosch, *Transforming Mission*, 295.
199. Larbi, *Pentecostalism*, 327.

James McKeown had a vision of training and equipping local leaders for ministry at every level in the church. He provided the opportunity for the organization to develop leadership that would suit its culture and its biblical doctrine. McKeown was not referred to as an apostle, yet he ordained others in the office of apostle. However, documents point to his being an apostle. For instance, a general quadrennial conference held in May 1954 included him as one of the 54 apostles and prophets.[200]

The basic leadership concept of the CoP is similar to that of Apostolic Church in the UK.[201] The pattern emphasizes the restoration of the New Testament leadership as apostles, prophets, evangelists, teachers, pastors, elders, deacons, and deaconesses. Appointments and callings into leadership positions are based on character, charisma, and the leading of the Holy Spirit. Leadership developments in the CoP began from the grassroots with members being nurtured through subgroups, movements, assemblies, districts, and areas. Team spirit and unique mentoring shape the talents and develop the individual's ministry among both the clergy and laity. The CoP nurtures and trains leaders right from conversion.[202] This kind of orientation has raised indigenous leadership from within to continue in service to the church without recourse to any external intervention. Therefore, the church did not lack indigenous manpower to fill the gap after McKeown's retirement.

By 1982, the church had raised enough indigenous apostles, prophets, and other leaders. The first indigenous executive chairman, F. S. Safo, served from 1982 to 1987. At the time of his demise, before a new chairman was elected according to the constitution, Apostle D. Y. A. Owusu became the acting chairman. He was replaced temporarily by Apostle F. D. Walker, until a General Council meeting held at Takoradi in 1988 saw the election of Prophet M. K. Yeboah (1988–1998) as the substantive replacement through prophetic utterance and confirmed by voting. Prophet M. K. Yeboah retired after serving two terms, that is, 10 years. He was replaced by Apostle M. K. Ntumy, who also served for 10 years, from 1998 to 2008. The much-younger Apostle M. K. Ntumy was brought to the office through prophetic utterance and confirmed by voting. Ntumy was replaced by the current chairman, Opoku Onyinah, who assumed office through nomination by the Executive Council and was confirmed

---

200. Opoku Onyinah cites this as from Tenobi, *Short History*, 23.

201. CoP, *Constitution*, 2010, 13–34; Apostolic Church, *Apostolic Church*, 22–44.

202. Leonard, *Giant in Ghana*, 121.

by vote of the General Council (2008–present). In 2009, M. K. Ntumy was sent as a missionary and a national head to Germany, not having attained the age of 65 required for retirement according to the church's constitution.[203]

The general secretaries, all indigenes, who had served in succession are Apostle Egyir-Paintsil (1952–1981), Apostle D. K. Arnan (1982–1988), Apostle R. Ato Addison (1988–1993), Apostle Albert Amoah (1993–2003), Apostle Alfred Koduah (2003–2013), and Apostle Alex Kumi-Larbi (2013–present). By June 2013, the church recorded 87 ordained apostles, three prophets, six evangelists, 1,189 ordained pastors, 26,491 elders, 19,335 deacons, 35,462 deaconesses and other leaders.[204] The 2016 statistics recorded 1,307 minsters in Ghana (which include 69 apostles, five prophets, and three evangelists), 32,656 elders, 23,683 deacons, and 44,054 deaconesses. Some of the area heads were retired in the period between 2013 and 2016, bringing down the number of ministers who were active apostles, prophets, and evangelists. Given that CoP ministers are due for retirement at 65, it is expected that in the next five years (2016–2021), 141 of CoP's active ministers, including 28 experienced area heads, should be proceeding on retirement.[205] These area heads are all experienced apostles or prophets. At this stage in its history, the CoP needs to consider how to replace these leaders and also how to effectively use the retired ministers who are still physically strong. They could be engaged in areas such as pastoral counseling for younger minsters and as lecturers in the Pentecost Theological Seminary. For 2016, the international missions recorded a total of 913 ministers, 6,385 elders, 5,841 deacons, and 10,732 deaconesses.[206]

Over time, the organization has developed its own means to equip its indigenous leaders. These training and equipping sessions are simply referred to as "retreats," which take place at different levels. The highest level is the Apostles and Prophets November Retreats. At this meeting colleague apostles and prophets meet to share intimate challenges in the ministry.[207] They engage with contemporary challenges and issues confronting the organization and discuss the way forward. It is also a

---

203. CoP, *Constitution*, 2010, 13.
204. CoP, Statistical Department Report, 2013.
205. CoP, General Council Meeting Minutes, 2016.
206. CoP, Worldwide Summary Statistics, 2016.
207. That was the reason for the November Heads' meetings given by then Chairman Apostle M. K. Ntumy.

time of fellowship, fasting, and prayer, out of which many of the church's progressive visions are divinely received. A much larger and more current version of the Apostles and Prophets Retreat is the gathering referred to as the Heads' Meeting, a kind of consultative meeting involving all departmental heads. This comprises all the apostles, prophets, evangelists, national and area heads, directors of ministries, and lecturers at the church's university. This is the most prominent ministerial forum for all senior office holders. It serves as a meeting point to discuss important business and review major theological discourse, church practices and traditions. Every year, the Executive Committee of the church proposes vision-driven policies and a theme to boost its focus. These annual corporate vision policies and themes are discussed at and implemented through this forum.

The decisions taken from the Heads' Meeting in turn come down to the area retreats, the orientation forums for all ministers and office holders such as elders, deacons, deaconesses, and ministry leaders in a designated area. The area retreat provides a forum for fellowship, prayer, fasting, and discourse on biblical doctrine and practices of the denomination. It serves as a forum where experienced ministers share with their progeny. It has recently been rebranded as "Apostolisation."[208] The annual themes that focus the corporate vision policy for any particular year are discussed and taught at these meetings. Ministers and their Wives Retreats are also held. These are refresher meetings aimed at orienting the ministers and their wives to be able to concentrate on their field assignments. They are convened two or three times a year by the area head, who also determines the facilitators. A more current development in leadership training that was started by the current executive chairman, Apostle Opoku Onyinah, in 2010, is the Ministers and Wives Conference held annually for all ministers and their wives in Ghana. All these forums aim to orient Ghanaian nationals and nationals of other nations to carry out the church's ministry.[209]

---

208. "Apostolisation" is a special designation by the chairman to indicate the passing on to another generation.

209. CoP, General Council Meeting Annual Report, 2010.

Development of Manpower, Training, and Education

The history of the CoP shows that it places great value on developing internal manpower. Historically, the denomination has been a grassroots organization, and the early leaders raised indigenous leadership. The church, by the nature of its activities, depends largely on its laity for ministry, many of whom have had little or no education. The early leadership was not very educated.[210] After several decades, children born into the church now are educated, and developments such as the Pentecost International Worship Centres (PIWCs) have seen the full entrance of academics into the denomination. Since the CoP depends largely on its laity, who are largely uneducated, for ministry, this poses a challenge in the present modern climate, which is typically knowledge driven. How then is the CoP prepared to meet these challenges and others? In answer, the denomination is addressing this situation through trainings.

Much of the training of manpower has been in-service, beginning from the local congregational level. Leonard affirms that the CoP operates in such a way that leaders are trained right from conversion.[211] However, over a period of time, the church developed a process of rudimentary training for its lay leaders known as Lay-leaders' School. The Lay-leaders' School is a two-week residential program that all lay leaders and upcoming leaders are encouraged to attend. Study manuals for the topics to be taught are put together for the participants by the church's Department of Theology at its university.

The church also develops its ministers through formal training. Requirements for entry into full-time ministry as a pastor are independent of one's educational background. A recommendation comes in through the local assembly's presbytery based on one's perceived gifting and commitment. In the initial stages, many of these ministers were called through prophecy.[212] Others were handpicked directly by the area apostles. As the church began to expand and ministry became more attractive to the younger generation, the process changed. Interviews were therefore conducted at the district and area levels, culminating in an interview at the level of the National Ministerial Committee, a five-member body appointed by the Executive Council. It comprises two members from the International Executive Committee, two other ministers, and the rector

---

210. Leonard, *Giant in Ghana*, 118.
211. Leonard, *Giant in Ghana*, 121.
212. Leonard, *Giant in Ghana*, 117.

of the University College.²¹³ Candidates who go through the national interviews successfully undergo training at the church's Bible Training Institute.

The idea of setting up a formal training institute or center was proposed and accepted at the General Council meeting at Winneba in 1963.²¹⁴ It was actually started in February 1972 by Pastor David Mills, an Elim Pentecostal missionary who was working with the CoP in Kumasi.²¹⁵ From 1972, the Bible Centre prescribed a ministerial training scheme where batches of ministers of the church spent three months in training sessions. The original idea was to run a one-month refresher course for pastors already in the field.²¹⁶ The pioneers of this training were S. O. Adipah, R. K. Amponsah, A. K. Atsu, S. K. Ayinor, J. K. Annin, Yaw Frimpong, S. A. K. Karikari, John Mensah, S. K. Nketsia, R. N. Otumfuo, R. K. Owusu-Ankomah, D. Y. Tieku, S. J. A. Tiase, and M. T. Wayoe.²¹⁷ The college was closed in 1973 and reopened in May 1982 at New Abossey Okai in Accra. It was later relocated to Madina, near Accra, in 1984. The Rev. Lionel Currie took over from the Rev. David Mills as the principal in 1984.²¹⁸ The Rev. L. A. Nyarko served as dean from 1986 to 1989. In 1992, the Rev. L. Currie was replaced by the Rev. John Waller, also from Elim Pentecostal–UK. From 1984 on, new ministerial candidates called into the CoP ministry spent eight months from January to August at the center. Ordained ministers continued to attend refresher courses. The subjects taught included studies on 1 Corinthians, systematic theology, and church history.

In 1995, the center was renamed the Pentecost Training Institute. The Rev. Michael M. Kopah took over from the Rev. John Waller as the first African principal of the Pentecost Bible Institute, 1997 to October 2002. It was upgraded to a Bible college in 1999 and also relocated in 1999 to a new campus at Sowutuom, a suburb of Accra. In March 2003, the Rev. Dr. Opoku Onyinah succeeded the Rev. M. M. Kopah as rector of the Pentecost Bible College. The following have served as dean of students:

213. CoP, *Constitution*, 2010, 109.
214. CoP, General Council Meeting Minutes, 1963.
215. Pentecost University College Dairy, Presentation of College History, 2012.
216. Interview with Apostle M. M. Kopah, former principal of CoP Bible Training Centre, March 13, 2014.
217. Bredwa-Mensah, "Church of Pentecost in Retrospect," 52.
218. Interview with Apostle M. M. Kopah, former principal of the Training Centre, Kasoa, February 12, 2014.

the Rev. M. K. Yeboah (1984–1986), the Rev. L. A. Nyarko (1986–1989), the Rev. Emmanuel Parker (1989–1992), the Rev. Samuel Opoku-Adipah (1992–1999), and the Rev. Kwame Blankson (1999–2003). The Rev. Dr. Emmanuel Amponsah-Kuffour was appointed the director of studies at the center from 1992 to 2003. Those who served as lecturers in the college include the Rev. J. S. Gyimah, the Rev. J. A. Mbillah, the Rev. Albert Amoah, Mrs. Matilda Mensah, Elder Joshua Adjabeng, the Rev. Peter Ayerakwa, the Rev. Opoku Onyinah, the Rev. D. K. Noble-Atsu, and the Rev. Emmanuel R. Bonney.[219]

The college has now attained university status. During the 34th session of the General Council meeting held at the Sowutuom campus on May 22, 2003, then-president of the Republic of Ghana, His Excellency Mr. J. A. Kuffuor, commissioned the premises.[220] The Pentecost University College Council was inducted on May 6, 2004, at the 10th session of the Extraordinary Council meeting held at the Sowutuom campus. The university was accredited by the National Accreditation Board, Ghana, in November 2004. The college is affiliated with the University of Ghana, Legon. In its current status, new entrants into ministry are obliged to go through a one-year certificate training before they are posted to a station. The church is also building on its scholarship program as it encourages some ministers to pursue a bachelor's degree at the university, School of Theological Education by Extension, or Canada Christian College. Others are encouraged to pursue a master's degree in theology and doctor of philosophy (PhD) degree to augment the faculties at the university. During the 33rd session of the General Council meeting, five ministers were sponsored to pursue various PhD courses in different universities.[221]

The school has a facility in the theological department that runs a special program for the CoP lay leaders—the Lay-leaders School, organized once every year for two weeks for all the church's lay leaders. The courses that have been taught from 2010 to 2013 include Leadership Development I and II, Old Testament Survey I, Marriage Counseling, Primary Health Care, The Incarnation of Christ and Discipleship, Personal Evangelism, Follow-up, Aspects of Marriage and Family Life, Holistic Child Development, Pentecostal Doctrine and Distinctive Character, Pentecostal Spirituality and Worship, Hermeneutics and Homiletics, and

219. Information in Bible Training Centre, *School Prospectus, 1992–1998*.
220. Pentecost University College, Diary, 2012. The facts concerning 2003–2004 events in this paragraph all come from this document.
221. CoP, General Council Meeting Minutes, 2012.

Church Administration and Finance.²²² At the end of 2013, all participants who successfully completed the three training sessions were given participant certificates designed by the church.

In 2013, as part of its new vision policy, *Vision 2013–2018*, the church created a separate institution for theological and missionary studies: Pentecost Theological Seminary. The 10-year vision for the institution is to strengthen the church's ministerial formation, higher theological education, and missionary training. It is also to continue the training for church lay leaders, as well as research and publish on vital church tenets and mission praxis. It is also to conduct special training programs and seminars on family life education and youth and children's ministries. The institution aims to give special attention to classical Pentecostal theology and spirituality, Christian doctrines, and pastoral responses to social, economic, cultural, and political issues that confront contemporary society.²²³

The vision document for the institution, though, is silent on the work and trend of evangelism and the Evangelism Ministry—a core value. This important aspect of the church's training should be formalized. An institution that claims to have evangelism as its core mandate should uphold it in its curriculum for pastoral and lay training. However, the principal of Pentecost Theological Seminary, Dr. Emmanuel Anim, has stated that the school's program on evangelism is incorporated into the Missions Studies Programme. He asserts that there is a specific course on Evangelism and Discipleship.²²⁴

Since 2014, a board, management, and staff have been put in place for the school's academic work. For the 2014/15 academic year, which began on September 22, 2014, there were 135 students enrolled. The seminary entered an institutional affiliation with Trinity Theological Seminary, Legon, through a memorandum of understanding (MoU), on June 21, 2016, signed by the Rev. Prof. J. O. Y. Martey and the Rev. Prof. J. D. K. Ekem for Trinity Theological Seminary and by Apostle Dr. Alfred Koduah and the Rev. Dr. Anim for Pentecost Theological Seminary.²²⁵ This is a requirement pending accreditation from the National Accredita-

222. CoP, Lay-Leaders Training Manual, 2010–2013.

223. CoP, Pentecost Theological Seminary, Ten-Year Vision and Development Plan based on the CoP *Vision 2018* document, 2013.

224. The writer's interaction with Dr. Emmanuel Anim, principal of Pentecost Theological Seminary, May 3, 2017.

225. CoP, Pentecost Theological Seminary, Annual Report, September 2016.

tion Board. The institution is headed by the Rev. Dr. Emmanuel Anim as its principal.

Engagement in Social Services

The CoP in its early stages, unlike the early missionary societies of the 19th century, did not focus on social services. Writers such as Wyllie, Leonard, Larbi, and Onyinah, who have written on McKeown as the missionary founder of CoP in Ghana, did not include social services as part of his legacy.[226] For instance, Larbi enumerated McKeown's major contributions to the development of the church as providing leadership, defining the priorities of the church in terms of evangelism, his personal integrity, and his uncompromising stand against sin, laziness, and misappropriation of funds. Opoku Onyinah has said that McKeown emphasized that his mandate was to focus on the core business, which for him was evangelism; presumably when the converts matured, they would go on to add other components such as social services.[227] This understanding dismisses the assertion that McKeown was averse to social services; rather, he proposed it for a generation that would be prepared to take it up without external dependency. For instance, a circular letter by McKeown to all local assemblies dated November 29, 1957, directed the establishment of a social service facility in Kade, Eastern Region. The circular reads in part:

> At the first meeting of the Ghana Apostolic Church Education Board, it was decided to establish an Industrial School at Kade. The School at Kade has granted the Ghana Apostolic Church 30 acres of land. The Chief and elders of Kade desire that this land given to us be used for the benefit of all Ghana. Young women can be taught dressmaking. Young men can be taught trades that will help them to earn a good livelihood, and be useful to help Ghana to rise to her high vision. We plan to have a Bible School in addition to the Industrial School. We have learned lessons from our past experiences with the Bible School. It is good that we continue the Industrial School with the Bible School. If the Bible teaching alone is given, in theory, men and women inclined to get to heaven will not be of earthly good. Yet we don't

---

226. Wyllie, "Pioneers of Ghanaian Pentecostalism," 113; Leonard, *Giant in Ghana*; Larbi, *Pentecostalism*; Onyinah, "The Man James McKeown."

227. Interview with Chairman Apostle Opoku Onyinah, February 10, 2014.

want people to get so earthly that they forget there is a "kingdom of Heaven."[228]

The circular establishes a clear premise that, though in the early stages the church did not completely rule out social services, it was careful not to be swayed from its main focus at that time: evangelization. Of course, some early denominations that placed emphasis on social services, to the disadvantage of evangelism, had laid a foundation for the CoP to build on. For instance, many of the early meeting places of the church were in classrooms of the mission schools.

In 1978, the finance board proposed an establishment for social services. McKeown apparently agreed on the issue of institutionalizing social services, but he cautioned that only elders head the program and not field ministers. A decision to commence social services was taken at the church's General Council meeting at Accra Academy in 1979, and the name Pentecost Relief Association was proposed. In 1980, at the same venue in the General Council meeting, the name was changed to Pentecost Welfare Association (PENTWAS). PENTWAS was registered with the Registrar General's Department on March 17, 1980, as a charitable NGO.[229] The primary aims of the PENTWAS at that point were to provide care for the poor, the needy, and the handicapped in the society, to train up children academically and morally and inculcate into them the fear of God, to train young people in agriculture, to build recreation centers, establish health care centers and orphanages, to embark upon evangelism through distribution of Bibles and other Christian literature, and establish libraries and render general relief services.[230] Elder A. H. L. Clottey was the first manager of PENTWAS, from 1981 to 1983. The church had previously pioneered some schools: Pentecost Preparatory Schools in Koforidua and Takoradi, in 1980. A school established at Kumasi could not be sustained. Farms had been set up at Trede and Ofankor; other farms were at Afram Plains and Wassa Simpa.

In early 1983, a restructuring committee chaired by Apostle Opoku Onyinah decided on restructuring the scope and mode of operation of the PENTWAS. According to Apostle Onyinah, it was felt to be time for

228. Circular letter from Pastor James McKeown, November 29, 1957. An extract of the circular can be found in CoP, Policy Guidelines for PENTSOS.

229. An extract of the circular can be found in CoP, Policy Guidelines for PENTSOS.

230. CoP, Policy Guidelines for PENTSOS. Information in the rest of this paragraph also comes from this document.

the church to start engaging in social services as a part of its contribution to society.[231] In June 1983, the name was changed to Pentecost Social Services (PENTSOS). In the same month Elder Bamfo took over from Elder Clottey, and Elder Anum Sampong was appointed the administrative secretary of PENTSOS. PENTSOS was registered as a church NGO with the Department of Social Welfare on January 6, 1992.[232] Under this new mandate, PENTSOS was to initiate and support community-initiated development programs such as education, educational support programs, health services, economic empowerment, income generation, disaster prevention and management, relief services, and advocacy for the equitable distribution of God-given resources and opportunities for development. In October 1986, Elder Johnson Adom-Yeboah was appointed as the schools manager and coordinator of PENTSOS. The PENTSOS program was managed nationally by a committee chaired by Elder Emmanuel Anane Boate from 1995 to 1998. Apostle J. K. Ampomah continued as the chairman from 1999 to 2011 and was relieved by Apostle J. A. Mensah, who served until August 2011. Since August 2011, Apostle Kingsford Kyei-Mensah has been the chairman of PENTSOS.

The eighth session of the church's Extraordinary Council meetings in 2000 decided to create a directorate for PENTSOS.[233] Adom-Yeboah continued as the first director of PENTSOS when it was given full directorate status. After his retirement, Elder Dr. Yao Yeboah took over as the PENTSOS director in September 2003.[234] By 2012, the CoP, through PENTSOS, had established 67 basic schools; two senior high schools, at Koforidua and Kumasi; two girls' vocational schools, at Goaso and Gbawe (Accra); and one boys' technical school at La, Accra. PENTSOS also coordinates an educational support scheme for brilliant but needy students. They also established a hospital in Accra (Pentecost Hospital at Madina) and six clinics in the following locations: Kpasa in Volta Region, Kasapin in Brong Ahafo Region, Yawmatwa and Tarkwa in the Western Region, and Twifo-Agona and Ayanfuri in the Central Region.[235]

In 2009, the church mandated PENTSOS to sensitize and mobilize the church populace in the various areas and districts to set up credit

231. Interview with Chairman Apostle Opoku Onyinah, February 10, 2014.
232. CoP, Policy Guidelines for PENTSOS.
233. CoP, Extraordinary Council Meeting Report, 2000.
234. CoP, Policy Guidelines for PENTSOS.
235. CoP, Policy Guidelines for PENTSOS.

unions that would serve as a means of relief from the socioeconomic challenges. By June 2012, the Pentecost Credit Union had been established at Tema, Kwashieman, Official Town Assembly, and PIWC-Kumasi, as other areas and districts were considering the program.[236] On September 2, 2014, the National Secretariat of the Pentecost Co-operative Mutual Support and Social Services Society (PENCO) was officially opened by the general secretary, Apostle A. N. Y. Kumi-Larbi.[237] They had 49 societies in 34 church areas (15 at the district level and 25 at area level) by 2016. The PENTSOS director, Elder Dr. Yao Yeboah, retired in 2014 after 12 years of service. He was replaced by Elder Afrifa.

Print and Electronic Media

Media has always played an important part in the propagation of the Christian message, especially for Pentecostalism. In particular, the Pentecostal periodicals, with their international circulation, were the most effective media used for spreading the message throughout the world before the advent of electronic media.[238] The CoP in Ghana is no exception. The early history of the church records that Apostle Anim was introduced to Pentecostalism through the reading of a periodical of the Apostolic Faith Church. Currently, in Ghana, one of the major appropriations and innovations of the Pentecostal and Charismatic movement observed to be aiding the process of Pentecostalization is the media.[239] Until 1965, the CoP did not have any official magazine; neither did it have access to the electronic media.

The birth of an official magazine of the church came through the establishment of an association, the African Pentecostal Evangelistic Association, by some church members. These include A. K. Asem and Mr. Adofo Marih. On March 6, 1965, the magazine *Pentecost Fire* was launched with its first issue. The first editor was Mr. Adofo Marih, who was later joined by A. K. Asem. The five years between 1965 and 1970 brought many difficulties, including financial setbacks. The first batch of

---

236. CoP, PENTSOS Annual Report, 2012.
237. CoP, PENTSOS Annual Report, 2016.
238. Anderson, *To the Ends of the Earth*, 9.
239. See Asamoah-Gyadu, *African Charismatics*.

5,000 copies financed by the church and some benevolent members was printed in 1970.[240]

The association started its religious broadcast, the *Pentecost Hour*, in 1972. The main brains behind the program were Elders A. K. Asem and Johnny Mallet, then presiding elder of the Osu Assembly. The early speakers included Pastors James McKeown, J. Egyir-Paintsil, Thomas Nyarko, E. K. Parker, Sister Eunice Addison, Elder E. K. Asem, and A. K. Asem.[241] The radio program and the magazine made a tremendous contribution towards the growth and development of the church. It was among the few religious programs in the country at that time. Leonard confirms that around 1969, Elim missionary the Rev. G. L. W. Ladlow and his wife, Margaret, became the radio pastors for three years and later helped in shaping the CoP radio ministry.[242] Margaret Ladlow spoke on the English program. The church took over the program from the association for effective management and appointed a substantive radio pastor in March 1975. The first radio pastor was Pastor L. A. Nyarko; he was assisted by the Rev. M. M. Kopah. In June 1979, the Armed Forces Revolutionary Council (AFRC) took over the governance of Ghana through a military coup. All religious broadcasts were stopped by the new government until the early 1980s.

The CoP set up an Audio-Visual Department to manage its audio-visual operations in September 1987, after the ban was lifted. The Rev. Johnson Agyemang-Baduh became the head and was assisted by journalist Mrs. Adutua-Amakye.[243] The Radio Committee coordinated the broadcasting, which was only through Ghana Broadcasting 2 (GBC 2). The Radio Committee and Audio-Visual Technical Committee were merged to become the National Radio and Television Ministry Committee (NRTVMC), which was headed by the Rev. Johnson Agyemang-Baduh. The original Audio-Visual Department became the Pentmedia responsible for audio and TV recordings.

The CoP commenced TV broadcasting in July 2001, under chairman of the NRTVMC Apostle M. M. Kopah. The 2013 national committee working with him included Pastor Daniel Tetteh Tackie as the radio pastor/secretary, Pastor Theodore M. Asare, Pastor Dr. Emmanuel

---

240. Larbi, *Pentecostalism*, 189–90.
241. Larbi, *Pentecostalism*, 190.
242. Leonard, *Giant the Ghana*, 156; see also Larbi, *Pentecostalism*, 195.
243. CoP, NRTVMC Annual Report, 2013.

K. Anim, Elder E. O. Donkor, Elder Matthew Nkansah, Elder Oppong Bio, Mrs. Hannah Adutuah-Amakye, and Miss Peggy Ama Donkor. The NRTVMC end of year report for 2013 showed that the *Pentecost Hour* was broadcast on 113 radio stations, eight at the national level and 105 in the areas across the nation. The national radio stations were Sunny FM, Unique FM, Radio Universe, Obonu FM, Channel R, Adom FM, Peace FM, and Spring FM. National TV coverage is on GTV, TV Africa, Multi TV, and GBC (Life) Digital. Many areas and districts have purchased airtimes in their catchment areas.[244]

In 1975, Elim Pentecostal Church in the UK donated one offset printing machine to meet the increasing printing needs of the CoP.[245] Currently, the CoP has its own press, which prints much of the materials of the church, including *Pentecost Fire*, the church's quarterly periodical. The Pentecost Press Ltd is a registered limited liability company. It prints an average of 72,000 copies of the *Pentecost Fire* in a year. At the General Council meeting in 2013, a publications officer, Overseer Isaac Annor, was appointed by the church to coordinate all programs, literary works, and the church's website.[246]

The records suggest that at the end of 2013, 3,030 messages had been preached, the result of which 1,415 people made a decision for Christ. The radio pastor's office received 4,954 telephone calls.[247] The response to media is very significant in the church's evangelization effort. Since 2015, the CoP has been running its own TV station, Pent TV. The radio pastor in 2015 received 6,201 phone calls and 57 text messages from listeners and viewers in Ghana and abroad; 515 listeners committed their lives to Jesus.[248] The aim of the Pent TV station is to counteract, in the church's perception, the current usurping of other TV stations propagating false doctrine and teaching. In November 2015, the board of the NRTVMC was reconstituted by the Executive Council of the church with the following members: Apostle Eric Nyamekye as the chairman, Pastor Daniel Tetteh Tackie as the secretary, Overseer Felix Dela Klutse, and Elders Justice Eric Kyei Baffour and Joseph Mbrokoh-Awol as members. The NRTVMC's subsequent report, in 2016, records significant strides in the

---

244. CoP, NRTVMC Annual Report, 2013.
245. Larbi, *Pentecostalism*, 195.
246. CoP, General Council Decisions and Appointments, 2013.
247. CoP, NRTVMC Annual Report, 2013.
248. CoP, NRTVMC Annual Report, 2015.

areas of technical training and broadcasts on the various radio and television networks. The radio broadcast increased from eight to 14 stations, and 8,089 calls from listeners and viewers across the country and abroad were recorded.[249]

Housing Facilities and Estate

Chapter 2 suggested that one of the features pointing to Pentecostalization on the Ghanaian scene is the erecting of massive structures such as church buildings. The CoP, after its secession from the parent body in 1953, lost most of its assets to the Apostolic Church of Ghana through a court ruling. Many of the congregations were said to have relocated to classrooms, rented places, and temporary spaces like under trees. At the end of 2013, the CoP's total congregations were 16,778 worldwide with 13,050 in Ghana. The CoP's system of congregational growth plants a community church in close proximity to the congregants. Larger community churches are divided with the intention of planting other churches in closer proximity to congregants. By 2013, among the 13,050 congregations, there were 1,652 permanent church buildings (12.7 percent), 3,682 uncompleted permanent church buildings (28.2 percent), 4,118 temporary structures (31.6 percent), 158 rented halls (1.2 percent), 342 receiving free accommodation (2.6 percent), 2,079 worshipping in classrooms (15.9 percent), 899 under trees (6.9 percent), and 120 in other undefined places (0.9 percent).[250] In this era when churches in the West are said to be empty and church infrastructure is being converted to warehouses and other uses, the CoP has members meeting in every available space, including under trees.

The church, by 2013, had 1,003 minister's residences and 1,100 road-worthy vehicles for its ministers at various levels. Among its numerous assets across the nation is an elaborate international headquarters in the heart of Accra, in Labadi. Recently, it has built the largest residential conference center in Ghana. The facility, named Pentecost Convention Centre, stretches over more than 100 acres of land. It is made up of a central auditorium that seats 5,000, with other smaller conference halls of 3,000, 500, and 200 seating capacity, and a 1,800-person capacity dining hall and an administration block. The facility was commissioned on May

---

249. CoP, NRTVMC Annual Report, 2016.
250. CoP, Growth Statistical Report for Mid Year, 2013.

8, 2013, by then president of the Republic of Ghana, His Excellency John Dramani Mahama.[251] In addition, there are four hostel blocks and an executive block. The facility also houses a two-block, four-story, modern, well-resourced Theological Seminary, which serves as a training place for its new entrants and for other training purposes. The corporate assets of the organization, both locally and internationally, are too numerous to count: This is remarkable, especially for a denomination in a sub-Saharan African country plagued with socioeconomic challenges. Ghana, between 2001 and 2003, was counted among the World Bank's Heavily Indebted Poor Countries (HIPC) of the world.[252] Yet the CoP in Ghana accrued, annually, sufficient internal financial resources to adequately support its budget and provide for several missionaries posted out of the country.

The church continues its efforts to provide decent worship places for its members, comfortable residences and auxiliary vehicles for its ministers, and other important infrastructure both in Ghana and abroad. In 2015 and 2016, through special targeted building projects dubbed Community Based Church Buildings (CBCB), many church buildings and worship centers in the rural areas were built to accommodate churches meeting under trees and to replace rented halls.[253] The church's financial report for 2016, delivered on May 4, 2016, indicated that more than GHC40,000,000 (an equivalent of $10,000,000) was released for construction of church buildings.[254] The State of the Church Address for 2016 by the CoP's executive chairman, Apostle Opoku Onyinah, confirmed that the National Estate Committee supervised the construction of 812 buildings, made up of 766 CBCB and other buildings.[255] This National Estate Committee is made up of professional engineers, builders, and architects, most of whom are ministers of the church. They include the general secretary, Apostle A. N. Y. Kumi-Larbi, who is a civil engineer, and the estate and development manager, Pastor Ignatius T. Buertey, who holds a doctorate in engineering. The budget presented for the year 2017 proposed an increase to twice the figure earmarked in 2016 for the same

251. CoP, General Council Decisions and Appointments, 2013.
252. www.worldbank.org/en/country/Ghana.
253. CoP, Estate Annual Report, 2016.
254. CoP, Financial Report, December 31, 2016, presented at the 15th session of the Extraordinary Council meeting, Pentecost Convention Centre, May 3–6, 2017.
255. CoP, Chairman Apostle Professor Opoku Onyinah, State of the Church Address, opening service of the 15th session of the Extraordinary Council meeting, Pentecost Convention Centre, May 3, 2017.

purpose.²⁵⁶ In every sense of the word, this organization can be considered a vibrant institution with the potential of ongoing real growth. Quite appropriately, authors regard it as self-sustaining, self-financing, self-propagating, and self-theologizing.

CoP and Ecumenism

The CoP's vision is to build a self-dependent institution. From the outset, the church assumed the characteristics of an indigenous church in terms of being self-governing, self-financing, self-propagating, and self-theologizing.²⁵⁷ Nonetheless, since its split in 1953 from the parent body, the UK Apostolic Church, it has nursed a strong desire to belong to a global movement. This desire is probably fueled by the idea that God has given the church a mandate through prophecy to reach out and impact the nations of the world.²⁵⁸ A prophetic utterance to that effect is claimed to have been given to the church in its early days.²⁵⁹

The earliest recorded affiliation of the church since it became independent was with Elim Pentecostal Church–UK, through its missionaries in Ghana, the Rev. and Mrs. David and Margaret Mills. At the CoP's General Council meeting in March 1971, the church agreed to affiliate with the Elim Pentecostal Church. Since then the Elim Pentecostal Church has made a great contribution to the development and growth of the movement in Ghana. The Mills initiated the Bible Training Centre, while the Ladlows, other Elim Pentecostal missionaries, supported the set up of the radio ministry.²⁶⁰ The Elim Pentecostal Church also made a great impact on the establishment of the CoP–UK in 1988. Through the Elim Pentecostal Church affiliation, the Norman Barnes UK Link International was born. Link International has provided drugs, tractors, and printing machines to the various establishments of the CoP.²⁶¹

---

256. CoP, Budget Proposals, 2017, presented at the 15th session of the Extraordinary Council meeting, Pentecost Convention Centre, May 3–6, 2017.

257. Larbi, "Sustaining Growth," 144.

258. This is a strong assertion from Chairman Opoku Onyinah, interview, February 10, 2014.

259. An excerpt of the Prophetic Utterance is published as God's Covenant with the church as an addendum in CoP, *Church of Pentecost Songs*, 147–49.

260. Larbi, *Pentecostalism*, 196.

261. Larbi, *Pentecostalism*, 196.

On the local front, the church has been instrumental in the formation and participation of the Ghana Pentecostal and Charismatic Council (GPCC). As indicated in the early history, the intractable relations between the Apostolic Church and Anim's group and later the divisions between the Apostolic Churches of Ghana eventually led to the formation of three distinct Pentecostal denominations of the same orientation: Christ Apostolic Church, the Apostolic Church of Ghana, and the Church of Pentecost. It is said that by 1968 the simmering embers of the feud between the churches had settled.[262] Some ministers made an initiative to have the four Pentecostal bodies in the country come together to form an ecumenical council in 1969. These ministers included Apostle D. K. Saforo of Christ Apostolic Church and the Rev. Gyan Fosu of the Assemblies of God.

On this basis, the Rev. Dr. Grau, the principal of Trinity College at the time, held an orientation exercise for the secretaries or representatives of the denominations; the participants included the Rev. S. K. Nkansah, Apostle D. K. Saforo, and the Rev. Egyir-Paintsil of the Church of Pentecost.[263] The weeklong meeting convened at Trinity Theological Seminary and had as its theme "The Building of the Kingdom of God."

The Ghana Pentecostal Council (GPC) was inaugurated on March 3, 1969, at the Evangel Assemblies of God Church, Adabraka. The GPC was registered under CAP XO17, on August 6, 1971.[264] The foundational denominations were the Assemblies of God, the Apostolic Church, Christ Apostolic Church, and the Church of Pentecost. The inauguration had in attendance the Rev. J. K. Gyan Fosu, the Rev. Robert L. Cobb, and the Rev. Edwin Ziemann of the Assemblies of God; Apostle Peter Newman Anim and Apostle D. K. Saforo of the Christ Apostolic Church; the Rev. James McKeown and the Rev. Egyir-Paintsil of the Church of Pentecost; the Rev. David Mills and the Rev. David Tenobi of Elim Pentecostal Mission; the Rev. Gregory Francis of World Evangelical Church Mission; George A. Nicholas of the Bible Society of Ghana; Calan Morris of Scripture Union; and Allan Konrad of the Lutheran Church of God.

On October 6, 1977, in order for the GPC to have an affiliation with Association of Evangelicals in Africa and Madagascar (AEAM), its name was changed to Ghana Evangelical Fellowship. It reverted to its

---

262. Saforo, "History of GPC."
263. Saforo, "History of GPC."
264. Saforo, "History of GPC."

original name Ghana Pentecostal Council on February 21, 1981. In the interim, the Rev. Allen Conrad was appointed chairman, with the Rev. J. K. Gyan Fosu as his secretary. The Church of Pentecost since then has played an important role in the body. Apostle F. S. Safo of CoP was the first substantive chairman of the GPC, with the Rev. Moses Afful as general secretary.[265] In the ensuing years, various chairmen of the CoP have chaired the council: Prophet M. K. Yeboah, Apostle M. K. Ntumy, and Apostle Dr. Opoku Onyinah. The last two successive general secretaries were seconded from the Church of Pentecost: Apostle Ekow Badu Woode (2000–2010) and Apostle Samuel A. Antwi (2010–present).

The CoP, however, has informal relations with the other Christian ecumenical bodies in the country such as the Christian Council of Ghana and the Catholic Bishops Secretariat. In the annual General Council meetings of the CoP, these bodies are invited to present their fraternal greetings, and these invitations are generally honored. The Catholic Bishop of Accra, Bishop Charles Palmer Buckle, was invited to the 13th Extraordinary session of the CoP council meeting as the guest of honor. The CoP, however, also has bilateral relations with many parachurch organizations in Ghana, such as the Bible Society, Ghana Institute of Languages, Literacy and Bible Translation, Gideons International, and the Scripture Union. Over a period of time, the Bible Society has consistently commended the CoP as its major financial contributor.[266]

In the year 2012, the CoP was registered as a member of the World Council of Pentecostal and Charismatic Churches. During the 2011 Conference of the Global Christian Forum, Apostle Opoku Onyinah, the CoP chairman, was asked to present a paper on behalf of African Pentecostals.[267] He saw it as indicating a unique recognition of the Church of Pentecost on the global front, making the church's contribution felt at the global level. In an interview he commented:

> For instance, we had the Global Christian Forum, the second of its kind with all the ecumenical bodies coming together, and then they ask me to present a paper for African Pentecostals. That helps the Church of Pentecost to add our contribution to World Christianity, and that is what God wants us to do. Feed the world with what he has given us. I see this aspect as part

265. Saforo, "History of GPC."

266. Presented by official of Bible Society at CoP General Council meetings, 2010 and 2012 sessions.

267. Interview with Chairman Apostle Opoku Onyinah, February 10, 2014.

of the fulfilment of God's Prophecy for the church saying he will use us to bless Africa and then later added the rest of the world.[268]

In a more recent development, the church received an invitation to be part of the founding members of the Lausanne Movement.[269] In this regard, the CoP, in anticipation of reaching the rest of the world as a fulfillment of certain prophetic utterances given to the church, sees its cooperation with other Christian bodies a vital factor.

CONCLUSION

The main thrust of this chapter has been the historical developments of the CoP after its formal, legal secession from the parent body, the Apostolic Church of UK, in 1962. Thus, it updates and continues Larbi's history of the CoP up to 1982, when James McKeown retired, chronicled in his work on Pentecostalism in Ghana.

The discussion has shown that the structures, which are also seen as religious and theological factors influencing its growth, were not necessarily deliberately and strategically formed, but rather produced in response to historical events such as the various acrimonies and conflicts. The evolving structures—also factors accounting for its growth—comprise functional ministries, church governance, administration and finance, pneumatic phenomena (Holy Spirit baptism, signs and wonders, and prayer camps), indigenous leadership, development of manpower, training and education, social services, print and electronic media, estates, and ecumenism. This chapter observes that the Holy Spirit, evident in pneumatic phenomenon, has been the central catalyst working through the individuals and the corporate institutions for its commitment and subsequent growth.

These factors have contributed to the CoP's increasing growth. For instance, through its functional ministries, the movement has been able to adapt to emerging challenges. The ministries are tailored specifically to

268. Interview with Chairman Apostle Opoku Onyinah, February 10, 2014.

269. Reported by CoP Youth Director after attending Lausanne Conference in August 2016 in Jakarta, Indonesia. The Lausanne Committee for World Evangelization, more commonly known as the Lausanne Movement, is a global movement that mobilizes evangelical leaders to collaborate for world evangelization. The movement grew out of the 1974 International Congress on World Evangelization (ICOWE) and promotes active worldwide evangelization.

check any changes that pose a challenge to the church's development both at present and in the future. We can see this, for instance, in the Children's Ministry, which addresses issues regarding children born into the church, and the Youth Ministry for young people in the church. The PIWCs provide an alternative for its educated youth to keep them from moving to attractive Charismatic services of some neo-Pentecostal churches or CMs, and they also provide a cross-cultural context for expatriates and others in similar categories. The management of these functional ministries, as in choosing its leaders, naming of the ministries, defining its functions, and other periodic restructuring, are avenues through which the growth of the church is managed. Although an Irish missionary was the CoP's missionary founder, the church has thoroughly developed and stabilized as an indigenous, independent, classical Pentecostal denomination that is self-sustaining. The CoP is ready to engage in any foreign missions as a local manifestation of African Pentecostalism. Chapter 4, a continuation of this updated history, addresses the modalities through which the CoP grows and extends its growth. The fifth chapter continues with the history of its missions and its branches abroad. This is followed by the sixth chapter, which centers on the character, theology, beliefs, and ethos that propel the movement.

4

Mission and Growth in the Church of Pentecost

A Case Study of African Pentecostalism

THE PREVIOUS CHAPTER ESTABLISHED that, by 1962 when the CoP legally and formally became independent from the British Apostolic Church, it had expanded numerically into every part of Ghana. Since then it has been establishing mission posts in other nations in a deliberate effort toward global evangelization and mission outreach. This chapter discusses the growth and mission pattern of the CoP as a local version of African Pentecostalism reflecting the missional character of general Pentecostalism.

MISSION AND GROWTH ANALYSIS

The CoP, as a denomination, has very important missions structures manned by an organized missions board and an international mission director.[1] Its annual calendar has established a "Missions Week" celebration to create missional awareness, and the CoP also organizes missions conferences, trains and sends out missionaries, and stresses the importance of missions in its daily teachings.[2] Historically, Christian

---

1. Asamoah-Gyadu, "On Mission Abroad," 91.
2. See the CoP Missions Committee Reports and Annual Missions Prayer Charts.

missions—evangelization, church planting, and mission across national frontiers—has been the bedrock of CoP's efforts since its inception. The previous chapters show how, from a humble beginning with a handful of adherents, an unstable administration, and various conflicts from the early 20th century, the CoP, as a Pentecostal denomination, experienced massive growth and planted large congregations both locally and internationally.[3]

Despite the numerous challenges and crises the denomination experienced in the first phase of its history (1937–1962), by the end of 1962, CoP membership, by a conservative estimate, was 26,000 adult adherents ages 13 years and above.[4] Membership in the CoP at this period was determined by one's having been baptized in water by immersion after conversion, regularly attending church services, and being 13 years of age or older.[5] A member was considered inactive or a backslider after staying away from church for more than three months not because of sickness or travel.[6] The church followed up with the backslider, however, until restoration to fellowship, even though not all were recovered.[7]

Criteria for adult membership have not changed. Any person who is 13 years or above, has accepted the Lord Jesus as his or her personal savior, has been baptized by immersion, and is in regular fellowship is considered a member.[8] Admittance into fellowship to participate in the Lord's Supper is by "extension of the right hand of fellowship"—a simple introduction to the congregation with a handshake from the minister or the presiding elder. Backsliders who return to fellowship after two months may also have the "right hand of fellowship" extended to them.[9] The CoP does not baptize infants or children below 13 years.[10] As already

---

3. See Larbi, *Pentecostalism*, 99–273.

4. CoP, Statistical Department Data, 1962. The CoP does not baptize infants, only adults above 13 years.

5. CoP, "Guide to Witness Activities," in *Witness Syllabus*, 1966.

6. The CoP has a column on its reporting form for every assembly, district, area, or ministry to report on backsliders and backsliders recovered. The status of a backslider is clearly spelled out.

7. CoP, *Constitution*, 2010, 114.

8. CoP, *Constitution*, 2010, 114.

9. CoP, *Constitution*, 2010, 114. The pattern of the "right hand of fellowship" comes from Galatians 2:9, where the Apostle Paul asserted that the leaders in Jerusalem extended to him and Barnabas the right hand of fellowship.

10. CoP, *Constitution*, 2010, 8.

stated in the previous chapter, child membership was not acknowledged until after 1971.

The second phase of CoP's history, from 1962 to 2016 and on shows a very different development. This historical epoch is characterized by a stable administration, aggressive evangelism, church planting, and external Christian mission outreach beyond the borders of Ghana into other African countries and nations in many parts of the globe, including the West. By 1973, about a decade after 1962, the number of adults 13 years and above had almost tripled, to 65,773.[11] In 1986, it claimed to have 182,417 adherents 13 and above, and 71,311 children below age 13.[12] From 2000 on, the statistical department recorded total membership as including both children dedicated by the church and baptized adults of 13 or more years. Thus, total membership numbers include both registered children and adult members. A reference to active or adult membership excludes children. The organization, as of December 31, 2013, reported its total worldwide membership to be 2,419,074, of which 2,078,166 (86 percent) are in Ghana. The remaining 340,908, making up 14 percent, represent congregations abroad or missions outside Ghana. The denomination claimed an established presence in 88 countries as of the end of 2013.[13] The total figure of members in Ghana decreased from 2,078,166 to 2,031,716 in the following year (2014) instead of increasing. This was due to the church leadership's concern to look critically at its statistical figures, especially for active membership, in an effort to properly evaluate its *Vision 2013–2018* policy. On April 29, 2016, the National Records, Statistics, and Archives Committee forwarded a memorandum on the subject, "Observation on CoP Membership Management" to the general secretary.[14] This memorandum indicated efforts by the church through this committee to streamline its membership statistics. This was done through head count and proper keeping of church attendance registers at the local assemblies. As of December 31, 2016, the chairman of the church, Apostle Opoku Onyinah, reported the worldwide statistical figures of the CoP in a State of the Church Address: operations in 91 nations, worldwide total membership of 2,804,861, and a total number of 19,941 assemblies (local congregations). This figure constitutes a total

---

11. CoP, Statistical Department Data, 2013.
12. CoP, Statistical Department Data, 2013.
13. CoP, Statistical Department Data, 2013.
14. CoP, General Council Meeting Minutes, 2016, appendix G, 100.

membership of 2,367,253 from Ghana, which forms 84.4 percent, and 437,608 from the external branches (15.6 percent).[15]

This chapter discusses and analyzes the growth patterns and missionary endeavors of the CoP. It addresses factors that have contributed to the church's growth and expansion into missions and discusses church growth principles, methods, and patterns in an effort to bring out the distinctiveness of CoP's methods or patterns in comparison to already existing patterns. These principles include discipleship and training, growing of small groups, effects of socioeconomic engagements, and other patterns, forms, or methods of church growth and missions. They also include factors exclusive to the CoP, such as ministerial formation and the transfer pattern of its ministers from duty posts.

PATTERNS, METHODS, AND PRINCIPLES OF CHURCH GROWTH AND MISSIONS

Basic Pattern for Church Growth: Biological, Transfer, and Conversional Growth

Generally, Pentecostal church growth has been evaluated in terms of soul-winning evangelism buttressed by effective discipleship, church planting, and missions, that is, multiplication of congregations both at home and abroad.[16] Arthur F. Glasser suggested, in three short phrases, what effective church growth and missions entail: "The centre is the proclamation of the gospel, the gathering of converts into existing congregations and the multiplying of new congregations."[17] In practice, however, the means by which a church grows numerically can be "biological," "transfer," "conversion," or a combination.[18] These basic forms are augmented by

---

15. CoP, Chairman Apostle Opoku Onyinah, State of the Church Address, opening service of the 15th session of the Extraordinary Council meeting, Pentecost Convention Centre, May 3, 2017. These figures are from the registers of the local assemblies and head count of the active members taken on December 31, 2015, and again on the same date in 2016.

16. Anderson, *Introduction to Pentecostalism*, 214.

17. Glasser, "Introduction to Church Growth Perspectives," 21. Arthur F. Glasser served as dean of the School of World Mission at Fuller Theological Seminary and associate professor of East Asian mission studies, 1946–1951.

18. McGavran and Arn, *How to Grow a Church*, 57.

discipling and training, growing of small groups, socioeconomic engagements, and other methods.

The CoP growth pattern appears to employ a combination of these methods (biological, transfer, and conversion). Biological growth takes place when the Christian community multiplies through childbirth. Members' offspring are thus trained and oriented (discipled) to become Christians, eventually increasing the church's numbers. Transfer growth takes place when Christians move or are made to move (for church-growth purposes) from one location to another, country to country, city to city, or from a rural setting to an urban area and vice versa. The other type of growth comes by winning others to the Christian faith through conversion—by causing them to turn, for instance, from other faiths towards Christ, in other words, becoming a Christian. In this case, new people are brought in to know and be part of the Christian faith for the first time. This type of growth is asserted to be central for real church-growth analysis, especially in Pentecostal circles.[19] It involves all forms of Pentecostal outreach or soul-winning endeavors such as gospel crusades, open-air gospel rallies, dawn broadcasts, personal evangelism, and cinema evangelism.

Transfer growth brings depletes one location while another increases. Thus, it can be evaluated as a negative trend, for example, in what is euphemistically called "sheep-shuffling." Green had suggested that a great deal that passes for evangelism in fast-growing churches is nothing more than transfer growth from some other section of the fractured church of God.[20] Transfer growth has been described by some missiologists and writers such as William Chadwick as "sheep stealing,"[21] which connotes the poaching of Christians from one denomination or church group into another. However, transfer growth should not always be seen as a negative trend because it can be a means to start another congregation that may multiply.

The CoP uses a form of transfer growth in a very positive sense. For instance, some of its members from one local assembly are ceded off to form the foundation of another congregation of the same denomination. This will be further explained later in this chapter. In practical church-growth mechanisms, all three patterns of growth (biological, transfer, and

---

19. See McGavran and Arn, *How to Grow a Church*.
20. Green, *Evangelism through the Local Church*, 4.
21. Chadwick, *Stealing Sheep*.

conversion) interact to produce a growth effect, as we shall see in these discussions concerning the CoP. Through an interplay of growth mechanisms, an enormous avenue for effective and sustaining church growth can be carried out. Missiologists Donald McGavran and Win Arn have written copiously about the enormous opportunities for church growth. They identify three possible setbacks to effective church growth: carnality in the existing church, nonresponsiveness to evangelization by already committed Christians, and the employing of wrong patterns or methods for this venture.[22]

This study on the CoP, as a pattern of growth in Pentecostalism, begins with conversion of the new adherents through evangelism (both personal and corporate), which is then made effective through discipling of the converts and other mechanisms. The winning of converts through evangelism is not an end in itself; it must be bolstered by other church-growth mechanisms for the required growth, church planting, and effective missions. Peter Wagner, a writer on church growth and missions, rightly commented, "Winning of souls in itself is not quite enough. True commitment to Christ carries with it a simultaneous commitment to the body of Christ. Jesus' great commission tells us to go and make disciples of all nations (Matt. 28:19, 20)."[23] The convert who comes into the church must then be located in a congregation and be discipled to become a conscientious Christian, able to continue the course of church growth.

Pattern of Growth and Missions: The Church of Pentecost

Four growth and mission outreach patterns in the CoP have been identified by this writer. The first is the internal growth generated in Ghana as the home country. The second, a subset of the first, is termed "internal missions." It refers primarily to evangelistic outreach and church planting in geographical locations within Ghana with fewer socioeconomic resources. These include three regions in northern Ghana (Northern, Upper East, and Upper West), parts of the Volta Region, and the Afram Plains. They are designated "internal" because that they are considered missions inside Ghana. These internal missions areas require, aside from the gospel, logistic or material support to stabilize the churches. They include places for worship, public address and musical equipment for

22. McGavran and Arn, *How to Grow a Church*, 6.
23. Wagner, "Three Growth Principles," 83.

worship services, and sometimes material provision for new converts who are very poor or deprived. Although an evangelistic outreach might not be explained as undertaken as an internal mission, mission directorate records specifically identify them as internal missions.[24]

The third and fourth types of CoP growth are its international missions outreach outside Ghana, designated by the church as its "external missions." The third comprises mission outreaches or church planting within other African nations, and the fourth, all evangelistic enterprises and church planting outside the African continent, including the West. Though the church regards both as "external or international missions," the writer has divided these into two groups—African missions and other international missions—in order to clarify how historically the mission outreaches of CoP emerged and progressed. This will also clarify a pattern of belief in the CoP (explained later in this chapter) envisaged as part of the reasons for its mission growth. Detailed discussions on the CoP external missions come in the fifth chapter, on CoP international missions.

In its early years, the evangelistic and missionary outreaches of the church were made by itinerant evangelists and individual adherents who had the zeal to evangelize. Later the Evangelism Ministry, other ministries (e.g., Women's Ministry), and the corporate church got involved. Annual and half-year reports document these evangelistic engagements: crusades, open-air rallies, conventions, personal evangelism, breakfast meetings, media evangelism, market street evangelism, outreach to specific targeted groups (e.g., prostitutes, parliamentarians, chiefs, footballers, Rastafarians, and others).[25] Other nonreportable evangelistic engagements could include dawn broadcasts (where individuals or groups proclaim salvation through Jesus Christ at dawn or in the early hours of the day) and gospel night (a monthly Sunday evening program set aside exclusively for the proclamation of the gospel). Through these crusades, rallies, dawn broadcasts, and gospel nights, individuals (new converts) are trained on how to evangelize effectively.[26] Reports of the number of these evangelistic engagements show, for instance, the number of rallies held through the Evangelism Ministry in Ghana in 2013 in comparison

---

24. See CoP, Missions Reports.

25. See CoP, Annual or Half-Year Reports and Evangelism Ministry Reports.

26. Evangelism Director Apostle Aseidu, in a presentation for follow-up training session in Lomé, Togo, recounted how he was oriented to evangelize through gospel nights and dawn broadcasts, then afterwards rallies and crusades.

with 2012: 16,067 and 12,970, respectively.[27] In 2016 the church recorded that 498,144 out of the 1,580,030 adult members (13 years and above) are engaged in active evangelism, which is 31.5 percent of its adult membership.[28]

Historically, as the church expanded, its evangelistic activities developed into missionary activities within and outside of Ghana. This zeal for evangelism is attributed to an ignited passion in the individuals through personal experience with the Holy Spirit after conversion.[29] The denomination, through its functional ministries (evangelism, women, and youth) also makes an effort as part of its rudimentary discipleship to train its members for rigorous evangelism and church planting as soon as they join. The ministries have effective soul winning as a prime aspect of their modus operandi, and it is an item on their regular progress reports.[30]

In the CoP, even secular structures meant for social service, such as the hospitals and schools, still have soul winning as part of their motives for operation.[31] For instance, the Pentecost Hospital at Madina in Accra has a chaplain whose duty includes counseling people and leading converts to Christ. The Pentecost Hospital in Madina has a time set aside for devotions every morning and very special services on Wednesdays in which patients are encouraged to make decisions for Christ. The PENTSOS report for 2016 records on evangelism as follows:

> Evangelism: According to reports received from the heads, many souls were won for Christ through their usual Wednesday worship periods and other social programmes organised, more than 100 souls were won. The chaplaincy department of Pentecost Hospital, Madina saw over 558 clients. Those who accepted Jesus are 31, those were haunted by past sins confessed their sins and were delivered from guilt were 122, 8 were baptised in water, 12 backsliders were restored and 364 were counselled.[32]

---

27. CoP, Annual Executive Summary Reports, 2013, 195.

28. CoP, Annual Statistical Report, 2016.

29. Larbi, *Pentecostalism*, 243; and Leonard, *Giant in Ghana*, 76. Interviews with the evangelism director and missions director of the CoP, Apostles M. C. Aseidu and Stephen Kofi Baidoo, confirm this.

30. See CoP, Ministries Reports Forms and Procedures.

31. See CoP, Social Services Manual (core philosophy, principles and values and mission policy).

32. CoP, PENTSOS Annual Report, 2016.

The CoP also has chaplains attached to the Ghana Prisons Services and the Ghana Armed Forces. Through the chaplains in the prisons several prisoners have become Christians. There are CoP local assemblies in the prisons, which have their own leadership structures just like the churches outside the prisons. For instance, the inmates' church at Nsawam Prison has a baptized membership of 1,231, according to their 2016 report.[33] Every block in the prison has a number of home cells of not more than 15 members. The church has constructed church buildings in some of the prisons in Ghana. These churches in the prisons have leaders who have been ordained as deacons, deaconesses, and elders. The church has also built 17 baptisteries in the prisons across Ghana. The Evangelism Ministry has Prison Ministry volunteers who are trained to minister to prisoners in custody and to provide aftercare for released prisoners. This is headed by the Chaplain General of Ghana Prisons, Chief Inspector James Tetteh, who is an ordained Apostle of the CoP and a National Executive member of the Evangelism Ministry. At the end of 2016, 2,405 souls were won for Christ, out of which 468 were baptized in water.

The CoP thus appears to engage in more corporate than individual methods of evangelism, involving the whole church. As a result, each member as well as the whole church community endeavors to take over communities and villages for Christ. This corporate involvement in the growth pattern and missions of CoP stems from very interesting traditional beliefs. The organization's adherents believe that its thriving fulfills prophetic utterances made by the pioneers of the organization. As a Pentecostal denomination, CoP believes in the efficacy of prophetic utterances as part of its spirituality.[34] This researcher holds the opinion that part of the CoP's drive and efforts in aggressive evangelism, church planting, and missions into other nations is propelled, apart from the scriptural mandates for evangelism (Matt 28:18–20; Mark 16:15–18) and other factors mentioned, by these beliefs of the CoP about these prophecies or prophetic utterances. The prophetic utterance stated that the CoP had been chosen by God to be the light from Africa that will spearhead and influence the outreach of the gospel into the whole of Ghana, Africa, and the rest of the world. This will be accomplished as a result of a special covenant relationship that the denomination has with God.[35]

---

33. CoP, Prisons Ministry Report, 2016. Data on prison ministry in the rest of this paragraph comes from this report.

34. Larbi, *Pentecostalism*, 250–51.

35. CoP, Covenant Document, 1993.

In its early history, the corporate body is said to have believed that it had a unique covenant with God as a prophetic mandate to spearhead the preaching of the gospel in every part of Africa. This belief existed from the early beginnings of the church when adherents numbered no more than 20. Later on, they assert, this prophetic utterance was extended to include reaching out not only into the African continent but also to the rest of the world.[36] Even though the scriptural injunction for global evangelization commands the whole body of Christ, the CoP considers itself to have a special prophetic mandate to reach the whole world with the gospel as a light from black Africa. Other prophetic utterances regarding its internal growth pattern were also said to have been made by God through the Holy Spirit to the early founding fathers.

In interviews, some of the leaders attributed much of the church's corporate effort in evangelism to the belief in these prophetic utterances. The denomination from time to time reaffirms this belief to its congregations through special orientations. For instance, on April 25, 1999, at the seventh session of the church's Extraordinary Council meetings held under the theme "Covenant Renewal," the church took the time to reaffirm what it describes as "God's Covenant with the CoP," in which the entire denomination was called upon to reaffirm their commitment to the part of the covenant that includes, among other concerns, aggressive evangelism and church planting in other nations.[37] Alfred Koduah, an apostle and former general secretary of CoP, presenting a lecture during the 50th Anniversary Celebration of the denomination, mentioned this ardent belief as the reason for the church's successful growth when he said, "Apart from the special covenant that the church believes to have with God, which serves as the invisible supernatural driving force behind the church's ministry, there are other theological and administrative factors."[38] In effect, Koduah placed this belief ahead of every other factor promoting the church's growth. Church leaders regularly remind those at various forums of these prophecies. And the church populace believes that the spread of the church hinges on their special covenant.

Larbi affirmed these beliefs as being the basis of the CoP's missions endeavors when he wrote, "This philosophy of mission is based on two main theological perspectives. First, based on some past prophecies,

36. CoP, *Minister's Handbook*, 2008, 3.

37. CoP, Circular Letter to All Assemblies from the Chairman's Office, April 25, 1999.

38. Koduah, "Church of Pentecost," 110.

reinforced by recent ones, it is strongly held that God has told them that, He would give the whole nation of Ghana to them and that, God has also promised to take them to various places of the world."[39] Second, he said, "the church believes it has a unique identity,"[40] referring here to the covenant relationship that causes the adherents to believe their teachings and doctrines are unique.

The members of the church feel an obligation to start churches wherever they find themselves and then report to the international office for them to send oversight leadership. The management of the church makes sure that the scarce resources generated from Ghana—which until recently was classified by the World Bank as a highly indebted poor country (HIPC)—be used not only for her congregations in Ghana but for other national branches as well. In reality, a good proportion of its internally generated funds are spread to every part of the globe where missions calls demand. Its periodic missions reports indicate property (buildings, plots of land, vehicles, Bible schools, and so on) bought with huge sums of money from Ghana in places such as the UK, South Africa, Nigeria, India, Pakistan, Portugal, Côte d'Ivoire, and Benin, to name a few.[41] The church also sends out very competent personnel, mostly the cream of its experienced ministers, administrators, and other logistics support to these mission posts. Recently, two national churches have been granted autonomy: the CoP in Côte d'Ivoire and in the Republic of Benin.[42] This implies that they will be operated by a constitution of their own and not directly under the International Executive Council of the CoP. The report at the end of 2013 indicated that the CoP in Côte d'Ivoire and Benin claimed a membership of 65,458 and 66,265, respectively.[43] The property acquired by the CoP in these nations through the efforts of the corporate churches—whether from Côte d'Ivoire and Ghana or from Benin and Ghana—became the national church property of these two autonomous nations.[44]

39. Larbi, *Pentecostalism*, 253.

40. Larbi, *Pentecostalism*, 252.

41. See CoP, Missions Annual Report, 2013.

42. See "Report on Autonomous Nations," in CoP, Missions Annual Report, 2013, 8.

43. CoP, Missions Annual Report, 2013.

44. CoP, Modality for Autonomy Report as part of Regionalization Committee report chaired by Apostle Opoku Onyinah, 1998.

Internal Growth in CoP: Discipleship and Training, Growing Small Groups, and Socioeconomic Intervention

As described above, the growth pattern and methods of the CoP does not hinge on evangelism alone, in the sense of proclamation of the gospel. Other mechanisms also grow the church and stabilize the converts who come in. These include discipleship and training, growing of small groups, socioeconomic engagements, and others.

Discipleship and Training and CoP Local Congregations or Assemblies

Discipling may be understood as the processes by which people who initially come to know the Lord Jesus Christ subsequently become baptized Christians and progress in perfecting or growing in grace through regular instruction of biblical truths.[45] Some church growth principles suggest that right from the outset the new converts must be made into leaders as part of the discipleship, alongside training and recruiting other leaders for church growth. MacGavran and Arn have noted that, in the New Testament, church growth involved the training of leaders by the church while they engaged in church activities, as a form of training on the job.[46] Thus, corporate principles of church growth, in addition to conversion, must include discipleship and training.

The CoP has its own particular pattern of discipleship and internal growth, which underpins the growth of every CoP local congregation at home or abroad. It can be described, from the writer's participatory point of view, as a system of local or community-based and lay-leadership driven congregations. The CoP designates each unit of its local or community-based congregations an "assembly," such as "Takoradi Assembly," "Effiakuma Assembly," or "Kaneshie Assembly," according to the location of the congregation. Thus, the CoP assembly is a congregational unit of adherents, referred to as members, living within a particular community where they are close-knit. The congregation is led or overseen by one or more lay leaders.

The CoP, until recently, has not emphasized large congregational church systems, or megachurches. The church thrives through

---

45. Hull, *Complete Book of Discipleship*.
46. McGavran and Arn, *How to Grow a Church*, 79.

multiplying its existing congregations. In addition to growth by planting new churches, the number of assemblies also increases through the division of or ceding-off part of an existing assembly to start a new one nearby, which grows both numerically and in spiritual maturity. In establishing the new congregations, sometimes factors such as the financial and material strength of both congregations (new and parent) and availability of leaders are considered for sustainability. However, such new congregations must strive from the outset to be independent and self-supporting. Thus, the CoP grows internally by increasing its membership through soul-winning evangelism and by establishing new congregations in particular local communities and appointing lay leaders to oversee them. However, the system does not come without challenges, including the non-availability of places for worship and adequately trained leaders to man them. Thus assemblies may be started in classrooms, rented premises, and even under trees in particularly remote areas.

Based on the need, availability, and numerical strength of the new congregation, the parent congregation planting the assembly may cede some leaders to the new branch. Subsequently, other lay leaders are raised or trained from the same community or from the church environs. In the initial stages the new congregation is considered a nursery assembly. In the CoP, a congregation is considered a full-fledged assembly when it has more than 12 congregants who are baptized in water and it can be self-sustaining enough to pay its monthly tithes.[47] The average active membership of a local assembly is between 140 and 158.[48] However, in some of the cities and larger towns, especially in the urban areas, some CoP local assemblies have several hundred or a few thousand active members. These include some "worship centres" and PIWCs. The PIWC of Atomic, an area in Accra, for instance, claims a membership of 1,500 and more.[49] The members of a local assembly are close-knit, and the assemblies are located within walking distance or where easily and quickly reached by public transport. Asamoah-Gyadu, trying to give a meaningful description for this pattern of the CoP's growth, wrote, "The CoP community-based approach to church planting makes assemblies

47. The tithe is a biblical injunction for adherents to pay 10 percent of their income or wages to the local church. In the CoP, tithes are paid monthly and used for the administration of the church and to pay the workers, especially full-time ministers. See the CoP statistical report form 2012.

48. CoP, Statistical Department Annual Report, 2016.

49. CoP, Area Annual Report, Madina, 2016.

within the same geographical area not only accessible to people but also, fostering stronger communal bonds as members were likely to be staying shorter distances from each other. The community-oriented congregations engender meaningful fellowship, discipleship and prompt pastoral care."[50]

The members of a newly opened assembly are thoroughly discipled and trained from the outset through participation in morning devotional services, Wednesday Bible teaching, vigorous Friday morning and evening prayer meetings, tarry night meetings (all-night prayer vigils), ministry participation (evangelism, women, youth), and open-air services (rallies and crusades), Sunday evening gospel nights, and so forth. It is not unusual for a new convert, a few days in the CoP, to be given a platform to testify about his or her conversion, share an experience with God, give a word of exhortation, or say a prayer. Most of the Friday prayer meetings emphasize the baptism of the Holy Spirit, culminating in the experience of glossolalia, or speaking in tongues. Apostle Michael Collins Asiedu, CoP Evangelism Director, asserts that the final expectation regarding the baptism in the Holy Spirit as part of discipleship for new converts is for aggressive energy for personal testimony and evangelism.[51] Many converts, especially in the rural areas, are unlettered. This kind of training, such as in the morning devotions, provides Bible knowledge. Participation in gospel night services prepares them for reaching out with the gospel to others. Further aspects of CoP's discipleship to train the new convert to be a responsible Christian and soul winner will be discussed in chapter 6.

The example of the Kaneshie Assembly demonstrates this pattern of growth. This CoP congregation has experienced growth and multiplied into other local community-based congregations in the manner described above. The Kaneshie Assembly was established in 1952 as a local congregation of the CoP.[52] Beginning from 1952, it periodically ceded off part of its membership or started a new congregation to form other assemblies as its membership increased. It therefore became part of Accra Central District, comprised of six local assemblies—Kaneshie, Korle Gonno, Bubuashie Number One, Bubuashie Number Two, Mataheko,

50. Asamoah-Gyadu, "'Promise Is for You.'"

51. Interview with evangelism director of CoP at Bolgatanga Crusade, November 2011.

52. Gakpetor, "Small-Medium Sized Church." Gakpetor used Kaneshie Assembly in his study as a case of a typical CoP medium-sized congregation.

and Odorkor—all its offshoots. It then multiplied by dividing itself into other communities within the Kaneshie environs until it had acquired the status of a CoP district known as Kaneshie District.[53] Most of the assemblies currently forming the Kaneshie, Dansoman, and Kasoa administrative areas of the church emerged out of this Kaneshie District.[54]

Around 1982, the membership (aged 13 years and up) of the old Kaneshie Assembly was 250, with 18 ordained lay leaders (six elders, six deacons, and six deaconesses). As the mother of all the congregations making up the Kaneshie, Dansoman, and Kasoa Areas, the Kaneshie Assembly had multiplied at the end of 2012 to an estimated figure of more than 321 local assemblies or congregations and about 120,913 active registered members.[55] As of 2014, the Kaneshie Assembly had grown again to an adult membership of 2,533 and a children's membership of 268, with 77 ordained lay leaders comprised of 25 elders, 27 deacons, and 25 deaconesses. The church now operates two shifts for its Sunday services.

"Single Assembly" District

Due to increased membership and the unavailability of space for the creation of new congregations, the CoP has adopted double services or shift services in the same worship centers. Each of these shift services operates under its own leadership and management. Many CoP congregations in the cities (such as Dr. Wyatt, Merry Villas) have adopted this means to address issues of growth and expansion caused by lack of space, changing trends, and other socioeconomic factors. They run separate assemblies under different management or lay leadership and are separate entities in respect to their management (accountability, oversight, etc.), but they are hosted in the same building and are under the same district minister. For instance, Kaneshie Assembly could have English Assembly, Kaneshie

---

53. A district, as explained in chapter 3, is a cluster of local congregations within a geographical area determined by the church. Most districts have between five and 40 assemblies. They are under the supervision of a full-time minister. Recently some single congregations have been placed under a full-time minister and referred to as worship centres. The worship centres have large congregations, some ranging between 500 to 1,200 members.

54. "Area" is CoP terminology referring to a cluster of districts (between eight and 25 or more) under the supervision of an area head, who is either a senior minister, apostle, prophet, or evangelist. See chapter 3.

55. CoP, Annual Executive Summary Reports, 2012.

No. 1, and Kaneshie No. 2 meeting in the same building, but they would worship at different times and with different lay-leadership teams and management.

Other assemblies with large congregations (between 1,000 and 3,000) have been placed under a pastor and designated a "single assembly district." That one assembly has a district pastor who is a trained minister and a set of lay leaders (elders, deacons, and deaconesses). Such assemblies are identified as worship centres. In line with this same pattern, the CoP in 1989 began raising megachurches in the cities and national and regional capitals to address the needs of its youth who were losing touch with the traditional taste of worship (due to long periods spent at school) and of members of academia and expatriates who might not be conversant with the local dialects. These PIWCs (Pentecost International Worship Centres) use English as the language for its services.

The assemblies in the CoP use predominately local vernaculars for their services. Due to its principle of establishing community-based congregations, the CoP majors in reaching communities in their local languages. This strategy is seen as one of its major advantages for acceptance, growth, and expansion. Nevertheless, partly due to the more recent trend of creating megachurches and partly due to other factors such as inability to manage its numbers, the CoP for the past few years (2010–2016), has been actively investigating other avenues for providing effective pastoral care and growth. Its major discussion since 2010 has been on growing small-group systems such as home cells and Bible study groups, as is done in many other Pentecostal denominations worldwide.[56]

Growing Small Groups as CoP Home Cells and Bible Studies

An arguably important follow-up to the cause of evangelism as part of discipleship is the growing of small-group systems. In numerically larger or growing congregations, the entire congregation is broken into small groups for effective management. These small groups, many suggest, provide a source of strength, power, and outreach to change and move churches and communities into growth and world mission.[57] Many of the largest churches in the world today, such as David Yonggi Cho's Yoido

---

56. CoP, National Bible Study, Home Cells and Lay leadership Training Report, 2010.

57. See McGavran and Arn, *How to Grow a Church*.

Full Gospel Church in Seoul, South Korea, have small groups as their foundational principle for growth.[58] Whereas in some cases small groups would have to be created, in others, the existing church structures have to be revamped. The ultimate result of such small groups should be church growth. Comiskey commented that "if small groups of existing Christians meet together, study the Bible together, pray together, get to know each other, feel kindly towards each other and the process stops there, much has not been gained or achieved." Every small group, he opines, must be open-minded towards the world and active in evangelism and church planting.[59]

The CoP, like many growing denominations, is seriously discussing and restructuring themselves into small-group systems.[60] Advocates argue that growing small groups in the church's system will be able to multiply ministry to meet the need of its adherents,[61] including being a tool for continually carrying out leadership development in church growth. At the same time, they hold that the growing church should not endeavor to break into small groups only for its enlargement and numerical growth, but rather must make its prime objective the multiplication of congregations in other nations.

Regarding these discussions, this study argues that the CoP in itself already has a system of small-group churches that effectively and adequately addresses its discipleship issues. The CoP, from the outset, was primarily rural based, and most of its congregations are community based, and its members and leaders are close-knit. These leaders are raised from within the community and closely associated with the members. The CoP assembly or congregation system, especially in the rural areas, provides fellowship, pastoral care, and also aid in raising leaders. These are characteristics of a home-cell system that its proponents use to argue for its value for church growth. In this writer's view, further breaking up the CoP assemblies, especially those in the rural communities, into smaller cells may be helpful, but could engender logistical, leadership, and other problems. However, the small-group system should be very appropriate for urban churches, which are growing in membership

---

58. Towns, Vaughan, and Seifert, *Complete Book of Church Growth*.

59. Comiskey, *Reap the Harvest*, n.p.

60. See CoP, *Vision 2018*. For other churches in the US, see Towns, Vaughan, and Seifert, *Complete Book of Church Growth*.

61. Asserted by Apostle Stephen Kofi Baidoo, current Bible study and home cell coordinator for CoP.

and have very limited space for breaking up. These include the single assembly districts and the PIWC structures.

Historically, the home-cell and Bible-study system of church growth cannot be considered entirely new in the CoP. Its origin dates back to 1979 in Kwadaso Assembly when Pastor David Mills was the district pastor (1974–1982).[62] Other pastors, such as Johnson Agyemang-Baduh, had used it effectively. The concept was put in practice during the early 1980s, mainly as morning devotions by some pastors, who went through pastoral training at the Bible Training School, under the leadership of Pastor David Mills. At the 1998 General Council meeting of the church, the first corporate stance was taken to use the system as a tool for discipleship, church planting, and growth management. The system faced a lot of challenges until it was relaunched in 2005 as mandatory for all CoP assemblies.[63] Some of these challenges included lack of leadership, nonattendance by district pastors, and a lack of convenient places for meetings. The writer sees these challenges as arising from the breaking up of a system that has been tested over a period as proactive or working.

Beginning from 2010, the CoP leadership has focused on turning the megachurches into cell-unit churches. In this regard, the smallest congregation of the CoP is the home cell and not the local assembly. A national committee was instituted comprising Apostle Dr. Stephen Kofi Baidoo as national coordinator, Apostle John Appiah Aidoo as deputy chairman, and, as members, Pastor Franklin Agbovi-Hushie, Pastor Matthew Wettey-Larbi, Pastor Ben Ali, Pastor Henry Ako-Nai, and Pastor Samuel Gakpetor. Their responsibility was to coordinate the running of the home cells and Bible studies in the church and particularly to provide the periodic home cell and Bible study guide for the Bible study leaders and the cell groups. They have been able to formulate a home-cell leadership training manual and a periodic home cell and Bible study guide since 2012.[64] In 2016, the leadership of the church decided that the work of the National Bible Study and Home Cells Committee and that of the National Lay-Leadership Training Committee were complementary enough for them to be merged into one, in order to avoid conflicts in carrying out duties. Thus, in 2016 the name National Bible Study and Home Cell Committee was changed to National Discipleship and Lead-

---

62. Agyemang-Baduh, "Home Cell System in CoP."
63. Agyemang-Baduh, "Home Cell System in CoP."
64. CoP, *Home Cells Leadership Training Manual.*

ership Development Committee. This committee therefore took charge of discipleship and lay-leadership manuals. The number of active home cells recorded in the church in 2016 was estimated to be 53,639.[65]

Evangelism and Socioeconomic Engagements as a Pattern of Church Growth in the CoP

As noted for Pentecostals in general, the CoP grows numerically primarily through conversion of souls from evangelism outreaches and other methods. "Aggressive evangelism" is their starting pattern after which other methods follow. As Anderson noted, "Pentecostalism is notorious for its sometimes aggressive forms of evangelism and from its beginning, was characterized by an emphasis on evangelistic outreach, its highest priority in mission strategy."[66] The CoP is no exception in this regard. Evangelism aimed at converting others through active witnessing and soul winning is clearly its starting point for growth and perhaps its major priority in mission strategy.

However, for effective church growth, evangelism alone cannot stand isolated. It must be undertaken together with other church-planting and discipleship methods buttressed by socioeconomic and political interventions (human welfare issues). This writer agrees with Donald McGavran that "the major task, opportunity and imperative in the church is to multiply churches in the increasing numbers of respective people of the earth."[67] Yet this must be done in conjunction with addressing other important socioeconomic and political factors that make for holistic mission. Addition of this component need not undermine the emphasis on self-propagation through evangelism and church growth, as some have contended. Rather, it prevents Pentecostals from being inward-looking, triumphalistic, and seemingly unconcerned with or oblivious to other serious human welfare issues, such as those affecting the socio-political context of the converted, especially where there is an oppressive government.[68]

65. CoP, *Annual Executive Summary Reports*, 2016, 258.

66. Anderson, *Introduction to Pentecostalism*, 214.

67. McGavran, *Understanding Church Growth*, 63. Donald McGavran was the founding dean of the School of World Mission and professor of mission, church growth, and South Asian studies at Fuller Theology Seminary, widely known for his writings in the areas of church growth and cross-cultural communication of the gospel.

68. Anderson, *Introduction to Pentecostalism*, 207.

José Miguez Bonino thoughtfully inquired of Pentecostals whether the "global challenge of missions can be ideologically diverted from a concern with the urgent challenges of situations at home."[69] This writer suggests that it cannot be ideologically diverted but must be inclusive. This work argues that, as part of a holistic mission agenda, Pentecostal mission such as that of the CoP must recognize a need for social services alongside evangelizing the nations. These social services must address the socioeconomic and political circumstances of the converted that prevent them from leading fulfilling and fruitful lives. In more recent years the CoP has encouraged evangelism alongside social intervention with the formation of PENTSOS, mentioned in chapter 3. However, this writer suggests that the church can do more in this regard than already achieved.

Much of the CoP has thought that James McKeown, the missionary founder, did not encourage such social intervention. Larbi, however, argues the opposite. He notes that James McKeown did encourage such social interventions, but it seemed his position did not encourage it at the expense of evangelism.[70] Despite the effort being made by the church in social interventions, very little effort in that regard appears in the church's mission fields. This is partly due to the fact that the work of PENTSOS is mostly situated in Ghana. The church's overemphasis on evangelism in the mission field at the expense of intervening to meet the social needs of the mission-planted churches leaves much to be desired. This applies particularly to nations in Africa found to be socioeconomically deprived. The church must therefore augment its program on social action as part of its missionary efforts in order to enhance its holistic ministry. This can be done through strengthening its mission churches in the West, considered socioeconomically able to support this course of action.

Ministerial Formation of the Personnel in the CoP

Another unique CoP characteristic important for its growth is the way human resources (such as ministers and lay leaders) are developed. The various discipleship and training programs and mechanisms aimed at growth in the CoP described above and in chapter 3 eventually become the avenue for developing human resources for the church's internal

---

69. Bonino, "Pentecostal Missions Is More," 284.

70. See James McKeown's circular letter on social issues, Accra, October 26, 1954.

growth and missions abroad. The CoP's unique system for nurturing, training, and forming its leaders—such as deacons, deaconesses, elders, pastors, and other senior ministers (evangelists, prophets, and apostles) who oversee the local congregations and mission posts—produces leaders who have a mark of maturity, dependability, fortitude, and sound character. This character of its leaders makes secession from the church minimal as compared to other emerging Charismatic churches.

The CoP forms leaders by passing the individual through the ranks in the local assemblies, as training on the job. The leader's progression to the next level is explicitly or implicitly subjected to proof of credibility and integrity. For instance, someone can be made (or rather called to be) a deacon through the observation of his voluntary services and his ability in handling positions in the functional ministries, such as being a secretary to the assembly's Evangelism Ministry. A deacon does not automatically become an elder, but moves up only when he has proved his service and commitment to authorities above him. Through the same procedure, recommendation to the pastorate in the CoP goes through the presbytery of the local assembly, which bears witness of one's gifting or calling and maturity for the task. In the early days of the church, ministers were appointed from among committed members of the Witness Movement.

The idea that any interested person could become a pastor as a vocation, for instance, by attending Bible training and applying to become a CoP pastor, is not the norm. An individual who has established his own church could be accepted in the ministry of CoP after relinquishing his previous position and agreeing to start afresh as a CoP member. Even in that situation one may not automatically become an elder or a pastor. The recommendation to a pastorate is first and foremost through the leadership of the local assembly, which bears witness of one's maturity, dependability, and integrity of commitment to the church.

A member or an adherent's observed potential in leadership and ministry is rigorously subjected to proof. One of the CoP's senior ministers who is an executive member commented after an ordination service, "You are recommended, assigned or posted after you have proved yourself."[71] This written requirement that forms part of cherished practice may include one's gifting, commitment, faithfulness, and sound moral character and integrity.[72] For instance, having ability for evangelism, per-

---

71. Apostle Ekow Badu Woode, comments at an ordination service for his new ministers called into the pastorate, Asokwa, Kumasi, August 2015.

72. CoP, *Minister's Handbook*, 2014; see also CoP, *Missions Handbook*, 2008.

forming miracles, healings, or signs and wonders does not necessarily qualify one as a recognized evangelist in the church. One may not be called into a pastorate in the CoP simply because of ability to organize and administer programs. One's worthiness, trustworthiness, and other capabilities would be tested. An unschooled or minimally educated but gifted and committed member may be preferred to an educated but uncommitted individual.

The church has records of district pastors and overseers who were not lettered yet performed their duties creditably through the influence of the Holy Spirit. They include Pastor Samuel Attah, who was called into the ministry of the CoP in 1977. He served meritoriously, according to church records, in four different stations: Sawla (1977–1980), Lawra (1980–1983), Nakpanduri (1983–1989), and finally Damango, where he retired in 1991 after working for three years. Though unschooled, Samuel Attah had learned to read his Bible though the help of Kweku Edusei, a church member, before being called into ministry. While still in ministry he undertook adult education and other church-oriented ministerial training to improve himself and his ministry.[73]

This same standard is observed for the rest of what the CoP refers to as "higher callings," such as area head, national head, ministry director, prophet, apostle, general secretary, international missions director, or chairman. Each subsequent responsibility in CoP leadership goes through the same process of training. This is an aspect of the way the church and its missions abroad grow. Through this pattern of ministerial formation, particular callings (pastors, evangelists, area or national heads) are harnessed and sent to oversee mission posts. This procedure of selecting, nurturing, and forming leaders in the church helps decrease secession of leaders from the church. This trend of ministerial formation and the part it plays in CoP's missions will be discussed further in the next chapter when dealing with postings of ministers as missionaries to other locations around the globe.

CoP Ministers' Posting and Transfers as a Mechanism for Growth

The next important aspect of the transfer growth mechanism employed by CoP is the assigning of the ministerial locations of the field workers. The CoP has a system of moving its field ministers from one location of

---

73. Asare-Duah, *Gallant Soldiers*, 3:105–7.

posting to another that is very different from other classical Pentecostal denominations. For instance, in the Assemblies of God, its ministers are stationed in the same location with the same congregation, only being moved on rare occasions. Further research on these two systems of posting of ministers may ascertain their effects on church growth.

In the CoP, apart from the three principal executive officers stationed at the church's headquarters (chairman, general secretary, international missions director) and other ministry directors who have mandated or stipulated periods of tenure in office according to the church's constitution, every other minister or field worker could be transferred from one posting location to another at any time. This is without regard to time spent in previous places by the minister, whether foreign or local locations, or the minister's educational background, tribe, ethnicity, age, or any such factors. The least amount of time a minster could spend in a particular posting is eight months, and the maximum is determined by the sending body, the International Executive Council of the CoP, when it is deemed appropriate or needful. The International Executive Council of the church is expected to prayerfully and carefully regulate and determine these postings under the leadership and guidance of the Holy Spirit. The chairman of the church, Apostle Opoku Onyinah, confirmed that this is the most difficult aspect of their task as a council.[74] The church sends its tested, proven, and very experienced ministers to the mission fields. They also send newly called and trained minsters to remote locations without regard to their tribal roots, educational background, or age. For instance, CoP congregations in northern Ghana are observed to be growing phenomenally because newly called ministers, who are young and energetic, some of them highly educated, are sent to these places to "prove" their ministry after a year in the seminary.[75] These are places in Ghana to which many churches will not send their ministers due to their remoteness and harsh economic conditions.

In his State of the Church Address presented on May 5, 2015, the executive chairman of the CoP named and commended the Walewale Area of the church, located in the northern region of Ghana, for establishing

---

74. Apostle Opoku Onyinah commented at the heads' and policymakers' meeting at Pentecost Convention Centre, November 2015, when addressing the area heads concerning their difficulties in the postings of ministers for 2016.

75. See CoP, Chairman's State of the Church Address, Pentecost Convention Centre, May 5, 2015, which points out that since 2011 areas in the north have successively led in the number of souls won and baptized as well as assemblies opened.

53 local congregations or assemblies in 2014. The area head of Walewale, Apostle Samuel Gakpetor, confirmed that this achievement was due to the posting of a new minister into that remote part of the region where there were no established churches.[76] The young minister, stationed at Temaa District, also won the chairman's award for opening the largest number of assemblies (16) in the Church of Pentecost in 2014. This trend in the CoP is not extraordinary; on the contrary, it is a regular occurrence, especially in the northern and upper regions of Ghana.

The chairman of the CoP has instituted an annual award as a motivation for districts in the church that open the most assemblies in the year. For instance, Temaa District was given GHC20,000.00 from the chairman's office for that feat.[77] Zabilla and Basyonde districts in the Upper East Regions, Bolgatanga Area of the church also received such awards in 2011 and 2012.[78]

Generally, though this type of transfer or posting of ministers in the CoP may have its own challenges, it appears to inject vibrancy into the congregations from time to time. They also relieve the ministers of familiarity in one location that might lead to work fatigue and in turn retard growth. In Ghana, where there are many tribes and languages, the CoP is one church that uniquely operates without tribal inclinations. Its ministers operate anywhere without complexities due to academic requirements. The church's records show that as new minsters move into different places, the congregations get revamped, leading to the opening of more assemblies and increased membership and financial contributions. However, it also happens that some such postings, instead of aiding growth, rather slow it down at particular ministerial locations. This is especially so in cases where the new minister does not live up to expectations. This can happen due to many factors, such as the receptiveness of the people to the new minister, the temperament and ministerial gifting of the individual minister, and other human relationship tendencies.

The church has a program in place by which, at the end of each year, the main stakeholders meet at a General Council to report on every responsibility. On the last day of the General Council meetings, the regulated mandatory postings and appointments to serve in various capacities and to upgrade positions to those the church refers to as higher

---

76. The CoP area head of Walewale, Pastor Samuel Gakpetor, confirmed this in an interview at Pentecost Transit Quarters in Accra, August 5, 2016.

77. Confirmed by the area head of Walewale, Pastor Samuel Gakpetor.

78. Confirmed by the chairman's cover letters dated in 2011 and 2012, respectively.

callings (pastor, evangelist, prophet, apostle) is read. This has come to be known as the reading of the "White Paper." Every year, anticipation of the reading of the White Paper in CoP's General Council meetings runs very high, as it comes with mixed expectations about appointments, new callings, and locations of new postings. The White Paper determines the future of the CoP minister as a worker of the church. Each minister is obliged to comply with the White Paper without question. This has become a procedure that sets the future direction of the individual minister and the church as a whole. The entire church sees it as direction by the Holy Spirit, which demands no questioning. Though there are incidents of discontentment after the reading of the White Paper, each minister is obliged to comply. The Rev. John Glass, the general superintendent of the Elim Pentecostal Churches in the UK, conceded, after the reading of the General Council decisions in 2012, at which he represented Elim Churches in the UK, that such a procedure might be difficult to implement in the Elim Church.

However, the present writer argues that this procedure makes the church's stability and growth more effective. The posting of the minsters in the CoP has become a very important aspect of its ministerial formation for the church's growth. For instance, in a regular army, such as the Ghana Army, one progresses in rank according to years of service. In the CoP, one's subordinate can rise to become one's senior or boss, and yet there is a cordial working understanding. Apostle Opoku Onyinah, the present executive chairman of the church, trained Apostle M. K. Ntumy, his immediate superior. M. K. Ntumy became the executive chairman while Opoku Onyinah served under him as an area head and a rector of the Pentecost University.[79] Subsequently, Opoku Onyinah became the executive chairman while Ntumy served under him as a national head of Germany and Director of Literary Works.[80] This type of posting arrangement is not unusual in the CoP, but rather forms part of the church's growth mechanisms. The church believes that it is part of the workings of the Holy Spirit in forming, shaping, creating, and training individuals to occupy various needed positions in the church.[81] Oppong Asare-Duah wrote in his book *The Gallant Soldiers of the Church of Pentecost* that part of the covenant the church believes it has with God is that he will

---

79. See CoP, General Council Decisions and Appointments, 2007.

80. See CoP, General Council Decisions and Appointments, 2014.

81. This was affirmed by both Apostle Opoku Onyinah and M. K. Ntumy at the Heads' Meeting of the church, Pentecost Convention Centre, May 10, 2016.

periodically provide ministers for the church. He wrote of that "aspect of this covenant which forms part of CoP's ardent beliefs is that God has promised to make or create leaders for the Church to steer its affairs from time to time."[82]

The White Paper, apart from the posting of ministers, appointments, and upgrading to higher callings, also announces other decisions. These include disciplinary measures against any person or group of persons whose actions may contravene the General Council's policies and granting temporary leave for the sick. The disciplinary measures include dismissals and downgrading of ministers whose misconduct in any way undermines the effectiveness of the church's growth. Such misconduct includes inefficiency at work, disregard of General Council policies, ethical misbehavior such as drunkenness or sexual misconduct, idolatry, or false doctrine.[83]

INTERNAL MISSIONS

The church's pattern of growth, through the mechanisms discussed, has not centered only in the southern parts of Ghana. Its expansion has extended to the whole nation, including the northern part and also outside the national boundary—in anticipation of fulfilling the prophetic utterances discussed earlier. In the period between the late 1940s and early 1960s, the CoP began to expand enormously, both internally and externally, into areas regarded as internal missions and some nearby African countries. While individual members endeavored to reach out with the gospel, two or three ministers were sent out with the commissions to establish more churches. In October 1953, after James McKeown had returned from the furlough in which he was dismissed from the British Apostolic fraternity, a General Council meeting was organized at Koforidua.[84] Three persons were said to have given a prophetic message that God was about to send them in twos and threes to other parts of the nation and other places to start new churches.[85]

---

82. Asare-Duah, *Gallant Soldiers*, 8.
83. CoP, *Minister's Handbook*, 2008.
84. Asem, *History of the Church of Pentecost*, 102.
85. This prophecy, purported to have been given by Pastors Frimpong, Apau-Asante, and Quaye on Thursday, October 15, 1953, is recorded by Larbi, *Pentecostalism*, 218.

These prophetic utterances are asserted to have been fulfilled in line with church patterns of growth outreach in this period. For instance, Pastor E. C. Apau-Asante and his family were sent to start the church in Tamale, in northern Ghana. They arrived there on April 28, 1953.[86] By the end of the year, they had established a church of 40 members. The church from Tamale subsequently reached out to Bolgatanga, Tumu, Wa, Damango, Gambaga, Yendi, Kete Krachi, Chinderi, Banda, and Kpandai within a decade.[87] Pastors S. K. O. Chemel, D. Y. A. Owusu, and J. A. Bimpong worked in the Brong Ahafo Areas in the late 1950s. They reached places such as Dormaa Ahenkro, Gyapekrom, Sampa, Wenchi, and Banda Ahenkro, areas where the gospel had never been heard.[88] Pastor F. D. Walker was delegated to reach the areas in the Eastern Region. In this period, the areas reached by CoP that had not been hitherto were the Akuapem areas in the Eastern Region, parts of Brong Ahafo, the Volta, Northern, and Upper Regions.

However, efforts to reach the Volta Region had begun previously. Between 1945 and 1949, the Apostolic Church of Gold Coast had sent itinerant preachers and evangelists to many parts of the Volta Region. Three ministers were stationed in the region by 1950 and 1951. They included Brother C. C. A. Hushie and Evangelist R. O. Hayford. Between 1951 and 1952 much of the Volta Region had been reached. Assemblies such as Peki, Kadjebi, Kpalime, Akpafu Mempeasem, Hohoe, Jasikan, and Kabu had been opened. By the end of 1952, Ho, Anloga, Keta, Kwamekrom, Dodo Amanfrom, Ahamansu, Tokurano, and Asukawkaw had all been established. Pastor A. S. Mallet was sent to Ho as the Volta regional head of the church in 1952.[89]

In 1960, the church asserted that another prophetic utterance confirmed the earlier one to the effect that the church should begin steps to expand into other territories and unreached areas, including other African countries.[90] This period in the history of the church also saw an expansion into other ethnic groups unreached with the gospel. For instance, Sawla in the northern part of Ghana, whose inhabitants are pre-

---

86. Asem, *History of the Church of Pentecost*, 153. His transfer was said to have been conferred through a word of prophesy in early 1953.

87. Asem, *History of the Church of Pentecost*, 105.

88. Bredwa-Mensah, "Church of Pentecost in Retrospect," 51.

89. Asem, *History of the Church of Pentecost*, 149.

90. See "First Covenant of Church of Pentecost," in CoP, *Minister's Handbook*, 2008, 3–6.

dominantly ethnic Lobi, was reached in 1960 through the enterprise of Pastor L. A. Nyarko.[91] The first local church was opened at Nyange with an ex-convict and his family as the first congregants.[92] The northwestern parts of Brong Ahafo and Akuapem in the Eastern Region areas, which were controlled by very powerful fetishes such as Akonnedi (a local deity worshipped by the people), were also reached with the gospel. This area had already been evangelized by the Presbyterian Church in the early 1800s. Pastor F. D. Walker and his team planted more Pentecostal churches in these areas.[93]

By the time Gold Coast Apostolic Church became completely independent from the parent British Apostolic fraternity and subsequently changed its name to the CoP, its local assemblies could be spotted in every region of the country.[94] What had to be done from this period onwards was to aggressively evangelize and establish more congregations in every village, town, or community and to disciple the converts. In effect, by 1962, the CoP was represented in almost every region in Ghana.[95] The areas in Ghana considered difficult for the penetration of the gospel for various reasons had all been reached. Within the Northern and Upper Regions, factors such as Islamic religion, traditional religion, varying linguistic patterns, and adverse socioeconomic conditions had been hindrances to the gospel. Yet these areas were penetrated.[96] From this period onwards the church saw expansion and church planting across international frontiers, beginning from the neighboring African countries. The church's vision for evangelism at this time was to reach out to all nations beginning from the neighboring West African nations.[97]

---

91. The Lobi ethnic group was then completely unreached with the gospel or Islam.
92. Asem, *History of the Church of Pentecost*, 153.
93. Asem, *History of the Church of Pentecost*, 154.
94. CoP, Statistical Department Data, 1963.
95. Asem, *History of the Church of Pentecost*, 153.
96. Asem, *History of the Church of Pentecost*, 62.
97. CoP, "Mission Statement and Vision Policy," in *Minister's Handbook*, 2008.

CHURCH OF PENTECOST HISTORICAL STATISTICS AND ANALYSIS OF GROWTH

The statistics of a Pentecostal movement such as the CoP can show various discrepancies, as can every religious movement's, due to its great size and to factors such as its rural nature and the illiteracy and constant movement of its adherents. Notwithstanding, the statistical growth analysis of the CoP shows phenomenal increase over the years. In the first six decades of its existence, from 1937 to 1998, the church claimed an adult membership of 496,000 with 415 new established churches.[98] By 1999, the membership had almost doubled to 863,401, with 7,049 new churches, and the church had reached out to plant new churches in 43 countries spanning all the continents. By 2002, the total membership reached 1,060,685, with 8,532 new congregations. The CoP's Annual Statistical Growth Report of 2010 stated that 11,874 of its congregations are found in Ghana, with another 15,167 congregations worldwide, claiming a total of 1,980,843 members worldwide.[99] The CoP, as of December 31, 2012, reported a membership of 1,938,411 locally and a total worldwide figure of 2,252,228, with 86 countries reached. The year 2012 witnessed the creation or opening of 12,801 new congregations both locally and internationally. A comparison of this era (1962–2012) with the earlier years (1937–1962) gives an indication of how the historical events discussed in chapter 3 reflect the church's growth pattern. The church's end-of-year policy makers' meeting held in Accra, November 10–16, 2013, with participants drawn from every area of the globe where it operates, approved a five-year policy plan to increase membership by 33 percent and open 3,000 new congregations.[100]

Table 4.1 and figures 4.1 and 4.2 show the total membership and statistical growth (1937–2012) in tabular, bar graph, and pie chart presentation.

---

98. CoP, General Council Meeting Annual Report, 1999.
99. In CoP, General Council Meeting Annual Report, 2010.
100. CoP, *Vision 2018*.

MISSION AND GROWTH IN THE CHURCH OF PENTECOST

YEAR	MEMBERSHIP IN GHANA
1937–1998	496,000
1998–1999	863,401
1999–2001	988,608
2002–2010	1,703,585
2011–2012	1,938,411

Table 4.1. CoP Total Membership in Ghana

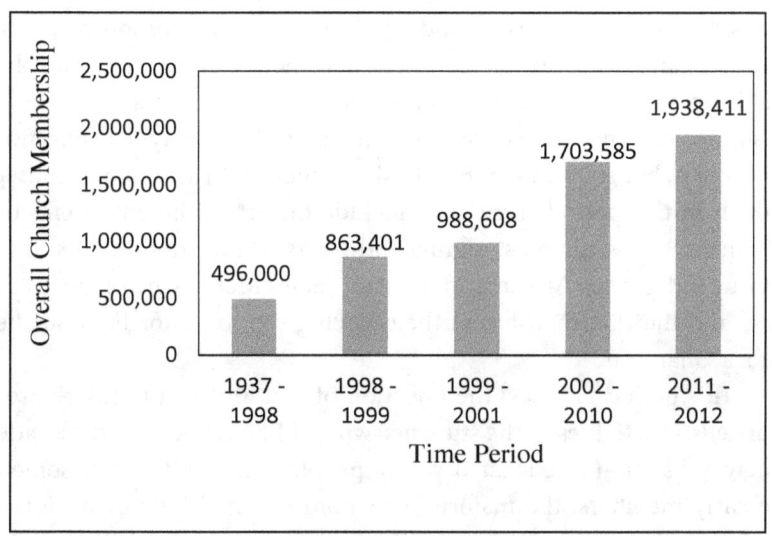

Figure 4.1. CoP Total Membership in Ghana—Bar Graph

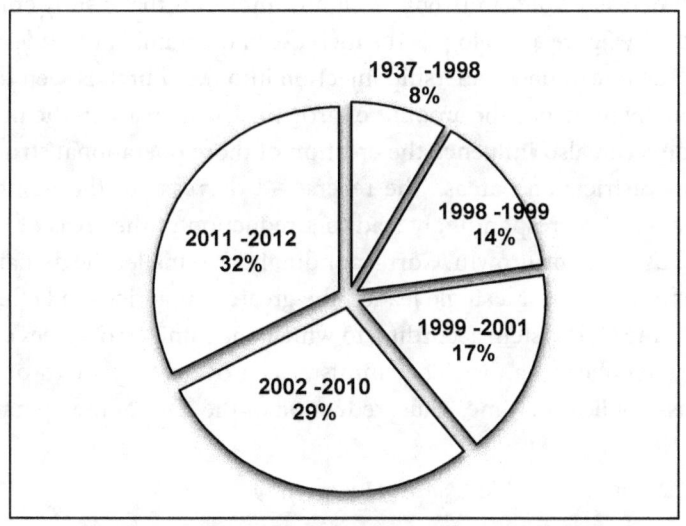

Figure 4.2. CoP Total Membership in Ghana—Pie Chart

Figure 4.1 depicts the progressive pattern of growth of the church from 1937 to 2012. The corresponding pie chart (fig. 4.2) gives the percentage increase in various periods during these years. From its inception to 1998, a period of 60 years (1937–1998) it grew by 8 percent. In the next two years (1998–1999), it increased by 14 percent. The succeeding three years (1999–2001) saw an increase of 17 percent. In the next eight years it increased by 29 percent. Then during the 2011–2012 two-year interval, growth increased by 32 percent.

The pattern of growth can be analyzed in two historical eras of development: between 1937 and 1998, when the institution had to go through various intractable conflicts, and then after 1998, when it had relatively stable and quiet administration, with minimal episodes of misunderstanding and conflict. Conflicts are invariably a disincentive for growth, but stability can be a basis for increase. Factors to encourage growth in this period since 1998 include the establishment of effective administrative structures; significantly, the administration was taken over by indigenous Africans after Pastor James McKeown's retirement in 1982 and the chairmanship of the church given to Pastor Fred Stephen Safo, a Ghanaian.[101]

This period also saw the injection of youthful zeal in the rigorous evangelistic activities of the students' wing (PENSA). After four decades, a new generation of educated young people arose, children of some of the early members, the majority of whom had had little or no formal education themselves. The activities of the newly formed PENSA and other changes influenced by these offspring effected a revamping of the church between 1986 and 1998. A significant factor that clearly emerges, depicted by figure 4.5 below, is the increase in the number of leaders after 1998. The rate of new leadership injection into the church is seen to proportionally influence the amount of growth. The increase in the number of leaders can also influence the creation of more operational structures such as districts and areas. The reverse—a decrease in the number of leaders—will correspondingly lead to a reduction of the areas of operation, thus reducing growth. Correspondingly, the smaller the demarcated area of operation for a single leader, the greater his anticipated effectiveness. In the CoP system according to which one minister oversees several local assemblies in a district, a minister can oversee up to 20 or more local assemblies at a time. Thus, reduction of the sizes of the operational

---

101. Asem, *History of the Church of Pentecost*, 69.

domain of the ministers through dividing the scope of supervision can promote effectiveness resulting in growth.

The following section compares two-year interval periods from 1962 to 2013 and also shows how the increase in the leadership has affected the growth of the church (fig. 4.5). The period between 2010 and 2012 had a fantastic growth rate of 32 percent. This sudden growth at this period could be a result of the combined effect of many favorable factors, including all the previously mentioned factors such as administrative stability, increase in leadership strength, and injection of a new breed of informed Christians—such as children born to the original pioneering members. But also, significantly, in this period the leadership aggressively sought growth and revamping of the church through developing small-group systems such as the home cell and Bible study.

The period is also characterized by a dramatic leadership decision to change some traditional church practices such as dress code (i.e., not requiring head coverings, allowing women to wear trousers, allowing dreadlocks) and seating arrangements (men and women were seated in separate places). The CoP, in line with its spirituality, had a strict dress code for women: They had to wear a head-covering to church services and could not wear trousers or any short dresses that exposed certain parts of the body. These were changed by a 2010 communiqué to address the ever-changing sociocultural environment in order to make the gospel message relevant to other people.[102] These changes encourage people such as Rastafarians, secular workers in their uniforms (police and prison personnel), and others to attend services without much restriction.

This change of some traditional church practices generated a lot of misunderstanding both in the church and outside. The major contention was the dress code of women, especially the head covering, which had been the church's practice since its inception. The older generation thought that dropping this might result in lowering moral standards. The younger generation seems to have a strong aversion to some of the church practices including, for instance, the use of head coverings. They question its usage based on scriptural interpretations and comparison with similar Pentecostal/Charismatic churches. They contend that such practices are archaic and therefore deter others from participating or joining the denomination. The review and removal of these practices

---

102. Communiqué issued by the apostles, prophets and evangelist of CoP at the end of their annual prayer meeting held at the Pentecost Pension House, Gbawe, Accra, January 19–21, 2010.

coincided with the sudden upsurge in growth and is therefore assumed to be a contributing factor.

This study argues that this move positively rebranded the CoP in the eyes of contemporary youth and may well be part of the observed growth pattern. A youth pastor asserted that many young people who would have left the CoP for other Pentecostal or Charismatic churches due to these issues have been retained and that many others who found the church too traditional have begun changing their perception. The communiqué was seen to have advanced the cause of the young people and situated the institution positively for contemporary emerging church trends.

The communiqué caused the major contention it did because the CoP was and still is seen as a standard for Christian morality and strict discipline worthy of emulation by other church organizations. Asamoah-Gyadu, for instance, argued earlier on that the uncompromising stance of the CoP with regard to Christian morality elicits a very high level of membership commitment evident in the intensity of participation in church life.[103] He argues in line with Rodney Stark's proposal that, in order for a religious movement to grow, it must, among other things, offer a strict distinctive religious culture that sets it apart from the general secular culture.[104] "Strict" in this context refers to the degree that a religious group maintains a separate and distinctive lifestyle or morality in personal and family life in such areas as dress, diet, drinking, entertainment, use of time, sex, child rearing, and the like. To Asamoah-Gyadu, "the Ghanaian public image of the CoP and Pentecostalism generally is that of a religious organization that is making up for some of the failures and weaknesses—particularly in the area of morality—that have come to be associated with Christianity in Africa."[105] Nevertheless, this writer agrees with the CoP's decision to shed practices such as strict hair covering and separate seating for men and women. The writer asserts that dropping such practices does not affect the CoP's strict discipline and moral stance but rather allows for more contemporary participation. The standards for discipline that carry immediate sanctions for both members and ministers, such as those Larbi referred to as strict disciplinary measures for any acts of immorality inscribed in its codes of conduct, are still intact.[106]

103. Asamoah-Gyadu, "'Promise Is for You.'"

104. Asamoah-Gyadu, quoting Rodney Stark, "Why Religious Movements Succeed or Fail," 137.

105. Asamoah-Gyadu, "'Promise Is for You,'" 79.

106. CoP, Rules of Conduct, 1983.

Larbi noted the official position of the CoP that states disciplinary actions may be taken against members of the church who make it a practice of going to questionable places, who fall into open sin, embrace or spread false doctrine, desecrate the Lord's day, divorce wife or husband, misappropriate church funds, fornicate or commit adultery, among others.[107]

COMPARATIVE GROWTH ANALYSIS (1962–2013)

Figures 4.3 and 4.4 display an analysis of the statistics from a non-variable two-year interval pattern to show the CoP's historical growth curve, beginning from 1962. The years 2015 and 2016 will be discussed separately for a current comparative growth analysis. The rationale is to examine the growth pattern after the CoP became an independent, separate registered religious body in Ghana. Figure 4.3 below shows the growth for every two years beginning from 1962 as a bar graph. The pie chart (fig. 4.4) interprets this data in percentages for easier analysis.

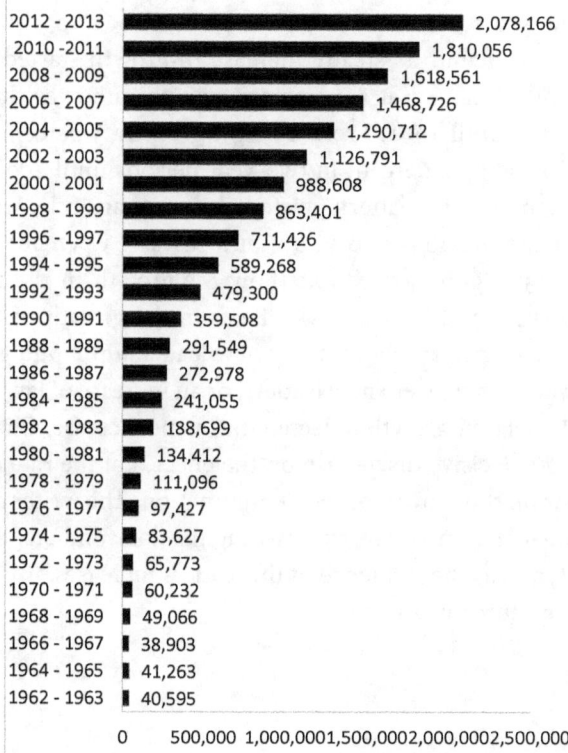

Figure 4.3. CoP Church Growth Analysis in Two-Year Intervals (1962–2013)

107. Larbi, *Pentecostalism*, 254.

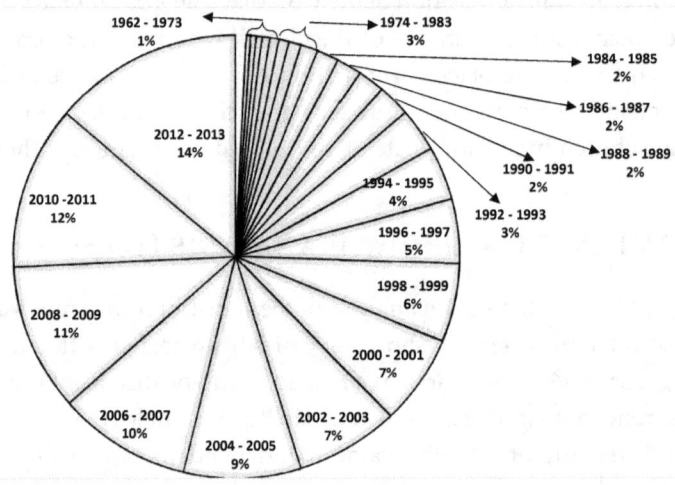

Figure 4.4. CoP Church Growth Analysis (1962–2013)—Pie Chart

The first few years after independence, from 1962 to 1983, showed growth of 0–1 percent. Its steady increase in growth started taking off after 1984 and remained at a 2-percent growth rate over the previous two-year period until 1991. From 1992, it grew by 3 percent, and then started increasing by 1 percent in two-year periods until 2004, at 9 percent. From 2005 on the pattern started changing again by increasing 1 percent over the previous two years until it was 14 percent percent in 2012 and 2013. Figure 4.5 exhibits how the growth in the number of leaders (ministers and lay leaders) reflects in the growth of the church as a whole. In the period without any new leadership input, growth was stationary. When there were new leaders, or an increase of lay leaders and ministers, the relative growth reflected that same increase. Chapter 7 will take up a more decisive discussion on the effect that the rate of increase of leaders has on the growth of the denomination. The writer asserts that when the organization is free from wranglings or conflicts, it is able to raise leaders, and as the influence of the leaders increases, this affects the growth of the church positively.

Figure 4.5. Comparative Growth Analysis of Ministers to Adult Membership of the CoP (1962–2013), Two-Year Intervals

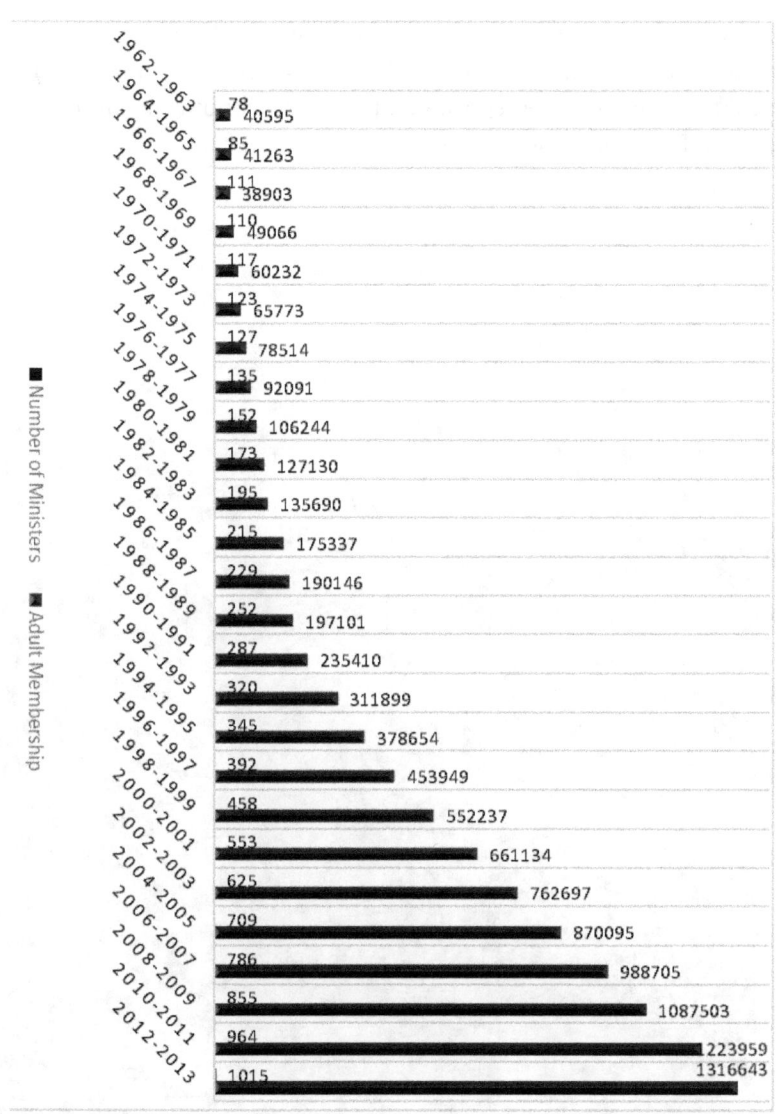

Series 1 = Total Number of Ministers   Series 2 = Total Adult Membership

ANALYSIS OF CURRENT GROWTH STATISTICS OF COP WORLDWIDE MEMBERSHIP

This section analyzes the growth statistics of the worldwide CoP for 2015 and 2016. The information in the tables and figures below have been generated from the statistical reports compiled and submitted by the church's Statistical Department for this period.[108]

---

108. CoP, Statistical Data, May 2017.

Statistic	Ghana 2016	Ghana 2015	International Missions 2016	International Missions 2015	Autonomous Nations 2016	Autonomous Nations 2015	Worldwide 2016	Worldwide 2015	variance	percent increase
No. of Nations	1	1	88	87	2	2	91	90	1	1.1
No. of Areas	61	58	-	-	37	34	-	-	-	-
No. of Districts	1,221	1,150	619	592	272	258	2,112	2,000	112	5.6
No. of Assemblies	14,980	14,352	3,008	2,796	1,940	1,786	19,928	18,934	994	5.2
Adult Membership	1,580,30	1,476,168	187,470	171,280	120,572	110,444	1,888,072	1,757,892	130,180	7.4
Children Membership	787,223	732,341	78,008	72,254	51,558	50,131	916,789	854,726	62,063	7.3
Overall Membership	2,367,253	2,208,509	265,478	243,534	172,130	160,575	2,804,861	2,612,618	192,243	7.4
No. of Elders	32,656	31,010	4,393	4,152	1,992	1,942	39,041	37,104	1,937	5.2
No. of Deacons	23,683	22,382	3,460	3,274	2,381	2,292	29,524	27,948	1,576	5.6
No. of Deaconesses	44,054	41,484	5,893	5,313	4,839	4,746	54,786	51,543	3,243	6.3
No. of Ministers	1,307	1,230	620	603	293	284	2,220	2,117	103	4.9

Table 4.2. Worldwide Growth Statistics

Membership Growth Analysis—Worldwide

As of December 31, 2016, the CoP operated in 91 nations with a worldwide total membership of 2,804,861, recording a growth rate of 7.4 percent over the year 2015. The total number of assemblies stood at 19,928, distributed across 2,112 administrative districts of the church. With a total membership of 2,367,253, the church in Ghana constituted 84.4 percent of the worldwide total membership. The remaining 15.6 percent was accounted for by external branches, including the two autonomous nations (Benin and Côte d'Ivoire) as shown in figure 4.6.

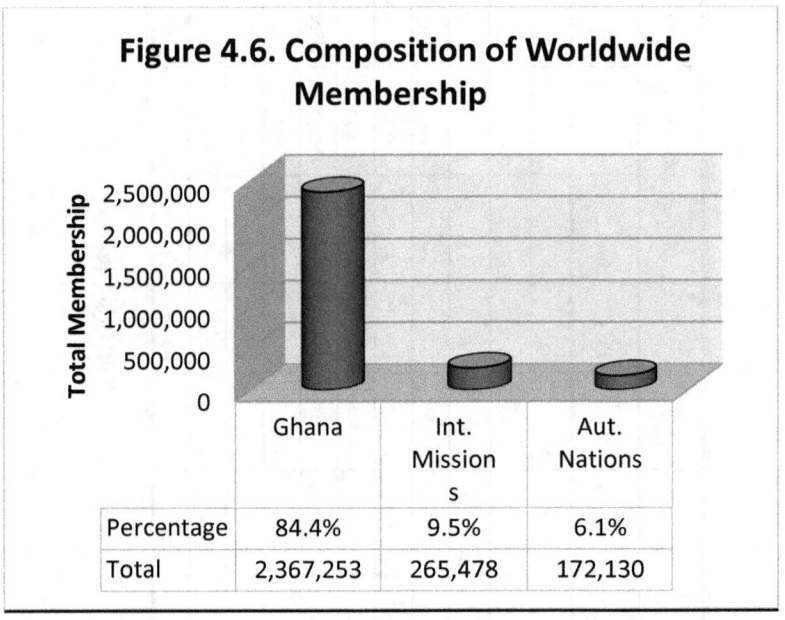

Figure 4.6. Composition of Worldwide Membership

	NON-AUTONOMOUS				AUTONOMOUS NATIONS			
Statistic	2016	2015	Variance	Percent Increase	2016	2015	Variance	Percent Increase
No. of Nations	88	87	1	1.1	2	2	0	0.0
No. of Districts	619	592	27	4.6	272	258	14	5.4
No. of Assemblies	3,008	2,796	212	7.6	1,940	1,786	154	8.6
Adult Membership	187,470	171,280	16,190	9.5	120,572	110,444	10,128	9.2
Children Membership	78,008	72,254	5,754	8.0	51,558	50,131	1,427	2.8
Overall Membership	265,478	243,534	21,944	9.0	172,130	160,575	11,555	7.2
No. of Elders	4,393	4,152	241	5.8	1,992	1,942	50	2.6
No. of Deacons	3,460	3,274	186	5.7	2,381	2,292	89	3.9
No. of Deaconesses	5,893	5,313	580	10.9	4,839	4,746	93	2.0
No. of Ministers	620	603	17	2.8	293	284	9	3.2

Table 4.3. Growth Statistics of the Church of Pentecost—External Branches

Membership Growth Analysis—External Branches

In 2016, membership in the non-autonomous nations increased by 21,944, making a total overall membership of 265,478. This represents an increase of 9 percent over the year 2015. The autonomous nations recorded an increase of 11,555 members, resulting in an overall total membership of 172,130, an increase of 7.2 percent over that of 2015. As of December 2016, the external branches of the church operated in 90 nations across the globe and recorded an overall membership total of 437,608, presenting an increase of 8.3 percent from that of 2015. Altogether, 41 new districts were created in the external branches in 2016, bringing the total number of districts to 891, whereas 2015 had 850, giving an increase of 4.8 percent. There were 3,008 assemblies in the non-autonomous nations in 2016—compared with 2,796 in 2015—an increase of 8.3 percent. The two autonomous nations recorded 1,940 assemblies in 2016 as against 1,786 in 2015, recording an increase of 154. The total number of assemblies in the entire external missions for 2016 was therefore 4,948 compared with 4,582 in 2015. The increase of 366 indicates an 8-percent increase.

Statistic	2016	2015	Variance	Percent Increase
No. of Areas	61	58	3	5.2
No. of Districts	1,221	1,150	71	6.2
No. of Assemblies	14,980	14,352	628	4.4
No. of Home Cells	53,639	47,650	5,989	12.6
No. of Active Home Cell Members	773,753	710,633	63,120	8.9
Overall Membership (Adults and Children)	2,367,253	2,208,509	158,744	7.2
Adult Membership (13 yrs and above)	1,580,030	1,476,168	103,862	7.0
Youth Membership (13–35 yrs)	891,277	795,471	95,806	12.0
Teen Membership (13–19 yrs)	387,636	340,506	47,130	13.8
Young Adults Membership (20–35 yrs)	503,641	454,965	48,676	10.7
Other Adults (above 35 yrs)	688,753	680,697	8,056	1.2
Children Membership (below 13 yrs)	787,223	732,341	54,882	7.5
No. of Elders	32,656	31,010	1,646	5.3
No. of Deacons	23,683	22,382	1,301	5.8
No. of Deaconesses	44,054	41,484	2,570	6.2
Total Number of Ministers in Ghana	1,307	1,230	77	6.3

Table 4.4. Growth Statistics—Ghana

Membership Growth Analysis—Ghana

The church's total membership in Ghana by the end of December 2016 was 2,367,253, which constituted approximately 8.4 percent of the total estimated 2016 Ghanaian population of 28,308,301.[109] It also constituted approximately 11.74 percent of the total Christian population in Ghana, which is estimated to be 71.2 percent of the Ghanaian population.[110] This makes the CoP's numbers a force to be reckoned with in Ghana with regard to national activities such as voting and other decisions. The 2016 statistics indicate that teen membership (13 to 19 years) increased by 13.8 percent, while overall youth membership (13 to 35 years) increased by 12 percent. Children's membership (below 13) increased by 7.5 percent. Within the same period, the total number of members aged above 35 increased by 1.2 percent, which points to the need for intensive evangelism and discipleship within the 35-and-above age group. Overall, the church recorded a membership growth of 7.2 percent in 2016. The data further shows that the youth continue to make up the largest segment (38 percent) of the church's membership, as shown in figure 4.7. Children's membership constitutes 33 percent, while those 35 years and above constitute 29 percent.

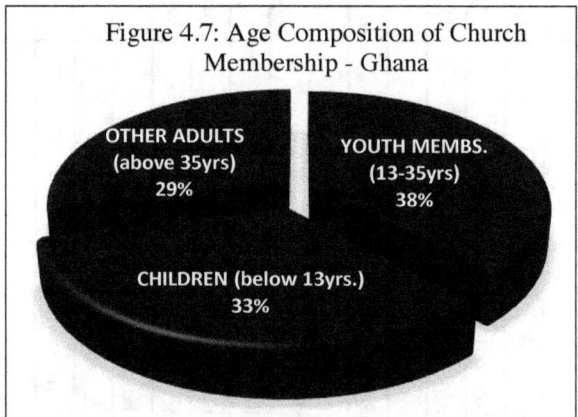

Figure 4.7. Age Composition of Church Membership

---

109. Data Production Unit, Ghana Statistical Service, September 16, 2016, http://www.statsghana.gov.gh.

110. "Ghana Demographics Profile 2016," Index Mundi, http://www.indexmundi.com/ghana/demographics_profile.html. Pentecostals and Charismatics constitute 28.3 percent. The CoP is about a third of this (30 percent).

A further disaggregation of the data shows that the youth membership is composed of 57 percent young adults and 43 percent teens, as shown in figure 4.8. This calls for the continuous need to effectively balance youth programs to cater to both categories.

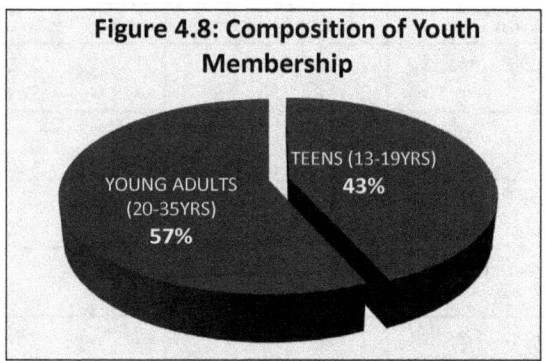

Figure 4.8. Composition of Youth Membership

The overall analysis implies that 71 percent of COP membership in Ghana is made up of children and youth. This is a healthy sign and an indication that the CoP is a thriving church with a great future. It is therefore imperative for the church leadership to focus its programs and activities towards effectively mentoring and nurturing young people to prepare them for leadership responsibilities, both within the church and in the nation as a whole. It is also important to ensure a healthy balance of both adults and youth in leadership. This will encourage the youth to learn from the adults. In 2016, three additional administrative areas were created in Ghana, bringing the total number of administrative areas for the church to 61. The church established an additional 71 districts in 2016. By December 2016, therefore, the church recorded a total of 1,221 administrative districts, which serviced the 14,980 local assemblies in Ghana.

Other Indicators of CoP Growth, 2016 Statistics—Ghana

In 2016, the Church in Ghana reported growth in some aspects of its operations, namely, rallies/crusades, backsliders won back, adult members engaged in active evangelism, marriages blessed, and assemblies opened (see table 4.5).

Indicator	2016	2015	Variance	Percent Increase
Children Dedicated	89,090	96,031	-6,941	-7.23
Rallies/Crusades	49,687	42,545	7,142	16.79
Adult Souls Won	170,748	171,716	-968	-0.56
Children Souls Won and Retained	54,158	55,083	-925	-1.68
Total Souls Won (Adults and Children)	224,906	226,799	-1,893	-0.83
New Converts Baptized in Water	131,280	137,200	-5,920	-4.31
New Converts Baptized in Holy Spirit	73,207	72,635	572	0.79
Old Members Baptized in Holy Spirit	110,687	114,245	-3,558	-3.11
Holy Spirit Bapt. (New Conv. and Old Members)	183,894	186,881	-2,987	-1.60
New Converts Retained in the Church	97,297	99,943	-2,646	-2.65
Backsliders Won Back	43,982	40,528	3,454	8.52
Number of Adults Doing Active Evangelism	498,144	398,451	99,693	25.02
Number of Marriages Blessed	6,906	6,604	302	4.57
Assemblies Opened	692	630	62	9.84
Assemblies Closed	64	49	15	30.61

Table 4.5. Comparative Statistics of Other Indicators for Growth—Ghana

In 2016, a total of 224,906 converts, made up of 170,748 adults and 54,158 children, were won. Out of the adult converts won, 131,280 were baptized in water, representing 76.9 percent, a slight drop from the figure of 80 percent for 2015. The number of rallies and crusades held increased by almost 17 percent. A total of 97,297 converts were retained in the church in 2016. This constitutes 74 percent of converts baptized in water. Although the church recorded a lower number of new converts baptized in water as compared to 2015, a greater proportion of such converts were baptized in the Holy Spirit in 2016: 55.8 percent, as compared to 53 percent in 2015. In terms of absolute figures also, more converts received baptism of the Holy Spirit in comparison with the previous year

(0.79 percent). This is an indication of improved efforts of discipleship. For Pentecostals such as the CoP, Holy Ghost baptism forms an integral part of its discipleship. The church recorded an 8.5 percent increase in backsliders won back. There was also an increase of 25 percent in the number of adult members engaged in active evangelism. The number of marriages brought to the altar in 2016 increased by 4.6 percent. Among these may be others who came into the church through marriage. It is also anticipated that children from such unions will add to the church's membership.

Ministry	December 2016			December 2015			Variance in Active Membership	Percent Increase in Active Membership
	Totala	Active	Percent Active	Total	Active	Percent Active		
Women	975,576	377,376	38.68	917,057	335,175	36.55	42,201	12.59
Men	604,454	169,398	28.02	559,111	149,645	26.76	19,753	13.20
Youth	891,277	347,497	38.99	795,471	305,518	38.41	41,979	13.74
Evangelism	478,306	327,828	68.54	363,224	289,028	79.57	38,800	13.42
Children	787,223	538,702	68.43	732,341	506,103	69.11	32,599	6.44

Table 4.6. Comparative Statistics of Functional Ministries' Performance—Active Members

a Women/Men total = Adults membership 13 years and above (Female/Male) Youth = Youth membership 13–35 years Evangelism = Total Class Membership as reported by the directorate Children = Children's membership below 13 years

Functional Ministries' Performance—Ghana

An analysis of the performance of the various ministries showed that almost all the ministries recorded increases in the percentage of active members in 2016 over the previous year. In 2016, the Evangelism Ministry recorded 68.54 percent of its members as being active in the ministry's activities. Children's Ministry followed with 68.43 percent of its members active in the ministry's activities. The Youth Ministry followed with 39 percent of its members participating in ministry activities.

Then came the Women's Ministry, with 38.7 percent of all adult women in the church active in the ministry's activities. The Men's Ministry came next, recording 28 percent of its members as active in the ministry. It is also interesting to note that more adult members are engaged in active evangelism (498,144; table 4.5) than in the Evangelism Ministry's activities (table 4.6). The ministry will have to find out why this is so and redefine its activities to attract more membership participation. It is noteworthy that the 39 percent active membership recorded for the Youth Ministry could be a result of most youth being in school for nine months of the year and often not counted as active members in the ministry's activities at the local level. Meanwhile, the same people are very active in the PENSA groups to which they belong on various campuses. In a final analysis, if all the active participants of the ministries are engaged in aggressive evangelism and effective follow-up, the church is set to double its membership figures every year or two.

Home Cell Analysis

The analysis of home cells and Bible studies indicates that out of an adult membership of 1,580,030, there are 773,753 actively participating in home cells. This indicates that 806,277 members, or 51 percent of adult members, are not involved in home cell activities. If the church aims to make the institution a home-cell unit church instead of retaining the assembly system, then it must encourage its ministers and leaders to work harder to ensure that its members are participating effectively in home-cell activities. Comparing the number of active home cell members (773,753) with the number of home cells (53,639) as presented in table 4.4 above shows that, on average, each home cell accommodates approximately 14 members.

Other Indicators of Growth, 2016 Statistics– External Branches

Other growth indicators come from the external branches through their operational activities, including seminars, retreats, conferences, conventions, rallies, Bible studies, home cells, and prayer and fasting sessions. The statistics in table 4.7 compare 2015 and 2016 numbers.

	NON-AUTONOMOUS NATIONS				AUTONOMOUS NATIONS			
Operational Result	2016	2015	Variance	Percent Increase	2016	2015	Variance	Percent Increase
Children Dedicated	5,658	5,444	214	3.9	4,457	5,066	-609	-12.0
Rallies/ Crusades Held	5,284	4,773	511	10.7	2,570	4,949	-2,379	-48.1
Souls Won	30,507	28,203	2,304	8.2	10,540	10,361	179	1.7
New Converts Baptized in Water	16,659	14,542	2,117	14.6	9,249	8,738	511	5.8
New Conv. Baptized in Holy Spirit	9,026	8,628	398	4.6	11,325	11,142	183	1.6
Old Memb. Baptized in Holy Spirit	13,516	15,655	-2,139	-13.7	0	0	0	0.0
Assemblies Opened	261	234	27	11.5	167	179	-12	-6.7
Assemblies Closed	49	19	30	157.9	0	4	-4	-100.0

Table 4.7. Comparative Statistics of Operational Results—External Branches

In 2016 the non-autonomous nations won a total of 30,507 converts, an increase of 8.2 percent over the 2015 performance. Out of the 30,507 total converts won, 16,659 were baptized in water, representing 54.6 percent, an increase of 52 percent over the previous year's figure. The two autonomous nations won a total of 10,540 souls. Out of this, 9,249 (87.8 percent) were baptized in water. This indicates growth in the mission fields.

	TOTAL EXTERNAL BRANCHES			
Operational Result	2016	2015	Variance	Percent Change
Children Dedicated	10,115	10,510	-395	-3.76
Rallies/Crusades Held	7,854	9,722	-1,868	-19.21
Souls Won	41,047	38,564	2,483	6.44
New Converts Baptized in Water	25,908	23,280	2,628	11.29
New Converts Baptized in Holy Spirit	20,351	19,770	581	2.94
Old Members Baptized in Holy Spirit	13,516	15,655	-2,139	-13.66
Assemblies Opened	428	413	15	3.63
Assemblies Closed	49	23	26	113.04

Table 4.8. Comparative Total External Branches Operational Results

The external branches won a total of 41,047 converts in 2016 as against 38,564 in 2015, representing a 6.4 percent increase. A total of 25,908 new converts were baptized in water in the external branches in 2016. This represents an 11.3 percent increase over the 2015 figure of 23,280. The percentage of converts who were baptized in water in 2016 was 63 percent, an increase of 2.8 percent over the previous year's figure of 60.4 percent. With respect to Holy Spirit baptism, the external branches recorded a total of 33,867 in 2016. New converts baptized in the Holy Spirit totaled 20,351, an increase of approximately 3 percent over the previous year. In reference to new converts baptized in water, 78.6 percent of them also received baptism in the Holy Spirit.

Infrastructure and Other Assets, Statistics—Ghana

An important factor in CoP measurement of growth is the infrastructure and assets accrued. Table 4.9 presents statistics for the infrastructure and assets reflecting part of the church's growth analysis for Ghana.

ASSET	Dec. 2016	Percent of Total	Dec. 2015	Percent of Total	Variance	Percent Increase
PERMANENT CHURCH BUILDINGS (Total Assemblies: 2016 = 14,980; 2015 = 14,352)						
Completed and Dedicated	1,456	9.7	1,215	8.5	241	19.8
Completed but Not Dedicated	343	2.3	439	3.1	-96	-21.9
In Progress	6,483	43.3	6,061	42.2	422	7.0
Not started due to lack of land	938	6.3	1,005	7.0	-67	-6.7
Not started due to lack of funds	5,491	36.7	5,342	37.2	149	2.8
Not started due to land litigation	84	0.6	76	0.5	8	10.5
Not started due to other reasons	185	1.2	214	1.5	-29	-13.6
CURRENT PLACES OF WORSHIP (Total Assemblies: 2016 = 14,980; 2015 = 14,352)						
Completed Permanent Church Buildings	1,799	12.0	1,654	11.5	145	8.8
Uncompleted Permanent Church Buildings	4,967	33.2	4,474	31.2	493	11.0
Temporary Structures on Church Plot	3,839	25.6	3,805	26.5	34	0.9
Temporary Structures on Rented Plot	412	2.8	401	2.8	11	2.7
Rented Halls	133	0.9	129	0.9	4	3.1
Free Accommodations	489	3.3	468	3.3	21	4.5
School Classrooms	1,787	11.9	1,828	12.7	-41	-2.2
Under Trees	1,296	8.7	1,351	9.4	-55	-4.1

Other Places	258	1.7	242	1.7	16	6.6
DISTRICT MISSION HOUSES (Total Districts: 2016 = 1,221; 2015 = 1,150)						
Completed and Dedicated	806	66.0	719	62.5	87	12.1
Completed but Not Dedicated	37	3.0	47	4.1	-10	-21.3
In Progress	332	27.2	326	28.3	6	1.8
Not started due to lack of land	13	1.1	20	1.7	-7	-35.0
Not started due to lack of funds	13	1.1	13	1.1	0	0.0
Not started due to land litigation	0	0.0	0	0.0	0	–
Not started because Head Office Residence is in use	5	0.4	16	1.4	-11	-68.8
Not started due to other reasons	15	1.2	9	0.8	6	66.7
DISTRICT MINISTERS' CURRENT RESIDENCES (Total Districts: 2016 = 1,221; 2015 = 1,150)						
Completed Mission Houses	843	69.0	766	66.6	77	10.1
Uncompleted Mission Houses	197	16.1	176	15.3	21	11.9
Rented Houses	124	10.2	145	12.6	-21	-14.5
Free Accommodations	37	3.0	44	3.8	-7	-15.9
Head Office Residences	7	0.6	12	1.0	-5	-41.7
Other Residences	13	1.1	7	0.6	6	85.7
VEHICLES IN USE BY DISTRICT MINISTERS (Total District Ministers: 2016 = 1,220*; 2015 = 1,150)						
District Cars	808	66.3	766	66.6	42	5.5
District Motor Bikes	230	18.9	183	15.9	47	25.7

District Push Bicycles	44	3.6	33	2.9	11	33.3
Private Vehicles	230	18.9	214	18.6	16	7.5
Head Office Cars	12	1.0	15	1.3	-3	-20.0
DISTRICT MINISTERS' VEHICLE STATUS (Total District Ministers: 2016 = 1,219; 2015 = 1,150)						
Ministers with Vehicle	1,172	96.1	1,088	94.6	83	7.6
Ministers without Vehicle	48	3.9	62	5.4	-14	-22.6
AREA MISSION HOUSES (Total Areas = 61)						
Completed	57	93.4	54	93.1	3	5.6
In progress	4	6.6	4	6.9	0	0.0
AREA HEADS' CURRENT RESIDENCES (Total Areas = 61)						
Completed Mission Houses	57	93.4	54	93.1	3	5.6
Uncompleted Mission Houses	3	4.9	1	1.7	2	200.0
Rented Houses	1	1.6	3	5.2	-2	-66.7

Table 4.9. Comparative Statistics of Infrastructure and Vehicles—Ghana

* Obuasi PIWC had no minister as of December 2016.

EVALUATION OF COP'S GROWTH AND MISSION WITHIN CONTEMPORARY CHURCH GROWTH AND MISSIONS DISCOURSE

This section evaluates CoP's total growth and missions endeavors in the context of current discussions on general church growth and missions. Contemporary missiologists evaluating church growth and missions patterns might consider the level to which a new church is self-propagating, self-supporting and self-sustaining, self-governing, and self-theologizing. Hodges advocated in the early 1900s that the aim of all mission activities was to build an "indigenous New Testament Church" that followed "New Testament methods." He emphasized that the church is "God's agent for evangelism" and that the role of the cross-cultural missionary was to ensure that a church became self-governing, self-supporting, and self-propagating. This has become a fundamental principle of Pentecostal mission strategy.

Recently, some African theologians such as Kwame Bediako and Lamin Sanneh have argued on the additional factor of self-theologizing. Earlier on, some of the principles of church growth and mission spearheaded by McGavran (1970s) and Wagner (1980s) were criticized as church growth ideology that sees the mission enterprise in terms of procedures and strategies that succeed in the United States. Fortunately, Hodges has taken a different tack. Yet in spite of Hodges's remarkable insight, as also noted by Anderson, he cannot escape the concept of missionaries being expatriates, white people who left home "for abroad," in contrast to nationals who must take over the missionaries' work when the ideal of an indigenous church has been reached. Hodges sees mission as an outreach to foreign lands. However, as Anderson affirms, the majority of world mission churches are now beginning to produce theologians and missiologists who challenge the presuppositions of the past and are not content to blindly follow foreign mission ideologies and strategies.

A typical example of such a challenge to past presuppositions is this present work, which seeks to unravel the theological and missiological factors behind the CoP's growth. This work analyzes CoP missions activity in its distinctive capacity as a Pentecostal denomination from the southern hemisphere (sub-Saharan Africa). It aims to bring out the general pattern through which a particular Pentecostal denomination or church has carved a niche for itself in engaging sound biblical and situational (theological and missiological) factors to grow a uniquely self-sustaining, self-propagating, self-governing, and self-theologizing church.

The CoP pattern of growth discussed is unique. Having established growth in the mother nation, Ghana, it moved into other nations just as in the New Testament the apostles first reached out to the Jews in the synagogues and later to the Gentiles. The CoP reaches out into other nations through its Ghanaian members in that particular nation, and eventually establishes indigenous churches that they aim to become autonomous in the future. Its branches in, for instance, Togo, Burkina Faso, Côte d'Ivoire, Malawi, and others are made up predominately of indigenes of those nations. The CoP in Malawi, for instance, has no Ghanaian membership. That of Benin is more than 90 percent Beninois. Its branches in the West may not have such indigenous membership, but still show a particular pattern, which will be discussed in chapter 5.

This pattern of the CoP's growth and missions confirms an earlier prediction by McGavran for churches of this caliber emerging from the Global South, especially sub-Saharan Africa. He rightly predicted in the 1970s the pattern that churches from Africa and Asia would adopt in this era. He then wrote, "In the coming centuries, as Christianity spreads throughout the myriad cultures of Africa and Asia, many factors varying from place to place and time to time will combine to give each church a unique growth pattern and to locate it at a particular place on each point." True to this foresight, the CoP from sub-Saharan Africa has emerged as a prominent global church denomination based on distinguished religious, theological, and missiological factors.

The CoP's pattern of growth into mission is akin to the New Testament pattern. The CoP enters a new nation through its migrant members in that nation. Afterwards it strives to reach the indigenes and create a purely indigenous New Testament church for that nation aimed at being autonomous. The following chapters further highlight the distinctiveness of this pattern: The next chapter (chapter 5) discusses the missionary endeavors and missiological factors promoting the growth of the CoP, while chapter 6 will deal with theological factors.

5

The Church of Pentecost International Missions

Exemplary African Pentecostal Missionary Enterprise

ONE OF THE UNIQUE ways that Pentecostalism in general is showing innovation and growth in this century is in its establishment of immigrant congregations by means of global missionary enterprises. The chapter demonstrates the distinctiveness of this mode of missions engagement by African immigrant churches across the globe, including the West, through CoP's international missions—referred to as its external missions—or church planting outside Ghana.

COP INTERNATIONAL MISSIONS

As of December 31, 2016, the CoP documented its presence in 90 nations across the globe, excluding Ghana.

The church claims a total membership in these 90 nations of 437,608, which is made up of an adult membership of 308,042 (adults 13 years and above) and a children's membership of 129,566 (below 13 years).

In these nations, the church has raised 913 ministers and 23,971 lay leaders (6,385 elders, 5,841 deacons, 10,732 deaconesses, and 1,013 other leaders) overseeing 4,948 local congregations.

This indicates that 15.6 percent of the church's total worldwide registered and baptized membership comes from these 90 nations outside Ghana. These figures include all congregations in African nations and congregations based in other Western and non-Western nations such as the United States, Canada, Germany, Holland, Australia, Belgium, Denmark, Czech Republic, Finland, France, Greece, Ireland, Italy, Norway, Portugal, Spain, Sweden, Ukraine, UK, Israel, India, and Nepal. CoP congregations dot the cities of these nations, and many of these churches have been duly registered as religious nongovernmental or charitable organizations. To clarify various factors in their historic emergence, this chapter distinguishes African missions from other international locations.

COP AFRICAN MISSIONS

CoP in Togo

The CoP's external missions commenced in Africa. The first neighboring West African nations to be reached were the Republics of Togo and Benin. Before 1950, itinerant preachers and evangelists had made efforts to reach these nations with the gospel through the Volta Region of Ghana. The entrance into Togo came as early as May 1951, when Alice Quist, a Togolese trader, led Pastor A. S. Mallet and Brother V. Y. Gogo to pray for her brother, who had taken to drinking. The miraculous healing of the man started a home prayer fellowship on the premises of Pauline Kpodo at Kukotime. The premiere evangelistic rally took place in 1952 in Lomé. The first resident missionary was F. K. Darkooh, who was sent in 1953 with an added responsibility to Benin, a neighboring country. In 1957, at a General Council meeting in Sekondi, the resident missionary for the work in Togo and Benin reported that the work was progressing and had 12 field workers in those two countries.

A crisis hit this work in 1959, caused by the mishandling of the church's finances. The resident missionary, F. K. Darkooh, was implicated in the financial mismanagement, which led to his dismissal. Later, upon his dismissal, he was found to have secretly started his own church in both countries. A section of the church broke away with the dismissed missionary. The mission's work in these two countries thus suffered a great setback. In 1960, Apostle Mallet was stationed in Lomé to revive the remnants. A Togolese national, Vincent Y. Gogo, took over from A. S. Mallet in 1963. There was also in Togo, at this time, an attaché British missionary, Stephen Westfall, and his wife. The responsibility of these white missionaries appears to have been to augment the evangelism initiatives and other sectors such as Bible training and also to act as a link for the affiliate institutions. By 1965, the General Council report recorded 3,006 members and 102 local churches in Togo and 1,056 members and 24 local churches in Dahomey, Benin.

The church in Togo was again hit by instability in 1966 when a misunderstanding arose between the youth and the church leaders. In 1966, the Rev. James McKeown's visit to them settled the initial rancor. Apostle F. S. Safo was then posted to Togo as the resident missionary. His presence eventually brought stability and led to the transformation of the church's administration between 1967 and 1976. Apostle C. C. A. Hushie continued the oversight responsibility in 1976 after Apostle F. S. Safo. The first crop of indigenous pastors in Togo were ordained on December 25, 1967. They were Boenor Apedo, Marko D'Almeida, Pierre Woglo, Pius Mensah, and Montcho Corneille. Apostle B. Y. Apedo, an indigene of Togo, took over the administration after two years and continued the work from 1978 to 1985.

The diplomatic relations between the governments of Ghana and Togo became strained for over 10 years beginning from 1978. Subsequently, a ban was placed on any Ghanaian-initiated church in Togo. This ban was reactivated between 1991 and 1992. The church in Togo suffered various degrees of persecutions, including imprisonment and physical torture of members. Although the activities of the church went underground by 1986, the church in Togo could report 6,525 members and 174 local churches in this period. Pastor K. E. Agbavitoh was the French translator attached to the church in Togo from 1988 to 1999. The CoP in Ghana sent two pastors to act as area heads in 1999 and 2000: Pastors K. K. C. Gadzekpo and J. K. Ocloo.

From then on the CoP in Togo made great strides. On April 16, 2003, the church was reregistered under the name Eglise de Pentecôte Internationale du Togo. Gadzekpo and Ocloo were replaced in 2004 by Pastors L. Y. Agogue, K. K. Mensah, and D'Almeida, who were Togolese. D'Almeida had been called into CoP ministry in Burkina Faso from 1973 to 1991. He was later ordained as an apostle and sent as a missionary attaché to the church in Togo in 2004. After D'Almeida transfer to Gabon in 2011, Apostle Ousmane P. Zabre took over as the national head of the church in Togo. By 2016, the church claimed a total overall membership of 53,973, from 802 assemblies located in 76 districts of the church.

The church in Togo has been receiving commendations since 2012 for winning and baptizing the highest number of souls among the mission churches. It baptized 4,265 converts in water in 2016 and opened 61 assemblies, the highest numbers in the year.

CoP in Benin

The CoP in Benin was separated from Togo and given its own oversight by the International Missions Board on December 25, 1967. Until then, it was jointly supervised with Togo by one overseer. In 1951, a resident evangelist, Atchia Ayao, seceded with a section of the church. Pastor Montcho Cornielle took charge in 1966. During his tenure, the church had many indigenous ministers as full-time workers. He improved the financial administration and set the church on a sound footing. Since Togo was considered the head of the administration in this region, money was periodically transferred from Benin to Togo for central administration. This later became a problem between the two national churches. The government in Benin intervened in the church's internal affairs when allegations of the transfer of money to Togo became an issue in the church. The internal wrangling in the church led to the government putting a ban on the Mono Area and freezing the assets of the church as well as disallowing non-indigenous leadership to lead the church.

The church in Ghana responded quickly in order to prevent the church in Benin from collapse. They sent a Beninese, Barthelemy Nato, to take charge, assisted by two indigenous workers. This marked the complete separation of the administration of the church in Benin and Togo. Many of the members who left the church during the period of the ban returned when it was eventually lifted. The first national head, a Beninese, appointed in 1985, was Germain Coffi Gbankpan. By 1985, the Benin church recorded 3,392 members and 57 local churches. The following ministers were sent to oversee the church in Benin from 1986 on: Pastor Coffi Gbankpan (1986–1991), Apostle B. K. Ephraim (1991–1996), Pastor E. C. Asante (1996–1998), Apostle René Coco (1998–2009). The church in Benin was the first to be granted autonomous status, on August 30, 2009. Apostle Marc K. Fastchao was the first chairman of the church, and his secretary was Apostle Konon Rogatien. Its growth pattern has been very steady and encouraging. The worldwide statistical report of the CoP for 2016 recorded an overall membership of 85,067, from 857 assemblies located in 116 districts in 17 areas of the church. They have 123 ministers, 766 elders, 1,267 deacons, and 3,151 deaconesses overseeing the churches.

CoP in Burkina Faso

Another African nation that opened up in the 1950s for the gospel through the CoP was Burkina Faso, formerly the Upper Volta. The church in Burkina Faso was administered by Apostle Apau-Asante from his station in Tamale. The progress of the church in Burkina Faso was rather slow for various reasons. Burkina Faso is an Islam-dominated country, which makes penetration with the gospel difficult. It is also claimed to be one of the poorest countries in the world, thus hampering financial commitment and making it difficult to support any national worker. At the 1962 General Council meeting of the church, held in Mampong-Ashanti, March 23–April 8, the statistics for the church in Burkina Faso indicated an improvement. The first indigenous full-time Burkinabe ministers were Ouedrago Billa Mossi and Pinogo Yanogo. Pinogo later became a pastor and was appointed as the national head. Other missionaries to Burkina Faso included Pastor E. D. Aninkorah (1968–1969), Apostle Léon Agogue (1973–1980), Pastor Moses Agyia Manu (1980–1984), and Apostle Kokoe Mensah (1984–1986). By 1985, the church in Burkina Faso had grown to 638 members. Other missionaries included Pastor Kenyon, a British national (1987–1988), Apostle B. K. Arthur (1989–1992), Apostle J. K. Ampomah (1992–1996), Apostle Koffi Kossonou (1992–1996), Pastor Lacou Coulibally (1996–2004), Apostle Badu Nyarko (1996–2000), Apostle Ousmane Zabre (1996–2009), Apostle Badu Woode (2009–2013), and Apostle René Coco (2013–2016). On September 1, 2016, Apostle Pierre-Marie Bayala, a Burkinabe national, was appointed as the national head in preparation for the autonomy of the church in Burkina in the next three years. The overall membership of the church is estimated to be 9,865, drawn from 126 assemblies in 37 districts with 37 ministers.

CoP in Côte d'Ivoire

The earliest attempt to establish the church in Côte d'Ivoire was in the 1950s when Prophet John Mensah, a former prophet of the CoP, tried starting a local congregation there. His effort was characterized by some acrimony. The CoP in Côte d'Ivoire actually began in 1956 under the leadership of Pastor J. B. Acher, stationed in Treichville as the first resident missionary from Ghana. The church was registered as a religious body under the name Eglise de Pentecôte, Côte d'Ivoire, in 1966. Apparently, the name "Church of Pentecost" had been registered by an earlier body. Other missionaries to the church in Côte d'Ivoire from the headquarters in Ghana included Pastor J. W. Sackey, Pastor B. K. Swanzy, Pastor J. K. Appiah, Apostle B. K. Arthur, Apostle B. Y. Apedo, and Apostle M. K. Ntumy. The church had an initial setback in 1978 when a faction seceded. They took away some major assemblies in the southern towns. By the end of 1986, the total membership was around 2,000 congregants, and there were 81 local churches.

In 2009, the leadership of the church in Ghana thought it prudent to make the churches in Côte d'Ivoire and Benin independent of the CoP Ghana as part of its proposal of granting the national churches autonomy to operate on their own. The strength of the autonomous Côte d'Ivoire CoP by 2013 was 65,458 adherents and 821 congregations. The CoP in Côte d'Ivoire at the end of 2016 claims an overall membership of 87,063, collated from 1,083 assemblies in 156 districts in its 20 administrative areas. They have 170 ministers, two of whom are missionaries sent out to other countries. Its lay leadership strength is 4,150, made up of 1,226 elders, 1,114 deacons, 1,688 deaconesses, and 122 other leaders (such as children's teachers and home cell leaders).

CoP in Liberia

The church was started in Liberia in 1962 through migrant fishermen. They included Kobina Awotwe and Kwadwo Kum and their wives. Following some disagreements, the group was destabilized until its reorganization in 1966. Apostle F. D. Walker became the first resident missionary from Ghana in 1976. Under his leadership, the church was said to have experienced phenomenal growth in the midst of great challenges in Liberia in those days, such as dread of witchcraft practices, ancestor worship, massive promiscuity and polygamy. The church made great strides into many areas in the country. They moved into places such as Monrovia, Logon Town, Popo Beach, Buchanan, Bong Mines, and Krakatau. Apostle Frank C. Ampiah took over from Apostle Walker as the national head from 1982 to 1988. Apostle D. K. Arnan (1988–1990) was helped by Pastor Michael K. Ntumy, also from Ghana, working under him as a resident missionary in Buchanan, another part of Liberia. The first acting national head, an indigenous Liberian minister, was the Rev. George Logan, stationed at Monrovia during the period prior to the Liberian political unrest in 1989. The others include Apostle Blessed Bonney (1995–2001), Apostle J. W. D. Cudjoe (2001–2002), Apostle Maasaboi M. Zuwu (2002–2012), and Apostle Nathaniel Ajayi (2012–present). The numerical strength of the church in Liberia by 2013 was 13,722 members and 121 congregations. Statistics at the end of 2016 indicated an overall membership of 16,220, carved from 165 assemblies located in 36 districts of the church.

CoP in Nigeria, Sierra Leone, and Others

Beginning in 1976, the CoP established congregations in many West African countries such as Nigeria in 1978. Moses Ladejo, a Nigerian born and raised in Ghana, was stationed as the first resident missionary from Ghana. He was assisted by Pastor A. K. Miah, also from Ghana. In 1987, the church reached Sierra Leone. In 1988 it was established in Gambia through the invitation of Mr. Eddy Carol, then director of Youth for Christ. In 1989, a resident missionary, Pastor S. K. Baidoo, was sent to Gambia, supported by Pastor N. A. O. Amegatcher. The church was later established in other nations in West Africa: Guinea Bissau, Guinea Conakry, Mali, and Niger. The history and statistics of the state of the CoP churches in these churches in West Africa and other nations can be found in the church's recent publication *Into the World We Go: The Missionary Enterprise of the Church of Pentecost*, by Onyinah and Ntumy. The present work does not provide enough space for all the history of the West African nations.

CoP in Southern and Eastern Africa

In the 1990s, the CoP spread out into places such as South Africa (1990), Malawi (1992), Botswana (1993), Zambia (1993), Gabon (1994), Mozambique (1994), Senegal (1994), Lesotho (1995), Tanzania (1996), Kenya (1997), and Zimbabwe (1997). Clearly the church began expanding in the 1990s from Ghana beyond its neighboring West African region into the southern and eastern parts of the African continent.

CoP in South Africa

The first country to be reached in this period was the Republic of South Africa. The expansion was pioneered by Deacon Evans A. Akuffo, a Ghanaian resident in Umtata, in the former Transkei homeland in apartheid South Africa. He thought it was time to have the CoP in the country after living there for five years and fellowshipping with other churches. On July 19, 1990, he obtained permission, in response to a letter he wrote to the church's Executive Council in Ghana, to commence a branch of the CoP in South Africa. CoP–South Africa duly commenced with Brothers Augustus Amegbley, Stephen Soglo, and Clement Obeng-Tuffoh. The first service was held on February 10, 1991, in a classroom at E. W. Pearce Junior Secondary Northcrest. The international missions director (IMD), Apostle Opoku Onyinah, visited the growing church June 18–22, 1992. His visit culminated in the sending of a missionary and his wife, Pastor and Mrs. M. C. Aseidu, as the first missionaries, on July 18, 1993. The CoP in South Africa was inaugurated by Apostle Opoku Onyinah (IMD) on July 25, 1993. Evans A. Akuffo was made an elder and became the national deacon. There were 144 members present at the inaugural service.

The church kept expanding as other assemblies were opened. Butterworth, Engcobo, Queenstown, Mount Ayliff, Johannesburg, and Port Elizabeth assemblies were opened between 1992 and 2000. The total recorded membership at the end of June 1998 was 250 adult members and 70 children. Elder Evans Akuffo was called into the pastorate as a tent minister and was ordained into the full-time pastorate in 2002, after serving for five years. The first National Executive Committee members were Pastor M. C. Aseidu, chairman; Elder Evans A. Akuffo, national deacon; Elder Yirenkyi Gyeke Darko, national secretary; and members Elder Benjamin Agyemang Coffie, Elder S. F. Ayesu Koranteng, Elder G. G. A. Smith, and Elder Clement Obeng-Tuffoh. The growth of the assemblies necessitated the sending of another missionary attaché from Ghana, Pastor Eric Nyamekye, accompanied by his wife, Mary. They were stationed in Umtata while Apostle M. C. Asiedu was moved to Port Elizabeth. The CoP national headquarters in South Africa was subsequently moved to Port Elizabeth in July 2000. Until Pastor Asiedu's tenure of missionary service ended, three persons were called into full-time ministry: Pastors Evans A. Akuffo (1997), Zola Mahlakata (2001), and David Nyoka (2001). Pastor Aseidu was transferred back to Ghana on September 24, 2004, after an 11-year stay in South Africa. Subsequent missionaries sent from Ghana after him were Apostle J. W. D. Cudjoe (2006–2011), Apostle E. K. Acquah (2011–2015), and Apostle Dr. Dela Quampah (2015–present). The membership strength of CoP South Africa recorded in 2015 was 5,515. They had 14 district pastors overseeing 49 assemblies located in seven out of the 10 provinces in the nation. Pastors Cameron Ndabesita Sikrweqe and Evans A. Akuffo were sent as missionaries to the Kingdom of Lesotho from 2005 to 2009 and from 2009 to 2015, respectively. In 2015 Apostle Dr. Dela Quampah was appointed to replace Apostle E. K. Acquah. The overall membership figures of the church indicated a drop of membership from 5,151 in 2015 to 4,648 in 2016.

CoP in Malawi

The CoP was started in Malawi in 1992 by a Ghanaian couple, John and Beryl Adu. It began as a prayer meeting in a refugee camp in Dedza, a small town in the central area of Malawi. Mr. Adu was a staff member of the United Nations High Commission for Refugees, on mission to take care of refugees who had crossed over from Mozambique to Malawi due to the war in Mozambique. Mr. and Mrs. Adu used the opportunity of having a Christian population to form a prayer group. They reported the rapid growth of the group to the CoP headquarters in Ghana. After periodic visits to the group by the IMD, Apostle Opoku Onyinah, in 1993 and 1994, the CoP was officially established. In 1994, Pastor Emmanuel Achim Gyimah was sent as the first missionary from Ghana to Malawi. The successive missionaries from Ghana who have overseen the CoP in Malawi are Pastor Emmanuel Achim Gyimah (1994–1996), Apostle Samuel Lord Agyin (1996–2004), Apostle Sylvester Arhin (2003–2009), Pastor Seth Kweku Asomaning (2009–2010), Apostle Johnson Agyemang-Baduh (2010–2013), and those from Malawi are Pastors Patrick and Andrew Pangani (2013–present). The church had a brief challenge in 2009 when an indigenous pastor appointed to take over the leadership, Esau Banda, declined the appointment and broke away with 58 percent of the members to form his own church. This setback notwithstanding, by 2015 the CoP in Malawi counts 7,356 members, all of whom are indigenous Malawians, with the exception of five Ghanaians and a Burundian. Pastor Patrick Pangani, appointed as the acting national head, was called into apostleship and confirmed as the substantive area head in 2017. The church operates in three of the four political regions with 81 local assemblies and 13 pastoral districts. The church at the end of 2016 claimed a total membership of 8,594 from 84 local assemblies in 13 districts.

CoP in Botswana

The CoP in Botswana was started in 1993 as a house fellowship by a group of Ghanaian CoP members resident in the country. The fellowship commenced through the initiative of Comfort Boamah, the wife of Brother Boniface Boamah, on a visit to her husband from Ghana. The membership of the initial group included Brother Boniface and his wife, Comfort, Brother Bonney, Deacon Daniel Amankwa, and Sisters Louisa Boamah and Juliana Boamah. The progress of the group was communicated to the CoP headquarters in Ghana, which wasted no time in dispatching the IMD, Apostle Opoku Onyinah, to pay a working visit on July 27, 1993.

He followed up his visit the next year, on July 27, 1994, and at this meeting Brother Boniface was ordained as an elder of the church. The process to have the CoP registered in Botswana was initiated. Mrs. Sarkodie-Mensah, Ghana's Consular General in Botswana and a member of the group, was mandated to help with this. Subsequently, the first missionary sent to Botswana was Pastor S. R. Odum in 1994. He had 26 members, three elders, and four deaconesses to continue with. After five years he had opened three other assemblies. The subsequent missionaries to Botswana include Pastor Osei Owusu-Brempong (1999–2005), Pastor Nii Kotei Djani (2005–2013), and Pastor George Prah Amonoo (2013). Pastor George Prah Amonoo's stay was cut short due to his inability to process his residential permit. By 2014 the CoP in Botswana had 11 assemblies in four districts and a total of 448 members. The church has two ministers who are Botswanan nationals. The absence of a resident minister or national head in the church since 2013 affected the growth and expansion of the church. Pastor Evans Akuffo from South Africa was made the national head, and he assumed duty on October 29, 2015. By the close of 2016, the CoP in Botswana claimed an overall membership of 561, with 12 local assemblies and four districts.

CoP in Mozambique

The CoP was started in Mozambique in 1994 by a Mozambican, Alberto Campira. During the civil war, which lasted 16 years, Campira was in Malawi as a refugee in the Dedza District of the Central Region, where CoP had started a church. As a member of the CoP in Malawi, Campira returned to Mozambique and started a branch of the CoP in Tete in 1994. Another group of refugees also started another branch in Milange in the province of Zambezia. The resident missionary in Malawi, Pastor Emmanuel Achim Gyimah, along with Apostle Alfred Koduah of Zambia and others, helped nurture the church in Mozambique. Between 1994 and 2000 the church operated in two provinces, Tete and Zambezia, with 21 assemblies and a total of 2,508 members. Pastors Asamoah Baah (2000–2005) and Jequessene (2005–present) have overseen the church since its inception. By 2014, the church operated in six out of the 10 provinces in the nation. The total membership is estimated at 4,279 in 28 assemblies and eight districts. The church in 2016 had 26 assemblies in two districts, and an overall membership estimated at 4,501.

CoP in Lesotho

The CoP in Lesotho was started when Brother Miah, a Ghanaian CoP member living in Lesotho, invited the church in South Africa to start a branch there. In 1995, Pastor Michael Collins Aseidu and Elder Evans Akuffo from CoP South Africa moved to start the church. They commenced at the home of Mr. and Mrs. Adu-Boansi, CoP members from Ghana resident in Lesotho. The pioneering members included Brothers Agyemang Oduro, Denis Bentil Adu, Vincent Badu Acquah, and Andrews Kwabena. The church was initially led by Elder and Mrs. Evans A. Akuffo, who traveled 1,500 km every weekend to oversee the congregation. Elder K. Osei Abunyewah was transferred from Umtata to head the church. Since the congregation was mainly Ghanaian at this time, it suffered a great setback from the 1998 political unrest in Lesotho. Many of the members relocated from the country to other places. In December 1998, Pastor David Tekper was sent to Lesotho from Ghana for three months. In 2000, a resident missionary, Pastor J. F. Asante-Ayeh and his family, were posted from Ghana to Lesotho. Pastor J. F. Asante-Ayeh was replaced by Pastor Cameron Sikrweqe from Butterworth District in

South Africa from 2005 to 2009. Pastor Evans Akuffo pastored Lesotho from 2009 until 2015.

The growth of the church was gradual. There was only one assembly from 1995 to 2005. Three more assemblies—Butha Buthe, Lithabaneng, and Ha Leqele—began from 2006 to 2009. Six more were added from then until 2014. As of 2015, the church operates in three geopolitical districts of the nation. The total membership is 564 adults and 250 children. During the General Council meeting held at the Pentecost Convention Centre in 2015, Pastor Peter Eshun was appointed a missionary and sent to replace Evans Akuffo. He assumed duty in Lesotho September 24, 2015. At the end of 2016, the CoP in Lesotho was located in three out the 10 political districts in the country. They claimed a total membership of 700, from five assemblies in two districts of the church.

CoP in Zambia

The CoP in Zambia started as an interdenominational Christian prayer fellowship in 1993. There were two recognizable groups or fellowships. The first was a Christian nondenominational fellowship group formed by Pastor Nelson Lukwesa, who was magistrate at the Copperbelt in 1990. Another group was also meeting in the Kafue Estates at Davies Munalula's house. Among them were Elders S. Y. Antwi and Ekow Badu Woode, both foreign teachers to Zambia and elders of the church from Ghana. The two groups joined together and started meeting as one congregation. After studying the CoP constitution, they decided to affiliate with the CoP in 1995. The group was registered with the Registrar of Societies in 1995 as The Church of Pentecost International–Zambia Branch.

Elder S. Y. Antwi was the first presiding elder. Nelson Lukwesa was sent to the Bible school in Ghana in 1994 and later returned as a full-time pastor in the church. Since its inception, several missionaries were sent to administer the affairs of the church in Zambia: Apostle Alfred Koduah (1994–1998), Apostle E. C. Asante (1998–2003), Apostle F. K. Andoh (2003–2008), and Pastor Nsiah (2008–2015). In 2015, the church had 11 districts made up of 42 assemblies, with 3,942 members. In 2016 they reported 45 assemblies from 10 districts and claimed a total membership of 3,525.

CoP in Senegal

The CoP in Senegal was planted by the church in Gambia. Though it is situated on the West Coast of Africa, CoP–Senegal only started there in 1994 through the initiative of the CoP resident missionary in Gambia, Apostle Francis Ofori Yeboah. A scouting was made by Pastor Alex Adwere to Dakar, and he managed to gather a few Ghanaians to start with. Among those who met was a deacon of the church, Charles Annor-Boakye, who was made the leader of the group. Subsequent visits by Apostle Ofori Yeboah and Pastor Alex Adwere yielded more abiding fruit by bringing more Ghanaians into the group.

On September 27, 1995, Pastor Emmanuel Gyesi-Addo was posted to Senegal as the first resident missionary. By 1998 the church was thriving as a continental church with members from Senegal and other countries such as Liberia, Benin, Nigeria, Togo, Congo, Cameroon, Côte d'Ivoire, and Ghana. Subsequent missionaries sent to oversee the church were Pastor Joe Ephraim (1998–2001), Pastor Yaw Annor-Adjei (2001–2006), Apostle Christian Kouakou Abissa (2006–2009), and Apostle J. O. Kessie (2009–2014). By the middle of 2015, the church in Senegal had eight districts, 40 assemblies, and 2,140 members. During the 41st session of the General Council meeting of the church held May 6–7, 2015, in Ghana, Pastor Alphonse Coly from Togo was ordained as an apostle and subsequently transferred from Togo to replace Apostle J. O. Kessie as the national head in Senegal. The overall membership figure for CoP in Senegal at the end of 2016 was estimated at 2,219, from 43 local assemblies located in eight districts.

CoP in Tanzania

The church's breaking ground in various parts of East Africa involved deliberate efforts, made especially by the CoP in Zambia through its resident missionary, Apostle Alfred Koduah. The method of establishing CoP congregations in East Africa was a departure from that of the western African churches, which started by house and prayer fellowships. In parts of East Africa, the church started through contacts and affiliations with other bodies or sometimes through the adoption of congregations already established by indigenes. These differences may be due to the language difference from West Africa (East Africans predominately speak

Swahili and English) or to difficulty in getting the CoP registered without an indigene's effort or intervention.

In Tanzania, for instance, Apostle Alfred Koduah attended a Morris Cerrulo conference in Dar es Salaam in 1995 to establish contact and explore avenues for church planting. From October 19 to 22, 1996, he, in the company of Brother Shadrack Nkata from the church in Zambia, visited Mbeya, Tanzania. Brother Nkata understands and interprets Swahili. On November 7, 1996, through many initial contacts and protocols, the CoP became affiliated with Pastor Gamanywa's organization in order to have an official cover. Three months afterward, an evangelist from Tanzania, Jackson Bisso Nntepa, wrote to express interest in working with the CoP to establish a presence in Tanzania. Efforts towards this were initiated by the IMD Apostle B. K. Arthur, who traveled together with Apostle Koduah to Tanzania to formalize this arrangement on August 6, 1997. They entered into understanding and affiliation with Gamanywa's organization and accepted Nntepa as CoP representative in Tanzania and moved him from Mbeya to Dar es Salaam to start the CoP Tanzania.

In October 1997, Pastor S. Y. Antwi was sent from Ghana to strengthen the church. He found no church on his arrival. With the help of the Campus Crusade for Christ office in Dar es Salaam and a Brother Faustin Kalambi, he held a crusade and opened an assembly in Tabata Mwenzi, a suburb of Dar es Salaam. The church was started in the house of Mr. Kasandra with 15 members. After staying for seven weeks, Pastor S. Y. Antwi left a strong congregation to the care of Jackson Bisso Nntepa. The International Executive of CoP sent Apostle E. K. Ekuban as the first missionary on November 11, 2000. Through his enterprise and effort, other assemblies were planted in Temeke, Ubungo, Usigala, Mkindo, Ilugu, Insimba, and Milanbo in the Tabora Region. The pioneering members include Sosthenes Edward, Stephen Urasa, Mr. and Mrs. Joseph Mbelwa, Joseph Kibiki, and Esther Nnetepa. The church was registered in the Home Affairs Ministry under the name The Church of Pentecost International on September 27, 2004. The church was advised to add "International" to the name because there was another church in the country registered with the name Kanisa La Pentecoste (Church of Pentecost).

Apostle E. K. Ekuban was replaced after seven years by Pastor Nicholas Appiah Missah on August 12, 2007. Subsequently Pastor Daniel Yeboah Nsaful took over from Appiah Missah on September 2, 2012. By the end of 2014, there were 16 assemblies from six pastoral districts within seven regions. The total membership was 1,723. There were three ministers and a field assistant, all of them Tanzanians. The close of 2016, however, showed a decrease in the total membership from 1,723 to 1,264 and in the number of assemblies from 16 to 15. At the 15th session of the Extraordinary Council meeting, Pastor Daniel Yeboah Nsaful was ordained as an apostle.

CoP in Kenya

The CoP in Kenya began through the initiative of the branch in Zambia. The first attempt at establishing the church in Kenya was made by Apostle Alfred Koduah, a CoP missionary to Zambia, October 26–29, 1996. This initial attempt to get the church started was unsuccessful.

A second attempt was made on August 8, 1997, through a meeting between Apostle Alfred Koduah and Pastor Yusuf Gowi Okumu, the general secretary of the Evangelical Fellowship of Kenya (EFK). The two met and struck an acquaintance at the Global Congress on World Evangelization held in July 1997 in Pretoria, South Africa. Based on their discussion, Pastor Yusuf Gowi Okumu aided the CoP in forming an affiliation between the CoP and the EFK in Kenya. Pastor Okumu also found Geoffrey Osolo, a student at an Assemblies of God Bible College in Nairobi, to assist in the pioneering of the CoP in Kenya. As a follow-up to this meeting, Pastor S. Y. Antwi visited Kenya as part of a mission to East Africa by the Executive Council. During this two-week visit, he formalized the starting of the church, place of worship, and payment of allowances to Geoffrey Osolo, who was still a student. In August 1999, Pastor E. K. Osei-Ofosu and Elder K. Ntiamoah, who were on a course at CORAT-AFRICA, were mandated by the International Missions Office to help Geoffrey Osolo to acquire a hall in Nairobi for church services. The maiden meeting was held on December 5, 1999, at a rented hall in Donholm Estate. Pastor E. C. Asante from Zambia officiated at this service, along with Pastor E. K. Ofosu, Elder Ntiamoah, and Geoffrey Osolo, with 30 adults in attendance. These included Elders Bonaface Owiti Anyango and Coleman Otage, who became the national head and national secretary, respectively.

Other local branches were adopted by Brother Geoffrey Osolo from the Busia District of eastern Kenya to the borders of Uganda. Pastor E. C. Asante, the missionary to Zambia, was given an additional responsibility to oversee or supervise the work in Kenya. He made three pastoral visits to Kenya from 1999 to 2000. In this period, the church also had 12 local assemblies from the Maasai-Kajiado Area, apart from the three local churches adopted from the Busia District. Vincent Ogesa supervised the assemblies in the Busia District, while Simon Ole Muntolol provided leadership for the congregations in the Maasai-Kajiado. Pastor Paul Jerry Adzah and his family were sent as the substantive missionaries to the branch in Kenya on August 2, 2000. Three more assemblies were opened in this period, including Eldoret Assembly.

An internal rift ensued between the missionary, Pastor Paul Jerry Adzah, and the caretaker, Brother Geoffrey Osolo. The rift eventually led to the dismissal in 2003 of Brother Geoffrey Osolo on the grounds of gross misconduct and failing to work amicably with his fellow ministers. In 2003, Pastor Paul Jerry Adzah was transferred back to Ghana and was replaced by Pastor and Mrs. Bright Yaw Senanyah from East Timor. They arrived in Kenya on September 5, 2003. The church was initially registered as an "International Centre," since the government of Kenya had placed an embargo on church registration from 1994. However, on June 17, 2004, the church was registered as The Church of Pentecost–Kenya. At the end of 2005 the total membership of the church was 1,687, with 26 local assemblies. Pastor Bright Yaw Senanyah was relieved by Pastor Emmanuel Offei Ankrah Badu in 2008. The church in Kenya is 80 percent Maasai, with the remainder made up of other tribes. The CoP headquarters in Ghana built and dedicated a 1,000-person capacity church and provided a Toyota Hillux pick-up truck for the Maasai area. Pastor Emmanuel Offei Ankrah-Badu was replaced by Pastor Samuel Berko from Ghana in 2015. At the end of 2016 the total membership of the church was estimated at 6,054, drawn from 77 assembles located in 16 districts of the church.

CoP in Zimbabwe

The CoP in Zimbabwe was initiated by Deacon Alexander Kporha, who was in Zimbabwe in 1994 to work for the United Nations Development Programme (UNDP). He was seconded to work with the Women's Bureau, an NGO involved in women's training. As is the tradition of CoP members when they travel abroad, he began to seek avenues to start a church in his local community, Charakupa Township in Kandava Village, near Harare.

Deacon Kporha's letter to the Missions Office in Accra for permission to start a CoP assembly in Zimbabwe received a positive response in 1996. Kporha encountered one Mr. Sibanda on his way to his rural home and presented the gospel to him. Though Mr. Sibanda himself did not make a decision for the gospel at that time, he led Kporha to his wife, who became the first convert to the CoP in Zimbabwe. Mrs. Sibanda mobilized other people in her area to form a Bible study group that met at her home. Kporha later witnessed to Mrs. Beholds Mbesa, the project leader of the Women's Bureau. The Mbesa family formed the nucleus of the fledgling church in Zimbabwe. These two groups—those from Mrs. Sibanda's group and the Mbesa family—joined together to form the first assembly. Mrs. Mbesa is a deaconess of the Zimbabwe church. Another assembly was later opened in Murewa.

The Zambian church and its missionary, Apostle Alfred Koduah, collaborated with Alexander Kporha in the expansion of the church in Zimbabwe. Apostle Koduah and his entourage, together with Kporha, visited the churches on April 22, 1997. The service at Munamba in Murewa was attended by 16 adults. The leader of the group was a 16-year-old form-four student. Mrs. Sibanda's group was attended by 13 adults.

Since 1997, the CoP in Zimbabwe has progressed tremendously. In subsequent missions to Zambia, Pastor S. R. Odum (September 1997) and Apostle E. C. Asante (1998) took turns to reinforce the stability and growth of the church in Zimbabwe. In July 1999, Apostle B. K. Arthur hosted the first conference for CoP missionaries from central and southern Africa and their wives. The first resident missionary sent to Zimbabwe was Pastor S. Y. Antwi in October 1999. He took over with one field personnel, five local assemblies, and 110 members. By September 2005, there were 20 local assemblies in five districts and a membership of 850, with three indigenous ministers and two field workers. The field workers are full-time ministers paid by the church in Zimbabwe, while the rest are paid from Ghana. Other ministers sent to Zimbabwe include Pastor and Mrs. E. K. Akpabli (2005–2008), Apostle Mark Obeng Andoh (2008–2012), and Pastor Isaac Tetteh Judah (2012–present). In 2014, the church in Zimbabwe had 10 districts and 31 assemblies with a membership of 2,338, 46 elders, 20 deacons, and 77 deaconesses. The total membership of the church in 2016 had increased to 2,675, in 32 local assemblies and 10 administrative districts.

CoP in Central African Countries

The prophetic utterances explained earlier in chapter 4, on which the church stands as its mandate to reach the whole of Africa with the gospel of Jesus Christ, continues to be relevant. It seems as though the CoP has a mechanism for the transmission of the Spirit of Pentecostalism from one African location to another. This CoP story is akin to that of Acts 1:8 in which Jesus mandated his disciples, "But you shall receive power when the Holy Spirit has come upon you; and you shall be witnesses to Me in Jerusalem, and in all Judea and Samaria, and to the end of the earth."

The CoP, based on its initial belief in this prophecy, clearly spread from Ghana into the neighboring West African countries, and thence into southern and eastern Africa. Since 1994, the CoP has been making inroads into locations in Central Africa. These Central African locations include Gabon, Angola, Cameroon, Chad, Central African Republic, Congo Brazzaville, DR Congo, Equatorial Guinea, and Ethiopia. The Missions Report presented to the 42nd session of the General Council meeting (2015) confirms this with detailed reports from these nations.

CoP in Gabon

The CoP in Gabon, unlike others, did not start as a fellowship or prayer group. It was a deliberate attempt to establish a church, which God graciously honored. In September 1994, a group from the International Christian Chamber of Commerce (ICCC), Ghana, led by Elder Kofi Amponsah of PIWC Accra, undertook a business trip to Gabon to participate in a fair of "Made in Ghana Products." The Executive Council of the CoP, through the IMD, Apostle Opoku Onyinah, asked Pastor A. K. Miah, who was the district pastor of Mamprobi, to join the ICCC group so that he could explore the possibility of starting a branch of the CoP in that country.

The group arrived in Gabon on September 24, 1994. Three days later, Pastor Miah met with Mr. Emmanuel Disse, who was the Honorary Consul General of Ghana. Through his efforts, it was arranged for Pastor Miah to meet with the Ghanaian community during their weekly meeting in Lafon-Dakar, Libreville. During the meeting, Pastor Miah had the opportunity to speak for 20 minutes. While he was preaching a message from Acts 1:8, there was a powerful outpouring, and seven people received Holy Spirit baptism. Three days later, 17 people joined in the first service. By the time Pastor Miah returned to Ghana, the number had increased to 48. These included Elder Amponsah Clement, Deacon Francis Baidoo, and Brothers Adjei Yeboah, Emmanuel Donkor, and Afful Shama. The church has been overseen by Pastor Anthony Kingsley Miah (1997–2004), Apostle Basili Kambire Luc (2004–2006), Apostle Emmanuel Gyasi Addo (2007–2011), and Apostle Komi Edina Agbavitoh (2011–present). By 2015, the apostle had 16 assemblies from six districts with a total of 1,512 members. These statistical figures had not changed much by 2016; the total membership decreased slightly to 1,502.

CoP in Northern African Countries

The CoP is also reaching out into North Africa, known to be predominantly Muslim. The CoP claimed its presence in Libya from early 2000 to 2011, until the political turmoil that ousted Libyan President Muammar Gaddhafi. Since 2011, the Missions Department has received no report from the CoP in Libya. But CoP records indicate its presence in North African locations such as Tunisia, where it was established in 2008. The period of its establishment is linked with the temporary relocation of the African Development Bank (ADB) from Côte d'Ivoire to Tunisia in 2003 due to political instability in Côte d'Ivoire in 2002. Elder N'Guamah Francis, an official of the ADB and a member of the CoP–Côte d'Ivoire, engineered the move. The government of Tunisia has laws restricting the operation of churches, allowing only three recognized churches, which are not evangelical. Elder N'Guamah Francis brought together all bank staff who were members of evangelical churches to form a single church. The total number of people he brought together was about 360. In the initial three months they prayed and had fellowship in hotels and in their homes.

Around the same time, Apostle Ebenezer Appiah from CoP–Côte d'Ivoire, on a mission to study the possibility of establishing CoP in the country, met with Elder N'Guamah. They therefore used the presence of the established group to form CoP out of the members who were willing. The initial nucleus of the church included Elder Francis N'Guamah, Brother N'Guamah Fréderic, Sister Rose Jolie Niamké, Deaconess Sinza Emilie and her daughter. They met in each other's houses sharing fellowship and prayer. In 2010, Elder N'Guamah requested the CoP headquarters to send a full-time minister to lead the congregation. Evangelist

Assemian Philippe and his family were appointed and sent from CoP–Côte d'Ivoire as the first CoP missionary to Tunisia. On September 18, 2011, the apostle was officially inaugurated by Apostle Sidiki Traoré, national head of the Church of Pentecost–Côte d'Ivoire. On September 15, 2013, Pastor Gnaoré Raymond Bernard went to relieve Evangelist Phillipe as the resident missionary. The 2013 Missions Report to the General Council reported the CoP in Tunisia to be progressing. The 2015 Missions Report indicated that evangelism was going on through door-to-door contacts because the nation prohibited open-air campaigns. They claimed membership to be only black African migrants from different nationalities. The 2016 Missions Report indicated a total membership of 117 in a local assembly. The CoP in Tunisia is not officially registered in the country; it is covered by the registration of an NGO operating in the nation, REMAR NGO. However, the missionary, who is from Côte d'Ivoire, has been granted a working permit to operate in the country.

GENESIS OF COP INTERNATIONAL MISSIONS IN OTHER LOCATIONS

As stated previously, the early fathers of the CoP conceived the future of the organization to be global and missionary in nature. Its overseas international missionary endeavors, designated external missions, extended into the West and other non-Western locations (apart from Africa) and during the late 1970s and 1980s became prominent as a result of some political and socioeconomic developments in Ghana.

During this era, the political developments in the African continent had resulted in massive emigrations of people of African descent to various other parts of the globe for varying reasons, including seeking asylum, greener pastures (lucrative jobs), and better education. This era saw many Africans migrating into countries north of the equator, including the United Kingdom. As Wout van Laar has shown, thousands of Africans stream to Europe yearly, "hoping for freedom, happiness and a future." A large number or even the majority of these African immigrants were purported to have originated from Ghana at the time, mostly from inland Ghana (Ashanti and Brong Ahafo Regions). This is not surprising.

Ghanaians already have a long history of migration for better job prospects, notably within their own borders and in neighboring countries. The inland people of Ghana, for instance, have a long history of migration due to their farming and trading activities. Apart from the international expansion of religions by mission, migration is one of the most important factors effecting religious dissemination. As Ter Haar pointed out, African migrants carry with them their own religious baggage everywhere they find themselves. The situation for the Ghanaian migrant Christians is no exception. Pobee has indicated that most of a Ghanaian's communal activities, as well as his social institutions, are inextricably bound up with religion. This applies to both the individual and the corporate Ghanaian community—at home and abroad.

The presence abroad of emigrant Ghanaian Christians, burning with the desire to have fellowship with their God and other believers, led to the founding of new congregations all over the US, Europe, and other destinations. The oldest of the African Christian congregations in Europe, according to Ter Haar, are in the former colonial powers, particularly Britain. As already suggested, the political, economic, and other reasons for migration at the time all led to the religious transmissions from Africa, including Ghana, to these Western locations. These home-bred developments culminated in the forming of African congregations, including African Pentecostal and Charismatic congregations such as CoP overseas missions.

As mentioned, people from Ghana have migrated into other places from antiquity. The nature of their primal vocations as farmers, fishermen, and traders has always caused movements of people, both internally and among the neighboring countries like Côte d'Ivoire, Togo, Burkina Faso, and Nigeria. The migration of Ghanaians into the nations of Western Europe and the Americas, however, has come in two phases. The first was the forced migration into the old and new worlds during the slave trade. The second was the voluntary emigration of free Ghanaians from the mid-1970s onwards. This second trend of migration has primarily been driven by political instability and economic factors of the time.

Modern Ghana became independent from British colonial rule in 1957. As a republic, its first president was Kwame Nkrumah. Nkrumah was overthrown in a military coup in 1966; the military handed over control to Kofi Abrefa Busia's Progress Party (PP) in 1969. Another coup was led by an army general, Ignatius Kutu Acheampong, whose government ruled from 1972 to 1978. By this time, Ghana was threatened with imminent collapse through this self-imposed governance. Yet another palace coup by the military in government tried to restructure the military government in 1978. In 1979, there was an uprising and military house-cleaning by junior officers in the army who subsequently handed over power to the third republic, led by Dr. Hilla Limann and his Peoples' National Party (PNP) administration. This political instability led to another military takeover, which brought the military into power again in 1981, led by a junior army officer, Flight Lieutenant Jerry John Rawlings.

These circumstances obviously give motivation for migration, especially since political opponents are bound to be looked on as enemies. Coupled with all this, Ghana was hit by severe drought—one of the worst in the country's history—in 1983, just about the same time that political differences between Ghana and Nigeria had led to the repatriation of over 1,000,000 Ghanaians from Nigeria. The economy of Ghana at this point was in a very bad shape. In a bid to salvage the collapsing economy, Ghana underwent a structural adjustment program imposed by the International Monetary Fund (IMF) and the World Bank, called the Economic Recovery Programme (ERP). This program, though hailed initially as a success story, did not work. By 1990, the economic situation in Ghana had clearly worsened, with 70 percent of the population earning less than one US dollar ($1.00) a day. Basic utility bills went up; healthcare was clearly out of hand since the government had introduced "cash and carry," a system that demands payment of medical bills before treatment; school fees were high, while the education system started collapsing with diminishing school enrollment. The country was almost totally dependent on foreign aid. This economic failure brought untold hardships on the people. The search for political asylum and economic opportunity led people to migrate in search of greener pastures to enable them to sustain their families. Though the prime destination in this period was Europe and United States of America, many found their way to nontraditional points of migration such as Israel, Japan, Taiwan, New Zealand, and Australia. By the mid 1980s, Ghanaians had become a recognizable category of migrant workers in the whole of Europe and other places in the West. By 2000, Ghana had the highest skilled migration rate for countries in West Africa, with a population of over 4,000,000 abroad.

Quite a significant number of these Ghanaian migrants were Christians, among them members of the CoP. Interestingly, what appears to be a misfortune for a nation from which, by the end of the century, one in every five Ghanaians purportedly lives abroad, is considered by CoP as a fulfillment of prophecy. Hanciles writes that "CoP Church annals have it that a prophetic message received in 1948 had warned of this development. The prophecy declared that God was going to instigate a worldwide spread of the Church by allowing life in Ghana to be very difficult; out of the subsequent 'scattering' the message of the gospel will spread."

The CoP adherents among these migrants began house group prayer meetings that eventually developed into full-fledged CoP congregations. The group would then make a request to the CoP headquarters to take over and send a missionary to take up the oversight responsibility. The CoP headquarters in response would send a resident missionary in a circular letter indicating a "call to missions," which indicated what the church intended to achieve. They were not sending a chaplain for their members abroad but a missionary with an assignment.

Beginning from 1984, the CoP was established in places such as the UK, Germany, Holland, Italy, Spain, Belgium, Portugal, Ukraine, Israel, Australia, and the United States. The CoP's annual statistical reports for 2016 give these details: The church has established 182 congregations spread out in different states in the US. There are also 77 congregations in Germany, 28 in Holland, 13 in Australia, 23 in Belgium, 95 in Italy, 43 in Spain, eight in the Republic of Ireland, and 33 in Canada, to name a few. Visible among these lists of Western nations is the United Kingdom, which is considered CoP's parent missionary country. The church claims to have 132 congregations in the United Kingdom. The account below traces the historic details of the CoP–UK.

COP IN THE UNITED KINGDOM

The establishment of CoP congregations in the West, such as CoP–UK, first and foremost affirms the presence of African indigenous independent Pentecostal denominations as immigrant religious establishments in the West. Furthermore, they represent the type of religious institutions these immigrant congregations are developing for Christianity worldwide and for themselves as African immigrants. Most importantly for this study, these international missions help us unravel the factors that promote the success of such missiological enterprise for the CoP and for the entire African Pentecostal mission enterprise.

The CoP–UK has been specifically selected for examination for two significant reasons. First, it demonstrates the extent to which missionary enterprise from a previously "missionary receiving" location (such as sub-Saharan Africa) is coming back to its parent "missionary sending" root (e.g., the UK), but in another capacity as an independent indigenous "missionary sending" organization. The second reason is to determine whether the numerous CoP congregations in the UK reflect current proposals of "missions in reverse" or function as immigrant churches for "chaplaincy," as being caretakers and conveners of their own kind (Africans), just as the early Western missions in Africa were described to have been. Another important enquiry asks whether other forms of emerging missions' trends are being engaged by these immigrant churches.

Scholars and writers are currently enquiring as to whether the non-Western immigrant churches springing up in the West are bringing back the gospel to today's secularized and postmodern societies of the West as reverse mission. The CoP–UK is representative of any African diaspora congregation, especially from CoP–Ghana. This is because the way that CoP diaspora congregations emerge and grow seems to follow more or less the same pattern, as will be seen later in this chapter. The main differences are found in the procedures through which the churches are registered as religious bodies, which may differ in the individual sovereign nations, and in how the churches initially begin. Whereas some of these congregations start as home cells, others begin as nondenominational fellowships or prayer groups. This notwithstanding, CoP–UK will be discussed first here also because it is among the earliest CoP missions to be established abroad.

Historically, the CoP broke away from the British Apostolic Church quite early on, in 1953, yet it appears to carry over some traits from the parent church's governance and structural systems. For instance, its appointment of ministries such as apostles, prophets, evangelists, and pastors, as in Ephesians 4:11, is copied from British Apostolic traditions and church governance. Turnbull noted that the Apostolic Church's governance by apostles and prophets distinguished it from other churches that likewise believe in the baptism with the Spirit. The CoP also differs from Pentecostal and Charismatic bodies such as Assemblies of God and some current Charismatic congregations in its administrative governance through apostles and prophets.

The Historical Beginnings of CoP–UK

From the early 1970s into the late 1980s the immigrant strength of the Ghanaian populace in the UK increased. Among those in London were Ghanaian Christians who found themselves worshipping with different

London-based Christian churches. Many of the Pentecostals among them worshipped with the Elim Pentecostal congregations at different locations, such as Elim Pentecostal Church, Kensington Temple; Newcourt Elim Pentecostal Church, Clement Road, Ilford, Essex; and Elim Pentecostal Church, Regina Road, Finsbury Park. In this period, African Christian Fellowship (ACF) sprang up where African immigrant Christians of different nationalities met periodically. This association of African Christian believers provided for the immigrant Christians a source of spiritual nourishment and an avenue for affirming identity and creating solidarity with one another. It provided the African immigrant students especially with a source of common fellowship and recourse to other socioeconomic support. Mr. Emmanuel Apea suggested that the ACP provided informal counseling on studies and marriage to members who were mostly students.

Later on some Ghanaian Christians among them grouped themselves into a separate nondenominational Christian fellowship, the Ghana Christian Fellowship, which met regularly at 5 Doughty Street, Holborn. The meeting place was later moved to Tavistock Square in the Kings Cross area. Their meetings were not patronized by only Ghanaian nationals; other African Christians in London also became members of the Ghana Christian Fellowship. In the early 1980s some individuals in these associations (ACP and Ghana Christian Fellowship), along with others who were or had been members of the CoP from Ghana, began having discussions about establishing CoP congregations in the UK. These discussions became necessary because some CoP members known in Ghana to be very dynamic in the Christian faith (in terms of Pentecostal spirituality) had either backslidden or become lukewarm upon reaching the UK. The Ghanaians also claimed to find the services at the Elim Pentecostal congregations unsatisfactory in their religious expressions such as language, songs, liturgy, and other elements of worship. They thought they needed to have a distinct Ghanaian/African flavor or identity in their worship.

The CoP in Ghana is known for its informal expressive and vernacular Pentecostal order of service. Services in most of the assemblies or congregations, apart from the PIWCs, are held in Twi, one of the dominant languages in Ghana. The pattern of CoP spirituality, as pointed out by Asamoah-Gyadu, emphasized, among other things, personal transformation, prayer, evangelism, holiness, healing, deliverance, and community living. These Ghanaian CoP members resident in the UK were thought to desire (individually and to some extent corporately) the same type of services as back home. For instance, they wanted to be able to engage in such activities as vibrant prayer sessions, aggressive evangelism, monthly revival meetings, and the like, as in Ghana. The meetings also gave them community in identity and self-perception as Ghanaians. These and other reasons pushed the agenda to start CoP churches in London.

In the late 1970 and early 1980s, Mr. Emmanuel Apea, an elder of CoP and an international civil servant then working at the Commonwealth Secretariat in London, along with others such as Daniel Clottey, a staff member of the Ghana High Commission in London, Kofi Asamoah, John Acheampong, Kabenla, Abraham Lawrence Doku, Sam Tuudah, Samuel Opoku Boateng, and brothers Sam Okwei-Nortey, Yaw Kontoh, and Newton Ofosuhene tried to rally together former CoP members from Ghana. The CoP branch was formed from Ghanaians then fellowshipping with Elim Pentecostal churches in London and other Ghanaians resident in London. This is the typical way CoP congregations are started. The growth pattern of the church has always shown a trend in which individuals or groups of members open up branches in the locations where they reside and request the headquarters in Accra to furnish them with pastoral oversight (see chap. 4).

In 1986, Mr. Sam Tuudah arrived in London from Liberia. Tuudah was an elder and a former national deacon of the CoP in that country. Upon arrival in the UK, he sought contact with Elder Emmanuel Apea through Elder Daniel Clottey. Based on the discussion on the progress of CoP's mission in Liberia related by Elder Tuudah, this group of people was inclined to use the influence and knowledge of Elders Apea and Tuudah to step up the establishment of CoP in UK. They subsequently formed an association in early 1986 that they named the Pentecost Association of UK and Eire (PAUKE). Through the organization of PAUKE, they began inviting—or gathering—all Ghanaian Christians resident in UK (especially those who were members of CoP back home in Ghana) whom they were able to contact. The initial discussions took place at meetings convened at the residence of Brother Abraham Lawrence Doku at 15 Lawrence Road, London, N15 4EN. Later on, the meetings shifted between the residences of Brother Doku, Elder Daniel Clottey, at 79 Axholme Avenue, Edgware HAB 5BD, and Elder Apea, at 78 Roll Gardens, Ilford, Essex.

Later in the same year, two pastors of the church in Ghana, Pastors Opoku Onyinah and Daniel Kwame Noble-Atsu, were granted scholarships to study at the Elim Bible College. Elder Apea convened a meeting of all the leaders and members at his residence, which the pastors were scheduled to attend. This meeting was to officially deliberate on the formation of PAUKE. At this meeting, the pastors conveyed the information from the chairman of the church, Apostle F. S. Safo, to the gathering, reinforcing the necessity and urgency of establishing a UK branch. They had actually been mandated to explore the feasibility of forming a CoP branch in UK. Having discovered the foundation already laid by these brethren, they went ahead to encourage them and officially helped them to launch and recognize the first leaders as executives for the PAUKE. The executives included Elder Emmanuel Apea as the convener, Elder Daniel Clottey as the secretary, Brother Abraham Lawrence Doku as organizing secretary, Elders Kofi Asamoah as treasurer, and Elder Sam Tuudah as the financial secretary.

The first official gathering of the PAUKE after this recognition was held at the Newcourt Elim Pentecostal Church premises on April 9, 1987. The meeting was attended by 28 participants, including Pastors Opoku Onyinah and Noble-Atsu. The group kept meeting regularly from this time on. Due to growth and expansion, the Executive Committee of PAUKE was expanded from five to seven. In January 1989, two more brothers, Elders Samuel Opoku Boateng and Nkansah, were added to the five. Later in the year, around March 1989, as welfare issues such as hospital visitation, childbirth, and immigration problems increased, Brothers Newton Ofosohene Nyarko and Yaw Kontoh Fosu Mainoo were appointed as welfare officers. Deaconess Emma Apea, the wife of Elder Apea, took on the leadership of the Women's Movement. By May of that year, the structures of the association had started taking shape. More CoP members from Ghana and others had joined. The chairman of the CoP, Prophet M. K. Yeboah, assisted by the general secretary, Apostle Rigwel Ato Addison, on a visit, formally inaugurated the PAUKE as a recognized CoP in the United Kingdom on May 6, 1989.

The inauguration was attended by a very significant representation from the Elim Pentecostal Church–UK. This included the Rev. Brian Edwards, Elim International Missions director; the Rev. Gordon Hills, Elim field superintendent; and the Rev. Adrian Hawkes, the senior minister of Newcourt Elim Pentecostal Church. Their presence was very important because, as stated in chapter 3, Elim Pentecostal Church–UK had an affiliation with the CoP. This affiliation had proved very necessary and quite helpful in many ways. Major among them is the part Elim played in helping train some CoP ministers in their college (Apostles Opoku Onyinah and Kwame Noble-Atsu and others were trained in Elim Bible College), granting CoP members in the UK a place for worship and fellowship, and subsequently aiding the church to regularize its registration and acceptance into the community of the United Kingdom.

Growth of CoP–UK

By the middle of 1989, much progress had been achieved by PAUKE in terms of organization, structure, and numerical growth. It was quite evident that the association had taken form as a full-fledged assembly of the CoP. Upon consultation with the other executives of PAUKE, it was thought prudent that a resident pastor be sought as a caretaker for the group. He was to provide shepherding and other ministerial obligations that the leaders could not provide, such as officiating at weddings, dedications of children, and so on. It also became evident that as the association grew, specific pastoral needs of individuals and some protocol concerns needed to be addressed. The need for a resident missionary was considered vital at this time because all the leaders had come to the UK for other reasons than church planting. This made it difficult for them to give their prompt attention to pressing church issues. Elder Emmanuel Apea, who was in Ghana for a vacation, was mandated to meet with the CoP Executive Council to put in a request for a resident missionary for the association. The initial arrangements for receiving the missionary were made by Elder Apea. He, with the help of the Elim Pastor Barry Killick and his board of elders, was to make sure that any CoP minister sent to facilitate the work of PAUKE would be received and helped to settle in the UK.

At the 1989 General Council meeting, Pastor Kwame Blankson and his wife, Ernestina, were posted as the pioneering resident missionaries to the PAUKE and the Pentecost community in the UK. They arrived in the UK in October 1989. The executives of PAUKE whom Pastor Blankson worked with had undergone a few changes: Elder Daniel Clottey, the secretary, had been replaced in July by Elder Okwei-Nortey because Clottey had been reassigned to Ghana by his employers. Elder Emmanuel Apea, the substantive leader, was to leave UK in December that year. He had taken an appointment as chief of the science section at the headquarters of UNESCO in Paris. Pastor Blankson's initial upkeep and accommodation was taken up by Elim Pentecostal Church in Ilford, where both Okwei-Nortey and Emmanuel Apea served as church elders under the pastorate of the Rev. Pastor Barry Killick. An official welcome ceremony was organized for the Blanksons by the group, officiated by Elder Okwei-Nortey and Deaconess Tina Anim.

Receiving Missionaries and Growth

Pastor Blankson and his wife commenced their work in earnest. By rectification of the PAUKE constitution after receiving a resident pastor, the National Executive was composed as follows: Pastor Kwame Blankson as resident missionary, Elder Edward Kwoffie as national secretary, Elder Kwesi Otoo as Missions Board chairman, Elder Samuel Obeng Tuudah as Finance Board chairman, Elder Kwame Nkrumahas as Charity Board chairman, Brother Edward Asare Afriyie as Literature Committee chairman, and Elder Kofi Asamoah as a member. Later in the year, Kofi Asamoah and Kwame Nkrumah relocated to Ghana and were replaced, respectively, by Elders Samuel Opoku Boateng and Newton Ofosuhene Nyarko. Samuel Tuudah left the association and was replaced by Elder Mike Etrue, then a student in the UK. Later yet, Elder Samuel Okwei-Nortey replaced Mike Etrue when he left for Ghana after his course.

The various positions mentioned above (such as resident missionary, Missions Board chairman) clearly suggest the group's intention; the sending authorities from Ghana and the group see their presence in UK as the starting of a new mission field and not as a chaplaincy or caretaking of its members abroad, although taking care of its members is part of its purpose. However, in the first few years from 1989 to 1994, the PAUKE ran as an auxiliary to the Elim Pentecostal Congregation in Ilford under the pastoral care of the Rev. Barry Killick and met on their premises. The Blanksons initially took up roles as both associate pastor for Elim Ilford and the overseers for PAUKE. As was conventional for CoP, it ran the PAUKE as Ilford Assembly while endeavoring to start other assemblies or congregations. In 1991, Vauxhall Assembly was started. Two more were opened in 1992 at Croydon and Wembley. Then in 1993 and 1994, respectively, Tottenham and Hackney began meeting. Following the structure of CoP, presiding elders (lay leaders) were assigned to the individual assemblies because the resident missionary cannot oversee all the assemblies springing up in the different parts of the city due to distance and the difficulties of effectively monitoring so many. Elder Kwesi Otoo was therefore appointed central assembly presiding elder in 1991. Elders Kofi Asamoah, Samuel Opoku Boateng, Ampoma Sakyi, Kwame Nkrumah, and Anthony Antwi Darkwah were made presiding elders at Vauxwell Assembly, Croydon Assembly, Wembley Assembly, Tottenham Assembly, and Hackney English Assembly, respectively. By the end of 1993, it had become evident that the PAUKE was becoming a significant church in itself.

From PAUKE to ELICOP

On January 1, 1994, the Elim Pentecostal outfit aided in registering the PAUKE as a full-fledged church under Elim Foursquare Gospel Alliance, with Elim Charity number 251549 and in the name of Elim Church of Pentecost (ELICOP). ELICOP came under the auspices of Elim Pentecostal as the branch that oversees its black community and immigrant congregations. Other assemblies were opened in subsequent years: East Ham Assembly, Tooting Bec, New Addington, and Deptford in 1995, and Highgate in 1996. The premiere presiding elders assigned to these various assemblies, respectively, were as follows: Elders Sam Okwei-Notey, Ntim Gyakare, Sylvester Wiafe, Osei Owusu Afriyie, and Kojo Yeboah. During this period the numerical strength of the ELICOP increased from a little less than 30 to 1,000 and more. Thus, following CoP's structural and administrative system for growth, two districts were created out of these assemblies: London North and South Districts. Two full-time ministers were called in London at the time to help manage the growing church: Elders Owusu Afriyie and Kwesi Otoo. The missionary responsibilities of the Blanksons were subsequently brought to an end in 1996. They were transferred back to Ghana, where Pastor Blankson became the dean of students at the Pentecost Bible College, where ministers are trained.

The Blanksons were replaced in the UK by Apostle and Mrs. Asomani Sarpong in October 1996. The period also saw the opening of more assemblies at locations such as Carter Place (English Assembly), Slough, and Edmonton. The Sarpongs were replaced in 1999 by Pastor and Mrs. N. A. O. Amegatcher. In Pastor Amegatcher's six years as the resident missionary until 2004, the assemblies began to expand outside London to other cities and towns such as Glasgow, Manchester, Birmingham, Milton Keynes, Harlow, Oxford, Bristol, Crawley, and Reading. This period saw the planting of PIWC congregations in all the major cities. The number of districts increased from two to 13. This means 12 other ministers were called and stationed as district ministers in the districts created. From 2005 on, the leadership changed hands when Apostle M. S. Appiah and his wife came from South Africa as the fourth missionary to ELICOP. Their missionary duty extended until 2011. Within this period, the number of districts increased to 16, with 17 district ministers, including the resident missionary as national head.

Becoming CoP–UK

This era also witnessed a leap in the developmental agenda of the organization. The organization was registered by the UK charity commission as CoP–UK, a company limited by guarantee on May 7, 2008. The CoP–UK then became an independent church distinct from the Elim Foursquare Fraternity in its financial regulations and administration. The church therefore became answerable directly to the charity office in UK. The registered trustees were Apostle M. S. Appiah as chairman, Pastor Kwesi Otoo as secretary, Elder Kwabena Arko Amoateng as finance committee chairman, and as executive members, Pastor Osei Owusu Afriyie, Pastor George Korankye, Pastor Edmund Appiah, and Elder Christian Dampare.

The constitution or charter of the CoP–UK does not mention the role of trustees. However, the membership compositions are thought to rotate concurrently with the tenure of office of the National Executives. Due to growth, the structural administration of the entire CoP–UK was divided into two areas for easier administration: Manchester and London Metropolitan Areas. The CoP–UK had expanded and ministers such as pastors and area heads had been formed and nurtured in the UK. The CoP–UK in this period pioneered missions into the Indian Ocean Islands of Seychelles, Mauritius, and Madagascar and also ventured the sending of missionaries to other places. The members of the CoP churches in these nations are entirely nationals or indigenes of these islands, except for the missionaries and their families. The CoP–UK membership consists mostly of Ghanaians or naturalized Ghanaians and their children who are born British citizens and a few from other African nations. Three of its ministers were sent to Greece, Israel, and France as national heads. Apostle Newton Ofosuhene Nyarko and Pastor George Korankye served concurrently as national heads for Israel and Greece. As Ghanaian-born British citizens, access to residential permits in these places was much easier for them than it would have been for someone from Ghana.

CoP–UK Ministers Assuming Administration

By 2011, the first CoP–UK bred minster was ripe to be given the responsibility of national head for the UK administration. Newton Ofosuhene Nyarko, notably a member of the pioneer leaders, called into ministry since 1993 from London, had risen to the position of an apostle in the CoP. Apostle Newton Nyarko replaced Apostle M. S. Appiah as the fifth national head. The missionary assignment of Apostle M. S. Appiah came to an end in 2011 when he was reassigned to Ghana as the area head of Berekum, in Brong Ahafo Region in Ghana. The readiness with which the missionaries move back to Ghana for their new postings without seceding is unique. These missionaries, as part of their duties, help equip and form capable ministers to take over their work. These ministers (pastors, area heads, apostles) are sent from their base in the UK as missionaries to other locations.

Until June 30, 2014, CoP–UK's statistical annals indicated three administrative areas (London Metropolitan Area, London South Area, and Manchester Area), 19 districts created from 113 congregations, and a total membership of 13,768 (comprising 8,237 adult members above 19 years, 1,580 teenagers, and 3,951 children). The CoP–UK had a resident missionary from Ghana as a national head, 24 full-time ministers (culled from different parts of the UK, most of whom held citizenship), and 1,216 lay leaders (elders, deacons, and deaconesses). By December 31, 2016, these figures had increased to 23 districts created from 132 local assemblies, and a total membership estimated at 16,748. This number was made up of 11,707 adult members of 13 years and above—which includes 1,719 youth members between the ages of 20 and 35 and 2,112 teens between 13 and 19 years—and 5,041 children below 13 years.

The CoP–UK is registered in England and Wales as a Company Limited by Guarantee, with Registration Number 6550075 and Charity Numbers 1123975 (England and Wales) and SC041242 (Scotland). The national headquarters is located in Dagenham, east of London, in an old cinema hall turned into a 3,000-person capacity hall with administrative offices. The offices are well resourced (both human and logistics) to adequately support its resident missionary (as the national head) for the administration of the 24 subsidiaries as districts. The structure also has offices for the national secretary (who is a pastor elected by the national presbytery) and for the administrative secretary and the financial team (comprising the area deacon, an accountant, and the clerk). The entire administration of the CoP–UK is responsible to the international missions director of the CoP through the resident missionary, delegated as the national head.

Achievements, Challenges, Assessment, and Proposals for Growth

The CoP–UK, which began as a small group of immigrants in the UK, has progressed into a self-propagating, self-sustaining, and self-governing church. As part of CoP diaspora missions, CoP–UK has made very meaningful achievements in its two decades or more. With regard to church planting, she has congregations in many important cities and areas in the UK, as described earlier. The reports on estate show 10 permanent acquired church premises, 98 rented premises, and four pastors' manses and cars as adequate means of transport for its ministers. Financially, CoP–UK is able to raise sufficient resources through projected monthly tithes and other offerings (monetary contributions) to sustain its expenditures. It has also been a significant progressive contributor to the church's missions offering, the main financial source of the church's missions endeavors. It has sent missionaries to various places such as Israel, France, Italy, and Greece and has pioneered the planting of the church in Cape Verde and in Madagascar. This is usually an advantage over sending people from Ghana, who struggle to obtain visas. Missionaries from the UK also have a greater working understanding of people in the diaspora than ministers coming directly from Ghana. As a missionary church, it also reports sending quite substantial amounts of money as missionary contributions to other nations where the CoP operates. Recently, the International Missions Board approved and contributed to the purchase of a defunct Christian college in Birmingham to be refurbished for use as a CoP–UK Bible college.

Having assessed the CoP–UK in growth and achievements, an unavoidable question of a religious historian or sociologist would be the percentage of adherents who are indigenous, that is, white British. James McKeown is asserted to have said concerning the planting of an indigenous church in Africa, "I have not come to African to plant an English Oak tree in an African soil." The opposite can be asked about CoP–UK. Can CoP–UK claim not to be planting a baobab tree in an English soil? As oak is a temperate plant suitable for a temperate zone such as England, the baobab is suitable to African soil. In other words, what religious institution is the CoP–UK developing by and for themselves in the UK where they reside? The 2013 statistics regarding adherents shows 16,556 Ghanaian nationals, 26 white British nationals, and 166 other nationals.

A cursory review of the whole structure right from its inception suggests that the church is skewed towards the gathering of its own kind (Ghanaian immigrants) rather than reaching out to the subjects of their sojourning location. A large majority, about 98 percent of the congregations, seems to be either immigrant Ghanaians, CoP adherents from other African nations, or young British citizens born to Ghanaian parents in the church. The indigene of Britain remains conspicuously untouched. The services lean more toward the African-tradition worship style (in liturgy, language, and music) than the English. Many of their services are for Twi-speaking congregations and follow an informal, expressive, and vernacular Pentecostal liturgical order as one would encounter in Ghana.

Of course the system serves largely as a means of identity and solidarity for the members as sojourners in another land. Another prime observation is that the congregations are led by lay leaders (presiding elders), many of whom double as salaried workers in other institutions. The trained ministers oversee a cluster of congregations as district overseers. The question is, How could such a system work efficiently in a complex society where everything is specialized and demands time and commitment?

Beginning around 1997, the missionary designate for CoP–UK, Apostle N. A. O. Amegatcher, in an attempt to confront the issue regarding indigenous congregations, made frantic efforts to have PIWCs instituted in all the district centers and major towns in the UK. More recently, the church is daring to raise youth churches that are led by young people who are British, uninspired by the traditional worship styles of the typical CoP congregation. The idea is for the young people who have been born in the UK—and whose culture and background is British—to be able to win their own kind. It is estimated that if these young people are oriented in this direction they may be able to dare where their parents have not ventured. This trend for CoP–UK can be seen as a pattern the rest of the diaspora missions of the CoP.

At the end of December 2016, the CoP–UK was made up of three administrative areas in the UK. Of its total membership, it counted 16,503 of Ghanaian nationality, 58 white British nationals, and 313 of other nationalities. It has lay-leadership strength of 1,582 (523 elders, 393 deacons, and 666 deaconesses), and a total of 27 ministers, which includes three apostles and a missionary sent to Israel.

With regard to the demographic make up of CoP–UK, the present writer personally observes and argues that CoP international missions such as CoP–UK are more complex than a vision of them as simply a reverse mission. This study argues that CoP missions also uses the Global North locations as a platform to launch missions into other locations in the northern hemisphere and other global locations. For instance, ministers were formed in the UK and nurtured to start churches in Madagascar and Cape Verde. In support of these assertions, the writer has used CoP international missions stations in other locations such as the USA, continental Europe, the Middle East, and the Far East as examples.

COP MISSIONS–USA

This section centers on other Western nations where CoP churches can be found. Apart from their presence in the UK, CoP congregations are located in several other Western countries and in some non-Western or nonconventional migration points such as Israel, India, Nepal, Japan, and Brazil. This section has selectively chosen the historical records of some of these congregations from different parts of the globe (USA, continental Europe, Middle East, and Far East) in an effort to authenticate the viability of African immigrant Christian mission in other parts of the globe as suggested by other scholars and seen with CoP–UK.

The CoP congregations, especially those in the diaspora, always commence as interdenominational Christian fellowships or home prayer meetings. The branch in the USA began as a home prayer meeting by CoP member Brother Eric Oppong and his wife, Theresa, who are Ghanaian immigrants resident in New York City. They started meeting at the Oppongs' home at Fish Avenue, Bronx, New York, in April 1986. Later, in July 1986, they were joined by other CoP adherents from Ghana living in the city. These included Maxwell Kusi, Ben Boakye, Emmanuel

Brown, Charles Baah, and Victoria Gyimah. Others such as Elder Festus Asare, Vida Asare, and Dennis Ababio joined later. The group named itself Church of Pentecost Prayer Group.

By 1987, the number had increased to 17. Brother Oppong moved into a larger residence at Corsa Avenue, Bronx. In 1988, the group was clearly taking shape: their number had increased to 25, activities and commitments had stepped up with weekly night prayer vigils and financial contributions of tithes and offerings. Monthly donations or contributions as tithes and offerings were sent to Ghana. Other people joined who were church members from Ghana: Yaw Yeboah-Asuamah, Thomas Asmah, and Sisters Beatrice Akuamoah, Georgina Boamah, and Victoria Opoku. The CoP considers a full-fledged assembly as one that has a congregation of at least 12 adults and that can pay tithes and offerings. It is more acceptable when there is an ordained elder to promote the group's spiritual growth. The group appointed leaders for themselves: Elder Festus Asare as the leader, Ben Boakye as the secretary, Eric Oppong as the organizing secretary, Maxwell Kusi and Emmanuel Brown as the prayer leaders, and Victoria Gyimah as the treasurer.

The prayer group, upon conferring with CoP headquarters in Ghana, changed its name to CoP–New York and converted to a church. On October 2, 1988, they moved with 35 members to rented premises at 137th Street between 7th and 8th Avenues in Upper Manhattan. The church was registered as a religious nonprofit organization with the state of New York on January 29, 1989, under the name The Church of Pentecost–USA, Inc. The Executive Council of the church in Ghana, upon deliberations with the group, sent a resident missionary, Pastor Anthony K. Awuah, and his wife, to take charge in February 1991. The growth of the CoP–USA became evident in a short while when other locations started gathering up members to start CoP congregations. Just after a year, in October 1992, an additional minister was sent to provide national leadership in the person of Apostle S. K. Ansong and his family. Pastor and Mrs. Awuah were relocated to help start branches in California. In this period, many congregations sprouted in different states and cities. The year 1992 saw branches planted in Atlanta, Greensboro, Charlotte, Tampa, Orlando, Norcross, and Raleigh; districts were created from the congregations for easy management. Within the period from 1989 to 2005, congregations were planted in 25 states, with a total of almost 12,000 adherents in 99 congregations.

The ministerial and administrative structures of the church in the United States were developed in the same pattern as CoP churches everywhere. By this period, they had in place all ministerial and administrative structures, boards, and committees. Other ministerial personnel sent to oversee the church in the US included Apostle A. Osei-Bonsu from 1997 to 2003, Apostle Albert Amoah from 2003 to 2009, Apostle Owusu from 2009 to 2016, and Apostle Michael Agyemang Amoako from 2016 to the present. Within this period, the church in the US raised some 36 ministers, including three apostles and 33 pastors, from its congregations to oversee the areas and districts created in the six administrative areas. At the end of 2013, the church in the US reported six administrative areas, 34 districts, and 140 congregations, with a total of 22,091 adherents, of which 16,465 were adults and 5,626 children. They also recorded a total of 625 elders, 487 deacons, and 722 deaconesses as ordained lay leaders, mostly from the CoP–USA. By December 31, 2016, the number of districts had increased to 55, with 182 local assemblies and 26,364 total members. The composition of their membership is 19,678 total adult members of 13 years and above and 6,686 children below 13. Within the adult membership are 7,663 youth ages 13 to 35, further broken down into 2,888 teen members between 13 and 19, and 4,775 young adults of 20 to 35. These figures comprise 23,060 Ghanaian immigrants, 2,158 nationals or indigenes, and 1,146 other nationals (not US or Ghanaian nationals). The CoP–USA also has a total of 66 ministers and 2,494 lay leaders (823 elders, 629 deacons, and 1,042 deaconesses).

The church in the USA spearheaded the planting of churches in Latin American and Caribbean countries (such as the Dominican Republic, Costa Rica, and Trinidad and Tobago). Many of the members or converts in these places come from the indigenous population. Currently, it has sent two missionaries to Canada and Japan, Apostle Yiadom and Pastor John Ofori, respectively. Pastor John Ofori has an additional responsibility for missions in Korea, Thailand, China, and Hong Kong. Thus, the CoP–USA mission has used its presence and ministerial formation in the US as a platform to reach out to locations in Latin America and Asia.

COP MISSIONS–CANADA

The planting of CoP congregations in Canada was engineered by the growing church in the USA. In September 1990, Elder Emmanuel Owusu

Bediako, the presiding elder of the New York congregation, visited his wife, Faustina, who was living with his brother in Toronto, Canada. Elder Owusu Bediako used the opportunity to gather some Ghanaian residents who were CoP members to start a prayer fellowship in Toronto. The initial meeting was held with 18 participants (11 adults and seven children) at the residence of Mr. Kusi-Akyeampong at 50 Trudelle Street in Scarborough, Toronto. At this opening meeting, a lady by the name of Doris Sackey made a decision for Christ and joined them. As has almost become the tradition, the group asserts that there were some prophetic utterances to the effect that the CoP would spread throughout Canada. This message served as an engine that sparked their enthusiasm.

The pioneering members included Elder and Mrs. Chris Asman, Mr. and Mrs. Danso, Elder Kingsley Mensah, Elder Eric Boateng, Deaconess Rosemond Effah-Adjei, Mrs. Faustina Bediako, and Brother Akuamoah Boateng. Within a month the group had increased numerically to 30. They formed their first leadership team comprising Elder Chris Asman as leader, Elder Kusi-Akyeampong as assistant leader, Elder Kingsley Mensah as secretary, Elder Eric Boateng as financial secretary, Mrs. Grace Akyeampong as treasurer, and Deacon Okyere Akyeampong as member. They kept moving their venues of meeting due to increasing numbers. They moved from Mel Lastman Square to Newtonbrook Secondary School when they exceeded 100 members. The General Council meeting of the church in March 1991 decided that Pastor A. K. Awuah in California would take on the additional responsibility of the infant church in Canada. In 1991, another assembly was started in Montreal, and Elder Emmanuel Anthony Owusu was assigned as the presiding elder. The churches in North America (USA and Canada) had a corporate Easter Convention in Toronto in which delegates from Ghana participated: the chairman, Prophet M. K. Yeboah; the international missions director, Apostle Opoku Onyinah; the general secretary, Apostle Rigwel Ato Addison; and Apostle B. K. Arthur. The meeting was held at Ramada Inn on Wilson Avenue in North York. Other assemblies, including Scarborough, North York, and Peel, were opened. Elders Dan Amponsah and Chris Asman were put in charge of these assemblies.

The main challenge of the infant organization at this level was meeting space and effective pastoral care. The leadership therefore requested a resident missionary from the headquarters in Ghana. The headquarters responded by sending one of its senior ministers to be in charge. In November 1992, Apostle Alex Osei-Bonsu was received in Canada as the missionary designate. From 1992 to 1997, when he was transferred to the USA, churches were planted in seven locations: Toronto, Scarborough, Mississauga, Montreal, Ottawa, Vancouver, and Hamilton. The statistics indicate a total membership of 2,265: 1,595 adults and 669 children, overseen by two minsters, two field assistants, 18 elders, 20 deacons, and 26 deaconesses.

In 1997, Apostle Kwesi Ackah-Baidoo replaced Apostle Osei-Bonsu as the national head. By 2004, congregations had been planted in Calgary, Winnipeg, Edmonton, London, Brampton, Read Deer, Kingston, and Toronto Downtown. In November 2004, Apostle Anthony Kingsley Miah took over from Ackah-Baidoo. By 2005, the Church of Pentecost could be spotted in 15 different locations in Canada, with a total of 680 adherents, 11 ministers, and a total of 182 ordained lay leaders. The church had acquired property such as manses for the ministers, offices, and church premises. The national office, which is a multipurpose facility with a banquet hall, an auditorium, conference halls, schools, and offices, is located at 2256 Sheppard Avenue West, in North York, Toronto. It was from this level that the church in Canada began to reach out into other nations such as Guyana and Brazil in South America. Again we see the same trend: the CoP–Canada using Canada as a platform to reach out into locations in South America. At the end of 2013, CoP–Canada reported two areas, 10 districts, 23 local assemblies, and 4,284 members: 3,377 adults and 907 children. The statistical figures by 2016 showed 11 administrative districts from three areas, with 33 assemblies and an overall total membership of 5,204. This is made up of 4,075 adult members (13 years and above) and 1,129 children (below 13 years). The total figure includes 4,821 Ghanaian immigrants, one white Canadian national, and 382 other nationals. They have 12 ministers, who include an apostle and an evangelist. They also have 397 lay leaders (132 elders, 112 deacons, and 153 deaconesses).

COP MISSIONS–ITALY

In Europe, the CoP has registered an enormous presence in Italy. The CoP in Italy commenced in earnest on June 17, 1990, at the premises of La Chiesa Evangelica-Colugna, Udine, with six Ghanaian immigrants who were CoP members from Ghana: Elder Daniel Prince Wiafe, Mrs.

Faustina Wiafe, Brothers Isaac Gyetuah, Francis Mends, Ebenezer Appiah, and Eric Nnipa.

By May 20, 1991, the initial number of participants had increased from six to 30. The group became financially sound enough to support a resident missionary. Information was sent to the headquarters in Ghana to request recognition as a branch of CoP in Italy and for a resident missionary to be sent. At the end of that year, Italy reported having planted churches in four provinces: Udine, Pordenone, Verona, and Brescia. Pastor Kwame Blankson (who was then the national head of CoP–UK) was delegated by the headquarters in Ghana to respond to the request. He was in Italy from November 29 to December 9, 1991. An interim National Executive Committee of five people was set up on December 7, 1991, made up of Elders Daniel Prince Wiafe (leader), Sylvester Berentumi (secretary), Kofi Owusu Ansah, Joseph Appiah, and Brother George Hooper. After Pastor Blankson's visit, a delegation from the church's Executive Council comprised of Prophet M. K. Yeboah (chairman), Apostle Rigwel Ato Addison (general secretary), and Apostle Opoku Onyinah (international missions director) was sent to affirm and regularize the church in May 1992. At their arrival, the interim national leaders were officially mandated as the National Executive of the CoP–Italy with the inclusion of Paul Osei Ameyaw as a member.

On October 17, 1993, when the assemblies had grown to 11 in number, the headquarters in Ghana appointed Apostle Stephen Kofi Baidoo and his wife as the resident missionaries to Italy. Apostle Baidoo restructured the administration and returned to Ghana due to difficulties in acquiring a resident permit. He came back from Ghana in 1995 to continue the administration. Until Baidoo's recall to Ghana in 2001, the church in Italy counted 47 congregations spread in 12 administrative districts in different provinces in the country. The leadership included nine minsters, 66 elders, 49 deacons, and 74 deaconesses. The membership was counted at 3,409, of which adults 13 years and older numbered 2,710, and there were 699 children below 13 years.

By the end of 2013, CoP–Italy had three administrative areas, 21 districts manned by 21 full-time ministers, 95 local congregations (assemblies) with over 7,755 members—5,726 adults and 2,029 children. CoP congregations were located in many towns and cities in Italy, including Milan, Vicenza, Verona, Brescia, Modena, Pordenone, Udine, Bassano, Valdagno, Mantova, Arona, Parma, Reggio Emilia, Verona, Ancona, Bologna, Bergamo, Napoli, Rome, and Palermo.

Apostle Baidoo was replaced by Apostle Francis Ofori Yeboah from September 15, 2002 until 2006. Apostle Daniel Prince Wiafe—from the church in Italy—became the national apostle in 2007. Daniel Prince Wiafe was the pioneer who initiated the planting of the first assembly in Italy. He later became a missionary to Belgium and then came back to head the church in Italy. Later he was sent as a missionary to Holland in 2012. In 2012, Apostle Osei Owusu Afriyie from CoP–UK was transferred from France to be the national head of the CoP–Italy. The CoP–Italy had sent missionaries to Spain, Belgium, Ukraine, and Portugal. The respective missionaries were Apostle J. K. Appiah, Apostle D. P. Wiafe, Pastor Emmanuel Quaye, and Pastor Emmanuel Aminssah. On September 12, 2016, Apostle D. P. Wiafe was sent to Holland as the national head. On September 18, 2016, Apostle Osei Owusu Afriyie was posted from Italy to the United Kingdom, and Apostle Newton Ofosuhene Nyarko replaced him from the UK as the substantive area head of Italy. By December 31, 2016, CoP–Italy claimed three administrative areas from 21 districts overseeing 92 assemblies. These comprise a total adult membership of 6,518 (13 years and above), and 1,731 children (below 13 years). This membership includes 6,119 Ghanaian immigrants, eight white nationals, and 307 other nationals. They have 17 ministers, including three apostles and 821 lay leaders (255 elders, 219 deacons, and 347 deaconesses).

COP MISSIONS–HOLLAND

The CoP branch in Holland, like many of the diaspora churches of CoP, also started as a home prayer and Bible study meeting in August 1990 with three married couples who had been members of the church in Ghana. These couples were Mr. Emmanuel and Deaconess Charity Konney, Mr. and Mrs. Opoku, and Mr. and Mrs. Asante Baah. They initially converged at Gravestein 720 in South East Amsterdam. Around the same time in 1990, other people had started a home fellowship in Amsterdam. Pastor Blankson, the national head of UK, brought the two groups together to start as one CoP congregation in Holland in 1990. Dr. Kenneth Aboah, an elder of the church in Ghana on course at the University of Maastricht Teaching Hospital was appointed the first presiding elder by the Executive Council in Ghana. He drafted the constitution and also registered the church as an NGO affiliated with the CoP in Ghana. That was the only possibility for registering the church at that time. Eventually, it was registered in Holland on February 3, 1992, under the name Stichting Evangelist Volle Pinkster. The board of trustees were Emmanuel Konney, Robert Oscar Mensah, Kwasi Atuah, Felicia Obeng, Theresa Koomson, and Sister Ama Serwaa.

The young church was saddled with a lot of misunderstanding and disunity among the presbytery as it grew. Peace was finally restored in 1998, after Pastor A. L. Angoh was transferred from La District in Accra to help resolve the crisis and maintain the congregations. The group was then finally registered as The Church of Pentecost–Holland. This time the board members were Elder Philip Sasu, Deaconess Theresa Koomson, Deaconess Suzzie Ampofo, the Rev. A. L. Angoh, the Rev. Samuel Obeng Eshun, the Rev. James Otchere, the Rev. Lassane Ouedraogo, Elder William Owusu Appea, and Elder Macdonald Ofori. Pastor A. L. Angoh was replaced by Apostle S. L. Agyin in 2007. The CoP in Holland could report for 2013 a total of six administrative districts, 25 congregations (assemblies), and 2,484 members (of which adults numbered 2,001 and children 483). The church in Holland pioneered the planting of the CoP–Belgium and sent Emmanuel Konney as the first minister in 1996. Apostle Obeng Eshun, formerly of CoP–Austria, who was sent as missionary to France in 2015, was a product of CoP–Holland. The CoP–Holland is growing. Apostle Dr. D. P. Wiafe is the area head, having been transferred from Italy to take over from S. L. Agyin in 2015. By December 2016, the CoP–Holland had an overall membership of 2,717 (2,218 adults 13 years or more and 499 children below 13). These are divided into six administrative districts managed by four ministers and 343 lay leaders (117 elders, 83 deacons, and 143 deaconesses). These members include 2,637 Ghanaian immigrants, 15 Dutch nationals, and 65 from other nations.

COP–INTERNATIONAL MISSIONS PRESENCE IN SOME NON-WESTERN LOCATIONS

CoP Missions–Israel

The CoP international missions has congregations in some nontraditional migration transit points such as Japan, Israel, Lebanon, Nepal, Pakistan, and India. Among the earliest to be formed was the branch in Israel. In early September 1983, Elders Samuel Aninkorah and Osei Bonsu, both working for a United Nations Peacekeeping mission in Israel, started a home cell prayer meeting at the home of Aninkorah in Naharriyah, in the northern part of the country. The group began with four people, Aninkorah and Osei Bonsu and his family of three, and it grew to 36 by May 1984. Aninkorah's group joined up with a nondenominational fellowship in Tel-Aviv to become the Bethel Fellowship, which later changed its name to Bethel Assembly. The nondenominational group was dominated by CoP members from Ghana. The assembly was officially inaugurated on August 18, 1989, at 2 Balfour Street at Bat Yam, a rented premises, with 50 members. The venue was later moved to Hamasger Street. Included among the earlier congregants were Elder Ofori Amanfo, Deacon Kwadwo Asante, Brother Atta Yeboah, Afriyie Boafo, Sisters Mary Asante, Susanna Atta Yeboah, and Baaba. Later on, they were joined by Major Boampong of UNIFIL, Brother Adu Dacosta, Kwesi Donkor, Kissiedu, Alex Febri, Abena Tawiah, and Ohenewaaah. By the end of 1989, the Bethel Assembly had grown to 130.

The Department of Christian Communities under the Ministry of Religious Affairs in Israel granted a place for a pastor to take charge of the African Christian Communities in Naharriyah and Tel Aviv. On October 14, 1993, the International Missions directorate sent Pastor Kwesi Ansah to take over as the first resident missionary. The congregation in Naharriyah became a nondenominational fellowship to serve the United Nations civilian community, and other congregations or assemblies were also created. By 1999, the total number of congregants for the entire CoP–Israel was 631,556 adults and 75 children. An English/French-speaking congregation was created for non-Ghanaians (which later became a PIWC), as well as seven other assemblies: two in Eilat and Red Sea, and five others in Tel Aviv, Bethel, Calvary, PIWC, and Zion.

Pastor Kwesi Ansah was replaced by Pastor Appiah Aidoo from 1999 to 2004. During the latter part of 2003, the church suffered a great setback due to a deportation order for all illegal immigrants living in Israel. A majority of the church members did not have the required resident permits and had to relocate to Ghana. Pastor Newton Ofosuhene Nyarko was therefore sent from UK to take oversight responsibility for Israel in addition to being the missionary responsible for the CoP in Greece. At the end of 2013, the records showed a decrease to 215,166 adults and 49 children, as well as a reduction in the number of congregations to just three under the leadership of Pastor George Kweku Korankye, a missionary called from CoP–UK. The General Council posted Pastor Raymond Odei from CoP–UK to relieve George Kweku Korankye as the resident missionary in 2015. By December 31, 2016, there was an administrative district overseeing three local assemblies. The overall membership was 313 (263 adult members 13 or more years and 50 children under 13). The church is made up of 258 Ghanaian immigrants and 55 members from other nations. There are no Israelis in the church.

CoP Missions–India

The formation of CoP–India and others like it in Asia and Latin America depart from the norm described in this chapter for the CoP's establishment in other countries. Unlike other CoP international congregations, whose members are predominantly Ghanaian immigrants, CoP India is completely indigenous, that is, members are native Indians. They have an Indian national head and indigenous Indian pastors. The mission's records at the end of 2013 show that CoP–India had 15 administrative districts, 73 congregations in various locations, and a total membership of 7,417 (6,229 adults and 1,188 children).

The CoP–India was started by a young Indian who went to Ghana as a business representative for a multinational company from India. His early association with the PIWC located at the heart of Accra endeared him to the service of the church. Particularly, his engagement with a home cell in the house of Elder Larkai was said to have been a life-transforming experience. After successful work for his company that year, he had to go back to India for a vacation. At the airport, Prophet M. K. Yeboah reportedly prophesied into his life and blessed him in these words, "Brother James Raj, the fire that is burning in you shall not keep you idle. You are going to spread the fire in your nation. Through you God will establish churches in India." James subsequently resigned his secular job in 1996. Starting in New Delhi, he established a CoP congregation with his brother David Stanley on a property donated by a new convert, a village headman, Mr. Rajappa. The church was helped through the benevolence of members of the PIWC in Ghana where Brother Raj had fellowshipped. After many visits by the leadership of the church through Apostle B. K. Arthur (IMD), Apostle Ayerakwa, and Apostle M. K. Ntumy, the churches were encouraged. Brother Raj was ordained as minister of the CoP by one such delegation in 2002, led by Apostle M. K. Ntumy and Pastor John Waller. Brother Raj received a short training at the Pentecost Bible College in Ghana, Accra, for three months and was released to continue his work in India. He led the CoP–India through 2016. The end-of-year 2016 report for CoP–India claimed 8,710 overall members (7,405 adults 13 years and above and 1,305 children below 13 years). The CoP–India has 15 districts administering 75 assemblies, with 16 ministers and 320 lay leaders (84 elders, 96 deacons, and 140 deaconesses). The entire membership is all Indian, with no foreign national.

CoP Missions–Nepal

The CoP in Nepal was similarly started by a Nepalese man who was challenged by the worldwide work of the CoP through Apostle Alfred Koduah. At an Advanced Leadership Course conducted by Haggai Institute in 1994, Apostle Alfred Koduah roomed with Timothy Rai of Nepal. Koduah challenged Rai to start a CoP branch when he went back home. The actual planting of the church materialized in early 2000. On April 5, 2003, at a ceremony in Kathmandu City, the Church of Pentecost–Nepal was inaugurated. By 2005, there were seven assemblies in six administrative districts in Nepal (Bhaktapur, Kabre, Mahottari, Morang, Ramechhap, and Jhapa), with a total membership of 222. The church was led by Timothy Rai as the general overseer and pastor, Bharati Rai as women's leader, and Pastors Simon Rai, Jeewan Rai, Peter Gurung, and Micheal Thapa. At the end of 2013, the figures had declined to two administrative districts, three assemblies, and a total membership of 161. The CoP in Nepal has a large percentage of indigene members. The nation of Nepal is a Hindu dominated country and requires missionaries to start up the churches. The CoP–Nepal's scanty annual report for 2016 suggests that the church is going through some challenges, a major one being the onslaught of Hindu fanatics against Christianity as well as general poverty in the country. There are two assemblies with 152 total members. From the report, the normal robust form of missionary dynamism one expects in the CoP's trained missionaries appears to be absent. The Nepal church is entirely dependent on the CoP–Ghana for support for its resident minister and other logistics.

CoP Missions–Japan

In the Far East, Japan is a struggling CoP congregation with a resident missionary posted from the United States who has an additional responsibility over the CoP branches in South Korea and other surrounding nations. The CoP–Japan still faces challenges with regard to registration as a religious body. The congregation was started on December 31, 1994, by a group of CoP members who had migrated to Japan. They included Elder Stephen Agyemang, Elder Stephen Gyempeh, Deacon Thomas Agyei Mensah, Brother Rexford, Brother Amoo Mireku, Brother Benjamin Amankwa, Brother Davis Ennin, Sister Emelia Amponsah, and Sister Amoo Mireku. These initially met at Brother Rexford's house to start a branch of the CoP since all of them were fellowshipping at different places. The group was visited by the international missions director Apostle Opoku Onyinah in 1996. The first resident missionary who was posted from the US was Elder Joseph Gyamfi, who with his wife started there as field workers and later became full ministers. By the end of 2005, there were three assemblies and a total membership of 101. There were four elders, six deacons, and five deaconesses. At the end of 2013 they had two assemblies and a total of 171 members (134 adults and 37 children). Among the main challenges for growth in some of these places are the strict migration rules such as regularization of working permits, which renders immigrants non-employed. Other factors include the dominance of Eastern culture and religions (Buddhism and Shintoism). In 2014, Pastor John O. Ofori was sent from CoP–USA to replace Pastor Gyamfi as the resident missionary. By December 31, 2016, though he had put in great effort, the church had not grown much. Its present overall membership is placed at 221 in two local assemblies. The membership is entirely composed of Ghanaian immigrants.

CoP Missions to Other Non-Western Nations: Brazil

In an effort to establish more indigenous churches and to branch away from becoming caretaker congregations for African immigrants and especially Ghanaian immigrants, the CoP has, since 2003, adopted a strategy of co-opting already existing churches started by indigenes. For instance, on July 9, 2003, collaboration between the CoP–Canada and Brazilian Pastor Geraldo Aredes started a CoP congregation in Itabirito-MG, where Aredes and his family lived. The church was started with Pastor Geraldo and his wife, Nilda; Wallyson and his wife, Sara; Dalila and her fiancé, Fabiano; Filipe and Willyam. Geraldo was commissioned as the head of the CoP–Brazil on August 1, 2003. In 2011, Apostle D. K. Sey and his wife were sent from Ghana to help Aredes as the resident national head of the church in Brazil. The CoP–Brazil numbered four districts, seven assemblies, and 312 members (259 adults and 53 children). By June 30, 2016, the CoP–Brazil had an overall membership of 600 drawn from 12 assemblies. Its membership is 522 Brazilian nationals and 78 Ghanaian immigrants. They have five Brazilian ministers and 40 lay leaders (11 elders, 13 deacons, and 15 deaconesses).

Other branches and assemblies are purely indigenous as well, such as CoP–India. Other churches have members from mixed nationalities that are not Ghanaians. For instance the CoP–Ukraine has assemblies that are headed by Ukrainians, and an assembly in South Bend, Indiana, USA, has mixed nationalities.

ASSESSMENT OF ACTIVITIES ENGAGED IN BY THE COP MISSIONS ABROAD

The pattern of activities engaged in by all these CoP international churches abroad, with a few exceptions, appears to replicate that of the parent church in Ghana. Among its mission churches that are purely or predominately indigenous, such as India, the pattern is the same. A few exceptions regarding activities relate to the communities or locations in which the churches are planted. The pattern of activities and growth aligns with the conclusions of this study described in chapter 4. The mission churches or congregations are mostly community based and lay-leadership driven. They include all the ministries (evangelism, youth, children, men, and women) in the church's normal pattern.

The general trend of activities of CoP missions abroad shows evangelistic engagements in all its forms (personal evangelism, crusades, gospel rallies, etc.). However, in many of the mission locations, indoor evangelistic activities are allowed or preferred to outdoor activities, due to strict laws in some of the nations and also the weather patterns; colder climates do not favor outdoor meetings. These activities include conventions, conferences, retreats, leadership trainings, ministry classes, prayer meetings, regular Sunday and midday services, and social activities.

In addition to the Ghanaian social activities, the churches abroad have adopted some of the sociocultural activities of their various sojourning locations. For instance, in the CoP congregations in the West such as the UK and USA, funerals, weddings, school graduations, naming ceremonies, bridal showers, and birthday celebrations abound. A major challenge in this regard is that even in the celebration of these social activities of the church, most of them favor the Ghanaian culture. This is a setback for mission outreach to the indigenes and other nationals. The CoP missions engage in other activities such as church planting in neighboring countries and offering of donations (in cash and in kind) to sustain them. The national churches aim at reaching out with the gospel to their closest neighboring nations.

COP MISSIONS BOARD, DIRECTORATE, AND POLICIES

The above discussion has highlighted and updated the extent of growth and the form and character of the international missions of CoP as a form of global African Pentecostal missionary enterprise. Some scholars engaging in discourse on religious transmission (especially Pentecostalism) from the African region to other parts of the globe, including the West, have commended the CoP African immigrant congregations abroad for their sound organization. Hanciles, for instance, acknowledges the CoP's diaspora missions as a classic example of how the extraordinary levels of African migration from the 1980s have radically transformed the outreach potential of African churches and Christian ministries. Asamoah-Gyadu, on the other hand, conceded that although African immigrant congregations may be fraught with some difficulties and problems such as administration, financial controls, and secessions, to which CoP may not be an exception, he could affirm that "CoP has some of the best-organized African immigrant churches abroad."

The present writer shares in these observations through his own personal involvement as a CoP Missions Board member for over 16 years and through personal observation of the CoP diaspora congregations. A significant observed factor that can account for CoP's missions' success is its deliberate agenda of having a separate centralized Missions Department. The CoP, under the stimulus of the unstructured migrant movement of its members worldwide has, since the mid-1980s, created a distinct Missions Department. This department may in part have been required because of the constant requests for resident missionaries from its members abroad who had organized themselves into a church. This department is so highly centralized that all congregations established by its members abroad form part of one polity. The CoP has an extensive missionary program under which Ghanaian missionaries have been sent to many parts of the globe. Members of the CoP everywhere make valuable contributions of prayer and monetary gifts and other material donations towards its missions in the nations, through the Missions Department.

The Missions Department is controlled by a Missions Board that determines its policies and major decisions. The policies and decisions are disseminated through a Missions Directorate headed by the international missions director. The directorate has a competent secretariat and workers who promote and help implement the board's policies to the local assemblies and members. Every local assembly has a missions committee. This missions committee sees to it that every decision or policy is adhered to at the grassroots level. This kind of hierarchical system of the CoP's Missions Department makes its operations and control effective and makes the CoP a thoroughly missions-minded church in which every member is involved.

The Missions Board in the CoP is a very important body. It is probably seen as next in administrative importance to the Executive Council, which recommends policies to be ratified by the General Council. It is chaired by the chief executive of the church, the chairman. The Missions Board has eight other members: general secretary, international missions director, an area head, a pastor, an elder (lay leader), chairman of the finance board, finance and administrative manager, and a representative from the Francophone nations.

The church has established an office for an international missions director, who also doubles as the secretary to the International Missions Board. The IMD's pastoral duty is to implement the policies of the board, disseminate its finances, train and supervise missionaries and their activities, and coordinate the religious activities of members migrating from Ghana. The IMD, who is also a member of the Executive Council, plans the church's entire mission strategy. This writer shares Asamoah-Gyadu's observation that, unlike other congregations abroad that may have independent status, the CoP has a measure of central control over its congregations, which ensures accountability and administrative and pastoral discipline. The office of the IMD is in charge of this aspect of the church's administration. Thus, the supervisory role of the mission's directorate accounts for part of the church's survival and credibility in missions abroad, within a context where secession is a primary option for dealing with differences that arise within local leadership.

A major aspect of CoP's religious culture towards missions is the members' generosity and attitude of giving. The members of the church generously donate in cash or kind in support of some specified programs and projects. The "McKeown Missions Week offering" is taken once a year in a weeklong program, and the "Missions Offering" is taken after tithes once every month. These donations are the main source of funding for the church's missionary work both within and outside of Ghana. The annual missions reports from the districts, areas, and nations also indicate massive missions' donations in cash and kind from individuals, districts, areas, and nations to different areas where mission posts are located. These items include cars, buildings, support for buildings, musical instruments, used clothing, and large sums of money in different currencies. They are channeled through the Missions Directorate for appropriate distribution and forwarding to designated mission posts. While the tithes and offerings are administered by the main CoP head office financial secretariat, all monies and items donated in the name of missions are administered uninterruptedly through the Missions Directorate by the advice of the Missions Board. These huge sums of money administered for mission in and outside Ghana bypass the budget of the main Ghana church. The Missions Directorate has the responsibility of administering all the allowances, monthly wages, and financial commitments of missions in the CoP. The Missions Directorate, in its financial commitment, makes efforts to steer the external branches on a course toward self-dependence. The mission branches are therefore made to share in the burden of the church until they can be self-sustaining, especially in terms of upkeep of indigenous workers and acquisition of capital property.

The directorate also plans programs, conferences, and various training sessions to sensitize missions awareness, and it disseminates them to the grassroots through the mission committees in the assemblies. The IMD is a very important figure with regard to contracting of personnel allowed to be minsters for the church, especially those intended to be sent on missions abroad. He is the chairman of the CoP's ministerial committee, the body that supervises and is responsible for the intake of ministers. The IMD, as a member of the International Executive, is part of the body responsible for ministerial callings, appointments, and sending out of missionaries. The missionaries are selected from the cream of CoP ministers who have been tried and tested over a period and found capable and competent.

COP MISSIONS PATTERNS AND ANALYSIS

The ongoing discussions have pointed out that the trend of global missions is shifting from the previous pattern of Global North to the South. It is currently moving instead from the South and East towards the West—to locations north of the equator. Some argue that this shifting trend is bringing missions in reverse from locations south of the equator to the north, into locations such as the UK and USA. Christian mission formerly came from the Global North—the center of global Christianity—towards the south, into locations such as Africa, Asia, and Latin America.

The analysis by this study further demonstrates that churches from locations south of the equator such as Africa, Asia, and Latin America are not just involved in reverse missions (as missions from the Global South to the North). They are also using the Global North as a platform through which missions are nurtured and launched to other parts of the globe, including the North, South, and East. We also observe a direct South-to-South missions movement pattern, as well as a movement via the North to the South and East.

It is evident that African immigrant congregations such as CoP congregations (from sub-Saharan Africa) have been established in various parts of Western nations. This affirms Ter Haar's earlier proposition: "Missionary initiatives from the old heartlands of Europe and North America are arguably diminishing in significance. A major reversal (and diffusion) of missionary enterprise is underway; one significantly tied to the fact that the direction of global migratory flow is now primarily south to north and east to west, where it was once primarily north to south." This argument is not contested; it has been proved by prominent scholars such as Hanciles, Asamoah-Gyadu, and Van Laar. Van Laar has categorically interpreted the presence of African immigrant congregations in the West as the representative face of the Christian faith in the modern West; Asamoah-Gyadu has affirmed Ter Haar's assertion, "Mission-minded African immigrants see Europe and indeed other Western countries such as USA as 'spiritual wastelands' which can be made fertile again with the help of African Immigrant Christianity."

Analyzing these arguments in light of the CoP's presence in the West gives rise to many questions. What pattern of missions are these institutions forming in the West? Are they chaplaincy structures just as the earlier European missions in Africa are claimed to have been? Are they indeed involving missions in reverse as a deliberate attempt to save a spiritually dead continent, borrowing from Ter Haar, back to life through conscientious Christian witness? In other words, does the kind of evangelism being undertaken by CoP immigrant congregations in the West demonstrate a missions effort from countries south of the equator, such as those in sub-Saharan Africa, towards the northern continents, such as the USA? Does the cream of mature ministers sent as missionaries from the CoP demonstrate reverse flow missions? As Ogbu Kalu noted, "It is surmised that immigrants come with a more conservative theology and practice, insist on using their languages and cultural expressions, prefer to import their own priests and challenge the authority of traditional hierarchy." Answers to these questions bring out the intentions of the mission enterprise of the CoP in the West and elsewhere.

This work argues, based on the history of the CoP's mission in the UK, that African Pentecostal mission enterprise such as that of the CoP has initially been intended for chaplaincy, but its presence in the West has actually evoked a Christian witness. As stated earlier in this chapter, references from the missionary sending body in the CoP such as "sending of resident missionary" and "creation of missions board" observed in the circular letters or correspondence indicate that they did intend a mission in reverse to the West. The evangelism targets of these CoP immigrant churches were originally people of African descent rather than the indigenes. This notwithstanding, their presence has filled a vacuum, as without them an otherwise secularized continent would have been yet more devoid of Christian presence. They have bought and occupied structures originally meant for Christian purposes that would have ended up in other secular usage for which they were not originally intended. Their witness may not have much affected the original indigenes of the places, but they still reached other Africans who are also migrants and not originally Christians.

Their generation of young people who have become Christians are sending the gospel as a reverse mission to their peers. The magnitude of missions in reverse may not at the moment be very profound, but it does exist. Hanciles wrote that "CoP is consciously utilising Ghanaian migration as a springboard to contribute to the Christianization of the world through evangelism." The composition of migrants involved in CoP missions abroad suggests a mixture of social status among the diaspora. They include students, officials from UNIFIL, United Nations, and staff in Ghanaian embassies and high commissions abroad. All these professionals and diplomats, together with those seeking greener pastures, are involved in missions. This is an indication of a well thought-out mission with the purpose of reaching out with the gospel in any place of sojourning.

Pockets of indigenes appear in some of the congregations, having come in through marriage and other ways. CoP structures such as PIWC and current youth churches are resources for future engagements in Christian enterprises. Thus, the CoP is actively addressing its cross-cultural missionary functions to embrace the indigenes of its sojourning locations without alienating the core constituencies on whose efforts its missionary actions depend.

This study further argues, from the various discussions of the histories of the formation of CoP mission churches across the globe, that mission in the CoP goes beyond chaplaincy and an intention for reverse mission. The trend suggests also a pattern in which the CoP uses its presence in the Western locations, such as the UK, US, Canada, Germany, and Italy as a platform to launch missions in other locations of the globe. They may be seen as missions from the Global South towards locations in the North and to southern and eastern locations. Actual examples of such CoP missions include that from Ghana to the UK, from the Global South to the North. Yet the CoP missions from Italy, for instance, have extended to Spain, Belgium, Ukraine, and Portugal as South to North ventures but via the North. In this case the northern country is being used as a platform to nurture missions. Again, CoP's missions from the United States to Latin American and Caribbean nations such as the Dominican Republic, Costa Rica, and Trinidad and Tobago can be seen as missions from the Global South to another Global South location but through the Global North. The northern locations in this instance are being used as a platform or springboard to launch into parts of the South. CoP missions can also be observed from Canada to Guyana, Brazil, and South America. These are missions from the Global South directed to other southern locations but, again, through the Global North. Another pattern of missions goes from the Global South directly to another southern location, such as the CoP mission from Ghana to India.

The trend of CoP's international missions therefore suggests a variety of patterns of movement. They can be seen, first of all, as missions extended from the Global South towards the North; second, as missions from the Global South towards other locations in the North but using the North as a platform; third, as missions from the Global South to other locations in the South but via the North; and fourth, as missions from the Global South to other non-Western locations.

The CoP achieves this global mission outreach described here partly through a distinct strategy discussed in chapter 4. This strategy seeks to form functional ministers for its international missions or branches through its immigrant churches in the West. The resident missionaries sent abroad might not be seen as reverse flow mission agents. Ogbu Kalu argues that the idea of a reverse flow is an initiative of the mainline churches in the late 1970s. He wrote:

> A historical excursus demonstrates that reverse flow was not an invention of Pentecostalism; rather, it originated from the mainline churches. In the nineteenth century, a forward-looking missionary anticipated a "blessed reflex" when the sending-churches of the West would be challenged and renewed by the churches then springing up in Africa, Asia and Latin America.[1]

The CoP missions are not a type of reverse flow. They are rather engaged in permanent missionary endeavors in their sojourning places. They are observed to facilitate the formation of functional ministers, such as pastors, area heads, and apostles, who are sent to other places in the West to start or overseer churches. They are first rudimentarily discipled, trained, and equipped, as discussed in chapter 4. Some of these individuals were founding members of CoP congregations in the UK, USA, and others areas in the West. They were trained and nurtured by the resident missionaries sent from Ghana to become functional ministers for their places of residence.

These functional ministers have the advantage of understanding the culture of their sojourning locations in the West. They also already have resident permits that enable them to move into other Western locations without many restrictions—due to EU migrational policies that encourage free movement among its member states. The resident missionaries sent to pioneer or continue the foreign missions, such as Pastor Blankson, Apostle N. A. O. Amegatcher, Apostle M. S. Appiah, and Apostle S. K. Ansong, gracefully and faithfully returned to Ghana to continue in their new ministerial postings. One exception is Pastor Anthony K. Awuah, who was sent to the US as resident missionary in 1991 and refused to go back to Ghana on transfer. The other is Apostle Alex Osei Bonsu, who resigned in the USA after pioneering the work in Canada and also serving

---

1. Kalu, "Anatomy of Reverse Flow in African Christianity," 30.

in the USA for six years (1997–2003). Apostle Alex Osei Bonsu could not take up his new position as the dean of the Pentecost Bible College but went back to stay in Canada.

However, before these resident missionaries (apart from the two mentioned) departed to their new stations in Ghana, they had nurtured and trained or made ready other functional ministers. The CoP used these ministers to spread its missions into other parts of the West and other non-Western nations that are not known to be traditional transit destinations for Africans. For instance, Pastor Newton Ofosuhene Nyarko was a founding member of the CoP–UK. He was raised as a pastor in the UK and later sent to Israel and Greece. He was brought back as an apostle to head the CoP–UK and was moved again as an apostle for CoP–Italy. Elder Daniel Prince Wiafe was a founding member of the CoP in Italy. Wiafe was sent as a pastor to Belgium and came back as an apostle to oversee the church in Italy. These individuals are pioneering members who are trained and sent out as pastors. They are then confirmed as matured senior pastors or area heads. After they have proved their worth as area heads, being capable of handling their postings successfully, they are brought back as apostles to head their nations. This pattern of raising functional ministers in CoP's international missions is unique, and this study argues that it is one of the factors that makes the rate of secession from the CoP minimal compared to other Ghanaian Charismatic churches.

TOWARDS THE AUTONOMY OF THE COP NATIONAL CHURCHES

The trend of CoP missions, especially its ministerial formation and postings of ministers in the mission field, indicates a deliberate pattern. Through this pattern, the CoP churches in the nations are prepared to become autonomous from the parent branch in Ghana. This is evident from the way that resident missionaries sent from Ghana are withdrawn and replaced by ministers formed in foreign or external churches. The process involves moving the new ministers around into different stations until they are considered mature. They are then sent back to their original home churches as apostles or national heads.

This process observed by the present writer is aimed at making the national branches autonomous and it promotes growth. One of the church's main missionary objectives is to establish and nurture the external branches until they are considered mature enough to assume autonomy. The mode of these operations is not clearly spelled out in the CoP's policy for missions. However, since the church created the Missions Department, two committees have been set up to address this issue. The first submitted its report to the Executive Council in 1996.

A second committee, made up of Apostle Dr. S. K. Baidoo, Apostle Dr. Opoku Onyinah, Apostle Traore Sidiki, Apostle Ousmane Zabre, Apostle René Coco, Elder Lawyer M. Z. Glover, and Elder Dwomoh-Amaniampong, produced a report with certain recommendations considered by the Missions Board.[2] These recommendations were as follows: The prerequisite for granting autonomy to an external branch is that it must be self-supporting, self-governing, self-propagating, and self-edifying. By self-edifying is meant that the church should have foundational leadership of at least two ministers, including an apostle or prophet qualified to ordain other apostles and prophets. In the CoP, ordination of church leaders such as ministers and lay leaders is done by apostles and prophets. The branch must not be dependent on the church in Ghana in these areas mentioned. Other recommendations are that it should have a national seat, national charter, national Executive Council headed by an elected president or chairman, and at least 60 percent of the total membership should be permanent residents of that particular country.[3]

The CoP has granted autonomy to two of its national branches—Benin and Côte d'Ivoire (see table 4.3). The chairman of the church, Apostle Opoku Onyinah, in his State of the Church Address delivered in May 2016, gave an analysis of the growth of both of these autonomous nations. They were estimated to have increased in membership from 148,087 in 2014 to 160,575 in 2015.[4] This study argues that, although the CoP has the intention and a modality in place for granting autonomy to its external branches, such action appears to be long overdue. Some of these churches, such as the church in Burkina Faso, are still dependent on CoP in Ghana after 40 years in existence. In contrast, other branches in the Western nations such as USA and UK can be considered more than due autonomy in regard to the criteria discussed. Their being autonomous

---

2. CoP, Autonomy Committee Report.
3. CoP, Autonomy Committee Report.
4. CoP, brochure for 42nd General Council meeting, 2016.

will encourage the initiative of forming churches that favor the particular nation's culture, language, and traditions.

In order for the church to expand in the foreign nations, leadership should expedite efforts towards autonomy of the qualified nations' churches. Afterwards the autonomous national churches of CoP could be formed into an interdependent commonwealth association, through which resources and manpower could be voluntarily distributed or shared. This recommendation for the continuous growth of the CoP will be further developed in chapter 7.

CONCLUSION

This chapter's review of the international missions of the CoP as an example of an African Pentecostal denomination engaged in global missionary enterprise confirms that the African version of the Pentecostal movement has become as an important international religious force. As such, it can offer insights regarding the changing face of global Christianity in this era.

By the end of 2016, the CoP had a presence in 90 nations across the world, apart from Ghana, including African nations, the Americas, continental Europe, the Middle East and Asia. The CoP–UK, as one of the earliest, demonstrates the pattern and trend of emergence and growth also followed by all the other nations, with only a few exceptions. These international churches emerged on the global scene beginning from the 1970s and 1980s, a period when unfavorable political and socioeconomic conditions on the African continent drove Africans migration to different locations. Some Ghanaians, including students, diplomats, asylum seekers, and others in search of better living conditions, joined this exodus. The CoP Christians among them grouped in fellowships that almost invariably turned into churches. Upon request by the group to the CoP headquarters in Ghana, an oversight minister, as a resident missionary, would be sent to oversee the congregations. This modus operandi led to the establishment of many CoP national branches in the diaspora.

The missiological factors that have led to the growth of the CoP include its having a centralized Missions Department and thus a very effective supervisory system in terms of pastoral care, effective administration, and monetary controls through the international missions director. Its missions method and pattern can be considered new and unique when measured against traditional missions' trends. Mission in the CoP, going beyond chaplaincy and an intention for reverse mission, uses its presence in Western locations such as the UK, USA, Canada, Germany, and Italy as a platform from which to launch missions to other locations of the globe. The CoP's international missions demonstrate various patterns in the directions of its movement: (1) missions extended from the Global South towards the North, (2) missions from the Global South towards other locations in the North but using the North as a platform, (3) missions from the Global South directly to other locations in the South but launched from the North, and (4) missions from the Global South to other non-Western locations.

The church's sending of resident missionaries to its mission posts indicates an intention for foreign missions. The CoP resident missionaries therefore do not represent a reverse flow in the same sense as the mainline churches intended it in the 1970s. The CoP's resident missionaries, apart from overseeing the churches, also train and nurture functional ministers such as district pastors, national heads, and area apostles, who mature to take charge of the foreign branches in different capacities. The CoP's international missions are structured towards growing the individual national branches into autonomous national churches without direct supervision from the CoP–Ghana. The next chapter, chapter 6, focuses on the character, theology, beliefs, and ethos that propel the CoP into missions, in order to discover the theological factors that have influenced the growth and efforts of the CoP.

6

"Spirit and Mission"
Toward a Theology of Pentecostal Growth in Africa

THROUGHOUT THE PREVIOUS FIVE chapters, this book has examined the history of the CoP in order to show the methods and patterns through which the church has expanded into global missions. The last three chapters specifically identified some salient religious and missiological factors accounting for this growth. This chapter now seeks to discover the key theological factors that underpin the character and spirituality that propels this growth.

Throughout this study, the main focus has pointed to the experience of the Holy Spirit—expressed as the Pentecostal and CoP spirituality and active in its adherents and in the corporate organization—as driving the growth of the Pentecostal movement (the CoP in particular). This pneumatic phenomenon underlies the character and spirituality of the CoP as a Pentecostal denomination. This chapter portrays the Pentecostal spirituality of the CoP through its theology of the Spirit, beliefs, pattern of worship, and other characteristics. It argues along the same lines as Asamoah-Gyadu: "CoP notably binds up the experience and the theology of the Spirit, with other Christological teachings, expressed in its tenets of beliefs, practices and other characteristic ethos to achieve its growth and global mission's agenda."[1]

---

1. Asamoah-Gyadu, *African Charismatics*, 78.

The main argument of this chapter is that the spirituality that influences the outstanding growth and mission of African Pentecostalism is a pneumatic phenomenon: the transformative power of the Holy Spirit that propels individual adherents and the corporate body to act. This chapter's effort to identify and describe the theological factors underpinning the CoP's growth will be discussed in three sections: Life and Ethos of the CoP, African Pentecostal and CoP Theology and Practice, and Toward a Theological Analysis of African Pentecostalism for Growth.

LIFE AND ETHOS OF THE COP

The CoP's Pentecostal Spirituality

The growth and expansion of the CoP can be attributed, among other factors, to its distinctive pattern of spirituality. This spirituality is evident, for example, in personal conversion through faith in the gospel message; water baptism by immersion; emphasis on Pentecostal phenomenon—as subsequent baptism in the Holy Spirit, discipleship, biblical prayer, aggressive evangelistic ethos, belief in the efficacy of prophesy, strict or uncompromising holiness ethics, belief in miracles, healings, and deliverance—and a closely knit community-based congregational lifestyle.

The CoP's spirituality, like most Pentecostal spiritualities, emphasizes personal transformation (conversion and subsequent baptism in the Holy Spirit), prayer, evangelism, holiness, healing, deliverance, and community living.[2] Hanciles affirms this image of the CoP as going back to its roots or inception. He emphasizes the CoP's founding in the classical Pentecostal tradition, which places major emphasis on prophecy, healing, holiness, and evangelism.[3] Through its spirituality, the CoP has gained enormous acceptance. For instance, its public image (particularly in Ghana) is that of a church making up for some of the failures and weaknesses—particularly in the area of morality—that have come to be associated with the traditional or mainline denominations and the early AICs.[4] The CoP's spirituality has been acclaimed be to restoring to the

---

2. Asamoah-Gyadu, "On Mission Abroad," 92.
3. Hanciles, "African Immigrant Churches in America," 351.
4. Asamoah-Gyadu, *African Charismatics*, 78.

church, especially Ghanaian Christianity, what the traditional mission churches could not sustain in terms of sound spirituality.[5]

Asamoah-Gyadu sums up the denomination's spirituality: "As a Pentecostal denomination, CoP is serious about religious experience and things of the Spirit."[6] He likewise describes the CoP as a Pentecostal church that is "serious with the Bible, prayer, and evangelism and above all serious with things of the Spirit."[7] The underlying factor, confirmed by almost every writer or interviewee on the CoP, is that the influence, manifestations, and experience of the Holy Spirit, portrayed in the life of the individuals and the corporate denomination through its theology, ethos, beliefs, and forms of worship, have influenced its growth. Almost every person interviewed concerning the factors that influenced the CoP's growth, especially those involved directly with its administration, mentions the Holy Spirit and his influence as the prime factor.[8] They agree too on factors such as fulfillment of divine prophecies, prayer, evangelism, holiness, church discipline, and prudent management of the corporate resources of the church.[9] Leonard writes that "people in the CoP will tell you the Church has grown because of the Holy Spirit." In addition, she affirms, "speaking as an outsider, I can see that it is true, but it would never have mushroomed in the way it did without James [McKeown] seeing many principles of church growth, long before anyone else ever thought of writing books about it."[10] She then suggests other factors such as evangelism, prayer, giving, discipline, and passionate love for Jesus.[11] Larbi describes CoP spirituality in the first 15 years of existence in these words: "The Spirit of God, prophecy, and the Lord Jesus were their guides, and the Word of God their food."[12]

---

5. Asamoah-Gyadu, "Born of Water and Spirit," 88.

6. Asamoah-Gyadu, "Born of Water and Spirit," 89.

7. Asamoah-Gyadu, "Pentecostalism and the Missiological Significance," 53.

8. Interview with Chairman Apostle Opoku Onyinah, now the international missions director, and Evangelism Director Apostle M. C. Asiedu, London, Mission House, July 14, 2014. Both consider the influence of the Holy Spirit to be the prime factor.

9. I have culled this from their interviews and writings.

10. Leonard, *Giant in Ghana*, 7.

11. Leonard, *Giant in Ghana*, 8.

12. Larbi, *Pentecostalism*, 188.

Baptism in the Holy Spirit:
The Prerequisite for CoP Leadership and Involvement

The periodic reporting of activities from all the denomination's functional bodies (ministries, committees, and boards) includes providing the number of adherents who have received the Baptism of the Holy Spirit.[13] It is the most basic requirement for active involvement in the denomination's regular activity, whether as a leader or active member of its units.[14] This prerequisite of having had a personal experience of baptism in the Holy Spirit (confirmed with initial evidence of speaking in tongues, or glossolalia), applies also for calling into leadership (deacon, deaconess, or elder) and for ministry as a pastor. The International Missions Director Apostle Emmanuel Gyesi Addo, as the chairman of the Ministerial Committee (the committee that interviews and accepts ministerial candidates), confirms that calling into a high position of the church's trust does not depend on one's educational background; it may have become more of a factor currently due to the complexities of society, but the level of education attained does not hinder the enrollment of those whom the Holy Spirit is seen to be directing into ministry or leadership.[15]

Leadership responsibility is first and foremost given to those whose lives demonstrate the influence of the Holy Spirit.[16] Other training and orientation for leadership comes on the job through "retreats" (periodic on-the-job orientation), short courses, and, recently, theological education by extension at the church's theological seminary. The major reason for the phenomenal success of the CoP is its cherished Pentecostal emphasis on the experience of baptism in the Holy Spirit, the premier indicator that influences all other theological factors that promote her growth and missions agenda.[17] This defines the theological character,

---

13. See table 4.5 for analysis of growth indicators.

14. See questionnaire forms of the church to be completed by proposed candidates for lay leadership and pastoral ministry in the CoP. The requirement strictly includes having been baptized by the Holy Spirit.

15. Interview with the IMD, Apostle Emmanuel Gyesi Addo, chairman of the Ministerial Committee, Pentecost Area Mission House, London, July 14, 2014.

16. See "Core Values," in *Minister's Handbook*, 2014, 14. This was also confirmed by the IMD, Apostle Emmanuel Gyesi Addo, chairman of the Ministerial Committee, in an interview at Pentecost Area Mission House, London, July 14, 2014.

17. The annual reports from the areas in Ghana and the external nations have almost equal numbers of converts baptized in water and those baptized in the Spirit, an indication that equal value is placed on each indicator. See table 4.5.

spirituality, and mission of the CoP, as seen in its history and growth, particularly as described in chapters 3 and 4. This observation confirms earlier assertions, such as those of Asamoah-Gyadu, which posit that the reasons for the phenomenal success of global Pentecostalism stems from its emphasis on the experience of the Holy Spirit and the pursuit of a mission agenda that takes seriously the authority of Scripture, active witnessing, discipleship, and the mediation of the Word of God in powerful, tangible, and demonstrable ways.[18]

Pneumatic Phenomena and "Conversion" into the CoP

The CoP asserts that the effects and influence of the Holy Spirit underpin every theological orientation, beginning from conversion as a first step to membership, through rudimentary discipleship, evangelism, and missions. J. V. Taylor points out that "the whole weight of New Testament evidence endorses the central affirmation of the Pentecostals that the gift of the Holy Spirit transforms and intensifies the quality of human life and that this is a fact of experience in the lives of Christians."[19] Thus, in the case of the CoP, the transformative experience of the Holy Spirit after conversion influences the individual for evangelism, discipleship, and effective Christian lifestyle and also works in the corporate church for growth and subsequently missions abroad.

To buttress this conclusion, the researcher presents an interview with a presiding elder of the CoP, Elder John Asare. In the late 1990s, Asare, who had no formal education, was leading a CoP congregation of more than 800 members at the Central Assembly of Wassa Akropong District, Western Region. This example is not unusual in the CoP, but may be more the norm. After Asare had preached an impressive, theologically sound salvation message based on 1 Corinthians 15:1–8, interspersed with biblical quotations and personal testimony, this writer had the opportunity of interviewing him to find out his level of training. Asare commented:

> I did not have the privilege of any formal education. I was a caretaker of my father's farm lands. My personal lifestyle had been that of a drug addict and a notorious fighter. When I accepted the Lord Jesus as my saviour through the hearing of the gospel

18. Asamoah-Gyadu, "'Promise Is for You.'"
19. Taylor, *Go-Between God*, 199.

and subsequently got baptised in the Holy Spirit, evidenced by speaking in tongues, the Holy Spirit taught me how to read my vernacular Bible consistently for three years, at every dawn just as you study in your classroom. My understanding of the things of God and theology is what He [the Holy Spirit] and the leadership of this church had impacted in me these years.[20]

Both members and leaders who were his close neighbors confirm Elder John Asare's transformative experience through the influence of the Holy Spirit.

John's testimony is not an isolated case. Larbi recorded other similar testimonies in his work. He categorically stated that not all who experience the Holy Spirit in this manner are taught to read by the Holy Spirit.[21] This example and others like it constitute evidence that the CoP's corporate spirituality (as attested to by its adherents and others) fits Ogbu Kalu's description: "a spirituality in which Jesus Christ saves from sin, empowers to live an exemplary Christian life, heals diseases, delivers from the powers of Satan and empowers to overcome in this life. This is achieved through the transformative power and experience of the Holy Spirit."[22] This is the distinct spirituality that recent African Pentecost scholars—as well as this researcher—argue to be the impetus behind the growth and missionary efforts and innovations of Pentecostalism in general and African Pentecostalism in particular. It is this Pentecostal pattern of spiritual life observed in the CoP that we see to be recovering the existential experience of the Holy Spirit for the contemporary church.[23] This study now examines how we see this Pentecostal spirituality rooted in the transformative experience of the Holy Spirit in its theology and practice.

AFRICAN PENTECOSTAL AND CHURCH OF PENTECOST THEOLOGY AND PRACTICE

The starting point of the Pentecostal experience in the CoP after one's conversion is the subsequent encounter with the Spirit as understood by

---

20. Personal interaction between the writer and Elder John Asare, at Takoradi, Affiakuma New Site Assembly, 1994.
21. See Larbi, *Pentecostalism*, 275–77; Larbi gives many examples to this effect.
22. Asamoah-Gyadu, "Born of Water and Spirit," 409.
23. Asamoah-Gyadu, "On Mission Abroad," 93.

the Pentecostal teaching about baptism in the Spirit with the accompanying sign of speaking in tongues, or glossolalia. This is what differentiates Pentecostal teaching from orthodox Christian theology.[24] Pentecostalism, as part of the larger Protestant body, shares much of traditional evangelical theological thought. However, it places its main theological emphasis, as part of global Pentecostalism, on what Anderson refers to as a theology of the Holy Spirit.[25] Through the experiential influence of the Holy Spirit, its adherents claim to have been transformed and empowered for service. Pastor Asomaning could interpret James McKeown's English preaching in his own local dialect (Twi) in public meetings under the inspiration of the Holy Spirit. Even though he had no formal education, he was filled with the Spirit.[26] Through the influence of the Holy Spirit, as in the case of John Asare and Pastor Asomaning, CoP adherents without formal education or theological training interacted with the Bible and gained biblical instruction through their leaders and shaped one of the most exemplary forms of the modern African Pentecostal movement in this century, the CoP.

The theology and practice found in the CoP were not theoretically developed by James McKeown, the early leaders, or some distinguished theological minds. The CoP as an indigenous church developed as a grassroots movement. Today the church can lay claim to prominent academics among its membership. However, the early founders, including McKeown himself, had very little or no formal education or training in theological studies. Leonard wrote that they were not men of status and learning.[27] Until recently, when the denomination began institutions such as the Pentecost International Worship Centre (PIWC), the majority of adherents had very little or no formal education. The CoP therefore thrives on a distinctly oral theology through "vernacularization" of its liturgy and forms of worship that appeal to the ordinary people. As pointed out by Asamoah-Gyadu, as well as this writer, the aspects of theology they consider important are the ones that address their religious and spiritual needs.[28] Their music for instance, is itself a theological form through which they verbalize their experiences, and it is an essential ingredient in

24. W. Menzies and R. Menzies, *Spirit and Power*, 24.
25. Anderson, *Introduction to Pentecostalism*, 179–97.
26. Leonard, *Giant in Ghana*, 118.
27. Leonard, *Giant in Ghana*, 118.
28. Asamoah-Gyadu, "Born of Water and Spirit," 406.

the CoP's Pentecostal pattern of worship. Members have composed local choruses that are easy to memorize and sing from their own experiences of the Spirit, most of which reflect their beliefs and theology.[29]

Genesis of the CoP Theology, Practice, and Ethos

The theology underpinning CoP practices, beliefs, and spirituality has emerged as a result of adherents' interactions with the Bible, their own experiences (as guided by the Holy Spirit), and of course the teachings they received from the leadership. In the very early days of the church, much of its theological belief was built on Peter Anim's readings of some periodicals, including some from USA-based Pentecostal churches, and from his personal experiences. This origin defends the international validity of the CoP's doctrine. Later, other encounters and challenges have caused changes that affect its present state. A few who facilitated the shaping of the CoP's early theological thought deserve mention: James McKeown, James Egyir-Paintsil (the first general secretary of the denomination), and others who through their own studies helped form CoP beliefs.

Pastor James Egyir-Paintsil is singled out as a brilliant, widely read man who entered the ministry in 1948. He was a great asset to the church and became its general secretary until his sudden death in 1981.[30] Larbi suggests that it was a corporate reflection or theologizing by some of the early ministers and illiterate peasants that gave shape to the beliefs, practices, and spirituality of the church. For instance, Kwame Bediako and his academic progeny, Philip Laryea, refer to Afua Kuma, an unschooled peasant farmer and a CoP member as a "grassroots theologian." The content of her vernacular prayer, praises, and appellations for God at church gatherings have been a subject of theological analysis and development of Christian thought as a foundation for Christian theology in the 21st century. Her contribution towards the CoP's theologizing will be looked at more closely later in this chapter. Larbi contends that, in the CoP, the role of "experts" as theologians shaping its practices and ethos, if any, may have been in the area of polishing and shaping the initiatives of these "peasants."

---

29. See Hayfron, "Theology and Spirituality."
30. Leonard, *Giant in Ghana*, 118.

Music and poems are some of the oral theological forms through which Pentecostals verbalize their experiences. Such oral theology is an essential ingredient of Pentecostal worship. And in the CoP members have composed local choruses that portray or bring out their theological orientations, practices, and beliefs that drive the movement. This understanding of the theology of the CoP, especially in its formative stages, can be described with Chan's characterization of "an ancient art of spiritual theology where reflecting on the nature of God and praying to him are indistinguishable acts."[31] A spiritual theology expresses itself through an oral theology in songs, testimonies, poems, and proclamations. Oral theological forms resonate with traditional African religious piety. Larbi affirms that its doctrines, ethos, and worship style can be ascertained best through the songs, practices, and to a lesser extent writings of some of the leaders and members.[32] These may include testimonies, poems, and appellations (proclamations addressing God). Simon Chan agrees with this observation and suggests that the strength of Pentecostal tradition lies in its powerful narratives. He affirms that Pentecostals through their testimonies of God's great works have quite successfully spread their experience to the masses, particularly among the poor and unlettered.[33]

Many in the CoP have received spontaneous inspiration. Among them are Mrs. Eunice Addison, Madam Eunice Johnson, Prophet P. B. Appiah-Adu, Mrs. Grace Gapetor, and most recently, the chairman of the church, Apostle Opoku Onyinah.[34] Apostle Opoku Onyinah seems to be inspired every year with songs that theologically interpret or reflect on the themes for the year proposed by the church's Executive Committee since 2010. Many of the earlier songs, such as those by Mrs. Eunice Addison, have been captured by Larbi.[35] An example of oral theology of the Spirit arising from among CoP adherents is one that has suddenly become a song in the CoP. In a recent gathering at Pentecost Convention Centre, dubbed *Kohinta Prayers*, the minister preached on the theme "Encountering the Supernatural." The pastor's wife, Mrs. Grace Gakpetor,

---

31. Chan, *Pentecostal Theology*, 12.
32. Larbi, *Pentecostalism*, 244.
33. Chan, *Pentecostal Theology*, 20.
34. See CoP, *Church of Pentecost Songs*.
35. See Larbi, *Pentecostalism*, 245.

inspired by the Spirit, spontaneously began singing out this song, which the entire church populace has recently taken up.³⁶

> *Mehyia no, Mehyia no*
> *Nia oma Nkwa no, Mehyia no (2x)*
> *Woa sesame, ayemefoforo, Woaye me wura, Naoni menam*
> *Mehyia no Mehyia no, Nia oma Nkwan no*
> *Mahyia no.*
>
> I have encountered Him, I have encountered Him
> He who gives life, I have encountered Him (2x)
> He has transformed me and made me anew,
> He has become my Lord, He directs my path
> I have encountered Him, He who gives life
> I have encountered Him.
>
> (Song given by Mrs. Grace Gakpetor)

This song expresses the CoP's belief in the transformative experience of the Holy Spirit for every person who truly encounters God through the Holy Spirit. According to Asamoah-Gyadu, "what differentiates the CoP from other Christian forms is their claim of the transformative experience of the Holy Spirit.³⁷ He argues that other Christian forms such as the mainline churches, though they believe in the work and ministry of the Holy Spirit, may not be as enthused with transformative personal experiences as is the CoP.³⁸ Thus he sees the CoP bringing renewal within Ghanaian Christianity. Developments and groups within the mainline churches, such as Bible studies and prayer groups, since the 1980s have proved more receptive to transformative experiences of the Holy Spirit.³⁹

Doctrines and Beliefs of the CoP

Article 1 of the CoP constitution contains its tenets and beliefs. Though in some of its writings the church identifies itself with the common fourfold

---

36. Interview with Pastor Samuel Gakpetor, the minister at the meeting and the husband of Mrs. Gakpetor.
37. Asamoah-Gyadu, "Born of Water and the Spirit," 394.
38. Asamoah-Gyadu, *African Charismatics*, 20.
39. Asamoah-Gyadu, *African Charismatics*, 30.

pattern in Pentecostal theology—Christ as Savior, Christ as Baptizer in the Holy Spirit, Christ as Healer, and Christ as Soon-Coming King, as described by Donald Dayton[40]—the tenets of its theology guide its practices and policies. These doctrines include the divine inspiration and authority of the Bible; the one true God revealed as Trinity; the depraved nature of man; man's need of a savior, repentance, justification, and sanctification; the sacraments of baptism and the Lord's supper or communion; the baptism, gifts, and fruit of the Holy Spirit; divine healing; tithes and offerings; and the second coming of Christ and resurrection in the next life.[41] Using these basic tenets as a guide, this study seeks to show how the denomination links the Holy Spirit to its theological orientations that promote its growth. As Chan argues, "Whenever movements seek to perpetuate themselves they evolve ways of passing on their ways of life by means of a systematized set of beliefs and rituals."[42] The CoP, like any other Pentecostal movement, is no exception. Its basic theological beliefs or tenets have been analyzed below as topics such as conversion and baptism; Holy Spirit baptism, gifts, and fruits of the Spirit, spectacular events, and prayer camps; community and discipleship; biblical prayer; holiness and moral ethics; vibrant evangelism programs; church discipline and accountability; liturgy and vernacularization; form and mode of worship; holy communion; and tithing.

Conversion and Baptism

The point of entry for becoming a recognized adherent of the CoP, unlike some mainline churches, is not through infant baptism or confirmation. In some mainline churches in Ghana, conversion to Christianity may not be as a result of the choices of individuals attracted by the message of Christianity, but through baptism (in most cases as an infant) as the first stage of becoming officially Christians. Such "Christians" may have no understanding of the Christian message. A minister who came out of a mainline church, Asamoah-Gyadu, states, "Parents scarcely know the significance of baptism and thus, are hardly able to give their children any education in accordance with it. Confirmation has all but lost its value as a means of personally affirming a faith that was affirmed on one's behalf

---

40. Dayton, *Theological Roots of Pentecostalism*, 21.
41. CoP, *Constitution*, 2010, 7–12.
42. Chan, *Pentecostal Theology*, 20.

as an infant in baptism."[43] Some ministers in the CoP, such as Apostle Opoku Onyinah, its current chairman, had confirmed their earlier baptism as infants in other mainline churches.[44]

The CoP does not baptize infants, who are not considered mature enough to make a decision for themselves. However, they dedicate infants at the consent of their parents, based on the premise that the parents are Christians and will nurture the child in Christian principles. The question still remains whether the CoP parent has the capacity to bring up the child with that knowledge. The child in the CoP, however, goes through Children's Ministry from age six and up. Trained teachers make conscientious efforts to bring the child to understand and accept the message of salvation. In the CoP, the major point of incorporation is through conversion by the individual, through the hearing of the message of the gospel of Jesus Christ and adhering to the faith. The individual is asked to make a decision for faith through a public declaration of faith. As discussed in chapter 4, the basic ways by which the CoP grows congregations are biological, transfer, and conversion growth patterns. However, it places primary emphasis on conversion of the individual. Ghanaian church growth expert Richard Foli identified "conversion growth," that is, church growth and discipleship through personal conversion, as the most sustainable kind of growth.[45]

This personal conversion in the CoP is largely attributed to the work of the Holy Spirit who himself convicts and brings the individual to repentance and eventually causes him or her to voluntarily own up to Christ. As Asamoah-Gyadu has written, one of the most enduring legacies in the CoP's heritage has been the emphasis that the missionary figure James McKeown placed on personal experience in the process of incorporation into the church.[46] The convert is thus, immediately or subsequently (not long after conversion) conscientiously baptized by immersion in water to ground his or her faith.

Only after water baptism by immersion is a convert considered a member and his or her name is added to the regular church register. The regular accountability reporting format indicates that the total number of converts baptized is added to the total number of congregants. The

---

43. Asamoah-Gyadu, "Pentecostalism and the Missiological Significance," 38.
44. Interview with Chairman Apostle Opoku Onyinah, February 10, 2014.
45. Foli, *Church Growth in Ghana*, 11.
46. Asamoah-Gyadu, "Pentecostalism and the Missiological Significance," 38.

reporting format therefore has columns specifically for converts won—those who made a decision for Christ—and converts baptized, that is, those who made a decision and went ahead to be baptized in water. For instance, the 2014 records claimed 111,168 souls won, out of which 83,453 converts were baptized.[47] This heritage of personal experience through the individual's conversion and water baptism is deemed the starting point of the discipleship that has enabled the CoP to maintain its missionary focus.[48]

Holy Spirit Baptism, Gifts, and Fruit of the Holy Spirit, Spectacular Events, and Prayer Camps

The next stage of incorporation, signifying one's readiness for work of ministry in the CoP, comes when one attests to having been baptized by the Holy Spirit, evidenced by speaking in tongues, or glossolalia. As incorporated in its constitution and factored into its teachings, the church expects that all who accept Christ as Lord are entitled to receive and should earnestly seek the baptism in the Holy Spirit and fire according to the commandment of the Lord.[49] They assert that this was the normal experience of the early church and that this Pentecostal experience brings power for effective preaching and bestowal of the gifts of the Spirit.[50]

The standard qualification for effective involvement in church activity, especially leadership (cell leader, deacon, deaconess, or elder), requires confirmation that one has been baptized in the Holy Spirit, evidenced by speaking in tongues as a subsequent experience after conversion and water baptism. There is evidence, however, of individuals who claimed to have received this grace before water baptism. The baptism in the Holy Spirit accompanied by speaking in tongues is the most significant symbol of incorporation in the CoP, as in any Pentecostal organization.[51] Prior to that, a converted and baptized adherent may not be eligible for any leadership or frontal role, no matter how long he or she stays in the church. This implies that, in the CoP, water baptism is the required evidence of membership, but the baptism in the Spirit is required to qualify for effec-

---

47. CoP, Annual Statistical Report, 2014.
48. Asamoah-Gyadu, "Pentecostalism and the Missiological Significance," 38.
49. CoP, *Constitution*, 2010.
50. Larbi, *Pentecostalism*, 278.
51. Chan, *Pentecostal Theology*, 13.

tive participation. One of the Executive Committee members, Apostle Ekow Badu Woode, confirmed this in his address to the church "Revisiting the Baptism, Gifts and Fruits of the Holy Spirit":

> The baptism in the Holy Spirit and the manifestation of the pneumatic gifts mark out our Pentecostal distinctiveness. History teaches that any group that substitutes the empowerment of the Holy Spirit in the work of the Church, sooner than later, loses her spiritual vitality. Recently, some in the Charismatic renewal have diluted a key Pentecostal doctrine. They are reinterpreting the speaking in tongues as not required as evidence that one is baptised in the Holy Spirit.[52]

Thus, in the CoP, the initial discipleship for new converts includes orientation to thirst for and vigorously pursue Spirit baptism.

The church also recognizes that the baptism in the Spirit, evidenced by the speaking in tongues, has more than evidential value. They see the glossolalia as prayer and the entire experience as attesting to one's acclamation or acceptance by the divine as "sealed" for future redemption and capable of undertaking a ministry position. Until recently, some of its early leadership (pastors and elders) had taught vigorously from Romans 8:9, that no one belongs to Christ without the baptism of the Spirit evidenced by speaking in tongues. The denomination believes that the Spirit baptism experience marks the first reception of adequate empowerment for work in the ministry and mission.

Calling into a leadership role, as lay leaders or into the clergy, does not depend entirely on the level of one's education. It depends first and foremost on one's attested experience with the Holy Spirit and one's commitment as observed by the local presbytery of leadership. They affirm this practice from Acts 6:3–4, "Therefore, brethren, seek out from among you seven men of good reputation, full of the Holy Spirit and wisdom, whom we may appoint over this business; but we will give ourselves continually to prayer and to the ministry of the word." Scripture envisages the Holy Spirit as capable of empowering and equipping for effective and successful ministry; therefore, to be able to serve well, one needs to be filled with the Spirit.

Those in the CoP recognize that at Spirit baptism one not only receives the glossolalia, but also a divine equipping in the gifts and fruit of the Holy Spirit, as in 1 Corinthians 12:8–12; Ephesians 4:11–13; and

---

52. Woode, "Revisiting the Baptism," 265.

Galatians 5:22. The Pentecostal recognition that the gifts of the Spirit remain relevant in this church age fosters the effectiveness in the church's use of lay leaders and also women's participation in church ministry. The CoP is a patriarchal church that does not ordain women into pastoral ministry. The church does not, however, deny women full participation in the life of the church. One of the major strengths of the CoP is its strong women's movement, with their participation dating back to the beginnings of the church. The unique roles women play include being leaders of prayer camps, which the equipping of the Holy Spirit makes possible, endowing women with different gifts and graces.[53] The distinctive appeal of Pentecostal Christianity lies in its empowerment through spiritual gifts offered to all and which can be experienced as present reality.[54] Lay people equipped with these graces are capable of fronting for the church in every capacity. Opoku Onyinah, the chairman of the church, has said,

> God has chosen not to work directly on earth, but to work through human instruments. He does this by giving His gifts to some people who then affect His intentions on earth. The person's responsibility has been to nurture the gifts of God placed in him or her for ministry.[55]

What distinguishes the CoP from other AICs, mainline churches, and some Charismatic churches is that they also stress the fruits of the Spirit as sound moral character, which balances the use of the gifts of the Spirit. Sound moral character becomes the test for the reality of the spiritual gift when in operation.[56] In the CoP, one's gift and ministry must correspond to one's character and way of life before one can be formally accepted. James McKeown wrote in 1939, "character is essential where the air is charged with demons and the atmosphere thick with sensuality."[57]

Chan pointed out that the Pentecostal doctrine of "Baptism in the Spirit is far richer in Pentecostal experience than in Pentecostal explanation."[58] To explain it as an experience, Hocken sees it as the "revelation" of the true God.[59] Macchia describes it as "theophany" of the God

---

53. Novieto, "Women Leaders," 92–93.
54. Asamoah-Gyadu, *Contemporary Pentecostal Christianity*, 6.
55. Onyinah, "Reviving the Gifts," 45–53.
56. CoP, *Minister's Handbook*, 2014, 9, 16.
57. Leonard, *Giant in Ghana*, 104.
58. Chan, *Pentecostal Theology*, 13.
59. Hocken, "Meaning and Purpose," 125–34.

of history and the eschaton.[60] In its more experiential form it is demonstrated through the gifts of the Holy Spirit. Through the equipping by the gifts of the Holy Spirit, the gospel is demonstrated through spectacular events as signs and wonders.

From the inception of the church, what characterized its evangelism and mission that brought growth were the accompanying signs and wonders. Reports say that McKeown instructed the church and the early leaders not to glory in signs and wonders. His reason for this instruction was that "men have the natural tendency, especially in Africa, to put signs and wonders before their relationship with Jesus."[61] This notwithstanding, the phenomenal growth of the movement cannot be deciphered apart from this equipping for evangelism. The chairman of the church, Apostle Opoku Onyinah, in his State of the Church Address in 2013, stated:

> We thank God for the manifestation of his continuous presence in his church through diverse signs and wonders. In 2013 the church recorded many miracles by the power of the Holy Spirit. Almost all the areas reported spectacular events which lead one to acknowledge that the ancient Pentecostal fire is still at work in the church of God today. Evil powers were neutralised, blind eyes were opened, and mentally challenged persons were restored to sanity, women who had been pregnant for two years and over gave birth and many childless couples were blessed with fruit of the womb.[62]

The CoP lays claim to the restoration of the fivefold ministry (Ephesians 4:11) and the supernatural manifestations in the book of Acts of the Apostles due to its claim of manifestation and experience of the Holy Spirit. Dayton asserts that having direct access to the experience of Pentecost leads to the claim of having the "apostolic faith" and all the supernatural elements reported in the New Testament restored. Among these are divine healings and miracles, which become not only a gift of God to his people in suffering but also a sign of the Spirit's presence to the believer and a form of witness to the unbelieving in the work of evangelism.[63] These giftings and supernatural graces in the earlier years of the church produced prayer-camp leaders who have in diverse ways pro-

60. Macchia, "Sighs Too Deep for Words," 47–73.
61. Leonard, *Giant in Ghana*, 36.
62. CoP, Chairman Opoku Onyinah, State of the Church Address, Pentecost Convention Centre, May 6–7, 2013.
63. Dayton, *Theological Roots of Pentecostalism*, 26.

moted the church's mission and growth.[64] The ministry of these prayer camp leaders, as noted in chapter 3, became a conduit for many people, including some prominent men and women, to join the church. Through the work of the prayer camps, women's ministry in the church rose in prominence because the work and ministry of some of these women prayer camp leaders were highly appreciated.

Community and Discipleship

The CoP expresses its Pentecostal experience and spirituality through its communal life and discipleship in a theological pattern similar to that of the early church in Acts of the Apostles. The denomination has a distinctive close-knit congregational system.[65] The members are encouraged to fellowship within the community closest in proximity, where they will be identified, pastored, and discipled. The early Christian church in the book of Acts, as noted by Asamoah-Gyadu, had a strong sense of community that held the adherents together on account of their common experience of the Spirit.[66] Chan, writing on Pentecostal tradition in the late 20th century, rightly suggests that Pentecostals depart from individualism in their conception of the spiritual life and move towards a more communal understanding of Christian faith and living. He argues that the Pentecostal Christian needs a Pentecostal community to make sense of his or her own spirituality. In this regard, he opines that Pentecostal experience and spirituality make much better sense when interpreted within its own communal-liturgical context.[67] This holds relevance particularly in African Pentecostalism because in African religiosity spirituality and a sense of community move together. The CoP has therefore shown a way in this direction. It is worth noting that, as an African Pentecostal denomination, one of the reasons attributed to its massive presence across the length and breadth of Ghana and beyond is its community-based methods of church planting and discipleship.

The individual is incorporated into church life through a very rigorous discipleship orientation. The aim is to make the individual a faithful

---

64. See Larbi, *Pentecostalism*.

65. See chap. 4, section on "Discipleship and Training and CoP Local Congregations or Assemblies."

66. Asamoah-Gyadu, "Pentecostalism and the Missiological Significance," 43.

67. Chan, *Pentecostal Theology*, 13.

and effective bearer of the Christian faith in word and in practice. The communal sense of fellowship becomes an avenue for social intervention in a spirit of hospitality and for care of the poor and needy just as it was characterized in the early Christian community in Acts 2:44–47. This sense of communal fellowship also serves as an avenue for effective pastoral care to all members by the leadership due to the proximity of their residences. The CoP discourages members from joining social clubs, such as lodges and other groups, whose activities are considered unhealthy to their doctrine. The church does not encourage complete alienation from one's extended family, but it encourages its adherents to be more closely knit in the church community. An elder of the church explained this: the church is a community capable of providing for each member just as well as the distant family or a social club could. This in a sense prevents the believer from otherwise getting involved in practices that the church considers idolatrous and ungodly such as traditional rituals for the dead, in which spouses are beaten and made to appear nude.

The communal solidarity of the church becomes a defense for the individual to stand against otherwise irresistible African traditional community practices. It is noted by Asamoah-Gyadu that "the problem that the older mission churches had with their members sharing allegiance with lodges, pseudo-religious welfare associations, and patronage of other problem-solving religious centres, as is common in African religiosity, is virtually nonexistent within the CoP."[68] The CoP is acknowledged as remarkable in this regard. In its overseas churches where a majority of the adherents are immigrants, this community-based system provides an avenue for identity, solidarity, and various social interventions. Without the church's discipleship, it is surmised, many immigrants would have been caught up by strange vices associated with their places of sojourning.[69] This has been acknowledged as one of the reasons for the massive presence of CoP congregations across Ghana and beyond.

Biblically Based Prayer

A most distinguishing feature of the CoP acknowledged by many who come into contact with its spirituality is its emphasis on prayer both at individual and corporate levels. Writers such as Leonard, Larbi,

---

68. Asamoah-Gyadu, "Pentecostalism and the Missiological Significance," 41.
69. See Asamoah-Gyadu, "On Mission Abroad."

Asamoah-Gyadu, and others have noted prayer as a major part of its spirituality.[70] Leonard points out that another reason for the growth of the CoP is its prayer life; the CoP is a praying church, she asserts.[71] Larbi describes prayer in the CoP as "perhaps the most significant mark of the church."[72] Prayer revolves around every program in the CoP. One of the major slogans of the early leaders stated, "Prayer is the work and the work is prayer."[73] As indicated by Asamoah-Gyadu, one of the key indicators of pneumatic movements in Christian mission is the desire for prayer, as evidenced by the ability to pray in tongues.[74]

In the CoP, as discussed above, membership commences with a personal salvation through a conscious decision to give one's life to Christ. Those who accept Christ are integrated into the church through baptism by immersion. Members are then expected to identify with the CoP's doctrine by seeking the baptism of the Holy Spirit with the initial evidence of speaking in tongues. Among other things, those with the gift of tongues testify to a new sense of empowerment to pray and confidence to intercede for others. It is common in the CoP to find groups of members frequently gathered for prayer. In this praying culture, the CoP stands in continuity with the life of the early Pentecostals, who "believed ardently in intercessory prayer."[75] The CoP, through its interpretation of the Bible and its application to existential situations, taught the principles of effective biblical prayer to be used by all who desire divine intervention in every area of life, including healing and spiritual warfare. As noted by Asamoah-Gyadu, in Africa, religion is a survivalist strategy, and so prayer and rituals often aim at achieving such practical ends as health, fertility, rain, protection, or harmony.[76] Pentecostalism is seen as a religion that advocates immediate experience of the supernatural and an interventionist theology that addresses these real-life issues.[77] For instance, through spiritual warfare prayers, it is able to address spiritual issues in such a precarious world, like Africa, which is rife with beliefs in evil

---

70. Asamoah-Gyadu, "Pentecostalism and the Missiological Significance," 41.
71. Leonard, *Giant in Ghana*, 7.
72. Larbi, *Pentecostalism*, 257.
73. Leonard, *Giant in Ghana*, 7.
74. Asamoah-Gyadu, *Contemporary Pentecostal Christianity*, 181.
75. Asamoah-Gyadu, "Pentecostalism and the Missiological Significance," 41.
76. Asamoah-Gyadu, "Pentecostalism and the Missiological Significance," 41
77. Asamoah-Gyadu, "'Promise Is for You.'"

spiritual activities and malevolent spirits. As pointed out by Asamoah-Gyadu, "That the power of Christ through prayer is effective to heal and deliver is one of the greatest lessons that Pentecostal Christianity teaches the church of Christ today in its attempt to continue his mission and discipleship in the world."[78]

Holiness and Moral Ethics

One of the major characteristic strengths within the theological constructs of the CoP is its cherished value for biblical holiness and its standard of ethical morality. It has been rightly pointed out that the Ghanaian public image and impression of the CoP and of Pentecostalism has been that of a religious organization that is making up for some of the failures and weaknesses, particularly in the area of morality, that have come to be associated with Christianity in Africa.[79] In the Ghanaian context, the historic mainline churches are thought to be very permissive in their attitude to holiness and other accepted ethical values, but not the CoP.[80] In keeping with its ethos, the CoP from its inception has been characterized by strict uncompromising holiness and moral ethics. The CoP discourages any practices of evil or appearance of unrighteous living. For instance, the church does not permit polygamy, adultery, sexual misconduct (fornication, homosexuality, and lesbianism), violence, theft, drunkenness, or any indications that suggest condoning or associating with idolatry and traditional fetish practices. It does not allow its members to visit places it considers questionable such as discos, hotels, drinking bars, shrines, or other religious organizations it considers cultic. These prohibitions include embracing false doctrine and not keeping the Lord's Day.[81]

The church has in place strict disciplinary measures and punitive actions against all who find themselves in such situations, ordinary members as well as leaders.[82] The sanctions and disciplinary measures are more intensive for pastors or paid clergy and frontline lay leaders. Issues of discipline will be discussed below in further detail.

---

78. Asamoah-Gyadu, *Contemporary Pentecostal Christianity*, 180.
79. Asamoah-Gyadu, "'Promise Is for You,'" 10.
80. Asamoah-Gyadu, "'Promise Is for You,'" 9.
81. CoP, *Constitution*, 2010.
82. CoP, *Constitution*, 2010.

The importance the denomination places on ethical morality and holiness is seen as a result of its emphasis on transformation emanating from the individual's encounter with the Holy Spirit. Though the strictness of some stances on the form of certain factors has been toned down with time and modernity, the denomination still maintains its strict adherence to holiness and morality. For instance, CoP conventions are now held in hotels, which would have been inconceivable some years ago. This is an indication that the church reviews its stance on certain practices with time. In 2011, the institution made major changes regarding seating arrangements and dress codes. In the CoP, men and women used to not sit together, and ladies did not attend church gatherings with their heads uncovered. These new arrangements allow women to attend church gatherings with or without head coverings. The seating arrangements now allow the genders to intermingle.

Vibrant Evangelism

The most obvious reason for the growth of the CoP from the writer's personal observation and also Leonard's observation is that its top priority has always been evangelism. Evangelism as active witnessing accounts for the successful mission of the denomination both at home and abroad. In the CoP, the deliberate focus or ultimate purpose for every function or gathering is to win souls through conversion. For instance, at child naming ceremonies, birthday celebrations, or funeral gatherings, the church creates a special context for people to make decisions through "altar calls" to join the church. Each functional ministry has enshrined in its aims or objectives for operation the winning of souls for Christ. The church's statistical or demographic sheet enquires about four ministry results designated particularly towards evangelization. It has a row for reporting numbers of rallies and crusades, souls won, converts baptized, and Holy Ghost baptisms. In 2014, 23,930 rallies and crusades were conducted in Ghana and 2,064 on the international front. Total souls won were 127,331, out of which 93,863 were baptized by immersion and 85,398 were baptized in the Holy Spirit.[83] In a ministry such as the CoP, where women could be addressing issues of keeping the home, Larbi has written that in the initial stages their focus was on prayer and evangelism. That was what the women in the church cherished most.

---

83. CoP, Annual Statistics, 2014, demography.

This aggressive approach to evangelism by the members and the corporate church is inculcated beginning right from the time of conversion and is considered the purpose for the baptism of the Holy Spirit. Members of the CoP everywhere, through their conviction and Pentecostal belief, openly and forcefully witness about their savior. Thus, personal witnessing in which members share their faith with others is a common feature in the CoP. The people of the CoP themselves verbalize one of the rewards of the baptism of the Holy Spirit experience as the power to witness effectively. One of their earlier evangelists and an area head wrote,

> Just as Jesus chose 12 disciples to understudy Him and carry on the work after He had departed to heaven, Pastor McKeown under the guidance of the Holy Spirit chose men for the ministry who followed his footsteps. The gallant men included Apostles S. R. Asomani, J. C. Quaye, F. D. Walker, J. A. Bimpong, A. S. Mallet, J. A. C. Anaman, Evangelist Adu Pare, Prophets Ankama, Gyimah, Duffour, to mention a few. With these he started the work after the Asamankese feud. Some of his followers were farmers, family heads and store keepers. When they received the Holy Spirit power they took to the streets and fervently preached the word. There was no public address system.[84]

Church Discipline and Accountability

A major hallmark of the CoP's cherished identity that emanates from its theological orientation—which has caught the eyes of many who have written on it, especially with regard to its growth—is its church discipline and forthright accountability in its dealings. According to some statements, the church believes the achievement of its current numerical strength depends on three pillars: prayer, evangelism, and discipline. Larbi wrote that "the church believes it has been able to achieve its numerical strength primarily because of its uncompromising stand in three main areas: prayer, discipline (in terms of ethical rigorism) and evangelism."[85] Earlier on, Leonard captured the comments of Opoku Onyinah, one of its apostles. Onyinah gave four reasons for the organization's growth: prayer, evangelism, discipline, and church structures. As Asamoah-Gyadu pointed out and as chapter 3 confirmed, the CoP has a certain measure of

---

84. Nyarko, "Zeal of the Fathers," 34.
85. Larbi, *Pentecostalism*, 180.

central control over its congregations, which ensures accountability and administrative and pastoral discipline. He commented that this is important for the survival and credibility of any church organization, especially within a context where a primary option for dealing with differences that arise within local leadership has been secession.[86]

Another reason observed is the effectiveness of the organizational structure, the church polity, which is attributed to the discipline mentioned above.[87] A major component of the CoP's spirituality that affects its growth is its stringent accountability strategy carried out through annual and quarterly or bi-monthly reporting systems from the grassroots to the top hierarchy. One of its senior ministers remarked, "In the CoP, everybody is accountable to another person." All participants at a meeting query both the strengths and inefficiencies. The local presbytery, through the local ministry such as Evangelism Ministry or Women's Ministry, has effective accountability periods. Each leader is called upon to articulate the efforts of the group in a particular period. The assessments include size of congregation, evangelistic campaigns held, records of Holy Spirit baptism, water baptism, projections achieved for the period, projections for the next period, challenges, reviews and appointments. These assessments are expected to be done in a spirit of truthfulness and objectivity. Recently, a system of appraisal has been set in place for all stakeholders in the CoP, especially the ministers' work. It is modeled on the kind of appraisal conducted in a business organization. In this system, the presbytery that the pastor works with appraises his work annually, while the area head also appraises him based on his personal observations and the reports from the district presbytery. The pastors in turn appraise their area head, through a set of guideline standards deliberately structured for this purpose. These assessments are sent to the executive chairman, the head of the organization, for him to evaluate, and to aid him in correcting and motivating every person. The chairman and his executives are also assessed by the area heads in like manner.

Liturgy and Vernacularization

The CoP is acknowledged to be a grassroots church. One of its strengths that attracts the Ghanaian populace, unlike some other Pentecostal

---

86. Asamoah-Gyadu, "On Mission Abroad," 91.
87. Larbi, *Pentecostalism*, 180.

denominations of its caliber, such as the Assemblies of God, is the informal and vernacular nature of its liturgy. Vernacularization makes the liturgy of the CoP so simple that the averagely trained lay leader is capable of handling the liturgical processes effectively without much difficulty. Apostle Stephen Kofi Baidoo, IMD for the church, has remarked that any intelligent person in the church could take hold of the minister's manual and administer its details.[88]

Such confidence put in lay leaders' grassroots participation enhances a sense of belonging, which encourages much growth. Lamin Sanneh drew attention to the effects of translation of the Scriptures in religious transmission. As Sule-Saa recently noted, the translation of the Scriptures into the vernacular languages has greatly aided Africans in bringing the Holy Bible into their communities, which has helped the church to grow.[89] In the CoP, for instance, members read and translate the Holy Bible in their vernacular languages in order to interpret the gospel message. In this way ordinary Christians, not just clergy, move with the gospel in the power of the Holy Spirit.

As also pointed out by Asamoah-Gyadu, "Vernacularisation in the CoP, which has been noted above, is given expression in the use of locally-composed choruses and songs, narration of personal testimonies, public Scripture reading and the preaching of sermons. This helps to give the CoP a certain appealing simplicity found neither in other classical Pentecostal churches like the Assemblies of God nor the traditional mission churches."[90] The import of the vernacularization policy of the CoP can be best appreciated against the backdrop of its wider demographic and geographical spread. For instance, the present chairman of the CoP, Apostle Opoku Onyinah, though a trained academic professor in theology, mostly addresses audiences in the vernacular language and style, especially in local gatherings. His programs on TV and radio use a very tailored vernacular Twi (a local Ghanaian Akan dialect).[91] This simple liturgy and vernacular nature that characterizes the church's mode of worship promotes real indigenization in the churches and allows free

---

88. Apostle Stephen Kofi Baidoo, at Area Heads' meeting, in an admonition for hard work by the area heads, Pentecost Convention Centre, May 3, 2017.

89. See Sanneh, *Translating the Message*, 188–89; and Sule-Saa, "Impact of Vernacular Bible Translation."

90. Asamoah-Gyadu, "Pentecostalism and the Missiological Significance," 46.

91. These are personal observations at various forums as a member of the church.

expression in the things of the Spirit, which characterize Pentecostal worship and growth.

Form and Mode of Worship

The CoP form and mode of worship very much displays the Pentecostal pattern of spirituality, whose distinctiveness is argued to be a key factor in the phenomenal expansion of Christianity on the African continent.[92] Worship in the CoP is characterized in the main by spontaneity and pneumatic manifestations.[93] In Ghanaian Pentecostalism, as in African Pentecostalism in general, this distinctive style of worship with its emphasis on experience of the Holy Spirit has introduced a nonnegotiable element into Christian worship.[94] The form and mode of Pentecostal worship exhibited in the CoP since the turn of the century as part of its spirituality has arguably added to the critique of and confrontation with the staid and over-formalized liturgical forms of worship in historic mission denominations. Pentecostal worship forms have thus tremendously influenced the modes of worship in the traditional historic churches. Although worship in the CoP is characterized in the main by spontaneity and pneumatic manifestations, its mode of worship is nevertheless very orderly, characterized by an informal liturgy in the vernacular or, based on the location and congregation, in languages such as English and French or another local dialect laced with vernacular forms.

The leadership in the CoP puts a lot of emphasis on worship that is meaningful, relevant, and experiential. A typical CoP worship service begins with a time of participatory and spontaneous prayer. This prayer time is most often dedicated to giving thanks for God's providence, protection, and provision. This is followed by a time of intense and expressive praise accompanied most of the time by clapping, drumming, singing, and dancing. This singing and dancing, though spontaneous, is quite orderly. Those on the platform (ministers and elders), women, men, and sometimes youth, take turns to dance so that there is no interruption. During such singing and dancing, people of different tribes and cultures are allowed to freely demonstrate their appreciation of their Lord through indigenous expressions in their various vernaculars.

92. Asamoah-Gyadu, *Contemporary Pentecostal Christianity*, 33.
93. Asamoah-Gyadu, "Born of Water and the Spirit," 392.
94. Asamoah-Gyadu, *Contemporary Pentecostal Christianity*, 18–33.

The time of praise with singing and dancing generally gives way to a period of verbalizing or expressive thanksgiving and testimonies, Bible readings or recitations, singing of songs or poems, and spontaneous appellations to God. During such times of testimonies, people recount various interventions of God in their lives, including healings, deliverances from precarious situations, childbirth, lorry accidents, and others. In some of these appellations, meaningful traditional imagery in local poetic and verse forms ascribing worth to a great being or king, as known in African culture, are offered to God. In some such appellations to God, seasoned theologians have observed an illiterate woman, Afua Kuma, a CoP deaconess from Sampa, offering deep theological expressions to God.[95] These appellations are typical pronouncements made upon kings and chiefs when they sit in African/Ghanaian palanquins at festivals that address their worth and dignity. The worshippers, overwhelmed by the mercies, grace, splendor, and dignity of their maker, call out such spontaneous pronouncements.

This leads to, as it were, the most solemn point of call for corporate worship, what Asamoah-Gyadu calls the highest form of religious expression and an outflow of the encounter with divinity.[96] This part of the worship service calls for spontaneous personal experiential interaction with an awesome reverence to God. It is laced with all forms of expressions such as kneeling, the raising of hands, crying, singing, and prophesying, all done in beautiful harmony. The congregation carries this out in spontaneous praying and singing, both intelligibly with understandable language and in tongues, as Paul discusses in 1 Corinthians 14:14–15.

The final segment of worship is dedicated to the sermon, offering, altar call, announcements, and benediction, in that order. This description of the CoP's mode of worship differs very little from Cox's description of research experience in other Pentecostal churches. He writes, "In each of the churches, the worship followed the pattern I have now learned to expect in Pentecostal churches: high amperage music, voluble praise, bodily movement including clapping and swaying, personal testimonies, sometimes prayers 'in the spirit,' a sermon full of stories and anecdotes, announcements, lots of humorous banter, a period of intense prayers for healing, and a parting song."[97] Hollenweger observed, for instance, that

---

95. See Kuma and Kirby, *Jesus of the Deep Forest*.

96. Asamoah-Gyadu, *Contemporary Pentecostal Christianity*, 18.

97. Cox, *Fire from Heaven*, xvi.

this mode of worship with its oral nature rooted in Pentecostal theology is consistent with primal piety and therefore does well in Africa.[98]

Holy Communion

In conformity with its strict holiness and moral ethics, the CoP uses the celebration of Holy Communion as an avenue through which members continually evaluate their lives to ensure their right standing in the Lord. As Larbi suggests, the soteriological understanding of the church is best understood through the main sacraments of the church such as Holy Communion and water baptism.[99] CoP churches set aside the last week of every month to prepare for it with prayer, fasting, and biblical teachings. Teaching focuses on the complete salvation work on the cross by Christ and his death for humanity, for one's salvation, and which thus requires a strict life of holiness and getting right with the Lord. In this preparation for and celebration of communion, the members are encouraged to work out their salvation with fear and trembling (Phil 2:12). The sinner who has been sanctioned refrains from participating. Others, such as polygamists, are encouraged and prayed for so that they would rescind their decision and participate in the communion. The session encourages fellowship and deeper brotherly interaction with members of various pedigrees.

An important aspect of this sacrament in the CoP is its drawing of awareness to the centrality of the cross and the suffering of Christ. This aspect addresses an area of theological reflection much neglected in Pentecostal circles—that of the Christian suffering. As Menzies notes,

> Pentecostals have been frequently chided for failing to develop an adequate theology of suffering. Our theology has appropriated and correctly emphasized the dynamic presence and power of God active in the lives of Christians. We have rarely, however, developed the breadth of perspective needed to handle suffering. In the mind of many, Pentecostals have a theology of Glory, but not a theology of the cross.[100]

The CoP, through its regular monthly solemn observance of the Lord's Supper (as they affectionately call Holy Communion) and its attendant

---

98. Hollenweger, *Pentecostalism*, 18.

99. Larbi, *Pentecostalism*, 3–13.

100. W. Menzies and R. Menzies, *Spirit and Power*, 171.

teaching on the cross, seeks to balance the teaching of deliverance and prosperity highlighted in the current Charismatic movement. This brings back into Pentecostal doctrine an awareness of aspects of teaching on the sovereignty of God in the lives of believers and also the place of Christian suffering, described by Paul in Philippians 3:10 as the fellowship of his sufferings.[101]

Tithing

An important aspect of the CoP's spirituality and discipleship, as for most Pentecostals, involves giving in the form of tithes and offerings. Tithes and offerings are the main sources of income for the church. In the CoP, these form part of the standards for evaluating the strength of an assembly and, in part, the commitment and spirituality of the individual. A newly created assembly (referred to in the CoP as a "nursing assembly") is considered a mature, full-fledged assembly when its tithes and offerings reach a certain level. The individual's maturity and commitment in a certain understanding is linked to his or her commitment to faithfulness in this giving. It is in a way part of the requirement that one be committed to effective church work before being called into leadership, whether lay or clergy. As the founder, James McKeown, is said to have stressed, when the Holy Spirit truly touches a person, he touches everything, including his finances. Many CoP leaders hold that James McKeown's intention from the inception of the church was to build an indigenous church with Ghanaian culture, Ghanaian ministers, and finances generated from within the church.[102] As one of the key factors in her success and growth, the CoP from its inception has been a self-supporting church financing its local and mission efforts from its own internally generated funds.

According to the theologically based practice intentionally instituted by James McKeown, members of the CoP, as an act of faith inspired by biblical texts for giving such as Malachi 3:10–11, Luke 6:38, and 2 Corinthians 8:9, give faithfully and without compulsion. Among other reasons, members of the CoP give as an expression of their love for their savior and Lord Jesus Christ, as a requirement of or act of obedience to injunctions from Scripture, and as expectation for rewards of financial blessings and prosperity from their master. The leadership of the church

---

101. See Gakpetor, "Christian's Response."
102. Onyinah, "Pentecostal Transformation in Africa," 17.

makes every effort to ensure that "giving" in the CoP does not become a pattern for deliberate manipulation or extortion of finances from its members but a true free-will giving. The leadership therefore periodically assesses and adjusts its form of giving or appeals for funds to make them conform to sound scriptural and ethical patterns so that members truly give out of their free will and not from a sense of compulsion.[103] Thus, through this effort, the CoP has succeeded in making financial commitment for the work of mission by the church a key part of its discipleship and spirituality.

TOWARD A THEOLOGICAL ANALYSIS OF AFRICAN PENTECOSTALISM FOR GROWTH AND MISSION

Attention to the above discussions prevents one from underestimating the CoP's—and African Pentecostalism's—understanding of the theology that underpins their spirituality and promotes their growth and mission. Martin E. Marty, of the University of Chicago, writing the foreword to Dayton's *Theological Roots of Pentecostalism* in 1987, rightly pointed out that "Pentecostals were not inconsistent, ecstatic ignoramuses."[104] Speaking in tongues should not be considered the only distinctive feature of Pentecostals, as was often the case during its early stages when they were branded "modern tongues movement."[105] As Dayton highlighted, the result of such typical theological analysis of Pentecostalism centered almost exclusively on questions of pneumatology, especially the doctrine of baptism in the Holy Spirit and gifts of the Holy Spirit.[106] However, Pentecostals, such as African Pentecostals, have fused experience of the Spirit with other theologically sound elements—as seen with the CoP—to produce, probably, the greatest or most fascinating religious phenomena in this century. Ogbu Kalu sums it up beautifully:

> The significance of aspects of the nineteenth century is that— as missionaries sowed the seed of the gospel—Africans appropriated it from a primal, charismatic worldview and read

---

103. A review of ministerial welfare practices was given in the Chairman's Circular Letter to All Officers of the Church of Pentecost, December 2, 2014.

104. Martin E. Marty, foreword to Donald Dayton's *Theological Roots of Pentecostalism*.

105. See Brumbeck, *What Meaneth This?*

106. Dayton, *Theological Roots of Pentecostalism*, 16.

the translated Scriptures from that hermeneutic. Indigenous agency subverted control through voice and exit; recovered the pneumatic resources of the Gospel and challenged missionary Christianity to be fully biblical. . . . Inexplicably, Charismatic and Pentecostal spirituality resurfaced to provide the energy for growth and sustainability in the midst of untoward circumstances.[107]

The African Pentecostals bound up the theology of the Spirit with other Christological teaching such as the elements of the foursquare gospel—Christ Jesus as Savior, Baptizer in the Holy Spirit, Healer, and Soon-Coming King—and other themes to enforce their theology.[108] These Pentecostal themes include the priesthood of all believers, spiritual warfare, and theologies on prosperity and deliverance. Its teaching on prosperity and deliverance, especially as taught in the current Charismatic movement, has been criticized variously from both inside the movement and also outside. Pentecostals are thought to be weak on the theology of suffering and ethical morality.[109] However, as described above, Pentecostal churches such as the CoP have strict interventions to balance such teachings.

The African Pentecostal movement, therefore, can be recognized as producing a Christocentric theology of the Spirit that has a keen emphasis on transformation and empowerment.[110] For instance, through Pentecostal orientation and teaching in its attempt to continue Christ's mission and discipleship in the world, we can observe the power of Christ in its effectiveness to transform lives, heal, and deliver to be one of the greatest lessons that Pentecostal Christianity is teaching the church of Christ today. Andrew Walls notes that Pentecostal theology, such as that of spiritual warfare, is a ministry cherished in African Christianity as a result of the spiritually precarious world in which people live.[111] In continuity with the African religious paradigm, Pentecostal and Charismatic Christianity have proven successful in Africa because of its openness to the supernatural, through its interventionist and oral theological forms that resonate with traditional African piety.

107. Kalu, "African Christianity," 38–39.
108. See Dayton, *Theological Roots of Pentecostalism*; Ntumy, *Tell the Next Generation*.
109. See Elorm-Donkor, "Christian Morality."
110. Kalu, *African Christianity*, 406–7.
111. Walls, *Cross-Cultural Process*, 15.

CONCLUSION

This chapter has identified a number of distinctive theological factors that ground the character and spirituality of the CoP and promote its growth. One can observe the CoP's Pentecostal spirituality in its character or ethos, beliefs, its doctrines and theology, patterns of worship, and other characteristics. This study has pointed out throughout this work that the pneumatic phenomenon that drive the movement's growth can be located in the experience of the Holy Spirit. This central Spirit theology is expressed in the church's spirituality, active in its individual adherents' lives, and a feature of the corporate organization. Thus, the main argument of this chapter—and the entire work—is that the transformative experience of the Holy Spirit in the lives of the adherents and the corporate body is what drives the church for growth.

This chapter has discussed the CoP's Pentecostal theologies, practices, character, and ethos in the areas of baptism and conversion, doctrines on the baptism of the Holy Spirit, gifts, and fruit of the Holy Spirit, and the contribution of spectacular events and prayer camps towards her growth. The aspects of its theology and practice that have been described include as well its community life and discipleship, biblically based prayer life, holiness and ethical moral life, and vibrant evangelistic programs driven by the power of the Spirit. It has also examined church discipline and accountability, liturgy and vernacularization, form and mode of worship, the sacrament of Holy Communion, and sacrificial giving such as tithing.

Because of these theological factors, the organization thrives, grows, and moves into missions. Thus, the present writer is convinced that the Spirit uses these factors to shape, drive, and influence the CoP and its adherents to grow the church. The study therefore concludes that, in continuity with the African religious paradigm, Pentecostal and Charismatic Christianity, as exemplified by the CoP, has proven successful in Africa because of its openness to the supernatural and its interventionist and oral theological forms that resonate with traditional African piety. In the late 1980s, Lamin Sanneh's *Translating the Message: The Missionary Impact on Culture* examined Christian mission with a focus on translation in its cultural dimension. This current study now points out how, in this era, Pentecostalism, such as that embodied in the CoP, is moving beyond translating the message to transmitting the Spirit in its own global missionary endeavors.

7

Summary and Conclusions

THIS RESEARCH HAS USED the history, growth, missions, and various innovations of the CoP to draw attention to African Pentecostalism and its many contributions to the current spread and missions of global Christianity. One main finding and conclusion of this study is that Pentecostalism is indeed growing, and African Pentecostalism must be acknowledged as a significant part of this growth. The CoP as a Ghanaian version of African Pentecostalism has been used to discuss some of the current innovations and contributions of the Pentecostal movement. It can be argued, therefore, that the CoP can offer viable answers on questions regarding the general growth of Pentecostalism, world evangelization, and Christian mission in this century.

This research has, first and foremost, updated the history of the CoP since Larbi's original work on its early history, *Pentecostalism: The Eddies of Ghanaian Christianity*. He captured the history of the CoP from its inception up to 1982, a period when the international missions of the CoP had not yet begun in earnest. Second, this work analyzes the CoP's history to identify the religious, missiological, and theological factors that have promoted its growth and missions. This research addresses the lack of scientific studies and discussion of the factors to which the tremendous growth of the CoP as an African indigenous denomination can be attributed.

Using a qualitative research method and a case study approach, this research has employed a historical-theological mode of study on the CoP's historical developments to achieve these objectives. To this end, the findings and observations were arrived at through personal observations, discussions, and collection of data from denominational documents, and analysis of the historical developments based on this full range of information.

The study confirmed the recent and ongoing proposal that Christianity on the African continent, including Ghana, is undergoing a "Pentecostalisation and Charismatisation."[1] It is particularly evident within the entire religious life and outlook in Ghana, where waves of Pentecostalism can be seen penetrating and influencing every religious sphere. For instance, such Pentecostalization appears in the historically Western-related churches as renewal movements, and it is currently the engine driving the new forms of indigenous Charismatic churches sprouting up.[2] The Ghanaian civic and public sphere also demonstrates this Pentecostalization in political, educational, cultural, and socioeconomic life, through its various engagements, including its media culture.[3]

SUMMARY OF FINDINGS AND CONCLUSIONS

This study updated and analyzed the history, growth, and missions of the CoP from the inception of the denomination to the present (2016). Yet the work focused mainly on the historical developments of the CoP after its formal and legal secession from its parent body, the Apostolic Church of the UK, in 1962, producing an update and continuation of Larbi's work on the CoP chronicled in his work on Pentecostalism in Ghana. Larbi covered the history of the CoP up to 1982 when James McKeown left the scene. He did not cover the leadership of the Ghanaian apostles, which this study does discuss.

In spite of the CoP's considering an Irish missionary as its missionary founder, the church has thoroughly developed and established itself as an indigenous, independent, classical Pentecostal denomination that is self-sustaining. Since the late 1940s it has engaged in missions outside Ghana as a manifestation of African Pentecostalism and has grown phenomenally as a vibrant missionary institution, planting churches all over its home country, Ghana, in other African nations, and in many parts of the globe. As an organization originating from sub-Saharan Africa with

---

1. See Asamoah-Gyadu, *Contemporary Pentecostalism*.
2. See Omenyo, *Pentecost Outside Pentecostalism*.
3. See Gifford, *Ghana's New Christianity*.

many well-known socioeconomic problems, it has grown independently and can be described as self-supporting, self-governing, self-propagating, and self-theologizing.

This work's analysis indicates that CoP administrative structures, religious character, theology, and ethos evolved from its historical trajectories and, in fact, are the same religious, missiological, and theological factors that have influenced its growth. It further argues that these factors may not necessarily be regarded as strategies that were deliberately formed to promote the church's growth. They were, rather, produced in the fallout from events in its history such as the various acrimonies, conflicts, and later developmental challenges. Having been thus produced in the context of a conflict or obstacle, they were further discussed, structured, and shaped to suit the pattern of the church at a particular time. In this way they served as means for further growth and development of the church.

These evolving structures discovered from the history, which are also the factors accounting for the church's growth, were identified as functional ministries (Evangelism, Women's, Children's, Youth, PIWC, Northern Outreach); church governance, administration, and finance; pneumatic phenomena (Holy Spirit baptism, signs and wonders, and prayer camps); indigenous leadership, development of manpower, and training and education; social services; print and electronic media; estates; and ecumenism.

The church appeared to be employing these factors to update its growth strategies. For instance, through its functional ministries, the denomination was able to adapt to contemporary challenges confronting its growth. Over time and changing circumstances, leadership tailored the functional ministries specifically to promote evangelism and to check developments that posed a challenge to the institution's growth at that time and in the future.

The Children's Ministry addresses issues regarding children born to members of the denomination. The Youth Ministry engages upwardly mobile young people in the context of their education and their particular issues such as contemporary postmodern challenges. The PIWCs provide correctives and check the effects of neo-Pentecostalism on the CoP's educated youth. They also provide a cross-cultural approach for expatriates and others of mixed cultural and language backgrounds. The Women's Ministry addresses issues pertaining to women; the men's fellowship, those of men; and the Northern Outreach Ministry reaches people from the northern region of Ghana living in the southern part of Ghana. All this demonstrates how the CoP adapts to deal with contemporary issues that confront its growth. Recently, the Northern Outreach Ministry was reintegrated into the larger church body because the leadership thought that factors leading to its establishment were no longer a challenge to its growth.

The primary aim and objective for the formation of these functional ministries has been effective evangelism and holistic growth of the individual adherents and the church as a whole. This culminated in the forming of the Evangelism Ministry in order to address the issues of effective evangelism; the Evangelism Ministry progressively developed from being a product of individual efforts, ad hoc participation, or unorganized evangelistic outreaches, into a more organized Young People's movement (*mbrentse kow*). Subsequently it developed into the Witness Movement and then the current Evangelism Ministry. With evangelism being the major activity or aim of the functional ministries, the Evangelism Ministry became a sort of mother to or prime focus of all these functional ministries. This observation is very important with regard to a recommendation in this work concerning the structuring of the functional ministries and growth of the CoP.

The growth pattern of the CoP draws upon a combination of the biological, transfer, and conversional growth patterns in Ghana and internationally. The CoP's major strength and its focus has been on conversion growth—growth through soul-winning evangelization. Yet in addition, its growth both at home and abroad makes use of transfer and biological growth mechanisms.

The denomination operates through a unique church growth method that can be described as a system of community-based and lay-leadership-driven congregations. Currently, it is vigorously growing small-group structures through home cells and Bible studies. Moreover, this study has observed the church engaging in growth patterns through active witnessing—evangelism—buttressed by socioeconomic engagements, effective discipleship, and the planting of churches.

The various discipleship and training programs aimed at growth in the CoP have also become means to produce manpower resources for its internal growth and missions abroad. The CoP develops leadership through members' personal engagement in ministries under established leaders to whom the newer leader is accountable. In this way the church forms its leaders such as deacons, deaconesses, elders, pastors, and other senior ministers (evangelists, prophets, and apostles) who oversee the local congregations and mission posts. Through this system, the church produces the kind of leaders who have a mark of maturity, dependability, fortitude, and sound character, which makes secession from the church minimal as compared to other contemporary Charismatic churches.

The formation of leaders also plays a role in the transfer growth mechanism employed by the CoP, which posts and changes the ministerial location of its field workers. The CoP system of moving its field ministers from one posting location to another differs greatly from other classical Pentecostal denominations, for instance, the Assemblies of God, which stations its ministers in the same location with the same congregation, only moving them on rare occasions. This study recommends further research to ascertain the effects on church growth of these two systems for posting ministers.

In the CoP system, every minister or field worker could be transferred from one posting location to another at any time. The only exceptions are the three principal executive officers stationed at the church's headquarters (chairman, general secretary, and international missions director) and the directors of the various ministries who have stipulated periods of tenure in office according to the church's constitution. This book argues that the CoP procedure of following the decisions of the General Council, especially regarding the annual posting of its ministers, stabilizes the church and makes its growth more effective.

Analysis of historical trends in the growth of the denomination shows that the periods having fewer conflicts and less rancor produced favorable conditions for increases in growth. Church growth patterns also seem to show that the growth of the church increases proportionally with an increase in the number of leaders, both lay and clergy.

An important aspect of the CoP's growth discussed was its international missions outreach, which began in the 1980s and which has since developed extensive diaspora missions in various parts of the West, continental Europe, the Middle East, and Asia. The members of the CoP traveling out of Ghana gather a few people for regular prayer and fellowship. As the gathering grows, the group then requests the headquarters in Ghana to send a responsible missionary to provide pastoral care and administration and also aid in evangelization and opening of other branches. These groups invariably end up becoming CoP congregations in these locations, and this mission and church growth method has resulted in the establishment of numerous CoP congregations all over the globe.

The most noticeable factor in CoP missions is the putting in place of a centralized Missions Department. The success of the CoP's diaspora missions has been attributed partly to the conscientious supervisory role of leaders provided by the international missions director for pastoral care, effective administration, and monetary controls. The orderly dissemination of mission policies from the top hierarchy through to the grassroots continues to ensure and to demonstrate that the CoP is mission-minded to its core.

This project argues, based on the history of the CoP's mission in the UK, that African Pentecostal mission enterprise such as that of the CoP initially began for chaplaincy purposes, but its presence in the West actually evoked a Christian witness.[4] The church's main intention, however, was to direct foreign missions towards the West as a mission in reverse to the West, much like the early European missions came to evangelize Africa as foreign missions. These CoP immigrant churches had originally focused on people of African descent, rather than the indigenes, as their evangelism targets. This notwithstanding, their presence filled a vacuum in an otherwise secularized continent by bringing a new Christian presence.[5] These Pentecostal Christians bought and occupied unused structures originally meant for Christian purposes that would otherwise have ended up in secular usage for which they were not originally intended. Their witness may not have affected the original indigenes of these places much, but they reached other Africans who were also migrants and not originally Christians.

The generation of young people born in Britain to Ghanaian parents and who have become Christians are sending the gospel as a reverse mission to their peers. The magnitude of this mission in reverse may not be very profound at the moment, yet to some extent we do see ongoing missions. Hanciles writes, "The CoP is consciously utilising Ghanaian migration as a springboard to contribute to the Christianisation of the world through evangelism."[6] The composition of migrants involved in the CoP's missions abroad suggests a mixture across the social strata of the

---

4. See Hanciles, "African Immigrant Churches," 351–54.
5. Goodhew, *Church Growth in Britain*, 107–93.
6. Hanciles, "African Immigrant Churches," 353.

diaspora, including students, officials from global organizations such as the United Nations and its various agencies, and staff in some Ghanaian embassies abroad. All these professionals and diplomats, together with those who appear to be seeking greener pastures, are involved in missions.

Some of the congregations include pockets of indigenes who came in through marriage and other relationships. The CoP structures such as PIWC and current youth churches are resources for future engagements in Christian enterprises. Thus, the CoP is actively addressing its cross-cultural missionary functions to embrace the indigenes of their sojourning locations without alienating the core constituencies on whose efforts their missionary actions depend.

The book further argues, from the discussion of the history of the formation of CoP mission churches across the globe, that mission in the CoP goes beyond chaplaincy and an intention for reverse mission. The trend suggests also a pattern in which the CoP uses its presence in the Western locations, such as the UK, USA, Canada, Germany, and Italy, as a platform to launch missions to other locations of the globe. These missions may move from the Global South directly to locations in the North and Global South and East, or via northern locations into other places in the North or Global South.

Practical examples of CoP missions from the Global South to the North include that from Ghana to the UK. But in addition, CoP missions from Italy, for instance, extend to Spain, Belgium, the Ukraine, and Portugal as South to North movement via the North. In these examples, the North serves as a platform to nurture missions elsewhere. Also, the CoP's missions from the USA to Latin America and the Caribbean nations—the Dominican Republic, Costa Rica, and Trinidad and Tobago—can be seen as mission from the Global South to another Global South location, but through the Global North. Again, the northern locations are being used as a platform or springboard to launch into other parts of the South. CoP missions have also been sent from Canada to Guyana, Brazil, and South America—likewise missions from the Global South directed to other southern locations but through the Global North. A different pattern of missions from the Global South to another southern location can be seen in the CoP's mission from Ghana directly to India. Therefore, the CoP's international missions display a variety of patterns of movement. This trend can be summed up, first, as missions extended from the Global South towards the North; second, as missions from the Global South to other locations in the North but using the North as a platform; third, as those moving from the Global South to other locations in the South but launching them from places in the North; and fourth, from the Global South to other non-Western locations.

The CoP achieves this global mission enterprise partly through the formation of functional ministers who are nurtured through its immigrant churches in the West. The activities of the CoP's resident missionaries sent abroad from Ghana must not be understood as a reverse flow in the way previous Western missions perceived theirs. Nevertheless, the CoP's resident missionaries, in addition to overseeing the congregations abroad, facilitate the formation of functional ministers such as pastors, area heads, and apostles who are then sent to other places in the West to start or oversee their churches. The resident missionaries disciple, train, and equip their constituents for the work of ministry. Some of these individuals who have been nurtured, who were also founding members of the CoP in the West, have become the heads of these CoP diaspora churches.

These functional ministers have an advantage of understanding the cultures of their sojourning locations in the West. They also already have resident permits that enable them to move into other Western locations with few restrictions, due to the migration policies of the European Union, for instance, which encourages free movement of people within its member states. The resident missionaries sent to pioneer or continue the CoP foreign missions gracefully and faithfully return to Ghana when given new ministerial postings. However, before these resident missionaries depart to their new stations back in Ghana, they would have nurtured and trained other functional ministers. These ministers the CoP then uses to spread its missions into other parts of the West and other non-Western nations that may not be traditional transit destinations for Africans.

Throughout this book, the study has worked with the hypothesis that a pneumatic phenomenon drives the African Pentecostal movement, and the CoP in particular, for growth. The study argues, as also observed by Asamoah-Gyadu and others, that this pneumatic phenomenon is the work of the Holy Spirit observed as the central catalyst bringing about Christian ministry and mission through the individuals and the corporate church. The dynamism of the CoP can be located in the experience of the Holy Spirit, expressed as its spirituality, active in its adherents and in the corporate organization. Thus, this study makes the main observation that the transformative experience of the Holy Spirit in the lives of the adherents and the corporate body is the drive of the church for growth. The wide acceptability of Pentecostalism, including the CoP, on the African continent is attributed to the fact that its religiosity and spirituality seem akin to those of the primal imagination of traditional African piety.

In the past, typical theological analysis of Pentecostalism centered almost exclusively on questions of pneumatology, especially the doctrine of baptism in the Holy Spirit and gifts of the Holy Spirit.[7] However, the CoP as a manifestation of African Pentecostalism has fused the experience of the Spirit with other theologically sound elements to produce, perhaps, one of the most fascinating religious phenomena of the century. The CoP integrated the theology of the Spirit with other Christological teachings, expressed in its beliefs, practices, and other characteristics to promote its growth. The CoP's Pentecostal spirituality is observed through its theology, character or form of beliefs, patterns of worship, and other aspects of its ethos.

This work discussed the CoP's Pentecostal theologies, practices, character, and ethos in the areas of conversion and baptism, doctrines on the baptism of the Holy Spirit, gifts, and fruit of the Holy Spirit, and the spectacular events and prayer camps, all of which contribute to her growth. Other aspects of her spirituality and theology that were examined include its community life and discipleship, biblically based prayer life, holiness and ethical moral life, vibrant evangelistic programs driven by the power of the Holy Spirit, church discipline and accountability, liturgy and vernacularization, form and mode of worship, the sacrament of Holy Communion, and sacrificial giving beginning with tithing. In contrast to the modus operandi of other Pentecostals, such as some contemporary Ghanaian Charismatic churches, which interpret the work of the Holy Spirit solely in terms of the Spirit's gifts and limit their application to healing and responding to existential needs, the CoP has a more holistic pneumatology that impacts all of the believer's life and the church's operations.

These theological factors fuel and direct the way the organization thrives, grows, and moves into missions. The present writer is thus convinced that the Holy Spirit uses these factors to shape, drive, and influence the CoP and its adherents through the organization's various systems to grow the church. This author concludes that, in continuity with the African religious paradigm, Pentecostal and Charismatic Christianity, such

---

7. Dayton, *Theological Roots of Pentecostalism*, 16.

as that of the CoP, has proven successful in Africa because of its openness to the supernatural, through its interventionist and oral theological forms influenced by a theology of the Spirit and other biblical Christocentric teachings and practices that resonate with traditional African piety.

RECOMMENDATIONS FOR THE COP'S GROWTH

Based on the update and analysis of the history of the CoP and these evolving factors (religious, missiological, theological) to which its growth is attributed, this author makes the following suggestions towards its continuing future growth.

Restructure the Evangelism Ministry into a Department

The analysis and discussions of the historic developments of the CoP's functional ministries show that the church's purpose for establishing the functional ministries is to grow the church through active evangelistic efforts. Evangelism therefore is the corporate church's main intention, which must be engaged in by all and not just by an identified group, such as the Evangelism Ministry. In the present writer's opinion, it is duplication to set up a special ministry, such as the Evangelism Ministry, as an option for individuals. Since other ministries, such as youth and women's, have the same primary aim, there are bound to be conflicts of interest and competition, as already seen between Evangelism Ministry and Youth Ministry, resulting in changes of names and functions over the years.

In an effort towards growth, this researcher recommends that the Evangelism Ministry of the CoP be structured as an outfit or a department that is responsible for mobilization, training, and instruction for evangelism within all the functional ministries and the entire body of the church. Evangelism would therefore be more clearly seen as imperative for every member of the church, as in the New Testament. Every member should be carrying out evangelism as a member of a functional ministry. This would enhance the main focus of the functional ministries—which is evangelism—by avoiding the duplication of duties and competition for certain groups of members, such as the young people. The Evangelism Ministry or Department would operate both in the local churches and the functional ministries. The headquarters directorate would become a department to collaborate with the functional ministries in their quest for effective soul winning by providing input into their syllabi and curriculum. It would provide training and aid mobilization for evangelism. In this regard, the ministries would have their own distinctive committees to work out the details for evangelistic campaigns, but they would be supported and equipped by the Evangelism Department.

Step Up Social Action as Part of Holistic Evangelism or Soul Winning

This study recommends that, as part of the CoP's efforts towards growth and mission, it should intensify social action as part of its corporate evangelistic efforts. In its early years, the church, upon the advice of James McKeown in particular, did not concentrate much on social interventions in order to not neglect evangelism. Evangelism was considered its main focus. Even though the church's social action has now come very far with the PENTSOS initiatives in schools and hospitals, more effort can be extended in this direction. The church's external missions especially should step up action concerning social interventions.

Having come this far with its growth, it is time for the church to fortify its evangelistic efforts with more social action on behalf of the needs of converts. This will ensure a more holistic effect on the poor and marginalized who encounter the faith. For instance, social and economic incentives can help its congregations in the Northern and Upper Regions of Ghana and other African locations that are not well endowed and are considered remote and deprived. In locations of intense poverty, the CoP churches in southern Ghana could mobilize efforts for poverty alleviation.

These commitments may include more initiatives toward formal education for the poor, medical relief, vocational and craftsmanship training for the disadvantaged, and avenues for micro financing small businesses and for educational scholarships for needy students. Youth and young adults with no means of support could be given basic training in crafts and job skills. This can be done through the strategic building of resource centers for computer training, secretarial classes, and various trades. Outreach evangelism should be accompanied by medical services to alleviate the health challenges of the poor and needy. This will ensure that the gospel becomes a tool for the holistic well-being of the converted in mind, body, soul, and spirit.

Examine the Establishment of Prayer Camps and the Place of Gifted Laity in the Church

The emergence of prayer camps across the religious landscape of the CoP was noted in this study as one of the factors in the CoP's growth. The church made efforts to reform and structure them to conform to biblical standards and practices. Because of practices in some of the prayer camps that the CoP considers unbiblical, the church put a ban on the establishment of new prayer camps. The ban may prompt more secessions that could hurt the church's numerical growth. This study pointed out a gap in the CoP structure as the cause for the springing up of the Prayer Camps. This gap should be addressed. We have observed that the CoP's ministerial formation has identified places or positions and direction for its gifted ministers. For instance, a minister could be made an evangelist, area head, apostle, or prophet with a defined scope and authority to work. However, such avenues are not apparent for gifted laypersons, for instance, those with gifts in the area of healing and ministry of power, which can be associated with evangelism. The majority of these laypersons are generally not well educated; some are women who do not have roles in the CoP leadership because ministers in the CoP are male.

These gifted lay people do not find official positions to fit into and therefore adopt positions known previously in the early AICs as prayer camp leaders. In the establishment of prayer camps, therefore, the layperson finds a means of expressing a God-given mandate. Other denominations, such as the Assemblies of God, have recognized this situation, and personal ministries can be developed in local congregations. These lay ministries can include leadership training, marital counseling, intercessory ministries, evangelism, healing outreach ministries, and others. The CoP can pattern recognized ministries in this direction to curtail the prevalent secessions of prayer camps established by lay members of the church.

Review a System of Community-Based Clusters of Congregations with One Pastor

One of the structures particularly unique to the CoP is its community-based churches, which are overseen by lay leaders and supervised by district overseers or pastors. A single pastor could be overseeing from two to more than 20 local assemblies or congregations. This system resembles some Ghanaian traditional chieftaincy systems headed by a paramount chief who has a cluster of chiefs reporting to him. The congregations are under the care of presiding elders who work voluntarily. The pastors act more or less as overseers. Even though this practice has many advantages and has worked for the CoP in Ghana and elsewhere, it may not be most effective at all times and places. The complexities of today's postmodern society and the demand for more pastoral attention in this era, especially in churches in the West, will require effort to get more committed stationary persons periodically to man each congregation. The system may not be suitable for other nations, as situations change from country to country. The system of the PIWC should be extended towards the entire church with the aim of having a single large congregation with one or more pastors. This will ensure more effectiveness in pastoral care, better output, and positive growth.

Develop Strategic Missions to the Nations Aimed at Long-term Missions

As part of its sustainable mission effort towards abiding and fruitful missions to the nations, this study recommends deliberate planned missions to specific locations. Specific nations could be targeted or earmarked for missions ahead of time, which would enable the church to prepare the type of personnel needed and to mold and enhance their specific abilities. For instance, individuals who have the grace for missions could be identified and then be specifically trained in particular languages and skills in preparation to go to a particular location. This will lessen the dependency on alliances with already existing churches, which have their own attendant problems, as this research observed. The church must specifically train people in languages such as French, Spanish, German, Arabic, Chinese, and Dutch to target its missionary focus. Such planning and training can prevent missions work from being done ad hoc and from being dependent on others who do not understand and have the same zeal as members of the CoP.

Take Action toward Autonomy of the CoP National Churches

The church should expedite the steps and take action toward granting autonomy to more of its national churches. The history of establishment of the CoP's national churches goes back more than 40 years; the commencement of missions outside Ghana dates from the 1940s. These churches have received missionaries and logistical support from the headquarters in Ghana for many years. In Africa, for instance, the church in Burkina Faso, one of the earliest to be planted, has been established for more than 40 years. However, it is still dependent on the church in Ghana for logistics and missionary support.

Admittedly, the CoP has so far granted autonomy to two of its national branches—Benin and Côte d'Ivoire.[8] Yet other branches in the Western nations such as the USA and the UK can be considered overdue for autonomy when measured by the agreed-upon criteria. Many of these churches overseas have become large national churches with several congregations and have grown their own leaders, including apostles and prophets. These nations appear to have fulfilled every requirement to stand on their own as autonomous national churches. These churches, though semi-autonomous in terms of administration, are still tied to the main headquarters in Ghana in policy and other matters. These churches should be granted autonomy and be encouraged to build the CoP national churches, adapted to suit their particular locations and contexts.

Some of the churches in the West should no longer be receiving missionaries from Ghana. They have raised enough manpower resources to stand on their own. The parent church should therefore commence action towards granting them autonomy. Coupled with this, the church must subsequently formalize a process towards collaboration for future relations among the autonomous churches and their members and for further evangelization into other nations. This will help the church in building a worldwide mission-minded church that will continue with a common missions agenda and policy.

Granting autonomy to these national churches will encourage their initiatives in forming churches that favor the particular nation's culture, language, and traditions. In order for the CoP to expand and to forestall some of the challenges that might be specific to particular nations—culture, law, language, and modes of administration—actions should be expedited for the formation of a well-structured, dependable

---

8. CoP, brochure for 42nd General Council meeting, 2016.

commonwealth association of the CoP's autonomous national churches, where resources and manpower could be voluntarily distributed or shared.

RECOMMENDED AREAS OF THE COP REQUIRING FURTHER RESEARCH

Alongside the specific recommendations outlined above, this writer believes the CoP, as an African Pentecostal institution, requires further scientific investigation and research to best promote its progressive global growth and mission. This writer recommends research in the following important areas:

1. How the lay-leadership-driven, community-based system being used by CoP in Ghana is adaptable for other external branches in other African nations and in other locations outside of Africa, including the West. This research is important for its global growth and expansion considering the diversity and complexities of other global locations.

2. The church's endeavors to sponsor and train some of its ministers and others as Christian scholars, especially in the area of postgraduate studies—with training from diverse institutions with different theological orientations and curricula. What does this training hold for the institution, the Pentecostal fraternity, and for the individual scholars themselves in the long term? What implications, for instance, does higher education at non-Pentecostal institutions hold for the future of the church's growth and Pentecostalism in general?

3. Comparative research with other church organizations of the same caliber, such as African Pentecostals, Redeemed Christian Church of God from Nigeria, and other non-Pentecostal churches, with regard to growth analysis.

4. Ways that the CoP can regulate and generate enough finances to sponsor its evangelism programs and also engage in effective socioeconomic intervention in its holistic missions agenda.

5. The person, ministry and missionary work of James McKeown, the missionary founder of CoP, as a missionary model that has produced the CoP.

6. Examination of the leadership qualities and style of the chairmen of the CoP African Executive in comparison to James McKeown and their effects on the CoP.
7. The impact of CoP music on Christianity in Ghana.

CONCLUSION

The CoP, as an African Pentecostal denomination, has moved from the periphery into the mainstream of global church growth and missions in this era. The denomination has adopted innovative and practical strategies for its continuing growth as a Pentecostal denomination and has thus become integral in the growth of global Christianity in this new century. Its whole process of growth and mission can be described as having moved beyond what Sanneh refers to as "translating the Scriptures" and into "transmitting the Spirit" in missions. This work, *Transmitting the Spirit in Missions: The History and Growth of the Church of Pentecost*, has repeatedly shown evidence that the influence and experience of the Holy Spirit serves as the pivotal and necessary main force or actor behind the church's growth and expansion.

Appendix A
Mission Report Form

THE CHURCH OF PENTECOST – INTERNATIONAL MISSIONS

ANNUAL STATISTICS REPORT FORM

NATION: PERIOD:

DEMOGRAPHY

STATISTIC			DEC. CURRENT YEAR	DEC. PREVIOUS YEAR	VARIANCE	PERCENTAGE INCREASE
No. Areas					0	-
No. of Districts					0	-
No. of Assemblies					0	-
No. of Home Cells					0	-
Overall Church Membership (Adults & Children)					0	-
Total Adult Membership (13yrs and above):		a) Total			0	-
		b) Male			0	-
		c) Female			0	-
Youth Membership (13yrs - 35yrs):		a) Total			0	-
		b) Male			0	-
		c) Female			0	-
Teens (13yrs - 19yrs):		a) Total			0	-
		b) Male			0	-
		c) Female			0	-
Young Adults (20yrs - 35yrs):		a) Total			0	-
		b) Male			0	-
		c) Female			0	-
Other Adults (above 35yrs):		a) Total			0	-
		b) Male			0	-
		c) Female			0	-
Children's Membership (below 13yrs):					0	-
Ghanaian Membership					0	-
No. of Nationals (indigenes)					0	-
No. of other Nationals					0	-
OFFICERS						

Appendix B
Photographs

COP IN ITS EARLY YEARS (1937–1962)

The Rev. James McKeown and Pastor Joseph Egyir-Painstil at a convention

APPENDIX B

One of the early conventions of CoP held at Nkawkaw in 1970

A cross-section of ministers at a convention in 1970

Some ministers' wives at a convention in 1970

Photograph of ministers after the CoP's General Council meetings held in Kumasi in 1977

APPENDIX B

COP EXTERNAL MISSIONS (1980–PRESENT)

The National Head Office of CoP–UK

A cross-section of the youth of CoP–UK during the annual National Youth Conference at Nottingham University, July 2017

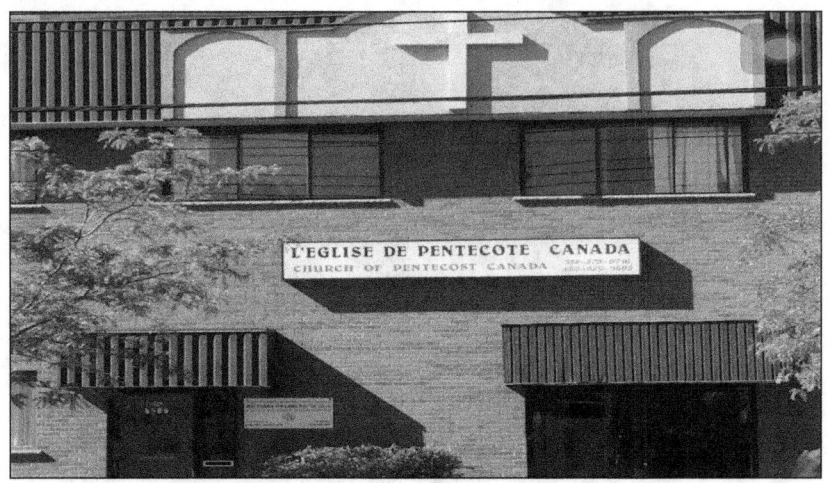

A branch of the Church of Pentecost in Montreal, Canada

The National Head Office of CoP–Canada

APPENDIX B

THE CURRENT STATE OF THE COP (AS OF 2017)

General Headquarters

Opening session of the Global Ministers and Wives' Conference of CoP, January 10, 2017, at the Pentecost Convention Centre

Pentecost University College, Sowutoum

Pentecost Theological Seminary

APPENDIX B

Pentecost Convention Centre

Aerial view of the Pentecost Convention Centre

Aerial view of some auditoriums at the Pentecost Convention Centre

Pentecost Press Ltd.

Pent TV

Bibliography

Adogame, Afe, Roswith Gerloff, and Klaus Hock, editors. *Christianity in Africa and the African Diaspora: The Appropriation of a Scattered Heritage*. London: Continuum, 2008.

Adogame, Afe, and James V. Spickard, editors. *Religion Crossing Boundaries: Transnational Religious and Social Dynamics in Africa and the New African Diaspora*. Leiden: Brill, 2010.

Adubofour, Samuel. "Evangelical Para-Church Movements in Ghanaian Christianity: 1950 to Early 1990." PhD thesis, University of Edinburgh, 1994.

Agyemang-Baduh, Johnson. "The Home Cell System in CoP." Presentation at Pastors and Wives Conference, Pentecost University College, Sowutuom, Accra, 2013.

Ali, Benjamin. *Prophetism in the Church of Pentecost in Ghana*. Accra: Advent, 2015.

Anank, Francis Kweku. "The Impact of the Northern Outreach Ministry on the Church of Pentecost." Long essay submitted for BA degree, Pentecost University College, 2013.

Anderson, Allan H. *An Introduction to Pentecostalism: Global Charismatic Christianity*. 2nd ed. Cambridge: Cambridge University Press, 2014.

———. *To the Ends of the Earth: Pentecostalism and the Transformation of World Christianity*. New York: Oxford University Press, 2013.

———. "Varieties, Definitions and Taxonomies." In *Studying Global Pentecostalism: Theories and Methods*, edited by Allan Anderson, Michael Bergunder, André Droogers, and Cornelis van der Laan, 13–29. Berkeley: University of California Press, 2010.

Apostolic Church. *The Apostolic Witness Movement Gold Coast: A Handbook of Twelve Studies for 1950 for the Young Peoples Work*. Cape Coast: Apostolic Church, 1949.

Asamoah-Gyadu, J. Kwabena. *African Charismatics: Current Developments within Independent Indigenous Pentecostalism in Ghana*. Leiden: Brill, 2005.

———. "'Born of Water and the Spirit': Pentecostal/Charismatic Christianity in Africa." In *African Christianity: An African Story*, edited by Ogbu U. Kalu, 388–409. Pretoria: University of Pretoria, 2005.

———. *Contemporary Pentecostal Christianity: Interpretations from an African Context*. Oxford: Regnum, 2013.

———. *The Holy Spirit Our Comforter: An Exercise in Homiletic Pneumatology*. Ghana: Step, 2017.

———. "'On Mission Abroad': Ghana's Church of Pentecost and Its USA Missions." In *African Christian Presence in the West: New Immigrant Congregations and*

Transnational Networks in North America and Europe, edited by Frieder Ludwig and J. Kwabena Asamoah-Gyadu, 89–102. Trenton, NJ: Africa World, 2011.

———. "Pentecostalism and the Missiological Significance of Religious Experience in Africa Today: The Case of Ghana 'Church of Pentecost.'" *Trinity Journal of Church and Theology* 12:1–2 (July/December 2002) 30–57.

———. "'The Promise Is for You and Your Children': Pentecostal Spirituality, Mission and Discipleship in Africa." Paper Presented at the West Africa Consultation of Edinburgh 2010, Akrofi-Christaller Institute of Theology, Mission and Culture, Akropong-Akuapem, Ghana, March 23–24, 2009.

———. "Renewal within African Christianity: A Historical and Theological Study of Some Current Developments within Independent Indigenous Pentecostalism in Ghana." PhD thesis, University of Birmingham, 2000.

Asare-Duah, Oppong. *The Gallant Soldiers of the Church of Pentecost*. Accra: Jospong, 2004.

Asem, E. Kafui, editor. *A History of the Church of Pentecost*. Vol. 1. Accra: Pentecost, 2005.

Baëta, C. G. *Prophetism in Ghana*. Accra: African Christian, 2004.

Barker, Peter, and Samuel Boadi-Siaw. *Changed by the Word: The Story of Scripture Union Ghana*. Bangalore: Bangalore Offset, 2005.

Barrett, David B. "AD 2000: 350 Million Christians in Africa." *International Review of Mission* 59 (1970) 39–54.

Barrett, David B., and Peter F. Crossing. "Christianity 2010: A View from the New Atlas of Global Christianity." *International Bulletin of Missionary Research* 34 (2010) 29–36.

Barrett, David B., G. T. Kurian, and T. M. Johnson, editors. *World Christian Encyclopedia: A Comparative Survey of Churches and Religious in the Modern World*. New York: Oxford University Press, 2000.

Bediako, Kwame. *Christianity in Africa: The Renewal of a Non-Western Religion*. Maryknoll, NY: Orbis, 1995.

———. *Theology and Identity: The Impact of Culture upon Christian Thought in the Second Century and Modern Africa*. Oxford: Regnuml, 1992.

Bonino, José Miguez. "Pentecostal Missions Is More than What It Claims." *Pneuma* 16:2 (1997) 284–95.

Bosch, D. J. *Transforming Mission: Paradigm Shifts in Theology of Mission*. Maryknoll, NY: Orbis, 1996.

Bredwa-Mensah, Yaw. "The Church of Pentecost in Retrospect: 1937–1960." In *The Church of Pentecost: 50 Years of Sustainable Growth; James McKeown Memorial Lectures*, edited by Opoku Onyinah. Accra: Church of Pentecost, 2004.

Brouwer, Steve, Paul Gifford, and Susan D. Rose. *Exporting the American Gospel: Global Christian Fundamentalism*. New York: Routledge, 1996.

Brumbeck, Carl. *What Meaneth This?: A Pentecostal Answer to a Pentecostal Question*. Springfield, MO: Gospel, 1946.

Chadwick, William. *Stealing Sheep: The Church's Hidden Problem with Transfer Growth*. Downers Grove, IL: InterVarsity, 2001.

Chan, Simon. *Pentecostal Theology and the Christian Spiritual Tradition*. Journal of Pentecostal Theology Supplement Series 21. Sheffield: Sheffield Academic, 2000.

Church of Pentecost [CoP]. *Administrative Manual*. Accra: Advocate, 2009.

———. Autonomy Committee Report on the External Branches of the CoP. 2013.

BIBLIOGRAPHY

———. Brochure for the 42nd General Council Meeting. Pentecost Convention Centre, May 11–14, 2016.

———. *The Church of Pentecost: 50 Years of Sustainable Growth; James McKeown Memorial Lectures*. Edited by Opoku Onyinah. Accra: Church of Pentecost, 2004.

———. *The Church of Pentecost Songs: Compiled for Council Meeting, Retreats, Conferences, Conventions, etc.* English and Twi. Addendum: "God's First Covenant and Promises with The Church of Pentecost (Revealed)." Accra: Pentecost, 2000.

———. *A Handbook for Pentecost Youth and Evangelistic Movement*. Accra: Pentecost, 1991.

———. *Home Cells Leadership Training Manual*. Accra: Pentecost, 2012.

———. Meeting of Executive Committees of All Ministries, Minutes. Tesan Transit Quarters, November 21, 2013.

———. *The Minister's Handbook*. Accra: Advocate, 2008.

———. *The Minister's Handbook*. Accra: Advocate, 2014.

———. *The Minister's Handbook for Financial Administration and Policy*. August 2014.

———. Missions Annual Report, 2013. International Missions Distribution of Church Statistics by Nations for January–December 2013. Compiled for the 14th session of the Extraordinary Council Meeting, May 7–10, 2014.

———. Missions Annual Report, 2015. Presented to the 15th session of the Extraordinary Council Meeting, 2016.

——— Missions Department compiled document, "History of Nations." 2006.

——— Missions Department compiled document, "History of Nations." 2013.

———. *Missions Handbook*. 2008.

———. Policy Guidelines for Effective Management of PENTSOS Institutions at All Levels. January 2012.

———. "A Short History of PENSA KNUST." In the brochure for the 30th anniversary celebrations for PENSA KNUST, Kumasi, April 2007.

———. *Vision 2018: Five-Year Vision for the Church of Pentecost Covering 2013–2018*. Accra: Pentecost, 2013.

———. *Witness Syllabus*. Oda: Jonaskey, 1966.

Church of Pentecost [CoP]–UK. Charter (an Elim Church Incorporated). Adopted by the National Executive Council on January 28, 2012 and rectified by the National Council on February 4, 2012.

———. "Short History of CoP-UK." In the brochure for the 25-Year Silver Jubilee Celebration, August 18–31, 2014.

Comiskey, Joel. *Reap the Harvest: How a Small-Group System Can Grow Your Church*. Houston: Touch, 1999.

Cox, Harvey. *Fire from Heaven: The Rise of Pentecostal Spirituality and the Reshaping of Religion in the Twenty-First Century*. Reading, MA: Addison-Wesley, 1995.

———. Foreword to *Pentecostals after a Century: Global Perspectives on a Movement in Transition*, edited by Allan H. Anderson and Walter J. Hollenweger. Sheffield: Sheffield Academic, 1999.

Daswani, Girish. *Looking Back, Moving Forward: Transformation and Ethical Practice in the Ghanaian Church of Pentecost*. Toronto, ON: University of Toronto Press, 2015.

Dayton, Donald W. *Theological Roots of Pentecostalism*. Metuchen, NJ: Scarecrow, 1987.

Docquier, Frederic, and Abdeslam Marfouk. "Measuring the International Mobility of Skilled Workers (1990/2000): Release 1.0." Research working paper series, no. WPS 3381. Washington, DC: World Bank, August 1, 2004. http://documents.

worldbank.org/curated/en/871711468125364867/Measuring-the-international-mobility-of-skilled-workers-1990–2000-release-1–0.

Doherty, Sam. *Why Evangelize Children?* Lisburn, Ireland: Child Evangelism Fellowship Specialized Book Ministry, 1996.

Elorm-Donkor, Lord Abraham. "Christian Morality in Ghanaian Pentecostalism: A Theological Analysis of Virtue Theory as a Framework for Integrating Christian and Akan Moral Schemes." PhD thesis, University of Manchester, 2011.

Foli, Richard. *Church Growth in Ghana.* Accra: Methodist Book Depot, 2001.

Gakpetor, Samuel. "The Christian's Response in the World of Different Voices." Presentation at All Ministers and Wives Conference, Pentecost Convention Centre, January 11–15, 2016.

———. "Small–Medium Sized Church Case Study in Missions: Critical Assessment through Global Case Study." Presentation at Church of Pentecost gathering, 2014.

"Ghana: A Brief Guide." A publication of the Ghana International Services Department, 1994.

Ghana Evangelical Committee [GEC]. *Survey of Churches in Ghana, 1989, 1993, 2010.*

Gifford, Paul. *Ghana's New Christianity: Pentecostalism in a Globalizing African Economy.* Bloomington: Indiana University Press, 2004.

Glasser, Arthur F. "An Introduction to Church Growth Perspectives of Donald Anderson McGavran." In *Theological Perspectives on Church Growth*, edited by Harvie M. Conn. Phillipsburg, NJ: P&R, 1976.

Goodhew, David, editor. *Church Growth in Britain, 1980 to the Present.* Farnham, Surrey, UK: Ashgate, 2012.

Green, Michael. *Evangelism in the Early Church.* Eastbourne, UK: Kingsway, 2003.

———. *Evangelism through the Local Church: A Comprehensive Guide to All Aspects of Evangelism.* Vancouver, BC: Regent College Publishing, 2012.

Gyekye, Kwame. *African Cultural Values: An Introduction.* Accra: Sankofa, 1996.

Haliburton, G. M. *The Prophet Harris: A Study of an African Prophet and His Mass-Movement in the Ivory Coast and the Gold Coast, 1913–1915.* London: Longman, 1971.

Hanciles, Jehu J. "African Immigrant Churches in America." In *Beyond Christendom: Globalization, African Migration, and the Transformation of the West*, edited by Jehu J. Hanciles, 350–73. Maryknoll, NY: Orbis, 2008.

———. "African Migrations." In *Beyond Christendom: Globalization, African Migration and the Transformation of the West*, edited by Jehu J. Hanciles, 207–28. Maryknoll, NY: Orbis, 2008.

———, editor. *Beyond Christendom: Globalization, African Migration and the Transformation of the West.* Maryknoll, NY: Orbis, 2008.

Hayfron, David Nyansah. "Theology and Spirituality of Songs of Eunice Johnson of Ghana." MA thesis, Akrofi-Christaller Institute of Theology, Mission and Culture, 2010.

Hock, Klaus. "Religion on the Move: Transnational Perspectives, Discourses on Diaspora Religion between Category Formation and the Quest for Religious Identity." In *Christianity in Africa and the African Diaspora*, edited by Afe Adogame, Roswith Gerloff, and Klaus Hock. London: Continuum, 2008.

Hocken, Peter. "The Meaning and Purpose of 'Baptism in the Spirit.'" *Pneuma* 7:2 (Fall 1985) 125–33.

Hodges, Melvin L. *Indigenous Church.* Springfield, MO: Gospel 1953.

Hollenweger, Walter J. "Evangelism: A Non-Colonial Model." *Journal of Pentecostal Theology* 3:7 (1995) 107–28.

———. *Pentecostalism: Origins and Developments Worldwide*. Peabody, MA: Hendrickson, 1997.

Hull, Robert, W. *The Complete Book of Discipleship: On Being and Making Followers of Christ*. Colorado Springs, CO: NavPress, 2006.

Jacobson, Douglas. *Thinking in the Spirit: Theories of the Early Pentecostal Movement*. Bloomington: Indiana University Press, 2003.

Kalu, Ogbu U., editor. *African Christianity: An African Story*. Pretoria: University of Pretoria, Department of Church History, 2005.

———. "African Christianity: An Overview." In *African Christianity: An African Story*, edited by Ogbu U. Kalu. Pretoria: University of Pretoria, Department of Church History, 2005.

———. "The Anatomy of Reserve Flow in African Christianity: Pentecostalism and Immigrant African Christianity." In *African Christian Presence in the West: New Immigrant Congregations and Transnational Networks in North America and Europe*, edited by Frieder Ludwig and J. Kwabena Asamoah-Gyadu. Trenton, NJ: African World, 2011.

———. "Ethiopianism in African Christianity." In *African Christianity: An African Story*, edited by Ogbu U. Kalu. Pretoria: University of Pretoria, 2005.

Koduah, Alfred. "The Church of Pentecost in a Postmodern Society." In *The Church of Pentecost: 50 Years of Sustainable Growth; James McKeown Memorial Lectures*, edited by Opoku Onyinah. Accra: Church of Pentecost, 2004.

Kodum, Micheal, and Osei-Wusu Brempong. "Evaluation of NOM Operations and the Way Forward." January 2, 2013.

Kpobi, David N. A. "African Chaplains in the Seventeenth Century West Africa." In *African Christianity: An African Story*, edited by Ogbu U. Kalu, 140–69. Pretoria: Department of Church History, University of Pretoria, 2005.

Kuma, Afua, and S. V. D. Jon Kirby. *Jesus of the Deep Forest: Prayers and Praises of Afua Kuma*. Accra: Asempa, 1980.

Larbi, Emmanuel Kingsley. "The Church of Pentecost: Sustaining the Growth." In *The Church of Pentecost: 50 Years of Sustainable Growth; James McKeown Memorial Lectures*, edited by Opoku Onyinah. Accra: Church of Pentecost, 2004.

———. *Pentecostalism: The Eddies of Ghanaian Christianity*. Accra: Centre for Pentecostal and Charismatic Studies, 2001.

Leonard, Christine. *A Giant in Ghana: 3,000 Churches in 50 Years—The Story of James McKeown and the Church of Pentecost*. Chichester, UK: New Wine, 1989.

Ludwig, Frieder, and J. Kwabena Asamoah-Gyadu, editors. *African Christian Presence in the West: New Immigrant Congregations and Transnational Networks in North America and Europe*. Trenton, NJ: Africa World, 2011.

Luzbetak, Louis J. *Church and Culture: New Perspectives in Missiological Anthropology*. Maryknoll, NY: Orbis, 1989.

Macchia, Frank D. "Sighs Too Deep for Words: Towards a Theology of Glossolalia." *Journal of Pentecostal Theology* 1 (1992) 47–73.

Markin, Amos Jimmy. "Ghanaian Christian Missions in North American Diaspora." MA thesis, University of Ghana, 2006.

McGavran, Donald A. *Understanding Church Growth*. Grand Rapids: Eerdmans, 1970.

McGavran, Donald A., and Win. C. Arn. *How to Grow a Church*. Glendale, CA: Regal, 1973.

McGee, Gary B. "Pentecostal Missiology: Moving Beyond Triumphalism to Face the Issues." *Pneuma* 16:1 (1994) 275–81.

———. "Pentecostal Phenomena and Revivals in India: Implications for Indigenous Leadership." *International Bulletin of Missions Research* 20:3 (1996) 112–17.

Menzies, William W., and Robert P. Menzies. *Spirit and Power: Foundations of Pentecostal Experience*. Grand Rapids: Zondervan, 2000.

Meyer, Birgit. "Aesthetics of Persuasion: Global Christianity and Pentecostalism's Sensational Forms." *South Atlantic Quarterly* 109:4 (2010) 741–63. doi: 10.1215/00382876-2010-015. http://www.academia.edu/5627193/Aesthetics_of_Persuasion_Global_Christianity_and_Pentecostalism_s_Sensational_Forms.

Novieto, Ernestina Enyonam. "Women Leaders in Ghanaian Pentecostal/Charismatic Churches." PhD thesis, University of Ghana, June 2013.

Ntumy, M. K., editor. *Tell the Next Generation: Lecture Notes on the Annual Themes of the Church of Pentecost Teachings*. Compiled by the National Literature Committee. Vols. 1–2. Accra: National Literature Committee, 2002, 2008.

Nukunya, G. K. *Tradition and Change in Ghana: An Introduction to Sociology*. 2nd ed. Accra: Ghana Universities Press, 1992.

Nyarko, L. A. "The Zeal of the Fathers." In *Tell the Next Generation: Lecture Notes on the Annual Themes of the Church of Pentecost Teachings*. Vol. 1. Edited by M. K. Ntumy. Accra: National Literature Committee, 2002.

Oduyoye, Mercy Amba. *Daughters of Anowa: African Women and Patriarchy*. Maryknoll, NY: Obis, 1995.

Omenyo, Cephas N. *Pentecost Outside Pentecostalism: A Study of the Development of Charismatic Renewal in the Mainline Churches in Ghana*. Zoetermeer: Uiteverij Boekencentrum, 2006.

Onyinah, Opoku. "The Man James McKeown." In *The Church of Pentecost: 50 Years of Sustainable Growth; James McKeown Memorial Lectures*, edited by Opoku Onyinah, 57–104. Accra: Church of Pentecost, 2004.

———. *Pentecostal Exorcism: Witchcraft and Demonology in Ghana*. Dorset, UK: Deo, 2012.

———. "Pentecostal Transformation in Africa: The Rise and Growth of the Church of Pentecost." *Pentecost Journal of Theology and Missions* [Ghana: Pentecost Press] 1, no.1 (July 2016) 17–22.

———. "Reviving the Gifts and Operations of the Holy Spirit." In *Tell the Next Generation: Lectures Notes on the Annual Themes of the Church of Pentecost*, edited by M. K. Ntumy, 2:45–53. Accra: National Literature Committee, 2008.

Onyinah, Opoku, and Michael Ntumy, editors. *Into the World We Go: The Missionary Enterprise of The Church of Pentecost*. Mumbai: Quarterfold, 2016.

Pobee, J. S. *Religion and Politics in Ghana: A Case Study of the Acheampong Era, 1972–1978*. Accra: Ghana University Press, 1992.

Robert, Dana L. "Shifting Southward: Global Christianity since 1945." *International Bulletin of Missionary Research* 24:2 (2000) 50–58.

Saforo, D. K. (Apostle of the Christ Apostolic Reform Church, formally of CAC). "History of GPC." 2014.

Sanneh, Lamin. "The Horizontal and Vertical in Mission: An African Perspective." *International Bulletin of Missionary Research* 7:4 (1983) 165–71.

———. *Translating the Message: The Missionary Impact on Culture.* Maryknoll, NY: Orbis, 1989.

———. *West African Christianity: The Religious Impact.* Maryknoll, NY: Orbis, 1983.

Shank, David A. "The Legacy of William Wade Harris." *International Bulletin of Missionary Research* 10 (1986) 170–76.

———. *Prophet Harris, the 'Black Elijah' of West Africa.* New York: Brill, 1994.

———. "William Wade Harris: A Prophet of Modern Times." PhD dissertation, University of Aberdeen, 1980.

Stark, Rodney. "Why Religious Movements Succeed or Fail: A Revised General Model." *Journal of Contemporary Religion* 11:2 (1996) 133–46.

Sule-Saa, Solomon Sunam. "The Impact of Vernacular Bible Translation on the Dagomba and Konkomba of Northern Ghana in the Light of Lamin Sanneh's Conception of Mission as Translation." Thesis, Akrofi-Christaller Institute of Theology, Mission and Culture, Akropong-Akuapem, Ghana, August 2007.

Synan, Vinson. *The Holiness-Pentecostal Tradition: Charismatic Movements in the Twentieth Century.* Grand Rapids: Eerdmans, 1997.

Taylor, J. V. *The Go-Between God: The Holy Spirit and Christian Mission.* London: SCM, 1972.

Ter Haar, Gerrie. "The African Diaspora in Europe: Some Important Themes and Issues." In *Strangers and Sojourners: Religious Communities in the Diaspora*, edited by Gerrie Ter Haar. Leuven: Peeters 1998.

———. *Halfway to Paradise: African Christians in Europe.* Fairwater, Cardiff: Cardiff Academic, 1998.

———. "The Religious Dimension in Migration and Its Reaction to Development: The Case of Ghanaians in the Netherlands." In *At Home in the World?: International Migration and Development in Contemporary Ghana and West Africa*, edited by Takyiwah Manuh. Accra: Sub-Saharan, 2006.

Towns, E. L., J. N. Vaughan, and David J. Seifert, editors. *The Complete Book of Church Growth.* Carol Stream, IL: Tyndale, 1982.

Turnbull, T. N. *What God Hath Wrought: A Short History of the Apostolic Church.* Bradford, UK: Puritan, 1959.

Van Laar, Wout. "Introduction: It's Time to Get to Know Each Other." In *Fruitful in This Land: Pluralism, Dialogue and Healing in Migrant Pentecostalism*, edited by André Droogers, Cornelis van der Laan, and Wout van Laar. Zoetermeer: Uitgeverij Boekencentrum, 2006.

———. "'We Shall Be Fruitful in This Land': Pentecostal and Charismatic New Mission Churches in Europe." In *Fruitful in This Land: Pluralism, Dialogue and Healing in Migrant Pentecostalism*, edited by André Droogers, Cornelis van der Laan, and Wout van Laar. Zoetermeer: Uiteverij Boekencentrum, 2006.

Wagner, C. Peter. "Three Growth Principles for a Soul-Winning Church." In *The Complete Book of Church Growth*, edited by E. L. Towns, J. N. Vaughan, and David J. Seifert. Carol Stream, IL: Tyndale, 1982.

Walker, Daniel Okyere. "The Pentecost Fire Is Burning: Models of Mission Activities in the Church of Pentecost." PhD thesis, University of Birmingham, 2010.

Walls, Andrew F. *The Cross-Cultural Process in Christian History.* Maryknoll, NY: Orbis, 2002.

———. *The Missionary Movement in Christian History: Studies in the Transmission of Faith.* Maryknoll, NY: Orbis, 1996.

Woode, Ekow Badu. Lectures at Pastors and Wives Conference, Pentecost Convention Centre, January 2013.

———. "Revisiting the Baptism, Gifts and Fruit of the Holy Spirit." In *Tell the Next Generation: Lectures Notes on the Annual Themes of the Church of Pentecost*, edited by M. K. Ntumy, 2:264–67. Accra: National Literature Committee, 2008.

Worsfold, James E. *The Origins of the Apostolic Church in Great Britain*. Wellington, UK: Zoe, 1991.

Wyllie, R. W. "Pioneers of Ghanaian Pentecostalism: Peter Anim and James McKeown." *Journal of Religion in Africa* 6:2 (1974) 109–22.

Yin, Robert K. *Case Study Research: Design and Methods*. London: Sage, 2003.

Zelditch, Morris, Jr. "Some Methodological Problems of Fieldwork Studies." In *Field Research: A Sourcebook and Field Manual*, edited by Robert G. Burgess. London: Allen and Unwin, 1982.

Index of Names

Ababio, Dennis, 219
Abeo-Tetteh, Victoria, 86
Abissa, Christian Kouakou, 196
Aboah, Kenneth, 224
Aboah, Victoria, 82
Abua-Ayisi (Elder; former FAD), 107
Abunyewah, K. Osei, 194
Acheampong, Ignatius Kutu (General), 204
Acheampong, John, 209
Acher, J. B., 189
Achim Gyimah, Emmanuel, 192, 194
Ackah-Baidoo, Kwesi, 222
Acquaah, Robert, 85
Acquah, Emmanuel Kwesi, 72–74, 192
Acquah, Vincent Badu, 194
Acquaye, Seth, 72
Adams, S. Amos, 94
Addae, A. K., 88–89
Addison, Eunice, 80, 121, 250
Addison, Rigwel Ato, 69, 111, 210, 221, 223
Addo, Gyasi. See Gyasi Addo, Emmanuel
Addo, Shadrack, 76
Adeti, I. J. K., 70
Adipah, S. O. See Opoku-Adipah, Samuel
Adjabeng, Joshua, 69, 115
Adjei, William, 69
Adobah, B. A., 85–86
Adogame, Afe, 6, 13
Adom-Yeboah, Johnson, 119
Adotey, S. L., 65–66
Adu, Beryl, 192
Adu, Denis Bentil, 194
Adu, F. Yaw, 77

Adu, John, 192
Adu-Boansi (Mr. and Mrs.), 194
Adutuah-Amakye, Hannah, 121–22
Adwere, Alex, 196
Adzah, Paul Jerry, 199
Afful, Moses, 127
Affum, Jacob Narh, 80
Afrifa (Elder), 120
Afriyie, Edward Asare, 212
Afriyie, Osei Owusu, 213–14, 224
Agbavitoh, Komi Edina, 186, 202
Agbemor, Joseph K., 72–73
Agbovi-Hushie, Franklin, 147
Agogue, Léon Y., 186, 188
Agyapong, Ebenezer, 75
Agyei-Agyiri (lawyer; of SSNIT Assembly), 89
Agyemang, Stephen, 229
Agyemang-Baduh, Johnson, 85, 121, 147, 192
Agyin, Samuel Lord, 80, 192, 225
Aidoo, John Appiah, 147, 226
Ajayi, Nathaniel, 190
Akay, Emmanuel, 94
Ako-Awuku, Godwin, 76
Ako-Nai, Henry, 147
Akpabli, E. K., 200
Akuamoah, Beatrice, 219
Akuffo, Evans A., 191–95
Akyeampong, Grace, 211, 221
Akyeampong, Okyere, 221
Ali, Benjamin, 23–24, 147
Amanfo, Ofori, 226
Amaniampong, Georgina Osei, 82
Amankwa, Benjamin, 229

INDEX OF NAMES

Amankwa, Daniel, 193
Amankwaah, David, 72
Amegah, S. K., 73
Amegatcher, N. A. O., 89, 190, 213, 217, 237
Amegbley, Augustus, 191
Ameyaw, J. E., 85
Ameyaw, Paul Osei, 223
Aminssah, Emmanuel, 224
Amoah, Albert, 111, 115, 220
Amoah, T. C., 80
Amoako, I. K., 89
Amoako, J. W., 54
Amoako, Michael Agyemang, 220
Amoateng, Kwabena Arko, 214
Amonoo, George Prah, 193
Amoo Mireku (Brother and Sister), 229
Ampiah, Frank C., 189
Ampofo, James Osei, 80
Ampofo, Stephen, 69
Ampofo, Suzzie, 225
Ampomah, J. K., 119, 188
Amponsah, Dan, 221
Amponsah, Emelia, 229
Amponsah, Kofi, 201
Amponsah, R. K., 114
Amponsah-Kuffour, Emmanuel, 115
Anaba, Eastwood, 45
Anaman, J. A. C., 57, 263
Anaman, Prudence, 60
Anane, Philip, 75
Anang, R. S. Nii, 86
Anank, Francis Kweku, 94
Anderson, Allan H., 2, 11, 148, 182, 248
Andoh, F. K., 195
Andoh, Mark Obeng, 200
Andoh, P. G., 86
Angoh, A. L., 225
Aniakwaah, Grace, 86
Anim, Emmanuel K., 116–17, 122
Anim, Peter Newman, 1, 18, 34–35, 52–55, 59, 126, 249
Anim, Tina, 212
Aninkorah, E. D., 80, 188
Aninkorah, Samuel, 225–26
Ankama, S. H. (Prophet), 64, 263
Ankamah-Lomotey, Stephen, 85–86
Ankrah-Badu, Emmanuel Ofei, 73, 199

Annin, J. K., 114
Annor, Isaac, 122
Annor, Philip, 54
Annor-Adjei, Yaw, 196
Annor-Boakye, Charles, 196
Ansah, Kofi Owusu, 223
Ansah, Kwesi, 226
Ansong, S. K., 85, 89, 219, 237
Antwi, F. E., 89
Antwi, S. Y., 195, 197–98, 200
Antwi, Samuel A., 127
Antwi, V. C. T., 88
Anum Sampong (Elder), 119
Anyango, Bonaface Owiti, 198
Apau-Asante, C. E., 84, 156
Apea, Emma, 210
Apea, Emmanuel, 208–12
Apedo, B. Y., 189
Apedo, Boenor, 186
Appea, William Owusu, 225
Appiah, Ebenezer, 202, 223
Appiah, Edmund, 214
Appiah, J. K., 66, 189, 224
Appiah, Joseph, 223
Appiah, M. S., 214–15, 237
Appiah Missah, Nicholas, 197
Appiah, Samuel Otu, 72
Appiah-Adu, P. B., 250
Appiah-Agyekum, Ebenezer, 70, 89
Aredes, Geraldo, 229
Aredes, Nilda, 229
Arhin, Sylvester, 192
Arn, Win, 135, 141
Arnan, D. K., 66, 111, 190
Arthur, B. K., 188–89, 197, 200, 221, 227
Asamoah, E. K., 88–89
Asamoah, Kofi, 209–10, 212–13
Asamoah-Gyadu, J. Kwabena, 5–6, 11, 19–20, 22, 31–33, 39–40, 46–48, 60, 97, 142, 162, 208, 231–32, 234, 242, 244, 246, 248, 251–53, 258–61, 263, 265, 267, 280
Asante, E. C., 187, 195, 198, 200
Asante, Georgina, 75
Asante, Kwadwo, 226
Asante, Mary, 226
Asante, S. O., 73
Asante-Ayeh, J. F., 90, 194

INDEX OF NAMES

Asare, Eric, 76
Asare, Festus, 219
Asare, John, 246–48
Asare, Kwaku, 54
Asare, Theodore M., 121
Asare, Vida, 219
Asare-Duah, Oppong, 154
Aseidu, Michael Collins, 66, 77, 143, 191–92, 194
Aseidu, M. C. (Mrs.), 191
Asem, A. K., 120–21
Asem, E. Kafui, 64, 68, 121
Aseyero, Patrick, 93, 95
Asiamah, Patrick, 66, 91
Asiedu, J. R., 57
Asiedu, Maxwell Adubofour, 72
Asiseh, Kate, 69
Asmah, Thomas, 219
Asman, Chris, 221
Asomani, S. R., 263
Asomaning (Pastor; McKeown's interpreter), 248
Asomaning, Seth Kweku, 192
Assabil, Rebecca, 82
Atsu, A. K., 114
Atta Kakra, Yaw, 64, 80
Atta Panyin, Yaw, 64
Atta-Mills, John Evans, 45
Attah, Samuel, 151
Atuah, Kwasi, 225
Atujona, Gladys, 82
Awotwe, Kobina, 189
Awuah, Anthony K., 219, 221, 237
Awuku, Georgina L., 85–86
Awuku, Offei, 69
Ayao, Atchia, 187
Ayerakwa, Peter, 66, 69–70, 115, 227
Ayinor, S. K., 114
Ayitey, M. T., 88–89
Baaba (Sister), 226
Baah, Asamoah, 194
Baah, Asante, 224
Baah, Charles, 219
Badu, Adjei, 85
Badu, Ben Ampea, 77
Badu, George Ankra, 58
Badu Nyarko, Samuel, 87–88, 96, 188
Badu, Seth Asare Ofei, 75

Baffour, Justice Eric Kyei, 122
Baidoo, Francis, 202
Baidoo, Stephen Kofi, 147, 190, 223–24, 239, 265
Bamfo (Elder), 119
Banda, Esau, 192
Barker, Peter, and Boadi Siaw, Samuel, 36
Barrett, David, 3
Bayala, Pierre-Marie, 188
Beddim (Pastor), 94
Bediako, Emmanuel Owusu, 220–21
Bediako, Faustina, 221
Bediako, Kwame, 3, 28, 182, 249
Berentumi, Sylvester, 223
Berko, Samuel, 199
Bernard, Gnaoré Raymond, 203
Bimpong, J. A., 54, 156, 263
Bio, Oppong, 122
Blankson, Ernestina, 211
Blankson, Kwame, 115, 211–13, 223–24, 237
Blay, J. B., 58
Boadu-Yirenkyi, Gideon K., 75
Boafo, Afriyie, 226
Boakye, Ben, 218–19
Boamah, Boniface, 193
Boamah, Comfort, 193
Boamah, Georgina, 219
Boamah, Juliana, 193
Boamah, Louisa, 193
Boampong, Major, 226
Boasiako, Emmanuel Antwi, 75
Boate, Emmanuel Anane, 70, 119
Boateng, Abraham N., 75
Boateng, Akuamoah, 221
Boateng, Eric, 221
Boateng, Samuel Opoku, 89, 209–10, 212–13
Bonino, José Miguez, 140
Bonney, Blessed, 190
Bonney (Brother), 193
Bonney, Emmanuel R., 115
Bonsu, Alex Osei. *See* Osei-Bonsu, Alex
Bosch, D. J., 109
Bredwa-Mensah, Yaw, 59
Bremansu, Patrick Kwabena, 72
Brempong, Osei-Wusu, 95
Brouwer, Steve, 39

Brown, Emmanuel, 218–19
Buckle, Charles Palmer (Bishop), 127
Buertey, Ignatius T., 124
Busia, Kofi Abrefa (Progress Party), 204
Campbell, Ross, 93
Campira, Alberto, 194
Carol, Eddy, 190
Chadwick, William, 134
Chan, Simon, 250, 252, 256, 258
Chemel, S. K. O., 156
Cho, David Yonggi, 145
Clement, Amponsah, 202
Clottey, A. H. L., 118–19
Clottey, Daniel, 209–11
Cobb, Robert L., 126
Coco, René, 187–88, 239
Coffi Gbankpan, Germain, 187
Coffie, Benjamin Agyemang, 191
Coly, Alphonse, 196
Comiskey, Joel, 146
Conrad, Allen, 127
Corneille, Montcho, 186–87
Coulibally, Lacou, 188
Cox, Harvey, 2, 267
Cudjoe, J. W. D., 86, 190, 192
Currie, Lionel, 114
Dacosta, Adu, 226
D'Almeida, Marko, 186
Dampare, Christian, 214
Danso (Mr. and Mrs.), 221
Darko, Yirenkyi Gyeke, 191
Darkooh, F. K., 185
Darkwah, Anthony Antwi, 213
Daswani, Girish, 22–23, 47–49
Dayton, Donald W., 252, 257, 270
Debrah, Juliana Asare, 82
Diaba, S. Y., 65
Dickson, K. A., 69
Dindiago, Amos, 94
Disse, Emmanuel, 201
Djani, Nii Kotei, 193
Doherty, Sam, 86
Doku, Abraham Lawrence, 209–10
Donkor, E. O., 122
Donkor, Emmanuel, 202
Donkor, Kwesi, 226
Donkor, Lord Elorm. *See* Elorm-Donkor, Lord Abraham

Donkor, Peggy Ama, 122
Duffour, S. W., 64, 263
Dwomoh-Amaniampong (Elder), 239
Dwuma, R. H., 54
Edusei, Kweku, 151
Edward, Sosthenes, 197
Edwards, Brian, 210
Effah-Adjei, Rosemond, 221
Eghan, Benedict, 75
Egyir-Paintsil, James, 65, 69, 111, 121, 126, 249
Ekem, J. D. K., 116
Ekuban, E. K., 197
Elorm-Donkor, Lord Abraham, 13, 21
Emilie, Sinza, 202
Ennin, Davis, 229
Ennumh, J. K., 80
Ephraim, B. K., 187
Ephraim, Joe, 196
Eshun, Peter, 195
Eshun, Samuel Obeng. *See* Obeng Eshun, Samuel
Essel, J. K., 85
Etrue, Mike, 212
Fastchao, Marc K., 187
Febri, Alex, 226
Foli, Richard, 253
Fosu, J. K. Gyan, 126–27
Francis, Gregory, 126
Francis, N'Guamah, 202
Fréderic, N'Guamah, 202
Frimpong, C. K., 54
Frimpong, P. Y. B., 77
Frimpong, S. T. W., 64
Frimpong, Yaw, 114
Gadzekpo, K. K. C., 186
Gakpetor, Samuel, 147, 153
Gamanywa (Pastor), 197
Gapetor, Grace, 250–51
Gbankpan, Germain Coffi. *See* Coffi Gbankpan, Germain
Ghansah, J. B. A., 88
Gifford, Paul, 39, 44
Glass, John, 154
Glasser, Arthur F., 133
Glover, M. Z., 89, 239
Gogo, Vincent Y., 185
Grau (Rev. Dr.), 126

INDEX OF NAMES

Green, Michael, 78, 100, 134
Gurung, Peter, 228
Gyakare, Ntim, 213
Gyamfi, Joseph, 229
Gyamfi, Onyinah, 89
Gyasi Addo, Emmanuel, 103, 196, 202
Gyekye, Kwame, 103
Gyempeh, Stephen, 229
Gyetuah, Isaac, 223
Gyimah, Emmanuel Achim. *See* Achim Gyimah, Emmanuel
Gyimah, J. S., 54, 66, 69, 115, 263
Gyimah, Victoria, 219
Gyinase, Robert, 94
Hagan, Ebenezer, 75
Hammond, Stanley M., 65–66
Hanciles, Jehu J., 6, 205, 231, 234–35, 243, 278
Harris, William Wadé, 9, 30–31
Hawkes, Adrian, 210
Hayford, R. O., 64, 156
Hayfron, David Nyansah, 74–75
Hills, Gordon, 210
Hocken, Peter, 256
Hodges, Melvin L., 181–82
Hollenweger, Walter J., 2, 11, 28, 267
Hooper, George, 223
Hushie, C. C. A., 65, 156, 186
Jacobson, Douglas, 10
Jequessene (Pastor), 194
Johnson, Eunice, 250
Judah, Isaac Tetteh, 200
Kabenla, 209
Kalambi, Faustin, 197
Kalu, Ogbu Uke, 235, 237, 247, 270
Karikari, S. A. K., 114
Kasandra (Mr.), 197
Kenyon (Pastor), 188
Kesseler, James S., 58
Kessie, J. O., 196
Kevin-Annan, Amos, 73, 75
Kibiki, Joseph, 197
Killick, Barry, 211–12
Kissiedu (Brother), 226
Kissiedu, C. N., 85
Kissiedu, W. N., 69–70
Klutse, Felix Dela, 122

Koduah, Alfred, 89, 111, 116, 139, 194–98, 200, 228
Kodum, Micheal, 95
Konney, Charity, 224
Konney, Emmanuel, 224–25
Konrad, Allan, 126
Kontoh, Yaw, 209
Koomson, Theresa, 225
Kopah, Michael M., 114, 121
Korankye, George Kweku, 214–15, 226
Koranteng, Henry, 70
Koranteng, S. F. Ayesu, 191
Kossonou, Koffi, 188
Kpodo, Pauline, 185
Kporha, Alexander, 199–200
Kuffuor, J. A., 115
Kum, Kwadwo, 189
Kuma, Afua, 249, 267
Kumi, A. Y., 88–89
Kumi-Larbi, Alex N. Y., 111, 120, 124
Kusi, Maxwell, 218–19
Kusi-Akyeampong (Elder), 221
Kutin-Buah, Mary, 73
Kwabena, Andrews, 194
Kwaffo, Beatrice, 80, 89
Kwakye, Stephen Owusu, 90
Kwoffie, Edward, 212
Kyei, Peter Ohene, 69–70
Kyei-Mensah, Kingsford, 66, 77, 119
Ladejo, Moses, 88–89, 190
Ladlow, G. L. W., 121, 125
Ladlow, Margaret, 121, 125
Larbi, Emmanuel Kingsley, 5, 13, 17–19, 34, 40, 52, 58, 60, 62–63, 69, 79, 91–92, 98, 100, 103, 109, 117, 139, 149, 162–63, 244, 247, 249, 259–60, 262–63, 268, 273–74
Larkai, J. A., 69, 227
Laryea, Philip, 249
Leonard, Christine, 13, 16–17, 85, 98, 103, 113, 117, 121, 244, 248, 259–60, 262–63
Limann, Hilla, 205
Logan, George, 190
Luc, Basili Kambire, 202
Lukwesa, Nelson, 195
Macchia, Frank D., 256
Magyam, James, 94

INDEX OF NAMES

Mahama, John Dramani, 124
Mahama, Kojo, 94
Mahlakata, Zola, 192
Mainoo, Yaw Kontoh Fosu, 210
Mallet, A. S., 156, 185, 263
Mallet, Johnny, 65, 121
Manu, Emmanuel Ayisi, 75
Manu, Moses Agyia, 188
Marih, Adofo, 120
Martey, J. O. Y., 116
Marty, Martin E., 270
Mbelwa, Joseph (Mr. and Mrs.), 197
Mbesa, Beholds, 200
Mbillah, J. A., 115
Mbrokoh-Awol, Joseph, 122
McGavran, Donald A., 135, 141, 148, 182–83
McGee, Gary B., 109
McKeown, James, 1, 13, 16–18, 34–35, 53–59, 61, 63, 79, 85, 98, 100, 103, 108–10, 117–18, 121, 126, 149, 155, 160, 186, 217, 244, 348–49, 253, 256–57, 263, 269, 274, 287–88
McKeown, Sophia, 34, 53, 79
McKeown, T. Adam, 79
Mends, Christiana Obo. See Obo Mends, Christiana
Mends, Francis, 223
Mensah, Anthony Peter, 89–90
Mensah, J. A., 119
Mensah, John, 114, 188
Mensah, K. K., 186
Mensah, Kingsley, 221
Mensah, Kokoe, 188
Mensah, Kwabena Darko, 76
Mensah, Matilda, 115
Mensah, Pius, 186
Mensah, Robert Oscar, 225
Mensah, Thomas Agyei, 229
Menzies, William W., and Robert P. Menzies, 168
Meyer, Birgit, 43
Miah, Anthony Kingsley, 190, 194, 201–2, 221
Mills, David, 83, 114, 125–26, 147
Mills, Margaret, 83–84, 125
Morris, Calan, 126
Mossi, Ouedrago Billa, 188
Munalula, Davies, 195
Muntolol, Simon Ole, 199
Nackabah, John, 31
Nambu, Elisha W., 94
Nartey, A. T., 66, 69
Nato, Barthelemy, 187
Niamké, Rose Jolie, 202
Nicholas, George A., 126
Nkansah (Elder; PAUKE), 210
Nkansah, Matthew, 122
Nkansah, S. K., 126
Nkata, Shadrack, 197
Nketsia, S. K., 114
Nkrumah, Kwame (Osagyefo), 58, 204
Nkrumahas, Kwame (Elder), 212–13
Nnetepa, Esther, 197
Nnipa, Eric, 223
Nntepa, Jackson Bisso, 197
Noble-Atsu, Daniel Kwame, 71, 73, 89, 115, 210–11
Noye, Ben, 75
Nsaful, Daniel Yeboah, 197–98
Nsiah, Stephen Safo, 76, 195
Ntiamoah, K., 198
Ntiri (Elder), 69
Ntumy, Michael K., 74, 89, 110–11, 127, 154, 189–90, 227
Nyamadi, Makafui, 75
Nyamekye, Eric, 74, 122, 191
Nyamekye, Mary, 191
Nyarko, Ebenezer Asamoah, 90
Nyarko, K., 54
Nyarko, L. A., 70, 114–15, 121, 157
Nyarko, Newton Ofosuhene, 210, 212, 215, 224, 226, 238
Nyarko, Samuel Badu. See Badu Nyarko, Samuel
Nyarko, Thomas, 121
Nyoka, David, 192
Obeng, Felicia, 225
Obeng, Kwadwo, 76
Obeng Eshun, Samuel, 225
Obeng-Tuffoh, Clement, 191
Obo Mends, Christiana, 59–60, 68, 80
Ocansey, E. D., 57
Ocloo, J. K., 186
Odei, Raymond, 226

INDEX OF NAMES

Odum, S. R., 193, 200
Oduro, Agyemang, 194
Oduro-Ampaw, Andrews, 85
Oduyoye, Mercy Amba, 78
Ofori, John O., 220, 229
Ofori, Macdonald, 225
Ofosu, E. K., 198
Ofosu, S. K., 80
Ofosu-Koramoah, Faustina, 85
Ofosuhene, Newton, 209
Ogesa, Vincent, 199
Ohenewaaah (Brother), 226
Okumu, Yusuf Gowi, 198
Okwei-Nortey, Samuel, 209, 211–13
Omenyo, Cephas N., 28
Onyinah, Opoku, 20–21, 63, 73, 89,
    91–92, 109–10, 112, 114–15,
    117–18, 124, 127, 191–93, 201,
    210–11, 221, 223, 229, 239, 250,
    253, 256–57, 263, 265
Opoku (Mr. and Mrs.), 224
Opoku, Raymond, 89–90
Opoku, Victoria, 219
Opoku-Adipah, Samuel, 114, 115, 132,
    152, 154
Oppong, Eric, 218–19
Oppong, Kwame Sampson, 9, 31
Oppong, Theresa, 218
Osei, Isaac, 76
Osei, Margaret, 82
Osei-Bonsu, Alex, 220–22, 225–26,
    237–38
Osei-Korsah, Philip, 72
Osei-Ofosu, E. K., 198
Osolo, Geoffrey, 198–99
Otage, Coleman, 198
Otchere, James, 225
Otoo, Kwesi, 212–14
Otu-Appiah, Gifty, 75
Otumfuo, R. N., 114
Ouedraogo, Lassane, 225
Owuo, Adelaide, 86
Owusu (Apostle; sent to church in US),
    220
Owusu, D. Y. A., 80, 88, 110, 156
Owusu, Emmanuel Anthony, 221
Owusu, Perpetual, 80
Owusu-Ankomah, R. K., 114

Owusu-Antwi, P., 88–89
Owusu-Brempong, Osei, 193
Pangani, Andrew, 192
Pangani, Patrick, 192–93
Pare, Adu, 163
Parham, Charles Fox, 11
Parker, E. K., 121
Parker, Emmanuel, 115
Peasah, Michael, 75
Peasah, S. Y., 77
Philippe, Assemian, 203
Pobee, J. S., 204
Pobee, S. E. A., 86
Quaicoo, Joseph, 90
Quainoo, Eric Abeiku, 76
Quampah, Comfort, 82
Quampah, Dela, 192
Quardson, J. G., 86
Quaye, Emmanuel, 224
Quaye, J. C., 263
Quist, Alice, 185
Rai, Bharati, 228
Rai, Jeewan, 228
Rai, Simon, 228
Rai, Timothy, 228
Raj, James, 227
Rajappa (Mr.), 227
Rawlings, Jerry John, 205
Rexford (Brother), 229
Rogatien, Konon, 187
Sackey, Daniel, 72, 75
Sackey, Doris, 221
Sackey, J. W., 189
Safo, Fred Stephen, 69, 80, 108, 110, 127,
    160, 186, 210
Saforo, D. K., 126
Sakyi, Ampoma, 213
Sanneh, Lamin, 29, 182, 265, 272, 288
Sarfo-Appiah, Faustina, 85
Sarkodie-Mensah (Mrs.), 193
Sarpong, Asomani, 213
Sarpong, R. Asomaning, 80
Sasu, Philip, 225
Senanyah, Bright Yaw, 199
Serwaa, Ama, 225
Sey, D. K., 229
Seymour, William J., 11
Shama, Afful, 202

Shank, David A., 30
Siaw, Omari, 75
Siaw-Adjapong, Joseph, 77
Sibanda (Mr. and Mrs.), 200
Sikrweqe, Cameron Ndabesita, 192, 194
Siriboe, Esme, 80, 84
Smith, G. G. A., 191
Soglo, Stephen, 191
Sowah, Robert, 86
Stanley, David, 227
Stark, Rodney, 162
Sule-Saa, Solomon Sunam, 265
Swanzy, B. K., 189
Swatson, John, 31
Tackie, Daniel Tetteh, 121–22
Tani, Grace, 31
Tawiah, Abena, 226
Taylor, J. V., 246
Tekper, David, 194
Tenobi, David, 126
Ter Haar, Gerrie, 204, 234–35
Tetteh, Andrew, 88–89
Tetteh, James, 77, 138
Thapa, Micheal, 228
Tiakor, Fred, 85–86
Tiase, S. J. A., 114
Tieku, D. Y., 114
Torso, E. Y., 70, 73
Traoré, Sidiki, 203, 239
Turnbull, T. N., 207
Tuudah, Samuel Obeng, 209–10, 212
Twerefuor, Kwadjo Asare, 86
Urasa, Stephen, 197
Van Laar, Wout, 203, 234
Wagner, C. Peter, 135, 182
Walker, Daniel Okyere, 12, 20, 85
Walker, Frederick Diabene, 66, 69, 110, 156–57, 189, 263
Waller, John, 89, 92, 114, 227
Walls, Andrew F., 3, 30, 271
Wayoe, M. T., 114
Westfall, Stephen, 186
Wettey-Larbi, Matthew, 147
Wiafe, Daniel Prince, 222–25, 238
Wiafe, Faustina, 214
Wiafe, Sylvester, 213
Wilmot, Tony, 37
Woglo, Pierre, 186
Woode, Ekow Badu, 127, 188, 195, 255
Woode, G. A., 80
Wyatt, Thomas, 55
Wyllie, R. W., 58, 117
Yamoah, Grace, 85
Yankey, Samuel, 75
Yanogo, Pinogo, 188
Yaw, A. K., 80
Yeboah, Adjei, 202
Yeboah, Atta, 226
Yeboah, Francis Ofori, 196, 224
Yeboah, Kojo, 213
Yeboah, M. K., 89, 110, 115, 127, 210, 221, 223, 227
Yeboah, Susanna Atta, 226
Yeboah, Yao, 89–90, 119–20
Yeboah-Asuama, Grace Lucy, 80–82
Yeboah-Asuamah, Yaw, 219
Yedu, Rita, 86
Yiadom (Apostle), 220
Yinger, James K., 94
Yirenkyi-Boadu, Gideon, 72
Zabre, Ousmane P., 186, 188, 239
Ziemann, Edwin, 126
Zinah, Micheal, 94
Zuwu, Maasaboi M., 190

Index of Subjects

African Christian Fellowship (ACF), 208
African Development Bank (ADB), 202
African Indigenous/Independent Churches (AICs), 1, 9–10, 19, 29–30, 32–33, 46, 79, 206, 243, 256, 284
African Pentecostal Evangelistic Association, 120–21
African traditional religion/piety/practice, 17, 32, 39, 42, 44, 93, 157, 250, 259, 261, 271–72, 281–82
Akan, 21, 103
Apostolic Church of Ghana (ACG). See under history of Church of Pentecost
Assemblies of God (AG), 10, 34, 46–47, 126, 152, 207, 265, 277, 284
Association of Evangelicals in Africa and Madagascar (AEAM), 126
baptism. See under doctrines and beliefs of CoP, conversion and baptism
baptism in/of the Holy Spirit, 37, 64, 98–100, 254–55, 256
prerequisite for leadership in CoP, 245–47, 254–56
Bombing group. See under Evangelism Ministry
British Apostolic Church (Apostolic Church-UK). See under history of Church of Pentecost
Campus Crusade for Christ, 197
Charismatic churches, 4, 10, 23, 33, 36, 38, 40, 43–44, 47, 150, 161–62, 238, 256, 281

Charismatic movements (CMs), 10, 33, 36, 38–40, 46–49, 92, 129
Charismatic phenomenon, 37, 64, 88, 99–100, 102, 128, 280
Child Evangelism Fellowship, 84
Children's Ministry, 83–87, 253
  activities, 84–85
  objectives, 84
Christ Apostolic Church (CAC). See under history of Church of Pentecost
Church of Pentecost (CoP)
  denominational organization and character, 34, 46–47
  administration and governance, 23, 17, 47, 60–61, 102–8, 207
  Bible emphasized, 28–29, 32–33, 66, 76, 79, 141, 143, 244, 246, 265, 271
  boards and committees, 107–8
  as a Classical Pentecostal church, 1, 12, 18, 46–51, 53, 55, 61, 98, 116, 129, 152, 243, 265, 274
  community based, 141–43, 208, 258–59, 276, 284
  CoP-UK organization, 214–18
  discipline and accountability, 17, 60, 263–64, 102, 232, 263–64
  evangelism as core value, 18, 59, 62, 64–65, 73, 75, 78, 95–97, 116–117, 137–38, 243–44, 262–63, 275–76
  governance of ministers/ministry, 103–4, 151–55
  housing facilities and estates, 123–25

INDEX OF SUBJECTS

Church of Pentecost (CoP) (continued)
  impact on Ghanaian life and culture, 40–44
  as indigenous African church, 16, 18, 47, 51, 53, 61, 125, 129, 182, 217, 248, 265, 269, 274
  indigenous leadership, 1, 13, 16–18, 29, 63, 108–13, 160, 186–88, 190, 192–93, 227, 229–30
  lay-leadership driven, 141, 230, 276, 287
  membership criteria, 131, 246, 253–54
  missionary mindset, 18, 20, 78, 140, 232, 278
  national churches' autonomy, 140, 187, 189, 238–40, 286–87
  and national/civic development, 44–45
  pneumatic phenomenon, 242–43
  and politics, 44–45
  rural base, 23, 143, 146
  Vision 2013–2018, 77, 82, 87, 116, 132
  worldwide, 19–20, 45–46, 132
  see also doctrines and beliefs of CoP; functional ministries; growth of CoP: measurement and analysis; growth of CoP: methods and principles; history of Church of Pentecost; internal missions; international missions; Pentecostal spirituality; worship
Classical Pentecostal/Pentecostalism (CP), 10, 12, 33–35, 37, 39–40, 46–49, 51, 152, 243, 277
  see also under Church of Pentecost denominational organization and character; history of Christianity in Ghana
clusters of congregations recommendation, 284
Community Based Church Buildings (CBCB), 124
conversion and baptism. *See under* doctrines and beliefs of CoP
deliverance, 20–21, 41, 46, 100, 208, 243, 260–61, 267, 269, 271

doctrines and beliefs of CoP
  biblically based prayer, 244, 259–61
  Communion, 268–69
  community and discipleship, 258–59
  conversion and baptism, 131, 246, 252–54
  discipline and accountability, 155, 162–63, 232, 263–64
  evangelism, 243–44, 262–63
  holiness and moral ethics, 162–63, 243, 261–62, 268, 271
  Holy Spirit baptism, gifts, prayer, 254–58
  liturgy and vernacularization, 264–65
  tithing, 269–70
  worship form, 208–9
ecumenism, 43, 125–28
Elim Church of Pentecost (ELICOP), 213–14
Elim Pentecostal Church of UK, 14, 122, 125, 154, 208–11
ethics. *See* moral character and practice
Evangelical Fellowship of Kenya (EFK), 198
Evangelism Ministry, 76–78, 81–82, 95–97, 136, 276
  Bombing group, 65
  history, 64–68
  through hospitals and schools, 137
  through local church, 61, 78
  Prison Ministry, 138
  rallies, crusades, etc., 64, 66, 76, 78, 136
  recommendation for, 97, 282–83
  Witness Movement/Apostolic Witness Movement, 65–68, 70–71, 76, 276
  and youth, 64–68, 73, 276
  see also PENSA; PENTYEM
Executive Council (of CoP), 105, 107, 110, 112–13, 232
exorcism. *See* deliverance
foursquare/fourfold gospel, 10, 251–52, 271
Full Gospel Men's Fellowship, 37
functional ministries of CoP, 63–97, 128–29, 275
  analysis, 95–97

as means for growth, 63, 95–97
owned and managed by church, 46
performance statistics, 175
as responses to specific needs, 96
see also Children's; Evangelism;
    Men's; Northern Outreach;
    PIWCs; Women's; Youth
fundraising practices, 233, 269–70
General Council (of CoP), 103, 105, 107,
    111, 232
Ghana Apostolic Church (formerly Gold
    Coast Apostolic Church). *See
    under* history of CoP
Ghana Congress on Evangelism, 37
Ghana Evangelism Committee (GEC), 93
Ghana Fellowship of Evangelical
    Students (GHAFES), 37, 68
Ghana Pentecostal and Charismatic
    Council (GPCC) (formerly
    Ghana Pentecostal Council
    [GPC]), 43, 126–27
global missions patterns, 20, 182–83,
    234–38, 241, 279–80
see also reverse missions
growth of CoP: measurement and
    analysis, 62–63, 128–29, 158
    comparative analysis (1962–2013),
        163–65
    composition breakdowns, 172–73
    CoP-UK, 214–16, 218
    CoP-USA, 220
    evaluation within church growth and
        missions discourse, 181–83
    external braches, 169–70, 176–78
    factors in, 16–19, 58–59, 78, 160–64
    increased number of leaders, 160–61,
        164–65, 277
    Ghana analysis, 171–73
    indicators of, 63, 173–75
    infrastructure and assets, 123–25,
        178–81
    recommendations, 277, 287
    statistics and analysis, 158–81
    theological analysis, 263, 270–72
    worldwide statistics, 166–69
    see also doctrines and beliefs of
        CoP; growth of CoP: methods
        and principles; Pentecostal
        spirituality; *under* theology, of
        Pentecostal growth
growth of CoP: methods and principles
    biological, conversion, and transfer
        growth, 133–34, 253, 276
    central Missions Department, 231–
        33, 240, 278
    change of certain traditional
        practices, 161–62
    discipleship, 141, 143, 258–59, 276
    dividing existing assemblies, 142–44
    evangelism, 135–38, 262–63
    experience of Holy Spirit /
        "pneumatic factor," 5, 12, 19, 22,
        97–100, 128, 137, 201, 242–47,
        272, 280–82
    functional ministries as engine, 63,
        95–97
    holistic mission agenda, 149, 276,
        287
    home cells and Bible studies, 145–48,
        161, 176, 276
    local assemblies' role, 141
    migration, 6, 20, 184, 203–6, 218,
        231–32, 234, 240, 278
    ministerial posting/transfers, 134,
        151–55, 237–38, 277
    prophetic utterances, 61–62, 125,
        128, 138–39, 155–56, 201, 205,
        221, 227
    self-sustaining, 59–60, 125, 129, 140,
        181, 233, 239, 269, 274
    single-assembly districts, 144–45,
        147
    socioeconomic engagements, 148–
        49, 276, 283, 287
    women's role, 78–79, 82, 256
    see also growth of CoP: measurement
        and analysis; internal missions;
        international missions;
        Pentecostal spirituality
head covering, women's, 161–62, 262
healing, 11, 17, 32, 46, 99–101, 208, 243,
    257, 260–61, 271, 284
    without medicine, 51–55

history of Christianity in Ghana, 7–10, 40
African Indigenous/Independent Churches (AICs), 1, 9–10, 19, 29–30, 32–33, 243
Classical Pentecostalism, 10, 12, 18, 33–35, 37, 39–40, 46–49, 51, 53, 55, 58
Charismatic churches, 10, 33, 36, 38, 40
Charismatic movements, 10, 33, 36, 38–40, 46–49
Charismatic revivalists, 30–31
neo-Pentecostal movements, 33, 35–39, 91
Protestant missions, 8–9, 27–29
Roman Catholic mission, 7–8
spiritual churches (SCs), 9, 31–33, 47–48
see also Pentecostal/Pentecostalism
history of Church of Pentecost, 34, 53, 58
1937 to 1962, 51–62
1962 to present (post-independence), 62–95
analysis of, 19
Apostolic Church of Ghana (ACG) (formerly Apostolic Church of Gold Coast), 18, 34, 46, 53–57, 61, 123, 126
British Apostolic Church (Apostolic Church-UK), 1, 14, 34–35, 50, 52–53, 55, 104, 110, 125, 207
Christ Apostolic Church (CAC), 18, 34–35, 54–56, 126
doctrinal conflict, 54–55
Ghana Apostolic Church (formerly Gold Coast Apostolic Church), 56–58
internal conflict and name change, 56–58
positive effects of early difficulties, 58–62, 128, 275
Holy Spirit
empowerment by, 247–48, 253–57
fruit of, 255
gifts of, 36, 42, 51–52, 104, 255–57
pneumatic phenomena, 9–11, 19, 31–33, 47, 51–52, 63, 98–101, 257

see also baptism in/of the Holy Spirit; deliverance; healing; prayer camps; spectacular events
indigenous leadership in CoP. *See under* Church of Pentecost denominational organization and character
internal missions of CoP, 135, 155–57
see also Northern Outreach Mission
International Christian Chamber of Commerce (ICCC), 201
International Executive Council (of CoP), 103, 105, 113, 152, 233
international (external) missions of CoP, 136, 184–85, 203–6, 277
assessment of activities, 230–31
Canada, 220–22
Central Africa, 201–2
co-opting existing indigenous churches, 229
exemplifying African Pentecostal missions, 184, 206–7, 218, 231
expansion beyond Africa, 136, 139, 203, 206, 236
Italy, 222–24
Global North as platform for launching new missions, 234, 236–38, 241, 279
governance and policies, 231–33
Holland, 224–25
local assemblies' support, 232–33
non-Western nations, 225–30, 236
North Africa, 202–3
recommendation for strategic long-term missions, 285
Southern and Eastern Africa, 190–200
United Kingdom, 125, 204, 206–18
United States, 218–20
West Africa, 157, 185–90
see also global missions patterns; growth of CoP: methods and principles; international missions director; Missions Directorate; reverse missions
international missions director (IMD), 91, 105, 108, 152, 216, 232–33, 240, 278

INDEX OF SUBJECTS

Inter-Tertiary Institution PENSA (ITI-PENSA), 68, 70–71, 73, 76, 91
Latter Rain Movement (LRM)/Latter Rain Evangelistic Team, 55
Legon Interdenominational Church (LIC), 68
Legon Pentecostals' Union (LPU), 69
media (use in CoP), 120–23
    National Radio and Television Ministry Committee (NRTVMC), 121–22
    Pentecost Fire, 120, 122
    Pentecost Hour, 121–22
    radio pastor, 121–22
medicine. *See under* healing
megachurch(es), 141, 145, 147
Men's Ministry, 87–90
    objectives, 88, 90
    Pentecost Men's Fellowship (PEMEF) Leadership Training Conference, 89
ministers (in the CoP)
    formation and training, 24, 65, 72, 110–13, 149–51, 245, 280, 287
    National Ministerial Committee, 113
    posting and transfer, 151–55, 215
    qualifications, 113, 150, 152, 245–46, 255
    retreats, 111–12, 245
    see also training and education; "White Paper"
miracles. *See* deliverance; healing; spectacular events
Missions Directorate (of CoP), 108, 232–33
    see also international missions director (IMD)
missions in reverse. *See* reverse missions
moral character and practice, 21–23, 33, 161–63, 243, 256, 261–62
music, 38, 41, 107, 217, 248, 250, 267, 288
Northern Outreach Ministry (NOM), 92–96
    and integration issues, 94–95
    people of northern descent living in south, 93

parachurch associations/movements, 7, 33, 35–38, 40, 127
Pentecost Association of UK and Eire (PAUKE), 109–13
Pentecost Bible Institute (PBI). *See* Pentecost University College
Pentecost Convention Centre, 123–24
Pentecost International Worship Centres (PIWCs), 90–92, 142, 145, 147, 227, 236
    recommendation for, 285
Pentecost Men's Fellowship (PEMEF). *See* Men's Ministry
Pentecost Students and Associates (PENSA), 67–76, 160
Pentecost Theological Seminary (PTS), 111, 116, 296
Pentecost University College (PUC), 41, 115, 296
Pentecost Youth and Evangelism Movement (PENTYEM), 67, 70–71, 76
Pentecostal, Pentecostalism, 10–12
    African, defining, 10–12
    and global Christianity, 1–4, 6, 44–46
    history in Ghana, 10, 27–40
    impact on Ghana, 40–45
    impact on politics, 44–45
    as missionary movement, 2, 46
    as non-Western movement, 3–4, 11, 39, 42
    prayer, 41–42
    worship, 38, 41–42, 249–50, 267
    see also African Indigenous/Independent Churches; Charismatic churches; charismatic movements; Classical Pentecostal/ism; history of Christianity in Ghana; spiritual churches
Pentecostal spirituality, 2, 20, 33, 38–39, 46, 48, 208, 242–44, 271–72, 281
Pentecostalization of Christianity in Africa/Ghana, 29, 35–36, 40–45, 50, 123, 274
PIWCs. *See* Pentecost International Worship Centres (PIWCs)
polygamy, 189, 261, 268

poor, poverty. *See* suffering, poverty
prayer camps, 42, 100–101, 257–58
    recommendation for, 101, 284
prayer intervention, 41–42, 100, 260, 282
prophecy, prophetism, prophetic
    utterances, 23–24, 55, 61–62, 110,
    155, 205, 227, 243
prosperity gospel, 48, 269, 271
recommended areas for research, 287–88
reverse missions/flow, 207, 234–37, 241,
    278
    see also global missions patterns
Scripture Union (SU), 37–38, 41, 127
self-governing, self-sustaining, self-
    propagating, self-theologizing,
    46–47, 59, 125, 129, 146, 181–83,
    216, 233, 239, 275
    addition of self-theologizing, 182
social services/action, 117–20, 148–49
    agriculture, 118
    economic and development, 119–20
    education and vocational training,
    118–19
    health care, 118–19
    McKeown's views on, 117–18, 149
    Pentecost Co-operative Mutual
    Support and Social Services
    Society (PENCO), 120
    Pentecost Social Services
    (PENTSOS), 119, 149
    Pentecost Welfare Association
    (PENTWAS), 118
    recommendation for, 283
spectacular events, 99–100, 257
    see also deliverance; healing
spiritual churches (SCs), *sunsum sore*, 9,
    31–33, 47–48
suffering, poverty, 48, 259, 268–69, 271
theology, 251–52
    African Pentecostal, 270–71
    and CoP practice and ethos, 249–51
    grassroots, 249
    oral, 248–51, 271, 282
    Pentecostal, 247–51
    of Pentecostal growth, 270–72
    of suffering, 48, 268–69, 271

see also doctrines and beliefs
tongues (speaking in), 11–12, 37–38,
    51–52, 99–101, 143, 245, 247–48,
    254–55, 260, 267, 270
training and education, 72, 111–17, 147
    at congregational level, 113
    lay leaders, 113, 115, 141, 147
    Pentecost Training Institute, 114
    see also ministers; Pentecost
    University College
Wesleyan anthropology, 21
"White Paper," 154–55
Witness Movement. *See under*
    Evangelism Ministry
Women's Ministry, 70, 78–83, 136, 256,
    258, 262
    leadership by men and transfer to
    women, 80–81
    younger women, 81–82
World Bank, 124, 140, 205
World Council of Pentecostal and
    Charismatic Churches, 127
worldview and cosmology, 17, 21, 28, 33
worship, 208–9, 217, 248, 264–68
    African/Ghanaian style, 38, 208, 217,
    265
    and church growth, 42, 264–65
    experiential, 267
    Pentecostal form, 41–42, 248–49, 266
    praise, singing, dancing, 266–68
    traditional imagery ascribed to God,
    267
    vernacularization, 248, 264–65
    youth churches, 217, 236
    see also music; Pentecost
    International Worship Centres
    (PIWCs)
Youth Ministry, 67–78, 82
    1996 separation of Youth Ministry
    and Witness Movement, 71
    PENSA restructuring, 70–71
    PENSA–Ghana traveling secretaries,
    72–76
    see also Evangelism Ministry; ITT-
    PENSA; PENTYM

www.ingramcontent.com/pod-product-compliance
Lightning Source LLC
Chambersburg PA
CBHW050616300426
44112CB00012B/1524